THE PURSUIT OF
ROBERT EMMET

Robert Emmet

Reproduced by courtesy of the National Museum of Ireland

THE PURSUIT OF
ROBERT EMMET

By

HELEN LANDRETH

BROWNE AND NOLAN LIMITED
THE RICHVIEW PRESS DUBLIN

First Printed June 1949

MADE AND PRINTED IN IRELAND
By
BROWNE AND NOLAN LIMITED
THE RICHVIEW PRESS DUBLIN

For

RICHARD LANDRETH PARKER

Foreword

THE young American to whom I dedicate this book was born in 1923. Robert Emmet was born in Dublin in 1778. One went to war allied with Britain, the other had her as his foe. And yet the things they fought for were the same, love of justice and belief in democracy. And it is devotion to those same principles that has made me write this book despite difficulties of many kinds.

I was in Dublin in 1939 when the Second World War broke out. I had gone there the year before to write a book on modern Ireland. What happened on the Continent outdated that work almost overnight. But by then I had become interested in a period in Irish history that, strongly influenced as it was by the American Revolution, had a great appeal for my Yankee blood.

I had not meant to write of Robert Emmet when I began my research in this period. For me, Robert Emmet was chiefly a few remembered phrases from his famous speech from the dock and a young lover whose tragic romance had been put into verse by his friend Thomas Moore.

But as I turned the pages of old letters housed in the manuscript room of Trinity College Library, the Royal Irish Academy, the National Library of Ireland, the Irish Public Record Office, and most of all the Irish State Paper Office, and read other letters and reports that had found their way into print, not only did his personality begin to emerge, gallant, tender, and idealistic, but I realised that I had stumbled upon a great mystery. For reasons that will become apparent, the true story of Robert Emmet's insurrection that took place in 1803 had never been told, and for generations efforts had been made to keep it a secret.

Official accounts of the rising spoke of it as a contemptible affair, a brief riot confined to a single Dublin street, which had engaged less than a hundred bloodthirsty ruffians. But secret and confidential official letters spoke of hundreds of men having been engaged in the fighting in Dublin, of Emmet's preparations as extensive and costly. Many of his fellow-conspirators had been as aristocratic and idealistic as himself. A simultaneous insurrection in the North of Ireland had been frustrated by the craftiness of a spy posing as a rebel leader. Other parts of Ireland, whose longing for liberty had never been quenched, had expected to take up arms after Dublin had been won.

All this was known, through spies and informers, to an under-secretary at Dublin Castle, Mr. Alexander Marsden. But far from nipping the rising in the bud, he had taken great pains that the rebels should not be frightened into giving up their plans for war and had deceived even the Lord Lieutenant and the Commander of the Forces in Ireland as to the rebellious state of the country.

For many years there has been a suspicion among persons interested in Irish history that Robert Emmet might have been tricked into revolt in 1803. In the 1880's Dr. Thomas Addis Emmet of New York City, a grand-nephew of Robert Emmet, got a hint of the mystery but was blocked from following it up. In trying to locate Emmet family papers, the Doctor had gone to the Irish State Paper Office at Dublin Castle, and, being denied access to the official archives himself, he had engaged the services of Sir Bernard Burke, Ulster King at Arms and Keeper of the State Papers.

Several years later Sir Bernard told the Doctor that years before he had read certain papers connected with Robert Emmet's rising in 1803 and others connected with the legislative union between England and Ireland that had taken place in 1800, which he had thought should not be made public at that time. Among the papers had been a letter from William Pitt to Alexander Marsden, under-secretary at Dublin Castle, the seat of the Irish Government, directing that another outbreak (there had been one in 1798) should be fomented in Ireland and suggesting that Robert Emmet, who was then in Paris, should be approached for the purpose. Burke also told Dr. Emmet that he had found " an unbroken chain of evidence " to show that an agent, carefully instructed for the purpose, went to Paris, approached Robert Emmet, and induced him by misrepresentations to return to Ireland. The papers also showed that from the time of Emmet's landing till the outbreak took place in Dublin (an interval of eight months) the police were perfectly aware of the conspiracy.

Sir Bernard had asked the Lord Lieutenant to have the papers sealed up. In proof of this statement he showed Dr. Emmet a roped and sealed box in an upper room of the Tower of Dublin Castle where the State papers are housed. On the box was a label saying that for the public good it was not to be opened for a certain period of years.*

Some years later Dr. Emmet made another visit to Dublin Castle and found that the sealed box was no longer in the Tower. He was led to believe that the contents had been destroyed. The Pitt letter, Sir Bernard told him, had disappeared. But the Doctor was offered an opportunity of buying, from a private source he does not identify in his book, certain documents relating to Robert Emmet's rising. These, he concluded, had been salvaged from the discarded contents of the sealed box by some one at the Castle.

A few years later when Dr. Emmet made inquiries about other Emmet family papers that he believed were at the State Paper Office, he was told, quite incorrectly, that they were not there. When he was in Dublin in the late 1880's, making inquiries from unofficial sources about his ancestors and particularly about Robert Emmet, he was visited by police officials a week after his arrival and requested to leave Ireland within twenty-four hours. Even after more than eighty years the real story of Robert Emmet's rising was still being concealed.

It was an exciting moment for me when, sitting in the Search Room of the Irish State Paper Office at Dublin Castle, I realised that the papers I was then turning over were some of the very ones Dr. Emmet had thought destroyed.† But

---

* *The Emmet Family*, Dr. Thomas Addis Emmet, p. 143.

† Sir Bernard Burke's official Report as Keeper of the State Papers, dated February 1, 1877, speaks of having received from the Chief Secretary's Office within the previous year the contents of two large boxes and books ranging from 1796 to 1808, which he was then incorporating with a series of letters received the year before covering the years 1796 to 1805. The indexing of these papers, however, did not begin until twelve years later. In that interval two historians, W. E. H. Lecky and W. J. Fitzpatrick saw in the Tower of Dublin Castle two boxes roped and sealed like the one Dr. Emmet had been shown.

In his book *Secret Service under Pitt*, Mr. Fitzpatrick said that, when the sealed chests were finally opened, they were found to contain (among other things) a bundle of 136 letters from Francis Higgins, the informer. In a series of papers now at the State

though he had been deceived to a certain extent, his conjecture that an effort had been made to destroy documents that betrayed the Government's knowledge of Emmet's rising previous to its outbreak is correct, at least as far as Marsden and the Chief Secretary, Mr. William Wickham, are concerned. Wickham, it has developed, also had fore-knowledge of the rising and not only helped Marsden conceal it from the Lord Lieutenant but later resorted to polite blackmail in an effort to prevent an investigation into the matter. There are gaps in the papers not to be accounted for by cartons sent to the Public Record Office in Dublin and destroyed in the great fire of 1922. The ones that remain are scattered through such an infinitely large mass of other material that their true significance would be overlooked by a casual observer. Many are unsigned letters from spies and informers, and their importance depends upon knowing the identity of the writers, a special knowledge gained only by long study of the papers.

But some obviously incriminating letters were overlooked, and in others of apparently little importance there are casual remarks that have tremendous implications to one who has made a serious study of the period. Small collections of State papers evidently salvaged at the time the obviously incriminating documents were destroyed have lately turned up elsewhere. Certain collections of manuscripts at Trinity College, Dublin, and the Royal Irish Academy supply some missing details, and so do others in private possession. The Public Record Office in London, where Dr. Emmet was once told there were no Emmet papers, has hundreds of relevant items.

Thus, bit by bit, like an enormous jigsaw puzzle, the real picture of Robert Emmet's rising has taken form. It is not complete in every detail, but enough of the outline remains to give an idea of the whole. The alleged Pitt letter seems to have disappeared completely, and proof of its one-time existence now rests only on Sir Bernard Burke's statement to Dr. Emmet. But though Sir Bernard did not act quite candidly with the Doctor and evidently regretted later having

Paper Office, covering the period 1796 to 1808, there is a bundle of 131 letters from Francis Higgins, the informer. The label of the carton holding it indicates that it was one of those opened by Sir Bernard Burke in 1876, and so do the labels of all the other cartons in the series. Hundreds of letters relating to Robert Emmet and the legislative union between Ireland and England are in those cartons.

mentioned the letter, there would have been no reason for him to have invented the story. Aside from that one point, his statements to the Doctor have all been borne out. The Doctor's integrity cannot be doubted.

Why should Pitt have sent for Robert Emmet to start a rising in Ireland ? He was out of office at the time, October of 1802, but he was expecting almost hourly that his successor as Prime Minister would be forced to resign, and that the King would again give him the seals of office. A renewal of the Anglo-French war was imminent. A French invasion of Ireland seemed inevitable, and that the Irish people would have welcomed it and taken the part of the French against the English Pitt knew only too well. His acute and ruthless statesmanship may have suggested the idea of a frustrated rebellion as an excuse for suspending the Habeas Corpus Act and thereby obtaining the means of keeping in gaol the most dangerously disaffected of the Irish people, not to mention the pacific effect that some well-publicised hangings would have on would-be patriots.* Pitt's return to office was delayed till 1804, but that was exactly the use made of the rising, under the direction of Wickham and Marsden.

Pitt was quite capable of originating and executing such a plan. As early as 1792 he had written the Lord Lieutenant of Ireland that he had long hoped that the " fermentation " in Ireland (the rebelliousness of the people to alien rule and their increasing devotion to democratic principles) might eventually lead to a legislative union between Ireland and England. Years of harsh and brutal treatment of the Irish people culminated in the rebellion of 1798. " You must use this moment of terror to frighten the Irish into a legislative union with this country," Lord Cornwallis was instructed when he was sent to Ireland as its new Lord Lieutenant, just after the outbreak of the rebellion. The words were written by King George the Third, but the idea was Pitt's.

His ability as a statesman and the efforts of idolising biographers have kept in the shadow one interesting aspect of

---

*As " gaol " was the spelling then in general use, and as there are countless references to specific gaols, Newgate gaol, Kilmainham gaol, which it would be impossible to modernise, it has been found convenient to keep this spelling throughout, instead of the modern "jail."

Pitt's character. He was an extremely sardonic individual, famous among his contemporaries for his bitter, freezing sarcasm and his love of a malicious joke. It may have amused him to think that in sending for Robert Emmet he was using the young man's blazing patriotism as a means of keeping enslaved the country he longed to free.

In casting about for someone who could call out all the disloyal, liberty-loving citizens of Ireland so that they could then be done away with, someone whose hopes and aspirations coincided so completely with those of the mass of the Irish people that his death and degradation would symbolise the destruction of their common cause, Pitt or any one else could not have made a better choice than Robert Emmet. He had the prestige of a name so reverenced in Ireland that it could recruit great numbers of men devoted to the principles it stood for, liberty, justice, and honour. His father was State Physician of Ireland, but politically liberal, nevertheless, and vastly popular with the mass of the people. His older brother, Thomas Addis Emmet, had helped to found the Society of United Irishmen, the organisation that spread the doctrines of democracy throughout the country. Four years of imprisonment for his principles, ending in exile, added lustre to an already honoured name.

Robert Emmet himself had been sworn a United Irishman while still at Trinity College. He had held high office in the Society, and in 1800 he went to Paris as its envoy. He was less practical than his brother and much too credulous and trusting for political intrigue. He was surrounded by spies and informers and false friends, but almost up to the outbreak of the rebellion in July of 1803 he suspected no one. Even then he had no idea that every move of the conspirators was watched.

Looking back on his life, it seems inevitable that Robert Emmet should have become the symbol of Irish nationalism, but not in the way his enemies intended. The very height of Emmet's idealism saved him. Caught as he was in a great and cold-blooded conspiracy, himself victimised and the safety of the girl he loved used as a threat to make him renounce his principles, he bore himself superbly. He struck a note so pure, so selfless, so lofty, that all the finer qualities of his fellow-countrymen responded to it, and in spite of the untruths told about him his name became immortal.

"I can serve my country as well on the scaffold as in the field," Robert Emmet wrote in his farewell letter to his brother Tom, and so it seems he can. For in the story of his life, filled with drama and fascinating for so many reasons, there is implicit much which is of value to the world to-day but which becomes dull and lifeless when reduced to generalities.

The use of the past as a help in understanding the problems of the present needs no apology. The great Italian liberal, Benedetto Croce, in his book *History as the Story of Liberty*, makes the case for the constructive use of history that seems particularly applicable in the present instance. "The past must be faced," he says, "or, not to speak in metaphors, it must be reduced to a mental problem which can find its solution in a proposition of truth, the ideal premise for our new activity and our new life."

And so I came to write of Robert Emmet and to reconstruct from thousands upon thousands of tiny, scattered fragments the picture of his life. It is a picture of a lover who could put duty before personal happiness, a picture that inevitably reveals him as an idealist even more than a patriot and so, though his patriotism and his concept of honour were entwined, lifts him for ever far above national boundaries and the dimming curtains of time.

One or two critics have spoken of the number of informers there were among the Irish, to the discredit of the national character. It is not my purpose to defend any of them, but I must point out that the critics are guilty of not seeing the forest for the trees. A policy of government which corrupts integrity through fear is to be condemned much more than the individual who yields to the temptation of saving his own life at the expense of others. To make clear the terrifying alternatives which were presented to one Irish soldier who had been caught in the net spread by a Government spy and *agent provocateur* I have introduced on page 274 a footnote showing how the moral problem was presented to him. Other persons in a position to help the Government by betraying their comrades were treated in exactly the same manner.

But for every one person who saved his neck at the expense of others there were dozens and hundreds of Irishmen who went quietly and undramatically to their deaths. Young Hart, the brother of Mrs. Dillon of the White Bull Tavern on Thomas Street, was one of them. Fourteen-year-old Billy Rodgers of Carnmoney, arrested for distributing Thomas Russell's proclamations in the North, was imprisoned for years while every effort was used to make him tell where and from whom he had procured them. They never were able to make him say one word.

Acknowledgements

BEFORE the printing press was invented, in the happy centuries when Ireland was the centre of learning of the Western world, Irish scribes began the tradition of finishing their manuscripts with petitions for the prayers of their readers, references to the conditions under which they had worked, or gracious acknowledgement of thanks to the persons who had provided the material they had copied. "A blessing on the soul of every reader who shall bestow a blessing on the soul of the writer, though neither his hand nor his script deserves it," one Rory MacMahon bargained in 1553.* "A prayer here for the students," another scribe pleaded, " for this is a difficult little story, and let me not be blamed for the script, for the ink is bad and the vellum defective and the day is dark."

One who has copied hundreds of thousands of words from manuscripts and documents in many libraries and archives, most of them in difficult script (and her own no better), may well repeat their supplications. Another colophon is even more appropriate : "A prayer of grace here for the man who gave me the copy for this book." To one man only was that scribe then indebted. I am under obligation to many persons and institutions, which I am happy to acknowledge here.

For permission to do research at the Irish State Paper Office I am deeply grateful to the then Taoiseach, Mr. Eamon de Valera.

For their kindness in making available manuscripts, documents, and books, and for allowing certain photostats to be taken, as well as for their unfailing courtesy and kindness in helping me with my research, I am most grateful to the Deputy Keeper and staff of the Irish Public Record Office and the Irish State Paper Office, particularly Mr. Diarmuid Coffey, who had the unhappy task of passing on my notes,

* In Gaelic, of course. The translation is by Doctor Charles Plummer, and the colophons and marginalia quoted here are taken from his monograph, *Colophons and Marginalia of Irish Scribes*.

and to Mr. Charles Dunne ; to the Director and staff of the National Library of Ireland, particularly Doctor Richard Hayes, Mr. Patrick O'Connor, and the late J. J. Bouch ; to the Librarian and staff of Trinity College Library, Dublin, particularly Mr. Joseph Hanna, Assistant Librarian ; to the Chief Librarian and staff of the City of Dublin Public Libraries, particularly Miss Roisin Walsh, Chief Librarian, Mr. Patrick Stephenson, and Miss Kinehan ; to the Directors and staff of the Royal Irish Academy, Dublin, particularly Dr. Anthony Farrington, Miss Caitlín Bonfield, and Miss Máirín Ní Dhomhnalláin ; to the Librarian and staff of the King's Inn Library, Dublin ; to the Deputy Keeper and staff of the Public Record Office of Northern Ireland ; to the Keeper and staff of the Public Record Office, London ; and to the Director and Librarian of the Royal United Services Institution, Whitehall, London.

I am deeply indebted to the Director of the National Gallery of Ireland and to Mr. Brinsley MacNamara for a photograph of the death-mask of Robert Emmet.

I am deeply grateful to the Director and staff of the National Museum of Ireland, particularly Mr. Liam Gogan, Keeper of the Art and Industrial Division, and Dr. Hayes-McCoy, for their kindness in supplying me with a photograph of the water-colour portrait of Robert Emmet, which is used as an illustration in this book, and for allowing the photograph of the rare drawing showing the inside of Emmet's depot to be electroplated.

For their kindness in procuring the loan of rare books from London, I am deeply grateful to the Librarian and staff of the Carnegie Students' Library, Dublin.

I am most grateful to the Very Reverend Myles V. Ronan, P.P., D.Litt., for his invaluable assistance, and for his great kindness in loaning me the manuscripts of *The Life of Anne Devlin* and *The Life of Michael Dwyer*, by Brother Luke Cullen, and for supplying me with other rare material.

To the anonymous owner* of Sarah Curran's music book in which she had sketched profiles of members of her family

---

* This refers to the late Very Rev. John Canon McGuirk, P.P., Rathfarnham, who received the book from an old parishioner in whose family it was preserved, apparently as a gift from the Curran family. It was given by the Canon to the Loreto Abbey, Rathfarnham, and the Rev. Mother has kindly allowed the drawings to be photographed for illustrations in this edition.

and of Robert Emmet I am most grateful for photostats of such sketches and for his allowing me to see other documents in his possession.

I am deeply grateful to Rev. Joseph Hurley, S.J., for his many valuable suggestions.

I am deeply grateful to Charles Dickson, M.D., for his kindness in loaning me transcripts of several documents.

I am deeply grateful to Richard Hayes, M.D., for permission to quote extracts from his book, *The Last Invasion of Ireland*, and to the publishers, M. H. Gill and Son, Ltd., Dublin, for concurring in such permission.

I am deeply grateful to the late Mr. John Butler of Ormond Quay, Dublin, for his kindness in supplying a photograph of the portrait of Sarah Curran used as an illustration in this book.

A selection of the Drennan Letters was published by His Majesty's Stationery Office in 1931 on behalf of the Public Record Office, Belfast, and acknowledgement is made of permission to reproduce certain material already included in the official volume. I am also most grateful to Dr. D. A. Chart, Deputy Keeper of Records of Northern Ireland, who edited the book, and to Mrs. Duffin of Summerhill, Belfast, for photostats of other Drennan letters.

I am most grateful to Mr. Seumas O'Connor, who conducted me through Green Street Court House, and explained the alterations made since Emmet was tried there.

To the late Mr. Michael MacDonagh and John Murray, Ltd., London, I am most grateful for permission to quote extracts from *The Vice Roy's Post Bag*.

My deepest gratitude goes to Miss Lydia Field Emmet of New York for her kindness in supplying photographs of several Emmet family portraits used as illustrations for this book, and for permission to use extracts from the text and the engraving of Anne Develin printed in *Memoirs of Thomas Addis Emmet and Robert Emmet* and *The Emmet Family*, by Dr. Thomas Addis Emmet of New York. I am also deeply grateful to her for several anecdotes of family tradition and for her invaluable assistance in checking certain details of family history.

Words cannot express the gratitude I feel to the many people both in Ireland and in the United States whose generosity and kindness helped make this book possible.

To the Whittlesey House editor, Miss Lois Cole, I have much more than the usual gratitude for her invaluable suggestions as to revising and re-writing this book.

I am most grateful to the late Albert S. Osborn for his kindness in examining letters and other documents written by Robert Emmet and giving his opinion as to authorship of unsigned ones.

"Three pen dips did that," a proud Irish scribe exclaimed at the end of a short poem he had just copied. Many more than three pen dips were needed to write this book, so I may truthfully end this litany of thanks with the words of a scribe who preceded me by centuries : " I will stop now, for my hand is weary, and weary is myself."

A blessing on the reader, and may Mary aid the ink.

HELEN LANDRETH.

Contents

I. BACKGROUND

Chapter		Page
1.	The House on St. Stephen's Green	2
2.	The Birth of the United Irishmen	10

II. PITT'S WEAPONS

3.	Intimidation and Rewards	29
4.	The Boy in the Background	42
5.	Informers and How they are Made	46
6.	The Rise of the Orange Order	56

III. INITIATION TO WARFARE

7.	Robert Emmet Becomes a United Irishman	65
8.	Robert Emmet Is Expelled from Trinity	76
9.	Two Questionable Characters	80
10.	The Red Harvest of 1798	87
11.	The Harvest of 1798, Second Phase	95
12.	Robert Emmet in Office	103

IV. INTERLUDE

13.	Robert Emmet in France	115
14.	The Mystery of the Summons	124

V. Emmet Prepares for Another Rising

Chapter		Page
15.	The Castle Watches	131
16.	Men and Arms	140
17.	Emmet's Communications with France	149
18.	The Disaffected outside Dublin	153
19.	Love and War	159
20.	The Explosion in Patrick Street	165
21.	" So Little Time "	170
22.	Thomas Russell and the North	175

VI. July 23, 1803

23. | Dublin Prelude | 185
24. | Action | 203
25. | Immediate Aftermath | 219
26. | The Rising Elsewhere | 226

VII. The Hunt

27. | Emmet in the Mountains | 245
28. | Man Hunt in Kildare | 255
29. | Harold's Cross | 260
30. | Reinforcements and Arrests | 266

VIII. Emmet's Capture and Ordeal

31. | Arrest and Examination | 281
32. | Building the Case against Emmet | 292
33. | Emmet Plans to Escape | 298
34. | More Trickery | 301

Chapter   *Page*

35. Major Sirr Raids the Priory   305

36. Russell Comes to Help Emmet   .   .   .   308

37. Into the Depths   312

38. Miles Byrne Reaches Paris   318

IX. THE TRIAL OF ROBERT EMMET

39. The Crown's Case in General   323

40. Crown Witnesses   332

41. The Crown Heaps Its Calumny   .   .   .   347

42. Emmet Answers   352

X. EXECUTION

43. Final Pressure   363

44. The Scaffold in Thomas Street   369

XI. USING THE RISING

45. Infamy and Arrests   377

46. Pitt's Fight for Office   398

Index   413

List of Illustrations

Robert Emmet . . . . . *Frontispiece*

Dr. Christopher Emmet and Rebecca Temple Emmet . . . . *facing page* 16

Dr. Robert Emmet and Elizabeth Mason Emmet . . . . . . „ „ 17

St. Stephen's Green . . . . „ „ 32

Trinity College, Dublin . . . . „ „ 33

Thomas Addis Emmet and Lord Edward Fitzgerald . . . . . „ „ 64

Theobald Wolfe Tone and Thomas Russell „ „ 65

The Upper Castle Yard of Dublin Castle . „ „ 80

Map of Dublin . . . . . „ „ 81

Michael Dwyer . . . . . „ „ 144

Emmet's Thomas Street Depot . . „ „ 145

Sarah Curran and Anne Develin . . „ „ 160

Sarah Curran's Letter to Emmet, her Music Book, Signature and Sketches . . „ „ 161

Trial of Robert Emmet : Scene in Court . „ „ 352

Emmet's Letter to Sarah . . . . „ „ 353

St. Catherine's Church and Thomas Street „ „ 368

Execution of Robert Emmet . . . „ „ 369

List of Illustrations

I
BACKGROUND

2—1854

CHAPTER ONE

The House on St. Stephen's Green

" AMERICA, America, the land of arts and arms, where the Goddess Liberty was wooed and won, and twelve young eaglets, springing from her nest, bore Freedom upward on their soaring wings. . . . "

Seventeen-year-old Christopher Emmet was practising an oration he was to deliver before the Historical Society of Trinity College. The time was 1778, the place the home of his father, Dr. Robert Emmet, on Dublin's St. Stephen's Green. Somewhere in the house was the baby of the family, little Robert Emmet, whose life was to be dedicated to the pursuit of that same goddess.

St. Stephen's Green was one of the stateliest squares of Georgian Dublin. The brick houses that faced the park on all four sides were classic in architecture and built on spacious lines. The brasses of their panelled doors shone with constant polishing ; their many-paned windows were draped with stiff brocades. Dr. Emmet's house on the west side of the Green was generously wide, and within the air was one of cultivated tastes and sumptuous furnishings, as befitted the State Physician of Ireland.

On the sideboard a huge silver salver bore the coat of arms of the ancient Emmet family with the motto *Constans*. Other Emmets in England and Ireland (spelling the name in a variety of ways) used *Tenez le Vrai*, but the basic idea was the same, and constancy was a family characteristic. From the Doctor's mother, Rebecca Temple Emmet, descendant of Sir Thomas Temple, came the talents of the famous line that had produced Sir William Temple, Algernon Sidney's friend and Cromwell's chaplain.

Dr. Emmet, the son of Dr. Christopher Emmet of Tipperary, had gone to France for his medical training and during his

3

holidays had travelled a great deal on the Continent. His years abroad had given him a cosmopolitan outlook on life and an easy, polished manner. On his return to Ireland he had practised for a time in Cork. There he had met Miss Elizabeth Mason, whose family came from Kerry.

Taking advantage of the poetic licence that allowed a gentleman to be more outspoken in rhyme than he could be in prose, he had wooed her with ardent verses :

> In vain, my dear Betty, your bosom you steel
>   Against the soft anguish you surely must feel.
> In the bloom of your youth, and so pleasing to sight
>   You'll be teased into love, and must yield to delight.

> Even now, while you slight me, examine your heart,
>   Yet a novice to Love, and a stranger to Art.
> Don't you feel some emotion you cannot explain,
>   A something you know not, of pleasure or pain. . . .

The *Dublin Journal* for November 22, 1760, carried the announcement of the marriage of " Robert Emmet, Esq., of Cork, Doctor of Physic and Corresponding Member of the Royal Academy of Sciences at Montpelia in France, to Miss Mason of said city." The ceremony had taken place six days before.

Together with her dowry of £500 Elizabeth Mason brought the first Irish blood to mingle with the Anglo-Norman strains of the Emmets. The Masons of Kerry were of English extraction, too, but they had intermarried with the native Irish families of their county and had acquired, together with an admiration for the old Gaelic culture that still survived there, the usual Kerry attitude toward free trading. In that district of deep bays, so tantalisingly close to the trade of France, smuggling was a common practice, and it was traditional to hold law and government in little respect.

This is not to say that the Emmet establishment was a disloyal one. Far from it. The Emmets were Castle people, part of the so-called Protestant Ascendancy that held the important offices of Ireland. About 1770, Dr. Emmet, probably through the influence of his kinsman, Lord Temple (later the Marquis of Buckingham, and the Lord Lieutenant of Ireland) was appointed (for a purchase price of £1,000) the State Physician of Ireland. The Emmets then moved to Dublin from Cork. At first, they lived in Molesworth Street, a pleasant enough neighbourhood, but as the Doctor's appointments, practice, and family increased, a larger and more fashionable house was appropriate. By virtue of his office as State Physician he was a governor of the Hospital for the Insane that Dean Swift had founded early in the century. In 1772, he became Licentiate in Physic of the College of Physicians, Dublin. But the inclination to Republicanism that Louise Imogen Guiney has claimed for the Temples made him critical of the faults of the Government that other officials were content to overlook. That was one of the reasons why young Christopher Emmet, at seventeen, was apostrophising the Goddess Liberty with so much eloquence.

There were only four Emmet children alive in 1778, though Elizabeth Emmet had borne one every year for the first eighteen years of her marriage, with a solitary exception. Many of them had died while they were very young. The last five had all been boys, each named Robert for his father. All but the last of these was dead before a new brother was born the next year. For him, Elizabeth Emmet wished only that he would be as tender and gentle and clever as his father.

Besides Robert, the baby, and the seventeen-year-old Christopher, already famous for his brilliance and eloquence, there was Thomas Addis Emmet, a rather shy boy of fourteen, who adored his older brother, and a little girl, Mary Anne. She alone of all the warm-hearted Emmets was cool and detached. She shared the family cleverness, but indolence kept her from exerting it very often.

Both the Doctor and Mrs. Emmet had been born to the tradition of *noblesse oblige*, which they automatically passed on to their family. Elizabeth Emmet spoke of honour as though, clothed with flesh and vital with the spark of life, it shared the house with her. She was equally intimate with the other virtues, and the horror of her life was the vice of vanity. Rather than let that corrupt her children she sternly repressed her pride in them. She was for ever pointing out their faults and delivering little lectures with morals attached. In her striving for improvement she included herself. She felt she was, as she once wrote Tom, "a most imperfect fabric and often in need of propping." The object of all this was to make her children and herself worthy of her husband, whom she passionately adored. Always, at the back of her mind was the thought that sometime he would die, and she would be left in the world without him.

There was a game the Doctor sometimes amused himself with when he was alone, and he may have played it with her when they were on long coach rides and darkness or rain shut out the landscape. He would imagine he was again a medical student at Montpellier, and on his holidays. He would choose a river of France, the Loire, the Seine, or the Villaine, and name the little villages that bordered the banks, from Nantes to Blois, from Havre de Grace to Paris, from Roche-Bernard to Rennes. Every poplar, every willow, every church spire and arching bridge he would recall and picture so vividly that he seemed to be floating along in some little boat, hearing the green whispers of leaves in the summer air or the sound of the Angelus coming over evening fields.

This was the household into which little Robert Emmet had been born. He had his mother's ardent nature. From her, too, he took his affection for the Irish people, his feeling of kinship with them. From his father's line he had the Temple face, dark and aquiline, the Temple promise of genius. The effect on his impressionable nature of his father's ideas on the bringing up of children was to make him live very much in a world of his own, idealistic and impractical. The Doctor, kind and loving parent though he was, did not believe in letting children intrude their immature thoughts into their elders' conversation. At the Doctor's door must be laid the greatest flaw in Robert Emmet's make-up.

The times he was born into also helped to make him what he was. The shot the embattled farmers had fired at Lexington in April of 1775 had been heard nowhere more clearly than in Ireland. In fact, thirty thousand or so of the rebellious inhabitants of the central provinces of America had lately gone there from the North of Ireland, taking with them the tradition of Republicanism they had inherited from their Scotch and English ancestors. The kinsmen they left behind in Ireland combined their democratic fervour with the national ambitions of the native Irish, who after six centuries of English rule were not reconciled to it.

They understood colonial opposition to the stamp tax, as they paid a similar one themselves, and Ireland's imperfect representation made her taxation seem equally tyrannous. Throughout Ireland sympathisers with America waited eagerly for news of the rebellious colonists' warfare against the English and rejoiced at the victories of Saratoga and Yorktown. A patriotic gentleman of Derry, one Thomas Cooke, who for his principles was later a prisoner in Newgate gaol, mixed in the entries of his commonplace book amorous passages from a French novel, notes on flax culture, Dr. Dodridges's *Lines On His Wife's Bosom*, and lengthy quotations from the speeches of Patrick Henry, including the inflammatory "If this be Treason. . . ." Later copies of *The American Museum*, a publication with a strongly patriotic outlook, were passed from one Irish hand to another and kept alive in Irish hearts the ringing words of Nathan Hale and General Israel Putnam. A "mischievous levelling principle was at work," one Irish Government official wrote nervously to another, "that sets itself up in opposition to all Law and Good Government, and seeks to destroy all Rank and Subordination, and to reap something from confusion." Robert Emmet was very truly a child of the American Revolution.

When Robert was five, the second son of the family, Thomas Addis, went to Edinburgh to study medicine, and he absorbed the intoxicating ideas about the inalienable rights of man and his innate nobility which the new Whigs there had distilled from the milder republican theories of Locke. They were still as dangerous to tyranny as when they had stirred Thomas Jefferson and the other framers of the American Declaration of Independence.

Christopher Emmet, who had become one of the most brilliant young lawyers at the Irish bar, died in 1789, just as Tom Emmet was finishing his medical course in Scotland. Tom's admiration for his brother was so great that he decided to give up medicine and take up Christopher's profession. He went to London to study law. The Temple was no such hotbed of democracy as Scotland had been, but Tom met there a witty and vivacious young Irishman named Theobald Wolfe

Tone. Tone's conversion to patriotism was soon to have a tremendous effect on the lives of both Tom and Robert Emmet.

By the time Robert was twelve, the Doctor had become an out-and-out supporter of parliamentary reform. The Irish House of Commons did not represent the people of Ireland in any way. No Catholic could sit there. No Catholic could vote. Only sixty-four of its three hundred seats were open to contest. The rest were rotten boroughs, held by the landed interests and the administration. The Government always could count on a clear majority, and it was shockingly brazen about adding to an already enormous pension list, very often for people who had no claim on the country whatever. Even if the Emmet children were not allowed to intrude on the family conversations, they absorbed the views of the grown-ups, and Robert learned by heart an essay on liberty that Dr. Emmet very much admired, written by a young Belfast man, Dr. William Drennan.

As a young Corsican corporal, who was later to come into Robert's life, had recently remarked, "It was surprising to see how the word Liberty set men's minds on fire." Robert Emmet's reaction was to try his hand at verse. Already he was an out-and-out rebel, at least on paper. His composition did not mark him as a poetic genius, but it did show the trend of his young thought :

ERIN'S CALL

Brothers, arise, our country calls.
  Let us gain her rights or die.
In her cause who nobly falls
  Decked in brightest wreaths shall lie,
And Freedom's genius o'er his bier
  Shall place the wreath and drop a tear.

Long by England's power opprest,
  Groaning long beneath her chains,
England's ill-used power detest !
  Burst her yoke ! Your rights regain !
The Standard raise of Liberty !
  Ireland, you shall be free !

> Brothers, march, march on to glory.
> In your country's cause unite.
> Freedom's blessing see before you.
> Erin's sons, for freedom fight.
> England's legions we defy.
> We swear to conquer or to die.

At the age of twelve, Robert Emmet had decided that it would be a glorious thing to give his life for his country.

CHAPTER TWO

The Birth of the United Irishmen

IN Ireland, which had suffered more than six hundred years of English rule without becoming reconciled to it, this was no unusual ambition. A proud, possessive, long-memoried people, now impoverished and oppressed, inevitably produced many men anxious to sacrifice themselves for the national honour. Ireland had once been the centre of learning of the Western world. Now its ancient schools were in ruins, its monasteries desecrated, its people kept in ignorance and forced to speak a foreign tongue. Once Irish poets had ranked next to its princes and had been rewarded with rich gifts. Now, though they might compose poems in Latin and Greek and English as well as their native Gaelic, they earned their living as *spailpíns*, spade labourers, or by furtively teaching their countrymen at alfresco hedge-schools. Once Ireland had sent missionaries to Scotland and England and the Continent. Now its people who adhered to the Catholic Church were deprived of property and practically every right as citizens. Once Ireland had been prosperous, with ships from Spain and Italy and France bringing goods to exchange for Irish cloth and marble, timber, salted fish, Irish works of art wrought from fine gold. Now most of the harbours were deserted. Irish trade had been throttled since it had competed with the English. Everything Irish had been sacrificed to enrich the invaders.

Naturally, a people with their heritage would not meekly accept poverty and subjection. From the time of the conquest of Henry the Second in 1171, they had fought the English whenever they could. Sometimes the resistance had been narrow and confined. Sometimes it had spread through most of the island. There were always people ready to take up arms whenever a leader appeared or times seemed opportune. In the fourteenth century Donal O'Neill, whose ancestor

Niall of the Nine Hostages had been High King of Ireland a thousand years before, tried to drive the English out of Ireland with the help of Robert Bruce. Henry the Eighth of England had had to put down an Irish rising led by the son of one of his own Irish ministers, the Ninth Earl of Kildare. He was a Fitzgerald called Silken Thomas, a descendant of Maurice Fitzgerald, one of the adventurers who had helped Henry the Second to get a foothold in Ireland. In four centuries the Fitzgeralds, known as the Geraldines, had acquired lands and castles and power. As Earls of Kildare and Earls of Munster they had become mighty men, and gradually " more Irish than the Irish." They were often in opposition to the English throne, and the Irish people looked to them for leadership as readily as they did to the native Irish princes.

Early in her reign Queen Elizabeth had had to put down a rising led by another Geraldine, the sixteenth Earl of Desmond, and one by Shane O'Neill, " the Lion of Ulster." Almost at the end of her long rule three great Irish princes, Hugh O'Neill, Hugh O'Donnell, and Hugh Maguire, had led the country in a nearly successful effort to overthrow the English. In the middle of the seventeenth century Owen Roe O'Neill, Spanish born and Spanish bred, a Spanish sword in his hand, had come back to the land of his fathers to lead an Irish army. When Patrick Sarsfield, the memory of the Irish defeats of the Boyne and Limerick still rankling in his mind, was dying at Landen, he mourned that his blood was shed for France and not to free Ireland. O'Mores, O'Briens, O'Byrnes, these and countless other Irish chieftains had led their clansmen against the alien enemy.

Since the English Reformation the Irish had combined resistance to Protestantism with their national cause, and each had reinforced the other. " For God and Our Lady and Rory O'More " had brought them out in arms in the middle of the seventeenth century. Their Catholicism had made them support James the Second against William of Orange at the end of it.

The Emmets were Protestants, but the self-interest that blinded most of the so-called Protestant Ascendancy in Ireland to the condition of the native Catholics was replaced in their case by clear-eyed devotion to the principles of liberty and justice. Their sympathy was with the Catholics.

For many years the Catholics in the North of Ireland had been subjected to raids by bands of bigoted Protestants whose aim was to drive them from that part of the country. The raiders were called Peep of Day Boys because they usually attacked at dawn. The Catholics, though forbidden by the Penal Laws to own arms, nevertheless banded together to oppose them and became known as Defenders. Throughout Ireland the Catholics had other grievances besides those imposed by the Penal Laws. They had to pay tithes of their harvest to clergymen of the Established Church, who extracted them with the aid of rapacious tithe-farmers. They had to pay enormously high rents for small tracts of ground, and absentee landlords spent the money elsewhere. All these conditions made for turbulence and dissatisfaction among the mass of the people. In the cities poverty was so extreme that one visitor earned a reputation for wit by remarking that he never knew what English beggars did with their old rags until he came to Dublin.

To make matters worse, in Robert Emmet's boyhood the always selfish Government had become more corrupt than ever, selling peerages to pay for seats to bolster its majority in the House of Commons and taxing the poor people beyond all endurance. The American slogan " No taxation without representation " had wakened the civic sense of the Irish people to such an extent that in 1790, in spite of the hopelessness of the situation, they were demanding a reform of Parliament. Napper Tandy, an energetic little man with an extraordinarily large flat nose, was getting additional stimulus by a correspondence with French Republicans.

Dublin's popular candidates were the veteran liberal statesman Henry Grattan and young Lord Henry Fitzgerald, a brother of the Duke of Leinster, the current head of the Fitzgeralds of Kildare. After an exciting interval of canvassing they went to the hustings at the head of eighteen bands, followed by fifteen hundred supporters carrying banners that proclaimed their Whiggish viewpoints. The crowds who lined the streets or leaned out of house windows cheered them all wildly. One little boy named Thomas Moore, hanging out of a window of the family home in Aungier Street, screamed so loudly that he was sure Grattan looked up at him.

Napper Tandy, marching behind Grattan, received a special ovation, and so did a well-dressed little Negro holding aloft the Cap of Liberty.

Dr. Emmet was so interested in reform that he made sure, during the election days, that Grattan was really in favour of a proper representation of the people in Parliament. " I and my young friend here," said Grattan, indicating Lord Henry Fitzgerald, " are by no means adverse to a reform of Parliament."

" Then, sir," said the Doctor, " the people enlisted under you as a party."

He was so pleased that he let Robert, who was with him, step forward and recite for Mr. Grattan the essay on Liberty that he had learned by heart.

Dr. William Drennan, the author of the essay, soon learned of the incident and was much flattered. He made a point of meeting Dr. Emmet and became a frequent visitor at the house on St. Stephen's Green. Dr. Drennan was a Protestant from Belfast and had studied medicine in Edinburgh. Probably it was the Whiggish point of view he had picked up there that made him so eager for reform. He was already turning over in his mind the idea of an organisation to bring about Ireland's independence, a society that really would effect improvements and not merely talk about them. He wanted something secret and ceremonial like the Freemasons, which would conspire benevolently and plot for the well-being of the people.

In the North young Robert Stewart, later to be known as Lord Castlereagh, and John O'Neill were also standing for Parliament as reform candidates. The people of Antrim and Down, determined to break the autocratic rule of Lord Downshire of Kilwarlin, the great landowner of the district, rallied to their support with enthusiasm and energy, as well as satiric and sometimes ribald ballads.

> A ——— for your freedom, a ——— for a Whig,
>   A ——— for your Grattan and Tandy :
> Go crack of your junction, I care not a fig,
>   The Laird of Kilwarlin's the Dandy,

began one of the raciest, in opposition to the Marquis's candidate.

'Tis mummery, boys, flummery, boys,
   Virtue and honesty are beggar-man's toys

ran the ironic chorus at the end of each verse.

He [the Marquis] seldom lets pedigree into his stud.
   For learning he cares not a louse, Sir.
He lifts Lawyer Gallipot out of the mud,
   And gives him a place in the House, Sir.

He dresses Religion as fine as his ————,
   His Sunday processions are grand, Sir.
Hacks, halberts, and burgesses rank at the door,
   And waddle away with the band, Sir.

Their opponents splattered equally malicious humour about
and, besides, had even more substantial inducements to offer.
A third liberal and literary physician, Dr. Alexander Haliday
of Belfast, writing to his friend the Earl of Charlemont, named
them with sorrow :

All the arts of Deceit, seduction, the weight of Bribery, the allurement of
promises, the terror of threats, the guilt of perjury, are all in action, without
a blush, nay, with exultation. Add to this the treachery of agents, the hired
industry of Bailiffs and tithe farmers, the countenance of government, the
sedulity of Revenue people great and small, the pious exertions of the
Church, perhaps the overflowing of the Treasury from the sale of Peerages !
What a formidable master ! What a horrid but too faithful picture.*

O'Neill and young Stewart were both elected, but by narrow
margins. Writing again to the Earl, Dr. Haliday lamented
the death of Benjamin Franklin and marvelled at the number
of votes the Downshire candidate had received.
" What cannot the weight of government, and of the
aristocracy do, and as noxious a vermin as any of them, the
tithe masters and [tithe] farmers do ? My lord, we must get
rid of them. St. Patrick knew nothing of them, or he would
have banished them along with the vipers and adders."
But the Government had no idea of letting any of its
servants be done away with, or its influence diminished. Two
liberal candidates had been elected here, but there was an old
established practice for use in such cases that shortly began to

* *Charlemont Manuscripts*, Royal Irish Academy, Dublin.

dampen the reforming ardour of those particular candidates. The Government began to dangle the prospect of a title before the eyes of Mr. O'Neill. Young Mr. Stewart was taken in hand by Lord Camden, his stepmother's brother, who was a member of the English Privy Council.

These moves, of course, were part of Pitt's basic imperial policy. Lord Chatham's brilliant younger son, who had himself once been an ardent advocate of reform, was now, as Prime Minister of England, an adroit and thoroughgoing politician. His chief objectives at this time were to build an empire and to entrench monarchy against the growing menace of democracy. The problem of Ireland was complicated by the spirit of revolt among the Catholics against the Penal Laws and the danger that ultimately they would demand the franchise. As they made up seven-eighths of the population of Ireland, the small Protestant minority that managed the country would then lose control of it. So Pitt was turning over in his mind the idea of eliminating the Irish Government and the Irish Parliament and merging the Irish people with the greater mass of Protestant Englishmen by means of a legislative union.

However, the time was not yet ripe for such a move, and until it was, Pitt was willing to give minor concessions to the Catholics to keep them quiet. But if a reform of Parliament were allowed in either Ireland or England, that, too, would make the Government lose control. So there was no softening, either in London or Dublin, of the official attitude toward men with liberal ideas. The members of the various Whig Clubs of London, Dublin, and Belfast, who counted men of great talents, rank, and wealth among their members, as well as people in more modest stations in life, were indiscriminately derided as low, loutish creatures of no consequence. The Irish Lord Chancellor, in a speech in the Irish House of Commons, spoke of a resolution of the Dublin Whig Club as " worthy of no more notice than those of any porter house assembly, except that it appeared authenticated by two of the hereditary Counsellors of the land, Lords Moira and Charlemont."

Hearing of this, the Secretary of the Northern Whig Club, Dr. Haliday, wrote to his friend the Earl of Charlemont, " I was about to have advertised a meeting of our Northern Guzzlers for the 12th August, but I shall now send them private notice to steal in by the back stairs, as Pitt did into the ministry."

The gay little man who wrote this in his cramped, precise hand did more good than he ever realised. His letters to the Earl (now preserved at the Royal Irish Academy in Dublin) were usually written to amuse his friend during his frequent illnesses. But inevitably they portrayed the viewpoint of a typical liberal Whig with more than typical wit and good humour. The Doctor once described himself as "having a fortunate flow of spirits." It was no exaggeration. Even in discussing his *bête noire*, the Prime Minister, there was no rancour in his humour. "The Government is at its wit's end, and that after no long journey," he once commented.

He was not an out-and-out democrat. The French Revolution led him to hope that "this new tyrant, Egalité, will not look Order and Subordination out of Countenance." But he loved justice ardently, and his dislike of Pitt's administration came from the fact that he believed the Minister was nullifying the liberties guaranteed in the British Constitution. All his political efforts were toward restoring that institution to a state of vigour and fighting the appalling corruption in the administration of his own country.

Tom Emmet came back to Dublin from London at the end of 1790 and was immediately admitted to the Irish Bar, where he felt both proud and diffident for being known as the brilliant Christopher's brother. Tom, though warm-hearted and sociable, lacked the gentle charm that instantly endeared Robert to almost every one he met ; but when he was among his intimates, he put aside his usual reserve and was obviously so anxious to be amiable that his very earnestness appeared as proof of his friendliness and had an appeal of its own.

Soon after his return to Dublin he married Jane Patten, a dark-haired girl of nineteen, whose uncle, Mr. Colville, was a governor of the Bank of Ireland. Her vivacity and charm made her a welcome addition to the family circle and balanced nicely the cool and indolent detachment of Mary Anne Emmet.

Dr. Drennan dined there in June of 1791, and wrote his impressions of the family to his sister, Mrs. McTier of Belfast ·

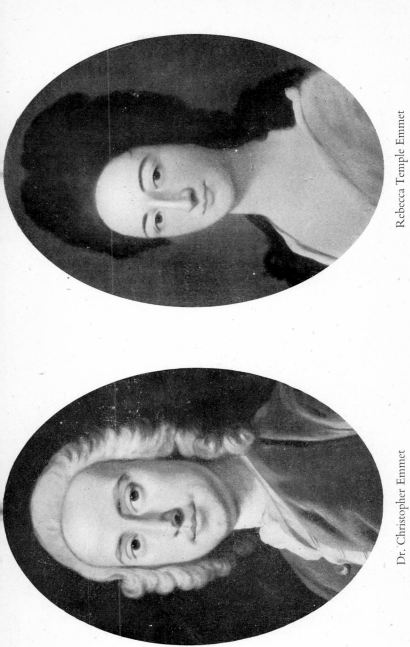

Dr. Christopher Emmet

Rebecca Temple Emmet

Grandparents of Robert Emmet
Reproduced by courtesy of Miss Lydia F. Emmet

Dr. Robert Emmet

Elizabeth Mason Emmet

Parents of Robert Emmet

Reproduced by courtesy of Miss Lydia F. Emmet

"Dr. Emmet, very civil; his wife, amiable; Mary Anne, not so much. The young counsellor, Thomas Addis Emmet and his lady live with the Doctor for the present. She is very pretty and he is very studious, or affects being so, very clever in speech, as all the family, through which a vein of elegance, taste, and all that runs."* Jane Patten, Dr. Drennan had heard, had brought a dowry of £2,000, but he told his sister, with characteristic scepticism, that he thought a quarter of that was probably nearer the figure.†

Besides Dr. Drennan, another young Irishman with advanced ideas about reform was also calling at the Green. He was Wolfe Tone, whom Tom Emmet had met in London. Tone was a slight, sharp-featured young man, whose very pigtail seemed charged with vivacity. His charm and wit equalled the brilliance of his mind. He came from a rather humble background, his father being a coachmaker who lived in one of the crowded and unfashionable streets near the north bank of the Liffey. But he had great natural abilities, and somehow his family had managed to send him to Trinity and then to the Temple in London.

He was given to planning things on a grand scale, and he used to quote Le Maréchal de Villars that he never sank to the mediocre until he was convinced that the great and the grand were impossible. Once he had conceived an idea in all its vastness, he could depict it in vivid and telling phrases. He had been called to the Irish Bar, but he was soon sick and weary of the law. He needed wider and more stimulating horizons than the Four Courts or the Leinster Circuit. While he was a flute-playing young blade at Trinity, he had eloped with a lovely young girl of sixteen. By now he had a family to support, no fortune, and a brilliant and thirsty mind. Some of his friends had gone into politics and written pamphlets. More or less out of boredom Tone thought of doing the same, and he cast around him for a subject. Reform being the popular topic of the time, he selected that. Looking at the sordid conditions of the country, he could see the cause of it, the connection with England. His metamorphosis as a patriot began.

---

* *The Drennan Letters*, edited by D. A. Chart, p. 55.
† Jane Patten's marriage settlement shows that her dowry actually was £2,000.

In the pamphlet that he wrote over the signature, "An Independent Northern Whig," he pictured the Irish people as "not that blatant beast that will bear any burden, provided their long ears be scratched, and they be indulged in the liberty of braying. They will see *who* they are that rule them with a rod of iron. . . . They will probe the ulcer that corrodes our Constitution to the bottom. They will look among themselves for the remedy."*

When Tone went to the Emmets, he sometimes took with him a young army officer then stationed in Belfast, Thomas Russell. He and Russell had met by accident in the gallery of the Irish House of Commons a couple of years before and had soon become bosom friends. They had a common liking for claret, as well as similar views on politics. "A great fool, and I have great trouble to manage him," Tone used to say of Russell deprecatingly, but he was very proud of his young friend.

Russell was remarkably handsome, dark, and several inches taller than Tone. Usually, he was a bit haughty to strangers and gravely courteous to ladies. But when he was with his intimates, and particularly when enlivened with a couple of bottles of claret, he was quite a different person. He had once been known—egged on by some fellow-officers from the regimental mess—to throw himself before a group of young ladies on the street in Belfast and address them with more ardour than discretion.

His diary for these days (besides showing the beginning of a hopeless love affair with Betty Goddard of Newry) says that he was often " playing billiards, supping, at dinners," etc.†
But the dreadful condition of the Irish people touched him even more deeply than it did Tone, and, like him, he was thinking how they might be helped. He knew most of the people in Belfast who were interested in reform, including Dr. Drennan's brother-in-law, Sam McTier, and he belonged to the Belfast Volunteers, a patriotic organization formed several years before.

* *The Life and Journals of Theobald Wolfe Tone,* I, p. 305, 1826 ed.
† Russell's papers were seized when he was arrested in 1796. Some are now at the Irish State Paper Office, and some at Trinity College Library. The particular sheets of pale blue paper on which Russell recorded this one are among the *Sirr Papers* at Trinity. Two note-books that he had started to use as a diary in competition with Tone's journal are at the State Paper Office.

Belfast was at this time so hotly democratic that it was called Little Boston. The Volunteers planned to advertise their principles by a celebration of Bastille Day. Tone and Russell talked over a set of resolutions to be adopted by the organisation following a parade ; and after Russell had gone back to the North, Tone put them into shape. He sent them to Russell with a letter that amounted to a private Declaration of Independence. " I have not said one word which looks like a wish for separation," he wrote, " though I give it to you and your friends as my most decided opinion that such an event would be a regeneration for this country."

He had been thinking about organising a society to effect reform. Its unique and daring feature was to have the Catholics, Dissenters, and Protestants with liberal views unite for the common good. This was almost as revolutionary an idea as his private wish to separate Ireland from England. He was a Protestant himself, but he realised that if the Dissenters— the Presbyterians and other small nonconforming sects—who suffered under almost as many disabilities as the Catholics, would unite with them and demand the rights of citizenship, they would form so great a body that the Government would have to listen to them.

Russell presented Tone's idea to the Belfast reformers, but it was so radical that a great many of them hesitated to act upon it. Whereupon Tone wrote a pamphlet about the Catholics that turned the tide strongly in their favour. It shortly made Tone so popular in Belfast that he was invited there in the autumn of 1791, the idea being that he should help organize a society that would bring together the elements he had pointed out.

He went to Belfast in October and, as he recorded in his journal, found Thomas Paine's *Rights of Man* to be the Koran of the place. After a few days of talking with the leading reformers (interspersed with a great many more convivial parties, late lobster suppers with Tom Russell at the Donegal Arms, and miscellaneous bottles of claret) a society was formed on the basis of both his and Dr. Drennan's suggestions. Dr. Drennan's brother-in-law, Samuel McTier, was in the chair at the first meeting, which adopted Tone's name, The Society of United Irishmen.

Having established this democratic society in Belfast, Tone
and Russell went to Dublin and helped to start a similar one
there. Dr. Drennan and Napper Tandy and thirty or more
others were present at the first meeting on November 9,
1791. They promptly sent out printed copies of their Constitution, and one reached Dublin Castle, the seat of the Irish
Government. There " Divide and Conquer " had always
been the policy. The Lord Lieutenant, Lord Westmorland,
who was in the habit of writing letters (in the most abominable
handwriting) to the English cabinet which customarily ran to
a dozen pages or more, was so upset that he dashed off one of
a single breathless paragraph :

> I have the honour to enclose to your Lordship [Lord Grenville, of the
> English cabinet] a printed copy of a paper dated the 9th (of November) by
> a Society just set up in this city which calls itself the Society of United
> Irishmen of Dublin, recommending *the Union of all the People* for a complete
> and radical reform of Parliament. The terms of the paper will probably
> bring it under the observation of the House of Commons. I need not
> trouble your Lordship with the Declaration of a similar Society at Belfast,
> as it is literally copied in the enclosed.*

The news was equally disconcerting to Pitt and the English
cabinet. They were bitterly opposed to anything that savoured
of democracy and always on the alert to ward it off. Only two
months before they had decided that nothing mischievous was
to be dreaded from the Irish Catholics adopting any of the
principles of the French Revolution, and thus they had not
considered it necessary to conciliate them in any way.† Now
they read the Constitution of the United Irishmen and Tone's
pamphlet in favour of the Catholics and decided the Catholics
might become something of a menace. Pitt sent for the Irish
Chief Secretary, Major Hobart, to come to England to discuss
how much would have to be given them to keep them quiet.

The Lord Lieutenant, who by now had his breath and a
good deal more information about the society he called the
Associated Scoundrels, kept Hobart supplied with the alarming
news. Thirty-three new members had been admitted at a
recent meeting, committees of correspondence had been
formed, and new branches were being established throughout

---

* Westmorland's draft of this letter, and a copy of it in the official letter-book,
are both at the Irish State Paper Office.

† *Fortescue Mss.*, II, p. 184. Published by Historical Manuscripts Commission.

the country. " Russell has certainly commenced a correspondence in Galway, Mayo and Roscommon, and I think,
Leitrim, but as it is all Russell, Tone and Tandy I hope nothing
of consequence."

Just here he was interrupted by the arrival of a letter from
Hobart in England intimating that Pitt was so alarmed that he
was thinking of giving Irish Catholics even greater concessions
than the English ones would get. Again picking up his quill,
the Lord Lieutenant swore that such an idea was ruinous and
for God's sake to discourage it. He hoped the Irish Catholics
would be satisfied with whatever concessions the English got ;
and if they were not, he thought they should be opposed. He
named several Catholic gentlemen who generally served the
Government who were now busy (at his suggestion) promoting
addresses from their tenants saying they had no idea of asking
any kind of relief.

However, these dutiful disclaimers did not carry much
weight even at the Castle. The apprehension that the bulk
of the Irish people were about to demand some voice in the
government of their country continued to worry the large
landowners and even many liberal people who wanted reform.
Tone said that Dr. Haliday's wig miraculously turned white
with fear of the Catholics, and it was true the Doctor thought
Tone had been too precipitate in stirring them up. Generous
and kindhearted and just as he was, the Doctor would have
restored to the Catholics the privilege of being educated before
opening up the professions to them and granting them the
franchise. As for sitting in Parliament, that was the very last
grace he would have granted.*

The Doctor's fears came from an honest distrust of the mass
of the Irish people, but at the Castle any thought of a reform
that included them was tied up with the foreboding that
the small group of Protestants who called themselves the
Ascendancy would lose their monopoly of the Government
and the wealth of the country. So the wrath and contempt
of administration was directed against any individual or
group that endangered it.

When the Catholic Committee petitioned Parliament for
the franchise, Sir Boyle Roche, who was hoping for a peerage,

* *Charlemont Mss.* R.I.A.

made a scornful speech in the House of Commons. Who were
the people who had signed the petition, he wanted to know ?
One, Edward Byrne, was a sugar baker, he said scathingly, a
seller of wines and other commodities. And John Keogh was
a retailer of poplins in Dame Street. They met in chop-houses,
and over their porter Byrne happened to dream he was the
nabob of Ireland. As for the other men who signed it, he
could not even recollect or describe them.

The two men he mentioned happened to be among the
leading Catholic laymen of Ireland, both extremely wealthy
and cultured men. Even Lord Grenville, who had private
sources of information and was keeping his eye on Keogh,
admitted that he and the members of the Catholic Committee
were people of weight and responsibility.*

Then the Irish Government, in the person of the Solicitor-
General, John Toler, took the floor against the United Irishmen. He was one of the champions of ridicule in Ireland,
famous for his wit, a roistering little man with merry grey
eyes, no inhibitions, no sensibilities, and no dignity. He was
called the Hanging Judge, from his love of capital convictions.
On one circuit alone he hanged ninety-seven men out of a
hundred who came before him. He was also called Puffendorf,
from his habit of blowing out his face while he was talking.

His method of discrediting the United Irishmen and everything they represented was to poke fun at Napper Tandy, the
secretary of the Society, for " lending his countenance to the
measure." As Tandy was far from handsome, this brought a
general laugh from the House.

" I do not wonder at the merriment of the House," Toler
commented with a smirk, " for when so important a measure
is being agitated it is droll that the reformers could not put a
better face upon it."

The United Irishmen bristled at this attack on their society,
and Tandy at the insult to his appearance. He demanded an
explanation. The Solicitor claimed too high a regard for the
dignity of his office to give one. Toler's famous hair-trigger
pistols, it was thought, would surely be brought out, for
among the Solicitor-General's other deficiencies was a total
lack of any sense of fear.

* *Fortescue Mss.*, II, p. 221.

But Tandy did not challenge. After some communication by letter, Toler took the position that the " privilege of the House' had been breached by the demand of a non-member for an explanation of a remark made there. Tandy was ordered into custody. He escaped from the messenger who had been sent to arrest him and went into hiding. A reward of £50 was offered for his capture.

The smallness of the reward was an added insult. " Poor Tandy," wrote Drennan, " after eighteen years struggle against his own interest in the public cause, has nearly lost his reputation as a gentleman in a quarter of an hour."

Tone saw the greater danger, that the whole Society was falling into disrepute. To bolster its reputation, he persuaded a wealthy and aristocratic landowner in County Kildare, Hamilton Rowan, to take the chair at the next meeting of the United Irishmen. He himself took Tandy's place as Secretary. He proposed resolutions that were an adroit mixture of dignity and insult, ending with the statement that the Society " resigned to merited contempt the scorn of official station or the scoff of unprincipled venality."

This last was intended as the overture to a challenge, and Tone, who signed the resolutions and had them printed in four Dublin newspapers, hoped that Toler and perhaps other members of the House would send their seconds to him. The least he looked for was to suffer the imprisonment that Tandy had avoided. But no challenge came. Instead, treating the matter as part of the Government's campaign against the Society, the Lord Chancellor of Ireland took the matter into hand privately.

This extremely able Irishman, John Fitzgibbon, then a baronet and later the Earl of Clare, was practically the directing head of the Government, with more influence than the Lord Lieutenant. He was violently opposed to anything Catholic, and he had long settled into consistent opposition to all proposals for reform. He seemed to pattern himself after Lord Jeffries of England, who had tried the aristocratic Republicans of England after the restoration of the monarchy. Like him, he called any one who advocated liberal ideas madmen, and charged them with being " politely insane."

Fitzgibbon now sent privately for the President of the United

Irishmen, the Honourable Simon Butler, brother to Lord
Mountgarret. Keeping the conversation on the personal level
of one gentleman to another, he hinted at the dire consequences that would follow if Mr. Butler continued to preside
over the meetings of the United Irishmen. He also spoke,
" in the harshest and most contemptible terms," of Wolfe
Tone.

Butler was not one to be menaced, however, and after
consulting with his friends he wrote the Chancellor stating
that, if he did not consider the conversation a private one, he
would like to publish the whole of it in the newspapers. This brought about a second interview, in which the
Chancellor retracted his criticisms handsomely.

All this Mr. Butler related at the next meeting of the
Society. No sooner was the meeting over when one of the
members went to his home, took out his writing case, and in a
neat and extremely graceful hand reported the whole matter
to the Government. He had done so after every meeting
since the Society was first formed.

In all this there had been no mention of Thomas Addis
Emmet, for he was not yet a member of the United Irishmen.
But he had been consulted through the whole affair and had
done his best to remedy Tandy's indecision and to get him to
fight. Now he had a brilliant idea. At the Society's orders
Tandy had returned to town the last day of Parliament's
session and had been committed by the House to gaol for the
remainder of the term. The United Irishmen, at Tom Emmet's
suggestion, moved to challenge in the courts the right of the
House to punish a man not a member of Parliament for breach
of privilege. The Lord Lieutenant, who had signed the proclamation against Tandy, would be among those summoned.
In the course of the trial, the validity of his patent would be
attacked, as it had been issued under the Great Seal of England
instead of Ireland.

The case came on in November of 1792, and one sentence
alone of Emmet's speech threw the Castle into consternation.
" I boldly assert that there has been no legal viceroy in Ireland
for the last six hundred years, and not only the counsel for
Lord Westmorland will not deny that fact, but will not dare
let his patent come under a train of legal investigation."

Hastily the proceedings were stopped. There is an unverified claim that Emmet was offered a legal post in the Government. Such a move would have been quite in policy of buying up the able opposition. Already the Government had tried to negotiate with Dr. Drennan without success. O'Neill of Antrim had given up reform for the promise of a baronetcy, and what Lord Charlemont called the " Pitticism " of young Robert Stewart had begun. Emmet's talents were equal to if not superior to both these men, and it is more than likely that the Government would have been glad to have acquired them for their own use. But as he did later, Emmet placed principle above private interest and refused. Instead, he took the oath of the United Irishmen and began to formulate for them a new plan for the representation of Ireland.

No man alive at that time could have perceived how this decision of Tom Emmet's would affect the brother who was only half his age, but, as always, what Tom did had a tremendous influence on Robert. With Tom a United Irishman, their destiny first became his, and eventually Robert's as well.

At fourteen the boy was still a romantic idealist. The city of Dublin swarmed with shoplifters, pickpockets, ringdroppers, counterfeiters, and every known variety of sharper and swindler, under disguises that ranged from clergymen's cloth to jockey's silks. An army of prostitutes paid tribute to the complacent constables of the watch. From the drawingroom window of the Emmet house Robert might have seen, a hundred times a night, the gleaming arc of a watchman's torch as it was lowered to inspect the face of one of the trulls who circled the Green looking for culls. If she were one of those who shared her earnings with the police, she went on unmolested. If not, off she was marched to the guardhouse.

Oblivious of such people, Robert believed as implicitly as Rousseau himself in the natural nobility of mankind, and that the only things men needed to make them act like angels were a government and a society that had some regard for their essential nobility.

He was nearly ready to enter Trinity now. Already he knew a great deal of Ireland's unhappy history, and he had begun the study of government. As if to send him another step further on his destined course, his text was John Locke on

The Origin, Extent and End of Civil Government. The margins of his copy of this foundation of democratic thought were full of notes in his own hand. One paragraph of text marked for special emphasis stated that a people owe no obligation to a government if force and not choice compels them to submission.

Simultaneously, unknown to any but a few intimates, Pitt was taking the first tentative steps toward a measure that would be the means of driving young Emmet into rebellion at a later date. The danger of the Catholics demanding the franchise was now so great that Pitt had decided the time had come to prepare the minds of certain officials for a legislative union between Ireland and England. About the time that Tom Emmet became a United Irishman, Pitt wrote confidentially to Lord Westmorland :

The idea of the present fermentation gradually bringing both parties to think of a Union with this country has long been in my mind. . . . The admission of Catholics to a share of the suffrage would not then be dangerous. The Protestant interest, in point of power, property, and Church Establishment, would be secure because the decided majority of the Supreme Legislature would necessarily be Protestant, and the great ground of argument on the part of the Catholics would be done away, as compared with the rest of the Empire, they would become a minority. . . .*

* *Fane Mss.,* I.S.P.O.

2

PITT'S WEAPONS

CHAPTER THREE

Intimidation and Rewards

THE evening that Tom Emmet became a United Irishman, December 14, 1792, the Society passed a set of resolutions urging the Dublin Volunteers to arm for the defence of the country. Then or later, one sentence in it must have burned itself into the mind of Robert Emmet, for he was to make use of the idea ten years later : " The sacrifice of life in the service of one's country is a duty much too honourable to be entrusted to mercenaries."

The informer of the neat and graceful hand thoughtfully obtained a copy of the resolutions for the Government's use. He sent it to the Castle with a letter mentioning that Thomas Addis Emmet had become a United Irishman and had attended a meeting of the Volunteers where the resolutions were distributed.

" Not one of the green linnets in uniform," the spy commented with dry humour.

Nevertheless, as the Volunteers were planning to parade in their uniforms, the Council of State issued a proclamation forbidding it, since the sight of the national colour made up into military dress might have had too stirring an effect on the citizens of Dublin. Two months later, the Irish Parliament was called upon to ratify the proclamation. The session provided Ireland with a new popular hero, whose influence was to linger so long in his native Kildare that later it had a great effect on Emmet's rising.

Using the opportunity to vilify both the United Irishmen and the Volunteers, the Chancellor pictured the members of both organisations as monsters with the most evil intentions toward their country. This was too much for Lord Edward Fitzgerald, brother of Lord Henry Fitzgerald, the liberal

29

candidate for Dublin who had been elected with Grattan in
the elections of 1790. He was not yet a United Irishman, but
he rushed to their defence. In a speech that probably startled
himself as much as any one in the House, he said to their faces
that the majority of the members of Parliament, and the Lord
Lieutenant as well, were the worst subjects the King had in
Ireland.

Half a dozen irate members jumped to their feet and
demanded a retraction. The authorities were vexed with a
problem of great delicacy. Lord Edward was too well born
to be disregarded and much too well connected to be punished
by the Chancellor's tongue or sent to Newgate for breach of
privilege. He was one of the ancient Geraldines. Carton,
the family seat of his eldest brother the Duke of Leinster, was
near the now-ruined Castle of Maynooth where for generations the Earls of Kildare had ruled with almost royal power.
He was of the same line as young Silken Thomas, who had
hurled defiance at Henry the Eighth. The Duke of Leinster
carried on the Fitzgerald tradition of respect and affection for
the Irish people, and he voted with the opposition in the Irish
House of Lords. Lord Edward sat in the House of Commons
as his member for Kildare.

Lord Edward's outburst, spontaneous though it was, was
quite in line with his political thought. He had just been
dismissed from the British Army for having made a speech at
a dinner in Paris where prominent Republicans from England,
France, and America had also spoken. He had spent much of
his boyhood in France with his uncle the Duke of Richmond
and had met there the very democratic Duke of Orleans.
Lord Edward's bride, whom he had just brought to Ireland,
was the famous Pamela, said to be the daughter of the Duke of
Orleans by Madame de Genlis. Through the father he had
met all the prominent Republicans in Paris and had been
invited to the now-famous dinner at White's Restaurant.
The British Government had heard that Lord Edward had
praised the French. As a reprimand and example it had been
thought fit to relieve Lord Edward of his commission as a
major in the British Army.

Naturally, his remarks about the Irish Lord Lieutenant and
the House of Commons could not be overlooked. He was

brought to the bar of the House. An apology was demanded. " No," said Lord Edward, the cupid's bow of his mouth flattened with firmness. He was sorry he did not understand the rules of the House, but he would say no more.

" By God," said his brother the Duke, who was in the gallery, " he shall not apologise."

Dr. Drennan met Lord Edward not long afterward and wrote his sister in the North that he was as plain and familiar in his manners as his dress, and an honest, zealous Republican. The Doctor feared he would soon be entrapped by some of the State inquisitors. " However," he concluded his letter, sceptical as always, " as the Leinster family are by nature capricious he may probably soon be diluted here."

But Lord Edward was not diluted. Within a month Dr. Drennan's sister was writing him from Belfast, " We have got Lord Edward on our jugs as the man of the people."

" That comedy, that buffoon, that dear delightful Eddy," as one of his aunts described him, was such a thoroughly ingratiating and affable person, so fond of writing to the dearest mother about his pretty little garden and his sweet little house in the country and his darling little wife, and so democratic in his manner that it was no wonder that, like Absalom of old, he stole away the hearts of the people. A disgruntled loyalist who heard that he even danced among the rustics at bonfires accused him of the theft, and there is no doubt that he was guilty of it. Lord Edward, Robert Emmet, and Wolfe Tone are still three of the most loved names in Irish history, and it was Lord Edward who set Kildare afire with the idea of democracy.

The resolutions of the United Irishmen urging the Volunteers to arm which brought Lord Edward into prominence were used by the Government to intimidate many of the principal members of the Society. Dr. Drennan was the first on the list, since he had presided at the meeting at which they were presented. A little while before that, he had been approached by Mr. John Pollock with an offer of patronage by the Government. Pollock came from Newry where Dr. Drennan had practised for a few years before coming to Dublin, and the two men had known each other there. The Pollock family were much admired for their great abilities and their national sympathies. But the allurement of office had brought John Pollock to Dublin some years before and had converted him completely to the Government point of view. He put at the disposal of the Castle all his keen intelligence, his integrity, and his really inexhaustible store of energy and industry. As Clerk of the Crown and Registrar for the Court of Judge Downs he had enough work to keep any man busy, but he had gradually added to these tasks the less pleasant ones of trying to soften the opposition of various individuals to the Government by private negotiations and of supervising many of the Castle's secret-service employees. By the time Robert Emmet was engaged in his conspiracy, Pollock was directing not only the most important spies and informers employed by the Government but even ragged and disreputable wretches who bought their own lives with the blood of others.

Pollock's first call on Dr. Drennan had no effect, and in April of 1793 he called for a second time. He insinuated that he had heard from official sources that Drennan was in danger because of his connection with the United Irishmen. The Doctor replied, with what he thought was gay assurance, that as he had done or written nothing to make him fear any inquiry, he could not alter his plan of conduct. They had some further conversation, and Pollock contrived to drop some sinister hints.

" I think," Drennan wrote Sam McTier, " that if on our former conference he meant to seduce, his aim at this time was to terrify or to find out whether there was really any grounds for terrifying me." *

The matter was dropped a second time, and the Government turned its attention to other would-be reformers.

In the North, which was still the hotbed of republicanism, the first of Pitt's coercive measures was being put into effect. A law controlling the possession of arms and gunpowder was used as a pretext for striking at any one with advanced political ideas. Their houses were almost certain to be raided for arms, and their possessions battered or removed in the process. In March, English dragoons billeted in Belfast and troops from surrounding towns suddenly burst from their lodgings at six

* *The Drennan Letters*, p. 150.

St. Stephen's Green, Dublin, in the 1790's. Dr. Robert Emmet's house is in the centre background

Malton's Views of Dublin

Trinity College, Dublin.   *Malton's Views of Dublin*

in the evening and began breaking the windows of houses showing portraits of Washington, Franklin, and other popular heroes of the times. The shop of a hatter who had supplied the helmets of the Belfast Volunteers was smashed, and so were the houses of many other prominent members of the corps. The military mob assaulted every person whom they met on the streets and cut and wounded many. They were just attacking an ale-house that displayed the portrait of Benjamin Franklin as a sign when the Volunteers began to assemble to protect the townspeople from further injury.*

The soldiers took to their heels. Some were arrested, but their officers had them released immediately. The Volunteers mounted guard all night, and in the morning the town met and appointed a committee to inquire into the attack. General White, the general in charge of the district, at first disclaimed responsibility for it, then tacitly admitted it and agreed to withdraw the dragoons. Later, other towns with a disposition to liberalism suffered similar attacks by the military. Always the individual victims were men prominent as Volunteers, United Irishmen, or Defenders.

A secret committee of the House of Lords began to inquire into the cause of disturbances in the North and other parts of the country.† This was presided over by the Chancellor, who insisted on examining witnesses on their oaths. Its first report claimed that the condition of the North was caused by the United Irishmen (the Society had not been formed until long after the disturbances had become serious), and that publications " which defame Parliament and extol " the French were also responsible.

As a body the United Irishmen were still quite innocent of anything but a desire for a just representation of the people, and they countered the report of the secret committee with a

* A Republican watchmaker, Thomas McCabe, would not repair his broken windows but put up a sign, "An Irish Slave."

† When war between England and France seemed imminent, secret committees of the Parliaments of both England and Ireland were appointed, ostensibly to inquire into the condition of those countries. The witnesses who were brought before them were all democratically inclined, and the expression of their views, which were made public in the committees' reports tended to alarm the loyalist element. It was soon suspected that this was the real motive behind the appointment of the committees. This was tacitly admitted in a letter which Lord Grenville, a member of Pitt's cabinet, wrote to Lord Auckland in January of 1793. " It (the appointment of such a committee) might be very useful in the view of embarking the nation heartily in support of a war, if unavoidable." Fortescue II, p. 362.

set of resolutions challenging the right of the committee to examine on oath. Such Star Chamber proceedings, they complained, were illegal, unconstitutional, and oppressive.

For signing these resolutions, the Honourable Simon Butler and Oliver Bond, a well-to-do Dublin merchant, were brought before the House of Lords and found guilty of a high breach of privilege. They were sent to Newgate gaol for six months, and each was ordered to pay a fine of £500. Lord Mountgarret, Butler's brother, and the Duke of Leinster left the House in protest.

The Society voted to pay their officers' fines, and seventy-one members subscribed a guinea each for wines and luxuries for the prisoners. Tom Emmet contributed £10 toward the fines, and Drennan £3. But the martyrs were soon living in such unmartyr-like extravagance that Drennan wrote his brother-in-law that he was disgusted and would decline giving another farthing.

Another victim of the House was Dr. James Reynolds, a Protestant physician from the North. He was summoned by the committee of secrecy to answer as to the state of his part of the country. He refused to take the oath until he knew by what authority they required it, as a legislative or judicial body. Dr. Drennan reported the case for his family :

If the first, he denies that they have any such right by the constitution, the principles of which he values as much as any of them. If in their judicial capacity, he protests against all secrecy as equally unconstitutional. . . . They think they will terrify this very young man, but they are mistaken. The Chancellor said to him, as Jeffries said to Sidney, " You are mad, sir." *

Reynolds refused to take the oath and was sentenced to gaol.

Tom Russell was the next victim of the secret committee. Since he had helped to found the United Irishmen both in Belfast and Dublin, he had been forced by need of money to sell his commission in the Army. For a short time he had been a magistrate in the County Tyrone, but he soon gave up the office. He could not reconcile his principles to a position where it was customary to ask a prisoner what his religion was before beginning a consideration of his case. He was now acting as Courier Extraordinary for the United Irishmen, as the anonymous informer in the Society had informed the Castle.

* *Drennan Letters*, p. 145.

This actually meant that Russell went through the country preaching the doctrines of the Society and urging turbulent Catholics who had become Defenders to align themselves with the United Irishmen to try to get reform peacefully.*   On orders from Pitt, the Irish Parliament had just voted to give certain qualified Catholics the franchise ; but without a reform of Parliament it was an empty indulgence.

As Secretary of the Dublin United Irishmen, Russell had recently signed an address to the people of Ireland explaining why the Government was persecuting the Society. This and his great popularity and influence with the democrats made him a target for the secret committee, and he was summoned to appear before it. He did not improve his position with the Chancellor by refusing to appear at that time, as he was going to Omagh to testify at a trial, and he thought it better to risk the anger of the committee than the lives of two men. He received a second subpoena, and since the United Irishmen had decided not to let their members be sent to gaol one by one, he was advised to appear before the committee. His journal for May 10, 1793, says that he was examined but would not swear to other people's opinions or answer such questions as might incriminate him. " The Lord's Committee evidently rascals. Stupid. Unfair and either ill-informed or pretending to be so. Ask opinions as to the French, volunteering and [Catholics] all of which are answered in such a manner as could not be pleasing to them."

He was so poor in worldly goods that, when his examination was over, he had no money to pay his expenses back to Belfast, and the committee refused to pay them. " Raise the wind by virtue of [Tone's] timepiece," he commented in his journal. Of the committee he simply said, " Sad Dogs."

When he got back to Belfast, he found that the Government had been trying to buy off the publishers of the *Northern Star*,

---

* An entry in Russell's journal about this time gives an example of what the poor people of Ireland were thinking politically. Near Randalstown Russell met a poor millworker and went to his cabin. " He makes bitter reflections on the spirit of the country," Russell wrote, " asks me was I not looked after by Government and whether they did not want to hunt me with Butler and Bond. . . . A wife and two children. Says : I should think Liberty worth risquing life for in a cause of that sort. ' I think I should have courage enough from reflection to brave death.' One of his children was climbing on his knee. 'As for my part,' says he, ' it does not much signify now as to myself but it grieves me to breed these children to be slaves. I would gladly risque all to prevent that.' "   I.S.P.O.

the paper the United Irishmen had started in Belfast. The approaches for the Government had been made by the erstwhile reformer, Mr. John O'Neill, now promised his baronetcy.

Young Robert Stewart had by now also completely deserted reform and had become Pitt's protégé. He was representing the Prime Minister in the British Parliament as his member from the Borough of Tregony. "He is Pittized with a vengeance, which he candidly admits," Dr. Haliday ruefully wrote to the Earl of Charlemont. Both these old Whigs were sincerely fond of the charming and clever young man, and the Doctor could not help showing his disappointment at his change of politics.

No doubt those gentlemen who with unwearied efforts and at great expense struggled hard and successfully for him, will think themselves rewarded by his deserting that station they have raised him to, and sinking into the mighty mass of the Body guards of a Minister whom they and all good Whigs detest and execrate ; at the instant too when he was become peculiarly obnoxious to them by his carrying through the House with indecent precipitancy the most formidable and unconstitutional measures which almost go to the establishment of Bastilles and Lettres de Cachet.*

The Doctor had also heard from the young man's mother the details of his marriage to Lady Emilia Hobart.

Lady Londonderry in her letter of the 9th speaks of Lady Emilia's fortune as noble beyond calculation, of the lady as truly amiable, her figure striking. They are to be married, she says, on articles in a fortnight ; so that probably this very day puts Robert into possession of both, and then Tregony and I suppose other honourable and good things under the Jesus Christ of Britain. You start, my Lord, but a worthy friend of mine just returned from London assures me that to his astonishment and horror he saw in many windows in England and Scotland "*William Pitt the Jesus Christ of Britain.*" Yet we are sending to the Devil the French for their impiety.

The parliamentary opposition in Ireland was further weakened by the desertion of Lord Shannon and his followers. For some time the Lord Lieutenant had been suggesting to Pitt that it might be well to find out if Lord Shannon were *à vendre*. Evidently he was, for he and several others went over to the side of the Government that summer, the price being Lord Shannon's appointment as First Lord of the Treasury.

* *Charlemont Mss.* R.I.A.

Pitt was breaking up the powerful Whig party in England, too, by creating new peerages and giving other favours to the followers of the Duke of Portland and Charles Fox. " Some quit him [Fox] from opinion," Lady Holland rather ineptly put it in her journal, " but most for the loaves and fishes which they were promised for their desertion."

In Scotland there were many prosecutions against people who were advocating ideas not approved by the Government. Thomas Muir, for one, was sentenced to transportation on evidence that he had advised a man to read Thomas Paine's *Rights of Man*.

In Ireland the battle against individual United Irishmen was taken up again when Hamilton Rowan was brought to trial in January of 1794 for having distributed the address to the Volunteers. He was found guilty by a jury carefully chosen by a new sheriff put into office for that very purpose and on evidence of a witness who notoriously perjured himself. Rowan was fined £500 and sentenced to Newgate gaol for two years. His imprisonment did not end his political activities, and these were soon the means, by an ironic turn of events, of allowing the Government to get rid of some of the leading men among the reformers.

A Dr. William Jackson, an English clergyman, had been living in Paris for some time in contact with the French Directory. Early in 1794 they sent him to England and Ireland to gather information about the political opinions of the people of those countries. While he was in London, he called on an old friend, one John Cockayne, a lawyer, and told him about his plans. Cockayne was not burdened with scruples, and he was a creditor of Jackson's to the extent of £300. Off he went to Mr. Pitt, and for promises that included making good the loan to Jackson he put himself under the instruction of the Prime Minister.

He was told to go to Ireland with Jackson and to keep an eye on his contacts and transactions. Mr. Pitt was to be informed of them all.

Cockayne knew Leonard McNally, a United Irishman who was already under some suspicion of being a traitor to his colleagues. At the time of the Napper Tandy case, the Government had mysteriously known what Tandy's brief

would be. Through McNally and Cockayne the unsuspecting
Jackson was introduced, some time in April of 1794, to
Hamilton Rowan in Newgate. Rowan in turn introduced
Jackson and Cockayne to Tone, Dr. Reynolds, and one or
two other United Irishmen.

No man at that time knew so well the state of Ireland as
Tone did. The paper he drew up at Jackson's request showed,
as well as the condition of the country, his great talents and
his disposition toward a separation between Ireland and
England. Jackson was delighted with him and suggested
that he go to Paris and tell the Directory personally what little
opposition a French invasion would meet with in Ireland.

Cockayne, of course, did not fail to get his hands on the
paper Tone drew up, and Rowan's copy of it. At last, the
Government was in possession of evidence of high treason by
an individual United Irishman, though the Society itself was
advocating nothing more radical than reform.

Warrants were sworn out. Jackson was arrested on April 29
at his lodgings in Palace Street. Tone, enjoying a musical
evening at a house in Merrion Square, received a warning
note from a friend, put down his flute, and went quietly away
to face a charge of treason. Hamilton Rowan escaped from
gaol and took a boat to France. Dr. Reynolds slipped away
to America. And some one called on Tom Emmet and tried,
with veiled threats and allurements, to make him withdraw
from the United Irishmen.

Since he had become a member of the Society, the anonymous spy had constantly kept Tom Emmet's name in the minds
of officials at Dublin Castle. He had proposed that a committee
prepare plans for a full representation in Parliament of all the
people of Ireland. He had served on that committee and had
drawn up a plan for it himself. He had acted for the Duke
of Leinster when a new society of which the Duke was Chair-
man, the Society of Friends of the Constitution, Liberty and
Peace, sent resolutions to the United Irishmen expressing their
profound respect and offering to act with them in all their
pursuits. He had moved for an address to the Catholics of
Ireland reminding them that without a reform of Parliament
the elective franchise was of no use whatever. He had suggested and served on a committee to investigate recent coercive

acts of the Government, and the report of the committee, sent to the Castle by the anonymous spy, showed how clear-sighted and fearless he was. A dangerous man to have against the Government ; a splendid acquisition if he could be persuaded to see things in a different light.

The man who made the approaches for the Government had been one of Christopher Emmet's friends ; and Tom, still devoted to the memory of his dead brother, took his assurances of friendship for himself at their face value. Remembering the manner in which John Pollock had approached Dr. Drennan, a modern reader is apt to be more sceptical. Who the so-called friend was is not now known. The only remaining evidence of the transaction is a rough draft of the letter Tom Emmet wrote in reply to the suggestions he put forward, and the veiled threats that had preceded them. It is now at the State Paper Office in Dublin, among those secret papers to which Dr. Thomas Addis Emmet was denied access in the 1880's. It is unsigned and has been lying unidentified for 160 years, but Tom Emmet's handwriting is most distinctive, and there is no doubt that it is his.* The salutation is simply " My dear F."

I have already delayed writing to you till the last moment that I might deliberate as materially as I could on our conversation of Sunday, and I think it right to assure you in the onset that the answer I am about to give is exclusively *my own*. Not having been able, by any consideration I could bestow on the subject, to raise a doubt within myself of the line of conduct I ought to adopt, I did not consult *even my father*, because I would not run the hazard of implicating him in any censure which may be cast upon me, if I am acting wrong.

You assure me that there is unquestionable proof of there being rebels in the country. I assure you in return that when I know who they are, I will by *my* conduct shew how much I disapprove of theirs. My object always has been an efficient reform in the House of Commons and *nothing more*. If any men with whom I have hitherto associated have views that carry them farther, I am ready to disclaim those views in the most explicit manner. But you suggest to me to withdraw from the Society of U.I. That I cannot do because I think it would be dishonourable and unjust. I have pledged myself to use my abilities and influence in favour of Reform, and I will religiously perform that promise, though I confess to you I do not consider the present moment as one, in which exertions in that cause can be made

* The draft is endorsed with the signature of the man who arrested Tom Emmet in 1798. All his papers were taken away at that time, which explains how the Government happened to acquire them.

with any prospect of success, and I am inclined to keep them for a more favourable opportunity, but I can never consent to do an act which would be construed by many as dishonourable dereliction of those principles to which I am pledged, and which must be construed by all as an imputation on that Society, of which I do not believe to be the fact, that its views are treasonable and rebellious. If any one attributed those views to me, I should say that he injured and calumniated me to the last degree. Would I then be warranted, My dearest Friend, in doing any act which as far as its influence extends, must injure and I believe calumniate a great number of individuals ?

You mentioned to me Professional Emolument : my fortune and situation in life is such as to make professional emolument an object of the greatest importance, but believe me sincerely when I assure you you mentioned another motive at least as persuasive, the friendship of my brother's friends. It has been my wish and ambition since I entered into the profession to enjoy that part of a brother's inheritance. I would do anything but abandon or belie my principles to obtain " the friendship of my brother's friends. . . ."

You said this was the crisis of my life. I believe you said truly, and therefore it is the moment in which I ought to adhere most strictly to those principles of honour and morality, which I have been taught to consider unerring guides. I believe this is the crisis of my life. God grant I may have decided prudently. I feel I have decided honestly.

If I should become involved in the general suspicion that will infallibly and indiscriminately be cast upon all with whom I have acted I entreat you, and those whom I love like you, to keep your minds clear from it. With regard to the Public at large, I have only to hope that time, and I trust, an uninterrupted good conduct will at length induce them to think more favourably of me. The censures of the world I shall lament, probably I shall feel them very severely, but if I can I will take care that *my own heart shall not reprove me as long as I live*. Believe me, My Dearest F, under very great obligations to you for the zealous interest you take in my welfare. I estimate it as I ought, and shall always remain,

Your very sincere friend
&
Obliged humble Servant

Wednesday
May 7th, 1794

That Tom actually sent a fair copy of this letter to F is indicated by the endorsement in his hand, " My letter to F."

Seventeen days later the Sheriff, some magistrates, and soldiers burst in on a meeting of the United Irishmen and formally suppressed the Society. The informer, who had been in gaol for debt for a few days before that, was bailed out by the Sheriff so that he could he present when the raid was made. He reported to the Castle :

Counsellor John Collis was the angry Duke from whom you took the books, and who is Sec'y for the present quarter.

On the breaking up of the meeting there was a proposal for adjournment to a Tavern, but I don't think it was carried into effect, but from extream (*sic*) and Real Indisposition and some other causes which I shall mention at meeting you I was under the necessity of going home.

I beg and request you that you may now plainly and boldly represent to your friends my very Dangerous situation and as the fact is that I cannot be of any more service in this country and that I hope and expect according to those promises which I am sure will be most honourably fulfilled that I may be enabled immediately to Quit, Suitable to my deserts.

The next letter in this exquisite hand is dated from London, asks for money and is signed Thomas Collins.

CHAPTER FOUR

The Boy in the Background

EVEN the Trinity students, Robert Emmet among them, were learning that any expression of liberal views brought an official rap on the knuckles. The suspicion that some of the members of the College Historical Society were tainted with Republicanism was the cause of their being locked out of their meeting rooms inside the college walls. They engaged a room in the city and, with more or less academic hilarity, rapped back.

According to them, a meeting of the Vintners, Publicans, and Courtesans of the City resolved on May 1, 1794, that their thanks be presented to the Vice-Provost and Senior Fellow of Trinity College, Dublin, for

. . . their public-spirited suppression of the Historical Society ; that the said Society had considerably injured their respective trades by employing the gentlemen of the university (formerly their best customers) one whole evening a week in literary pursuits, and wasting other evenings in preparation of it ; that the kind interference of the college would cause the custom of the young gentlemen to return gradually to them, and their time would again be more profitably employed than in pursuits of the said institution.*

In spite of a later and perfectly sincere assertion of Robert Emmet's that " Virtue is the mark of a Republick," it must be admitted that there were not a few of the young men associated with him who at times patronised all three classes of tradespeople named in the satiric resolution, but we have Thomas Moore's word for it that Emmet was not one of them.

This friend of Emmet's boyhood, who was later to help fix his immortality by the words of a song " He lived for his Love, for his Country he died," wrote of these years in his *Memoirs* that Emmet was " wholly free from the follies and frailties of youth." His interest in science, particularly in

* Madden, *United Irishmen*, III, p. 18.

chemistry, was the only thing that diverted him at all from his absorbing enthusiasm for Irish freedom. When he got up to speak in the Debating or Historical Society, Moore remembered, he would drop his customary manner of mildness and repose and become in an instant excitingly powerful and inspired, his eloquence and the political boldness of his opinions adding to the satisfaction of his personality.

On one occasion he took so ardently the side of democracy in a discussion " Whether an Aristocracy or Democracy was most favourable to the advancement of Science and Literature " that years afterward Moore felt as if his words were still sounding in his ears.*

Emmet, after reviewing the great republics of antiquity, showing how much they had all done for the advancement of literature and the arts, took as his final argument " the grand and perilous example of the young republic of France, and, referring to the story of Caesar carrying with him across the river only his sword and his Commentaries, he said, ' Thus France at this time swims through a sea of blood, but while with one hand she wields the sword against her aggressors, with the other she upholds the interests of literature, uncontaminated by the bloody tide through which she struggles.' "

Moore remembered another speech Emmet made in the Debating Society : " When a people, advancing rapidly in civilisation and the knowledge of their rights look back, after a lapse of time, and perceive how far their Government has lagged behind them, what then, I ask, is to be done by them in such a case ? What but to pull the Government up to the people ? "

Just once Emmet's eloquence failed him. It could hardly be imagined that such sentiments, uttered at a meeting of a society in a college over which the Chancellor had control, could go unchecked. A man of advanced standing in the college, and with a reputation for oratory, was sent to the Society expressly to neutralise the effects of Robert Emmet's speeches. Whether he was generally successful or not Moore does not say, but he recalls one evening when Emmet, in replying to one of the older man's dampening attacks, suddenly and unaccountably lost his electric quality and his usual

* Thomas Moore's *Memoirs*, I, p. 47.

easy flow of words and became confused and inarticulate.
He stammered on for a few limp sentences and then, to the
consternation of his friends, deserted the argument and sat
down.

Moore's *Memoirs* give another glimpse of Emmet during
his Trinity days which is so significant that no biographer can
omit it.   Moore, whose love of country was to find expression
in songs written to old Irish airs, was in those days filling
himself with the melodies collected from the vanishing race of
harpers and fiddlers by Edward Bunting of Belfast. Bunting was
a friend of Thomas Russell, Russell of the Emmets, Robert
Emmet of Thomas Moore.   Perhaps Bunting himself was
sometimes at Moore's with Robert Emmet. Edward Hudson,
another Trinity Republican, often was ; and his flute and
Tom Moore's pianoforte duetted through "Ancient Irish
Music" till the candles were burned to flickering stubs in
wax-dripping sockets.

But this day Robert and Tom Moore were alone, the one
absorbed in his thoughts, the other in melody. Moore had
almost forgotten that any one was there when, as he was
playing "Let Erin Remember," Emmet suddenly started up
from his reverie and exclaimed with that passion that could
so overwhelm him, " Oh, that I were at the head of twenty
thousand men and marching to that air ! "

Later, Moore was to have an experience with Emmet which
showed that, idealistic and impractical as he was, Emmet
believed that words were not enough and should be backed
by action.   Another Trinity student who was in college at
that time also remembered something Emmet said at one of
the Historical Society debates that indicated the same attitude.
The question of the evening was, " Is a complete freedom of
discussion essential to the well-being of a good and virtuous
Government."

Emmet was restricted in his oration by the rules of the
Society which forbade all allusion to current politics, but he
managed to imply that his words might have a practical
application. He showed the necessity and advantage of liberty
of discussion and the encouragement it deserved from a good
Government.   He cited the evil effects of despotism and
tyranny in the governments of antiquity.   In his conclusion

he said, as his fellow-student remembered, " If a government were vicious enough to put down the freedom of discussion, it would be the duty of the people to deliberate on the errors of their rulers, to consider well the wrongs they inflicted, and what the right course would be for their subjects to take, and having done so, *it would then be their duty to draw practical conclusions.*"

His interest in chemistry gave him a chance to demonstrate his self-confidence and courage. He and John Patten, the brother of Tom's wife Jane, who used to visit at the Green for weeks at a time, once performed an experiment using corrosive sublimate. Evidently some of the chemical got under Robert's fingernails, and when he was working on an algebra problem late that night he began to nibble at them. Soon he was seized with violent pains. He realised what the matter was, and that he was in danger. But rather than disturb the family who were all in bed, he looked up the antidote for the poison himself.

Finding that chalk was recommended, he broke open the coach-house in the rear, where he knew John Patten had been using chalk, took enough to neutralise the poison, and went back to his studies. Next morning his face was drawn and yellow, but he had finished his algebra problem, and no one's sleep had been disturbed.

Dr. Emmet sometimes worried about Robert's perennial boyishness, but he realised that under certain circumstances Robert would assume an extraordinary amount of responsibility. He once told John Patten that if Robert's mind were made up on any point, he had none of his usual diffidence, no distrust and no fear.

If Robert were looking out of that window [the Doctor told John] and saw a regiment passing that was about to be reviewed, and was informed the colonel had just fallen off his horse, and was incapacitated for his duty, and it was intimated to him that he might take the colonel's place, and put his taste for the reading of military tactics and evolutions to the test, Robert would quietly take his hat, place himself at the head of the regiment, and give the necessary commands without any misgivings or *mauvaise honte.**

* Madden, *United Irishmen*, III, p. 339.

CHAPTER FIVE

Informers and How They Are Made

IN 1795 a new Lord Lieutenant, Lord Camden, with Robert Stewart as one of his under-secretaries, went to Ireland as many such officials had before him, cherishing an ambition for the Garter and willing to work for it. His official instructions were to discourage the claims of the Catholics and to revive the spirits of the Protestants. But though they had ended with the injunction to " moderate, soothe, conciliate these jarring spirits," Camden chose to interpret that as meaning that the conciliation was to apply only to the Protestants. His policy toward the Catholics was admittedly one of harshness and repression, which he put into operation without reprimand from his superiors in London.

The Army and Militia soon learned that they could act as ruthlessly toward the mass of the people as they pleased.* In Roscommon, the Defenders had set up a little democratic community with a leader called Captain Stout and were demanding lower rents and higher wages, claims that Camden admitted were just. Nevertheless, he sent the Commander in Chief of the Army, Lord Carhampton, there to settle matters. He did it by wantonly shooting the people and burning their houses. Then he began the practice, carried on for years, of arresting and transporting without trial any man suspected of being either a Defender or a United Irishman.

The action in Roscommon was so outrageous that it shortly brought about the prospect of many lawsuits. Lord Camden, who had sent Carhampton the official thanks of the Government for his exertions, had to make arrangements for a Bill of Indemnity to cover the illegal transactions, but he did not

* Sir John Moore later explained this in his journal. See p. 88.

curb the Commander in any way. His only criticism of what he called Carhampton's *doctrine* was that it was so notorious.

Within four months of Camden's arrival in Ireland he could send to the Duke of Portland (who had been induced to leave Charles Fox's Whig party in England by the offer of the Irish department and its patronage) a business-like digest of all the informations he had received about the Defenders and the reorganised but now illegal United Irishmen. A Captain MacNevin of Carrickfergus had written the Castle that " the United Irishmen, being prevented from meeting publicly, have established clandestine Societies, who are well supplied with inflammatory publications, and calling themselves Book Clubs, Literary Societies, and Reading Societies, others saying their only view is, to defend themselves against the Freemasons." The real view of those societies, Camden thought, appeared in their oath, which bound them to seek parliamentary reform.*

He was getting information from all the secret sources Lord Westmorland had used, he told the Duke, and also he had some new additions to the corps of secret agents.

Every country, of course, has its secret service, and England's had long been established. Algernon Sidney had been persecuted by its agents in every country on the Continent where he had taken refuge. The buying of Benedict Arnold had been one of its achievements. During the American Revolution twelve young men were kept busy at the Post Office in London reading intercepted letters not concerned with military affairs. At this time Pitt's Secret Service was famous for its " soul-seducing gold." It went beyond the usual activities of obtaining military information for the use of the Army and Navy and was concerned with buying up ministers of foreign governments as well as civilians in every walk of life.† It

---

* I.S.P.O.

† Among the important persons who were secretly enticed into British service while ostensibly still acting for their own countries were the French Ministers Carnot and Barthélemy, Generals Pichegru and Dumouriez, and the Swiss Advoyer, M. De Steigeur, and many others. Mr. William Wickham was the real head of the British secret service on the Continent, though he always had some official situation to mask his activities in this line. The details of some of his transactions are given in his own published correspondence, and letters to and from him in the published correspondence of Lord Auckland, Lord Malmsbury, and Lord Minto, all fellow-diplomats ; in letters published in *Courts and Cabinets of George the Third,* edited by

was now giving to the Government in England and Ireland thousands of watching eyes, eager ears, and furtively written reports, mostly concerned with the activities of civilians with democratic aspirations.*

the Duke of Buckingham and Chandoes ; and in the *Fortescue Manuscripts*, particularly Vol. III.

In 1795 some of Wickham's most important spies were caught with very incriminating letters on them, and the French Directory began to ask for Wickham's dismissal from his post as British Minister at Berne. Many of the important men he had been acting with in secret were also anxious to have him leave and so avoid an inquiry which would bring their duplicity to light.

The demand of the French Directory for Wickham's recall was first placed in the hands of M. De Steiguer, himself one of the men involved, but he was powerless to have the matter dropped, and it went to the central Helvetic Body. Wickham wrote Lord Grenville, his chief at the Foreign Office, on October 13, 1797, that the proofs that the Directory could produce against him gave him very serious uneasiness, and he gave Grenville some of them in detail. He suggested that he withdraw from Switzerland, and that he give as his reason for doing so the affection of the British King for the Helvetic Body, and his wish to avoid committing them with a neighbour who knew neither faith, law, nor reason. This, he said, would avoid public discussion of the matter, which he, as well as the men involved with him, were anxious to avoid. He said that on withdrawing from Switzerland he would write a note " which might be so drawn as to augment the opinion (which the measure itself would certainly establish) of his Majesty's magnanimity and benevolence, to retort very severely to the French Government, and to elude every sort of accusation without either expressly admitting or denying any charge whatever." *Wickham Correspondence*, II, p. 50 *et seq. Fortescue Mss.*, III, p. 216.

Wickham was removed, and officially his recall was attributed to the very same high motives he had suggested. Later he got into difficulties in Vienna, where he also combined secret-service work with the duties of his diplomatic position, and while at home " on leave " he wrote to Lord Grenville tacitly admitting the truth of the charges against him. He was afraid they could not be concealed much longer, and he told Grenville he could not help feeling that the disclosures would carry something like stigma. To refurbish his reputation abroad, and to make him still useful to the Government, as well as for his own personal security, he asked some mark of distinction from the King, preferably the Privy Council. *Fortescue Mss.*, VII, p. 52.

This outline of Wickham's secret-service activities has been inserted here because he played such a large part in Ireland during the period Emmet was preparing for his rebellion and immediately thereafter. Then all Wickham's efforts were concerned with using the rising as an excuse for imprisoning all the principal men among the disaffected—besides the ones executed for their part in it—and enforcing the Suspension of the Habeas Corpus Act and the Martial Law Act, which were passed immediately after the rising, in such a way as would keep the country quiet, he hoped, for years. He had been sent to Ireland in 1802 at Pitt's request, while Pitt was still out of office, at exactly the same time that Emmet was summoned back to head a rising. Certainly he knew a great deal about the plans of the rebels which he did not tell to the Lord Lieutenant, and when Marsden and he were being criticised for not having prevented it, he used pressure that did not stop short of the threat of blackmail to prevent an official investigation of the affair. An understanding of his character and personality is necessary to enable the reader to judge if he would have been capable of taking part in Pitt's alleged plan to trick Robert Emmet into leading an Irish rebellion.

*A discrimination should be made between officials whose position required them to supply the Government with information, and so-called " mercenary informers." No stigma should attach itself to the former. But, particularly in Ireland, the second class is held in such disrepute for extracting information from unsuspecting friends and acquaintances which is then passed on to authority and used against them that the

Nothing was too large to be taken care of by this machine, nothing was too small, nothing was too far away. The British Minister in Switzerland, William Wickham, was head of the British secret service on the Continent for many years. He traded so freely with *agents provocateurs*, enemy ministers, and generals that twice he was expelled from countries where he was officially credited for abusing his diplomatic position. He was as meticulous in gathering details about young Irishmen travelling on the Continent as he was of transactions involving hundreds of thousands of pounds, foreign princes, kings' mistresses, and General Buonaparte's secretary.

A Frenchman whose name first appears as an emissary to the disaffected of Ireland and Scotland took up residence in London. Ostensibly he was a refugee. But privately he was employed to relay to Dublin Castle the plans and hopes of the democratic party in Ireland. These he gathered from the letters of former friends who did not suspect the change of his sympathies and the source of his income. He was part of the system. A bankrupt merchant named Bird, who used the name of Smith, escaped from an English prison, wormed his way into the confidence of the Belfast reformers, and betrayed them to the Castle. He was part of the system. A tavern-keeper of Carrickfergus got himself sworn as a United Irishman and listened to the conversation of his customers. He was part of the system. Captain Mumford, the owner of a small sailing vessel that Irish nationalists were in the habit of hiring to make furtive trips to France, sold himself to the British Government. He kept up his old trade, but now officials in London and Dublin were made acquainted with the names and plans of his passengers. He was part of the system.

Government there takes precautions that, even if they lived more than a hundred years ago, their descendants may not be branded. Licence to use the documents at the Irish State Paper Office is qualified by the rule that the name of an informer may not be disclosed if his unethical activity has never before been known and the discovery is made through the state papers. For that reason, I am not able to give the name of several persons who were acting as informers at the time of Robert Emmet's rising. Such persons I have given names which have some similarity to their real ones, or which have an association in my mind, and have written them in quotation marks. "Fine Hand," for instance, who will appear shortly, is named for his beautiful script. His letters are not signed, and it was only by a careful study of the contents of the three letters in that lovely hand that I was able to deduct who he was. For the benefit of later research workers, I am depositing with the Keeper of the Public Record Office (Dublin) a sealed envelope giving the real names of these persons.

A versatile countryman known as B. Senior, whose interest
in horses was used as an excuse to take him to all the Irish
fairs, feigned an interest in Catholic emancipation and reform.
He and eventually two brothers were part of the system.
Belle Martin, a barmaid of Belfast, whose vocabulary was
entirely lacking in negatives, listened to the suggestions of one
of Mr. Pollock's intermediaries, as well as to the customers she
so saucily served. She was part of the system. A degraded
priest from County Roscommon got into the good graces of
the Defenders, so that he could betray the people over whom
he had had spiritual sway. He was part of the system, but
not for long. After trapping unsuspecting Defenders in
Dublin at the suggestion of the Castle, he was sent by the
Government to spy on the Defenders in Belfast. There the
canny Northeners found him out, and he was mysteriously
drowned.

Francis Higgins, a newspaper proprietor who had long ago
parted from what few principles he ever possessed for the
privilege of printing Government proclamations at a substantial rate, developed an acquaintance with dozens of individuals whose ears he found useful. He not only sent reports
to the Castle about the disaffected but seduced two of Ireland's
most infamous informers, Francis Magan, the man who was
to betray Lord Edward Fitzgerald, and Samuel Turner, who
became, while ostensibly acting as envoy for the United
Irishmen at Hamburg, one of Pitt's most valued sources of
information about the activities of the Society on the Continent.
Another newspaper publisher, William Corbett, kept in
contact with printers in every printing establishment in
Dublin—a most convenient way of obtaining manuscripts
that might be termed seditious—and as such made the basis
for prosecutions against men in the Black Books at the Castle.*

One of the most notorious of the men in the secret service
of the British in Ireland was Leonard McNally, a Dublin
barrister, who for more than a century has been known as a
mercenary informer and a traitor to his clients. McNally had
started life as a tradesman, one who sold groceries " in the
smallest quantities " in St. Mary's Lane, Dublin. He then

* A Black Book was, and still is, a compilation of names of persons suspected of
being dangerously disaffected to the Government.

studied law at the Middle Temple in London and practised there for a while. He was also called to the Irish Bar. In London he had several plays produced without much success, but his ballad " The Lass of Richmond Hill " is sung to this day, and he married the lady who inspired it.

He returned to Dublin about 1790, and his first case there put a blemish on his reputation. He was openly charged in court with having brought over from London some witnesses of rather dubious integrity. McNally sent a challenge to his accuser, but the Irish bar, at a general meeting, held that McNally was not worthy of taking part in an affair of honour. Thereafter, he was shunned by many of his colleagues in the courts and as a defence mechanism he took to patriotism.

Part of his unpopularity probably came from the fact that he was not attractive physically. Most of the descriptions of him show a somewhat soiled and saturnine creature but with handsome features and piercing, hawk-like eyes. Because his legs were not the same length, he walked with a limp, and everything about him seemed disarranged and ill-matched. But he could be good-natured, whatever his motives. He had friends who were loyal to him even after his later and greater infamy became known. He was hospitable when he had money—which the Castle sometimes provided for just that purpose—and at his own table picked the brains of his guests for the benefit of the Government.

By means of information thus obtained, added to what he learned from his unsuspecting clients, hundreds of men, all of them acting in the name of patriotism, and many of them innocent of any crime, were imprisoned, hanged, or transported half-way around the world to the convict colony of Botany Bay. He helped materially to defeat the cause of democracy and Irish freedom. But though there was nothing he would not stoop to do, one shred of decency remained in him. Every now and then, in the letters he sent to the Castle, there sounds a note cf utter despair at the plight of his country, like the cry of a lost soul pleading for mercy for those he has helped to damn.

He had become a United Irishman soon after the Society was formed, and Collins's informations from the beginning mention his activities as a member. He wrote several patriotic outbursts that were printed in pamphlet form. But almost before their ink was dry, he was suspected of betraying the secrets of the Society to the Government.

When Thomas Addis Emmet was conducting Tandy's case against Lord Westmorland in 1792, McNally was one of his legal aides. The Crown lawyers showed an uncanny knowledge of the line the case would take, and it was supposed that McNally had given Emmet's brief to the Castle. He acted suspiciously a few months later, and Dr. Drennan wrote that he had forfeited all confidence in the Society, and that Emmet was inclined to denounce him.*

That he became a member of the secret United Irishmen after the suppression of the Society in 1794 shows how plausible he must have been. Tom Emmet was very active in regenerating the Society a few months after it was suppressed. A committee of twenty-one balloted on the whole membership, and one in five was rejected. Dr. Drennan spoke in favour of McNally, thinking then that he had not been treacherous, and that his levity was not a good ground for objection.

He was admitted, but Richard McCormick, one of the leading Catholics, hearing of his election, told Emmet he would never attend the Society again, and Drennan began to regret his recommendation. "We admit Tone, Russell etc., . . . Emmet very staunch and even active, notwithstanding McNally's admission, whom he deservedly despises, and I really do wish now he had been rejected, though I thought it wrong to make such a man a declared enemy." †

The scepticism concerning McNally's integrity was quite justified. Having lost Collins as a spy on the Dublin United Irishmen, the Castle needed a new one, and McNally became their man. John Pollock, who had had considerable practice in matters of this sort, was probably the man who conducted the negotiations for the Government.‡ He was the man who "managed" McNally thereafter, and the first letters the informer wrote over his now-famous *nom de plume*, J. W., were

* *Drennan Letters,* p. 131.
† *Drennan Letters,* p. 214.
‡ Besides his unsuccessful overtures to Dr. Drennan, Pollock had represented the Government in the case of a printer, W. P. Carey, whom Pollock wanted to give information against the Doctor ; James McGucken of Belfast, who became an informer in 1798 ; an ironmonger of Thomas Street whose secret activity has never been brought to light ; and many others.

directed to Lord Downshire, a great friend of Pollock's. In
December of 1794 he sent an account of the political state of
the country to Lord Downshire that must have made that
gentleman shudder. The Catholics, McNally wrote, were not
satisfied with having got the elective franchise but were
demanding admission to both houses of the Irish Parliament.

> Paine's *Age of Reason* is sought after with as much industry as his *Rights
> of Man*. . . .   One consequence of these publications is a strong union
> between the better classes of papists and dissenters. They have been brought
> to think alike, and they now appear as determined to act on the same
> principles, as when they joined for the purpose of raising the National
> Volunteers. . . .
> The principles are beyond all doubt *republican*. . . .*

Two months after writing this, McNally sent Edward
Cooke, an under-secretary at the Castle who had a great deal
more authority than his title implied, an account of a Whig
Club meeting that had been unanimous in deciding " to unite
with the people, and to support them in all justifiable measures
as necessary for obtaining redress for their past sufferings, and
full security against every oppression." He promised to write
again the next day, but that letter has now disappeared.

McNally would have been of no value to the Castle if he
had not been trusted by the United Irishmen, and he must
have used his peculiar abilities to good advantage to reinstate
himself in their confidence. From this time on, he posed as
a violent democrat, and was given most of the important cases
involving United Irishmen and Defenders. In April of 1795
he went to Cork and evidently attended meetings of the
United Irishmen there. " By the debates of the United Irishmen at Cork," he wrote for the Castle on April 13, 1795, " it
appears that they wish to establish a democracy."

Later in the month he acted as defence counsel for the
Reverend William Jackson, the gentleman who had come
from France the year before and had been trapped, along with
Tone, Hamilton Rowan, and Dr. Reynolds, by Pitt's agent
Cockayne. McNally, of course, passed on to the Government
everything he learned from his client, who had no suspicion
of his treachery, and called McNally " his dearest friend."
Jackson was so sure he would be found guilty that, to save his

---

* *Downshire Letters.* P.R.O. (Belfast).

small estate for his family, he took poison in the dock before
he could be sentenced. He had given a letter to McNally
concerning his wife and family. Instead of looking after
their interests, McNally kept the letter for two weeks and then
turned it over to the Government.

Still, the Castle could not have felt too sure of its new agent,
because it was about this time that he was threatened with the
noose.*   A letter now at Dublin Castle dated May 6, 1795,
begins : " Your friend and mine have met in London. The
latter [McNally always referred to himself as ' my friend ']
you may be assured, will be found as you wish." So evidently
the final negotiations had been made in London, and the
" wishes " had been for information, for the letter goes on to
give information about certain individual United Irishmen.
It has one paragraph that shows that though the Society was
aware that it had a traitor among them, it did not now suspect
McNally. " Reynolds was at first suspected to be the person
who gave information to the Government from the upper
department of organisation, but Col. Keating is now the
man." The Society, McNally said, now relied on foreign aid.†

About September the informer wrote for the Government
a series of reports on conditions in the country. The first of
the series now available is No. 6, dated September 12, 1795.
It is most emphatic in pointing out the danger of invasion from
France. The whole peasantry of the country would join the
French troops, he said. The Government could not depend
on the loyalty of the regular Army or the Militia.

The sufferings of the common people from high rents and low wages,
from oppressions of their landlords, their sub-tenants, the agents of absentees,
and tythes, are not now the only causes of disaffection to government and

* Lecky, *England in the Eighteenth Century*, VII, p. 139, from papers in the Public
Record Office, London. When I was doing research there in January and February
of 1946, volumes of Home Office Papers for 1795 had not yet been returned from
their place of war-time keeping, so I was unable to consult the document Lecky
refers to. He calls McNally's treachery to Jackson his first service to the Government,
but in this he was mistaken. His research " of a few weeks " at the Irish State Paper
Office had been during the period when the " secret " papers were in the locked
chests in the Tower. Otherwise, he might have found the Whig Club letter of
February 4, 1795, and a report of Lord Camden's that quoted McNally's Cork letter
of April 13, 1795. He could not have known of the *Downshire Letters*, as they were
then in private possession.

† To protect themselves, informers always made it a practice to throw suspicion on
some other individual.

hatred to England, for though these have long kept the Irish peasant in the most abject state of slavery and indigence, yet another cause more dangerous and of course more to be feared pervades them all, and is also indeed almost universal among the middle ranks, by whom I mean the upper classes of artists and mechanics in the cities and farmers in the country. This cause is an attachment to French principles, in politics and religion, lately imbibed, and an ardent desire for a republican government. . . .*

The next letter in the series showed that the United Irishmen, even though they had been suppressed legally, were secretly extending their membership throughout the country, and that the Republican hopes of the people were strong and widespread. Paine's *Rights of Man* was still widely read, McNally said, and was influencing many people. He thought it was responsible for the Republican spirit that was pervading the country. Another letter of this series warns the Castle :

A kind of seditious convention is now forming in America composed of Hamilton Rowan [who had escaped from gaol and fled the country], Napper Tandy and Doctor Reynolds [both of whom had felt it expedient to leave Ireland], Wolfe Tone [who had been banished after his connection with Jackson had become known] and other fugitives from Ireland. These men have it in their power, and no doubt it is their wish to give every possible information and assistance to France. Tone is a keen sensible man, argues with plausibility and cunning, and writes with perspicuity and elegance. . . .

McNally was wrong in including Hamilton Rowan and Dr. Reynolds in the seditious convention of Irish exiles but quite right as to Tone and Napper Tandy.† Tone, indeed, was already in communication with the French minister in Philadelphia and was making arrangements to leave for France. His modest ambition was to arrange for a French invasion of Ireland.

* I.S.P.O.
† Hamilton Rowan's only ambition now was to be pardoned by the Irish Government and be allowed to return home. Dr. Reynolds, with whom Tone left copies of his journals and other papers when he set off for France, was evidently prevailed on to give them up. At least, when Tone's wife and son tried to get them years later, the Doctor could only show them the empty chest where they had been stored.

CHAPTER SIX

The Rise of the Orange Order

FROM the autumn of 1795 on, the term Orangeman appeared in the letters of Castle correspondents with increasing frequency. Orange had been the Protestants' colour since the Dutch Prince William of Orange had been invited to England to take the throne from Catholic James II. In Ireland, Armagh was a centre of Protestants who for years had been preying on the Catholic population, which was in the minority there. They had been known successively as Protestant Boys, Peep of Day Boys, and Wreckers.

The increasing political activity of the Catholics naturally made the bigoted Protestants of the North more aggressive. They banded together in larger and larger groups. In September of 1795 there was an engagement between armed Protestants and Catholics at a place called the Diamond in Armagh. Twenty or thirty Defenders, Catholics, were killed. The Protestant casualties, if any, were very few, a fact that naturally makes one somewhat suspicious of the Protestants' charge that the battle had begun by a surprise attack on their people by the Catholics.

The Orange Order grew out of the action of that day. Its avowed purpose was to defend the laws and peace of the Protestant Constitution and to defend the King and his heirs as long as they should maintain the Protestant Ascendancy. The real policy of the Orangemen was to drive the Catholics out of that part of the country entirely, as notices tacked to the doors of countless Catholics warning them to move will testify.

The Castle soon began to hear of instances where this policy was being carried out with great brutality. In March of 1796 a magistrate in the North wrote to the Castle that Catholics in his neighbourhood were receiving threatening

notices from Orangemen. These were signed Oliver Cromwell and warned the occupants of the houses on whose doors
they were posted to quit their homes for good or have everything belonging to them destroyed. The magistrate continued :

I have within a few days got information that I can depend on that there
is an association formed between Drum and Clones in County Monaghan,
under the title Orange boys, that they already amount to some hundreds
and that they have sent a Debutation (sic) to a number of Presbyterians and
Protestants in their County to associate with them, that a night is fixed for
their meeting at which an Oath of Loyalty to His Majesty and Secrecy to
the Rules of the Association is to be taken. . . . They are all armed and
can form a very great body.

Shortly after this the magistrate began to act as apologist
for the organisation. He wrote to the Castle :

It is folly to shut our eyes to the State of the Country. It is teeming with
Treason, and Treason methodized. It will surely be wisdom to oppose
System with System. If it be true that the conspirators are formed into
companies, or ready to rise at the shortest notice, ought we not to take a
lesson from them, ascertain our strength, and have a rallying point in each
district ? If they are *up* before us we are lost.

A couple of months later he wrote, semi-officially :

As to the Orangemen, we have a rather difficult card to play. They must
not be entirely discountenanced. On the contrary we must in a certain
degree uphold them, for with all their licentiousness, on them we must rely
for the preservation of our lives and properties should critical times occur.

He did not elaborate on the licentiousness of the new
organisation, but many others did, including Dr. Haliday.
The Doctor, though he had no desire to see the Catholics in
power, was shocked by the way they were being treated by
the Orangemen. He wrote Lord Charlemont :

A worthy gentleman, well acquainted with the County of Down, told
me two days ago, he had a list of 57 houses wrecked (that's their phrase) by
the Orangemen, since the Assizes of that County, and 10 in the County of
Armagh. Wrecked in the cruellest manner, unroof'd, doors, windows and
furniture destroyed, webbs cut out of the looms and with the yarn carried
off and burned, the wretched inhabitants of course obliged to fly (under
threat of being murdered if they do not) many to the south and west of
Ireland, where they may eventually do good in diffusing manufactures,
thousands to America. Our friend A. Johnston, who lately returned from
Derry, saw many fine American ships lying there, and was assured that they
would carry off 5000 passengers, a large proportion of them proscribed
Catholics.

Eighteen of Lord Charlemont's Catholic tenants were murdered by Orangemen shortly after this, and the horse-fancying informer, known as B. Senior, wrote Secretary Cooke at the Castle about it. " They came further up in the County Armagh than they ever did before, and killed a very respectable man, a Mr. Cummins of Market Hill, whom they mangled in a most inhuman manner. . . ."

General Dalrymple, stationed in the North, wrote down to Dublin that the roads were covered with decent-looking people going they knew not where. Lord Moira, always liberal and sympathetic to the interests of the people, sent a list of nearly three hundred names of his tenants driven from their homes by the threats of Orangemen. From the west the Earl of Altamont transmitted one giving more than a hundred. With it he sent his own offer to subscribe £1,000 toward building houses for " those unhappy sufferers who have been obliged to fly from their homes by a merciless and unheard of persecution." He wanted the Government to double the amount. The suggestion was not adopted.*

Instead, the fermentation of the country was increased by the formation of yeomanry corps that rigidly excluded Catholics from membership. The war between England and France now made a French invasion appear inevitable, and the Castle knew only too well, that if it put arms into the hands of the Catholics, many of them would be used against the forces of the Irish Government rather than the French.

As for the great mass of the Irish people, they watched for such an invasion with eagerness. It had been traditional with them, from the time of the Jacobite wars on, to look to France for assistance. No Stuart supporter in England or Scotland was more fervent than the Irish in their devotion to Old and Young Pretenders, and the love of Bonny Prince Charlie was embedded as deeply in the songs of Gaelic poets as it was in Border ballads. To the Irish peasants whose ears had always been listening for the sound of " French drums coming to set them free " it was almost instinctive to look to France.† To

---

* The Earl, who was not completely disinterested in making this offer, later became the Marquis of Sligo and as such was one of the Government's greatest aides in ridding his part of the country of nationalists. See p. 241.

† In 1666, the Most Reverend Dr. John O'Moloney, Bishop of Killaloe, and a friend of Colbert, Louis XIV's great minister, had persuaded him to prepare a great expedition for Ireland. At the last moment Louis changed his foreign policy, and the fleet never left the French ports.

the enlightened Irish nationalists, France was the land that had helped America establish her independence. What she had done for the colonists they hoped she would do for Ireland.

Wolfe Tone, who had reached France early in February of 1796, was then conferring with Government chiefs and had taken to soldiering himself. He wore a blue coat, he wrote his wife with characteristic vividness, but when he got to Ireland he would wear one " green as a leek." Lord Edward Fitzgerald, by now a United Irishman and more democratic than ever, had also been in France to urge assistance for Ireland. It was promised, and William Wickham, about to be expelled from Switzerland for abusing his diplomatic position, reported that the French General Hoche spent six hours each day conferring with the French Directory about the project. He was not able to buy Hoche off, but other Frenchmen were more mercenary.*

Dublin Castle was particularly interested in finding out who the leaders in the North now were, and so when an English bankrupt named Bird, who called himself Smith, made some contact with them by claiming sympathy with their cause, the Castle was glad to make use of him. Lord Camden considered him of enough importance to write Thomas Pelham about him on July 30, 1796 :

A man of the name of Smith, which however, is not his real name is an acquisition we have lately made and he appears to me to have more address and sense than any of those we have employed. The tenor of all the information is, that the Republicans have sollicited (*sic*) the assistance of the French, that they have endeavoured to corrupt the Militia in which they have to a degree succeeded, that they have established societies throughout the Kingdom, that they possess arms to a certain amount but that they want ammunition. This we know of their actual situation and intentions.

We are aware on our part that the Orangemen in the North and the Defenders in the West are only kept down by the force which is stationed there. It is impossible to have much confidence in some of the militia regiments and we have often agreed that there is not much dependence to be placed on our generals.†

B. Senior, the Government agent who specialised in fairs and taverns, was busy at this time following a rich farmer

* See p. 47.
† *Pelham Transcripts.* P.R.O.B.

named Patrick Carey and a companion, the informer referred
to as "the Frenchman." Carey, who had fled the country
the year before for his democratic principles, had since been
in America and France. Who his companion was is still a
mystery, but B. Senior followed the pair from the farmhouses
of Meath to the city of Belfast, and always the reports he sent
back to the Castle were of assurances Carey and the Frenchman
had given the people of French assistance.*

General Lake, then commanding in the North, poked a
playful finger at a friend's parrot and was aghast to have it
croak at him, "Are you up?" the slogan of the United
Irishmen. His loyal hostess hastened to explain to the
general that her servants had taught the bird the seditious
phrase while it was at her country home.

Generally the Defenders assembled under the pretext of
digging the potatoes of some neighbour who was in gaol.
After making good the excuse, they used their spades as
dummy muskets and were drilled in military manoeuvres.
Fifers usually enlivened the proceedings, and the companies
were headed by boys carrying green boughs to symbolise a
tree of liberty. One magistrate of Derry, Sir George Hill,
sent down to Dublin an account of a mammoth potato digging
where, in spite of suspicions that the Government might have
spies watching them, 5,000 men appeared. They handled
their spades like muskets, Hill observed, and, by the manner
they balanced them and their erect gait, showed they could
manage real weapons as well.†

Sir George rode his horse among them and tried to find out
their political opinions. They answered warily, said they

* William Corbett, the publisher-informer, once sent a report to the Castle of the
political complexion of all Dublin priests. Carey's two brothers were characterised
as "violently democratic."

One of B. Senior's reports describes the Frenchman as being smartly military in
dress and manner. He was, ostensibly at least, an advance agent for the French. But
when, in the summer of 1798, the Castle officials were making up lists of rebels to be
exempt from the Amnesty Bill, they were assisted by several of their informers, who
gave them lists of the disaffected with whom they had been in contact. The source of
several of the names listed is given as " the Frenchman." Whether Carey's companion was this man, or the Frenchman mentioned on p. 80 is not now known.
Later, B. Senior's brother John accompanied by a scallawag named G——, who posed
as a Frenchman, travelled through the County Kildare, where they passed as " friends
of the cause." As such, they were sent to Carey's farm just before Robert Emmet's
rising and were there when Emmet's summons to Carey and his sons arrived. I.S.P.O.
See p. 171.
† I.S.P.O.

could not oppose the French if they came since they had been made to give up their arms. They would not be soldiers to protect what they did not care for. The unhappy Sir George was certain that two-thirds of the country were planning rebellion and that any accident, or the landing of even a few Frenchmen, would make them break out.

In September, John Pollock went up to Belfast to help Lord Downshire and Robert Stewart, now Lord Castlereagh, superintend the arrest of the Northern leaders of the United Irishmen. Tom Russell, Samuel Neilson, and Charles Hamilton Teeling were among them. Pollock, with his usual industry and attention to detail, listed the characteristics of every man arrested. Of Thomas Russell, whom the Government had come to fear because of his great popularity and his military knowledge, Pollock said simply, "Take great care of this man."

The arrests were made by soldiers with the greatest roughness and aroused the indignation of the town. Dr. Haliday's description of the transactions tallies with many others written by irate citizens who, though they were not in sympathy with the United Irishmen at this time, saw in the manner of their suppression danger to the civil liberties of the whole community.

I am writing this on Friday [September 16, 1796], our market day, but all business in the streets, the Linen Hall, and at 'Change has been put down by dragoons, and with the war-like Marquis [Downshire] at their head. Espionage flourishes as well here as in France, under the old government, or in England under the new one. In consequence of this blessed system the town was carried sword in hand at a very early hour, and five or six United Irishmen have been taken up. I am told 42 have been informed against by a disguised corporal.* Not all here. Some have been secured at Lisburn, some respectable Linen drapers siezed on their way to our market. The confusion you may believe is great and the timid women truly frightened.

The good people of this town early exerted themselves to be discriminated from those whose principles they did not like. To no purpose, to no purpose. They were confounded in one common mass and the town reprobated and devoted (sic) without exception. As to amity to the constitution, they no longer behold it in Britain as what is entitled to respect and love, much less, in this proconsular province: . . . Depend upon it, my Lord, never was so great and unnecessary an insult offered to the civil power, as has been

---

* Dr. Halliday meant a sergeant from Carrickfergus, but Smith had supplied the most important informations.

witnessed this day. The ordinary Magistrates and Constables could and would have the business done, as well and quietly. . . . Speaking as a Belfast man, what is it to me whether I am to be destroyed by an unconstitutional government or an illegal mob ? †

The Marquis of Downshire and Lord Castlereagh were two of the most powerful and loyal supporters of the Orange regime.

† *Charlemont Mss.*   R.I.A.

3
INITIATION TO WARFARE

Thomas Addis Emmet, brother of Robert Emmet

Lord Edward Fitzgerald

Prints reproduced by courtesy of Miss Lydia F. Emmet

Thomas Russell

Theobald Wolfe Tone

Originals in the National Library of Ireland

CHAPTER SEVEN

Robert Emmet Becomes a United Irishman

In December of 1796, about the time that Wolfe Tone, in the laced regimentals of a French Adjutant-General, was hopefully setting out from Brest with an expedition intended for Ireland, Robert Emmet was sworn a United Irishman. It was inevitable that he should have become one. He was eighteen now, and his whole ambition in life was to help attain the freedom of his country. The condition of the mass of the people there was increasingly deplorable and dangerous, and hope to reform by peaceful means was now seen to be impossible.* Both Tone and Lord Edward Fitzgerald had been urging the French to go to Ireland, and at last an expedition was known to be in preparation at Brest, known to English and Irish officials as well as to the United Irishmen.

In order to organise the Republicans among the students at Trinity, Robert Emmet and some other members of the Historical Society withdrew from it and, under the pretext of forming a debating society, formed a college association of the United Irishmen. Thomas Addis Emmet and a man named Corbet who had a young brother in the college administered the oath to the new members, thereby placing

---

* Samuel Neilson, one of the charter members of the Belfast United Irishmen, made a declaration of principle that showed the prevalent attitude toward armed revolt. The paper found its way to the Castle, probably just after Neilson's arrest in September of 1796, when all the papers of the prisoners were sent down. Besides Neilson's papers, Russell's were seized and sent down, and the papers of the Teelings of Lisburn, a prominent Catholic family whose sons carried on a correspondence that showed, besides their interest in politics, great affection for one another, Bart Teeling's mare, and the boys' sisters, in the order mentioned. They will be mentioned later.

Neilson's declaration of principle, among other things, said : " With regard to the Progress of Truth by discussion and not by Arms I agree with Goodwin, but when the discussion is utterly at an end, I know of no means of resisting Tyranny but by Force."

all their lives in jeopardy.*   Robert Emmet and Michael
Farrell of Longford were the Executives, empowered to
administer oaths and to communicate with the different
branches of the Society in Dublin. They received their
instructions from the National Executive through Tom
Emmet, Arthur O'Connor (nephew to Longueville and a
great friend of Lord Edward Fitzgerald), and John Chambers,
well-to-do printer and bookseller, at Chambers' place in
Abbey Street.

The Castle shortly learned that Robert had become a
United Irishman. The report came through the new Town
Major of Dublin, Charles Henry Sirr, just coming into prominence as the head of as brutal and bullying a secret police
as the times could produce.† He was building up a staff of
spies, informers, and suborned witnesses supported by secret-
service funds which had no difficulty in operating among the
young gentlemen of the college.

But Emmet's ambition to take up arms was frustrated for
the time being, by the weather and possibly by political
intrigue.‡ The French expedition was separated by storms

* This information was given the Castle years later by a tall, dark young man with
ingratiating manners who had been a student in Trinity at the time. He was expelled
(not for political reasons) in 1797, went to England, and became involved with
George Orr, a Trinity graduate who was then spying on the disaffected Irish in
London. The two went to France together (Orr to watch the Irish exiles there), and
they both volunteered for an Irish expedition under Napper Tandy in 1798. On the
arrest of the young man in England in 1799, he was prevailed upon to become an
informer. Since he was ostensibly an international courier for the United Irishmen
and travelled much between Ireland, England, and France, he kept the Governments
of Ireland and England supplied with information about disaffected Irishmen at home
and abroad. His secret-service name was " Jones." At the time of Emmet's rising he
wrote many long reports for the Castle about all the prominent men who had been
acting with Emmet. The letter about Emmet's initiation was one of them.

† Besides being Town Major of Dublin and a Police Magistrate, Sirr did secret-
service work for the Castle ; in fact, that was his chief activity. The men he employed
were paid from " Secret Service Money applied in Detecting Treasonable Conspiracies, Etc." An account-book covering payments of this money from August 21,
1796 to March 28, 1804, is now at the Royal Irish Academy, and Sir John Gilbert
edited it in Documents Relating to Ireland.

‡ Dr. Richard Hayes' Last Invasion of Ireland says that English secret-service money
played a large part in causing the failure of the French expedition to Bantry Bay. He
points out that several government departments in Paris had among their employees
Frenchmen who had been bought over by Pitt, a statement that can be verified in
countless important instances. Dr. Hayes continues : " Writing a hundred years ago
Crofton Croker, who was an official in the English Admiralty and had access to many
of its private documents, states that Hoche and De Galles, the military and naval
Commanders in Chief respectively of the expedition, were very strangely on board
the same ship. He might, indeed, have added that all the money for the expenses
of the undertaking were also stored in that same vessel. Croker stresses the fact that

and never made a landing. Tone, after being close enough to
toss a biscuit from his ship to the shore, sailed back to France
with the broken fleet. He was seasick and raging with disappointment, but his determination to take French assistance
to Ireland was not broken.

In Ireland, the people who had been full of hope at hearing
of the approach of the French fell into deep gloom. But in
spite of the fact that their leaders tried to keep them in check,
they went ahead with plans for a rising. Blacksmiths became
extraordinarily busy, not merely with the shoeing of horses.
While watchers guarded the doors, they hammered out long
blades to be fitted to pike shafts. These were best fashioned
from ash, and gentlemen with plantations of ash-trees began
to notice that their forests were being robbed by night. The
people assembled as for a potato digging, by the hundreds,
and shouted and cheered at the fall of each tree.*

The authorities, now allowed by a recent Insurrection Bill
to take up " idle and disorderly persons " at will, interpreted
that to mean any who held political views they did not approve
of. They filled Irish gaols with prisoners and sent hundreds of
men to serve in the British Fleet or to indefinite captivity on
the prison ships that rode at anchor in many Irish harbours.
A proclamation from the Government ordered all subjects
to surrender their arms, and General Lake got orders to take
them from the people by force. A private note from Secretary
Pelham at the Castle suggested that of course the order did not
apply to those loyal to the Government.†

Many officers disliked service of this kind, but General
Lake, now in command of the Northern district, was not

he had his information from ' the most unquestioned authority,' and states that the
captain of the vessel had accepted a considerable bribe to sail the vessel away from the
Irish coast. ' He performed this delicate little task so well,' adds Croker, ' that he
boldly drew on the English government for double the amount agreed upon, which
moreover, was ultimately arranged to the perfect satisfaction of all parties concerned.' " Hayes, p. 256.

In the Archives Nationales in Paris, Dr. Hayes himself found a letter, written in
November of 1796 by General Hoche [Wickham had found him " impenetrable "],
who was evidently exasperated at the strange delays and frustrations he met with in
planning the Irish invasion. " The next thing I expect to hear from them," he wrote
angrily to the Ministry of the Marine, " is that there is not enough water in the sea."
Studies, XXIX, No. 116.

* Downshire Letters. P.R.O.B.

† I.S.P.O. Copies are also in the British Museum and with the Pelham Transcripts
at the P.R.O.B.

among them. He dropped a hint to some men of the Monaghan Militia that the *Northern Star* was not exactly under his protection and then discreetly left town. The soldiers took the hint. They broke into the office of the paper and destroyed the press and the house of the printer and for good measure the house of a man who had been supplying some political prisoners with food. " They dealt their blows about freely all day," the General confided to a fellow-officer stationed at Derry, " and carry a great many sore heads. I heartily urge this must go on. The whole garrison seems amazingly exasperated against the people who are uncommonly frightened. All this you must allow most fortunate."*

Dr. Haliday, though he had not been in sympathy with the views of the paper, referred to the incident with gentle sarcasm as a masterly and well-timed *coup-de-main.* " The people have been kept ever since in wholesome ignorance with respect to all the governmental and military outrages, except what few Irish truths they can pick up from the London Courier." †

The terror inspired by this act of vandalism was increased by raids made on the houses of individual United Irishmen. The peace officers and soldiers who carried them out were sometimes accompanied by a little man wearing a black mask. He was shortly identified as one Edward Newell, an amateur artist from Dublin who had recently been preaching devotion to liberty, but who was now a mercenary informer. Two brothers named Murdock, with whom Newell was living, were also pointing out United Irishmen and Defenders to the military and accompanying them on some of their raids. Belle Martin, an ex-barmaid, who had caused a great many men to be arrested before this, went down to Dublin and talked to Lord Carhampton himself. When she went back to Belfast, the peace officers there were irritated by the great airs she put on, but they were glad to make use of her services.

Towns surrounding Belfast had their own local informers, and so many arrests were made that men with timid hearts began to slip away into hiding or exile, or (providing they were important enough to be useful to the Castle) became secret agents themselves. Two very important men in the

---

* *Lake Manuscripts.* National Library of Ireland.
† *Charlemont Manuscripts.* R.I.A.

North were won over in the early part of 1797, Nicholas Maguan of Saintfield, County Down, and Samuel Turner of Newry.

Maguan stayed at home and provided the local officials and Dublin Castle with information about the men of the surrounding territory and their plans. Turner was even more important and was sent to the Continent. He was a Trinity graduate, an attorney, and had often been in Dublin on business for the United Irishmen. He was a friend of Lord Edward Fitzgerald and knew many of the Dublin leaders. His travels through the North on circuit as a defence counsel for members of the Society who had been arrested had given him a wide acquaintance there. In some way Francis Higgins, the newspaper proprietor who was so useful to the Castle, learned that Turner was under obligations to Lord Carhampton and that Carhampton might influence him.

Though he boasted a great deal about his bravery and sometimes swaggered around in a green stock, Turner was an extremely timid man. He slipped away from Higgins once or twice before he was finally landed. He demanded a promise that, if he became an informer, his name should never be known, and he was considered such a valuable acquisition that this was agreed upon. Naturally, he also spoke of reward.*

He did not wish to stay in Ireland, and it was arranged that he should go to London and eventually to the Continent, ostensibly because it was not safe for him to remain at home. He had been prominent enough to make this plausible, and his friends had no suspicion of him. Lord Edward was so concerned about him that, having to go to London himself at that time, he looked Turner up and gave him letters of introduction to Lady Edward, then visiting relatives at Hamburg.

Turner's future as an informer was planned in London by Mr. Pitt himself, Mr. Wickham, and Thomas Pelham, then the Chief Secretary at Dublin Castle. Soon he was settled in Hamburg, and, as he was vouched for by Lady Edward Fitzgerald and her family, he had no difficulty in learning all

---

* Higgins's letters revealing his part in seducing Turner are in the bundle of 131 written by him which Fitzpatrick said were in the secret chests in the Tower. At least, Fitzpatrick said 136, but there are now only 131.

the secrets of the democrats of the city. These he handed on surreptitiously to Sir James Crauford, the British representative there, or sent to London. Within a short time no Irishman on a seditious mission could fail to come under Turner's observation, and through him to the attention of the highest officials in Dublin and London.

While these sordid negotiations, which were later to have such a serious effect on Robert Emmet, were going on, he was composing a sermon in verse. Presumably it was intended for the edification of Mr. Pitt and his ministers. It told the story of a shamrock and a London pride that grew beside one another, and of how the London pride stole away all the life juice of the little shamrock. Finally, the abused plant was forced to speak :

> Neighbor, we're born with equal right
> To feel yon sun and see his light,
> T'enjoy the blessings of this earth—
> Or if right follows prior birth
> In this still stronger is my claim—
> Long was I known, and great my fame
> Before the world e'er heard thy name.
> But letting all these strong claims lie,
> Pray tell me, is it policy
> To thwart my offspring as they rise,
> To break my heart, to blind their eyes?

> Sure, if they spread the earth along,
> Grow handsome, healthy, stout and strong
> They will as usual happy be
> To lend that happy strength to thee :
> Thus would we keep each other warm,
> And guard us from all coming harm :
> We'd steady stand when wild winds blow,
> And laugh in spite of frost and snow. . . .

The Londoner, however, far from profiting from the rebuke, turned angrily on the shamrock. But its threats of extinction were cut short by a timely flash of Jove's anger, which completely annihilated the domineering interloper. The gentle trefoil thereupon grew once more to strength and calm. An almost redundant moral embellished the tale :

Take heed, learn wisdom hence, weak man,
And keep a good friend while you can ;
If to your friend you are unkind,
E'en Jove will be against you joined ;
Reflect that every act you do,
To strengthen him doth strengthen you ;
To serve you he is willing, able,
Two twists will make the strongest cable,
To bind a friend and keep him steady,
To have him e'er in reach and ready.*

Considering that Toler and the Chancellor were still threatening to throw out of the House by the collar any man who mentioned reform or Catholic emancipation, and that the measures of tranquilisation they advocated were so brutal that even a captain of Militia protested at the practice of shooting bands of unarmed peasants, Robert Emmet's forbearance and optimism seem almost celestial.

However, it must have been soon after this that he began the study of military science. Toward the end of 1797 the heads of the United Irishmen, disappointed and disillusioned at the way the Government had blocked the latest efforts to bring about a reform of government, were again thinking of rising. Robert Emmet was appointed one of the leaders of the college division. His cousin, St. John Mason of County Kerry, John Lawless, son of a prosperous Catholic brewer of Dublin, Edward Hudson, to whose flute Thomas Moore's pianoforte had often played accompaniments, John Keogh's sons, and others were sworn into the Society.†

Thomas Moore was never a member, but he wrote a violently inflammatory address to the students of the college which was printed in the *Press*, the Dublin organ of the United Irishmen. In it he urged them to study to be a scourge to tyrants and to study to deserve well of their country, their sunken and degraded country. Could they see her tortured, degraded, without burning to be revenged on her damaged tormentors ?

The publication drew a gentle rebuke from Robert Emmet. Walking with Moore one day, Emmet told him he could not

* Dr. T. A. Emmet, *Memoir of Thomas Addis and Robert Emmet*, II, p. 12.
† Information by the Trinity boy, "Jones." I.S.P.O.

help regretting that the public attention had been thus drawn to the politics of the university. He was afraid the college authorities would now try to frustrate the progress of the good work there. The rebuke, delivered, as Moore said, with the almost feminine gentleness of manner that Emmet possessed, carried, as Moore also admitted in his *Memoirs*, the intimation that in the circumstances in which they were, men should not talk or write about their intentions but act. Probably the rebuke was a bit more pointed than Moore admitted. Emmet no doubt meant that no man should urge others to rebellion who did not mean to take up arms himself.

The newspaper in which Moore's article had been printed had recently been established by Tom Emmet and other prominent United Irishmen. It had immediately become so popular that the Government had put both McNally and William Corbet to work to find out who financed it and who was writing its articles. McNally managed (with £50 provided by the Government) to buy a share of the newspaper's stock and so was able to tell the Castle everything it wanted to know. Corbet bought over the editor and got hold of some manuscript in the handwriting of the authors.

Tom Emmet was doing a series for the *Press* signed Montanus, which painted too accurate a picture of conditions in the country to suit the Castle. At. John Pollock's direction, Corbet wrote for his own newspaper, the *Hibernian Telegraph*, some articles signed Whipcord, which attacked Emmet bitterly. Tom had heard of Pollock's connection with the *Telegraph*, and he wrote Pollock asking an explanation of the attack. In righteous indignation Pollock replied that he did not have, never had had, and as long as he lived never would have, directly or indirectly, any share, connection, intercourse, privity, or acquaintance with the *Hibernian Telegraph*, or any newspaper that ever was or ever should be published. If there were black marks against Tom Emmet's name at the Castle before this, they must have been increased and deepened as a result of the correspondence. A letter Pollock had written Dr. Drennan's sister a few years before showed that, when his anger had been aroused, he could be an extremely unpleasant and vindictive person.

As the Castle knew from McNally, Tom was now one of

the National Executives of the United Irishmen. The majority of them were for moderate measures, Tom most of all. Arthur O'Connor, however, was more violent in outlook, and with the help of an even more violent and vindictive little man, Walter Cox, he started a paper called the *Union Star*, which he claimed was an official organ of the Society.*

Inking his type with venom, Watty turned out a paper that blackguarded Lord Carhampton, and any one connected with him or the Castle, and listed the name of those men he thought fit subjects for what he called " public justice," in other words, assassination. This was so far from the actual policy of the Society that Tom Emmet wrote an article in the *Press* repudiating the *Union Star* and the principles it preached. " Robespierre and Marat preached the same doctrine and their example should afford an instructive lesson," he concluded, throwing light on his own attitude toward the terror in France.

But the impression created by the *Union Star*, that the United Irishmen were a bloodthirsty crew, exactly suited the Castle. The paper was not suppressed, but agents were sent to find out the publisher. When a reward was offered for his discovery, Cox went to the Castle himself. He claimed the reward, saying that he knew the man, and then revealed it was himself. He got impunity for his editorials, if not the reward promised, and agreed to let the Government know everything he learned of the plans of the United Irishmen.

There was a split in the Society in December, and McNally wrote the Castle that Arthur O'Connor and Lord Edward were for violent measures. They drew their followers, he said, from a few priests and a number of mechanics and from the lower order of society.

---

* Cox's animosity toward the Government had been aroused in 1797, when his father had been sent on board a prison ship by Lord Carhampton. Cox was an extraordinarily unscrupulous, cunning, and witty little man who had started life as a gunsmith. For forty years he managed to be intermittently an informer and a thorn in the side of officials at the Castle. Marsden sent for him in the spring of 1803 to give information of the rebels' plans, and he was undoubtedly giving information to the Castle at that time. But in 1807 he started a publication, *The Irish Magazine*, which was so displeasing to the Government that he was sued for libel, sentenced to Newgate, fined, pilloried, and finally bought off and sent to America. But after as stormy a career there as he had had in Ireland he returned home and lived on a Government pension of £100 a year until 1835 when it was withdrawn. He died soon after in great poverty and squalor.

The moderate party who wish for the independency (*sic*) of Ireland, though of republican principles, and who are adverse to everything treatcherous (*sic*) or cruel, consist of the men of Education and wealth. Among them are Lawless [William Lawless, a surgeon, relative of Lord Cloncurry, and one of the owners of the *Press*], Emmet, the two Leesons, McCormic, Dillon of Parliament Street and Dillon of Bride Street.

The moderate party triumphed, and Thomas Addis Emmet became a member of the Directory, as he had been earlier in the year. He needed some insignia of office, and Robert sketched for him, at one of the last of the pleasant family gatherings at the Green, a design for a seal. Early in the autumn the *Press* had printed a poem of Dr. Drennan's calling Erin the Emerald of Europe. One line spoke of her as " striking her high harp to the ocean's deep roar." Robert used this as his inspiration and sketched a woman touching the strings of a harp. Some time before, Sir John Temple, a cousin of Dr. Emmet, had made him a gift of a fine emerald he had brought from India. Evidently, the Doctor presented the stone to Tom, and the design was engraved on it—at a cost, Dr. Drennan carefully noted, of six guineas. For himself Robert had a less costly seal with a similar design.

Having learned through a new and very important informer of a meeting of the Leinster Executive that was scheduled for March 12, 1798, the Government decided to arrest them all and to send magistrates and soldiers to their homes to seize all their papers.* Most of the wanted men were found at the meeting at Oliver Bond's in Bridge Street. Tom Emmet

* The new informer was Thomas Reynolds, whose wife was a sister of Mrs. Wolfe Tone's. Reynolds had been only mildly interested in politics until he was induced by Mr. William Cope, a wealthy silk merchant who had opposed Catholic resolutions in the Dublin Corporation in 1792, to develop his connection with the United Irishmen so that he could betray them to the Castle. Reynolds was deeply indebted to Cope, who probably felt that this was a fortunate way of turning Reynolds from a liability into an asset.

From February 3, 1798, on, Cope was getting information about the United Irishmen from Reynolds. Cope was also getting information from a Northern delegate to the Dublin meeting, all of which indicated that in spite of the efforts of the moderates in the Society, there was great danger of an insurrection within a few weeks.

Reynolds learned for Cope the time and place the Executive would meet. He found out the password that would admit the police officers to the upper part of the Bond house where the meeting was to be held. He even drew a plan of the premises. But he himself stayed away and thus avoided arrest.

Not being suspected at once, Reynolds went to Kildare and got more names of important local United Irishmen for the Castle. Originally he had not intended to prosecute his victims publicly, but the Government induced him to change his mind by quartering soldiers at his house until he agreed to do so. He got the enormous reward of £5,000 for his work, and a pension of £1,000 a year, which was paid for

had not arrived at the meeting when the raid was made but was arrested at the house on St. Stephen's Green.

Here the raiders made a special search for Tom's new seal ring. They even invaded the nursery looking for it and tipped some of the children out of their cribs, but Jane Emmet had it safely concealed on her person. Tom's papers, however, were all taken away, and with them an address Robert Emmet had written only four days before. It was addressed to the United Irishmen :

My Countrymen and Fellow Citizens. At a time when you are urged to acts of imprudence by every effort of malice, cunning and tyranny ; when illegal and unconstitutional measures are employed to force you into insurrection, and when the members of a most corrupt and infamous Administration are earnestly hoping, and anxiously watching, for the first appearance of Rebellion, that they may make it a pretence for destroying some of the most respectable and amiable men in your society, and crushing to the ground the whole body of United Irishmen, I conjure you to guard with the utmost care against being irritated to the degree they wish by their machinations, or imposed on in the way they hope by their real or pretended apprehensions.

Is it necessary that I should use any arguments to convince you that the view of the satellites of Government is to provoke you to insurrection before the proper time ? Is it not the glaring object of all their actions ? . . . The hour will ere long arrive when your purposes may be effected without the horrid effusion of blood that must be shed in the event of an ineffectual attempt. . . .

Remember that all your prospects of success depend on a resolute calmness. Let your sleep be the sleep of a Lion, and when the hour of awakening comes you will be invincible. Use every effort to encrease your numbers, but be cautious whom you trust ; place no confidence in man of bad moral character, and do not fail to encourage all the virtues in your society. Remember that Virtue is the true principle of a Republic. Remember that this is the hour of repose, and Remember that a time will come when you shall sleep no more.

March the 8th, 1798.*

thirty-seven years. Besides this he held various posts in foreign countries that brought his gross return from the British Government up to above £50,000. Mr. Cope also received a pension of £1,000 a year, which reverted to his last surviving daughter, and which eventually amounted to more than Reynolds' recompense. Between Reynolds and Cope, the cost of this transaction was over £100,000, paid eventually by the poor people of Ireland. The new material for this note is from letters at the I.S.P.O. See also Fitzpatrick's *Sham Squire,* p. 227, *et seq.,* 1895 ed.

* I.S.P.O.

CHAPTER EIGHT

Robert Emmet is Expelled from Trinity

TOM EMMET's arrest did more than shatter the happiness and security of the two families in St. Stephen's Green. It ended abruptly his brilliant career in Ireland. It started him on four years of imprisonment in Dublin and Fort George ; ultimately it sent him to exile in the United States. Never again would the Emmets be united. Not for years would they be free from anxiety and danger. It also increased tremendously the prestige of the family name among the great mass of the Irish people, a prestige that the Castle regarded as dangerous to the " quiet " of the country.

Within a few weeks Robert's prospects of a career in Ireland also came to an end. He had been right in telling Thomas Moore that the authorities would probably turn their attention toward Trinity. Already two students had been expelled from the college for their Republican politics, David Power of Cork and Arthur Ardagh of Tipperary. Young Ardagh thereupon sent a challenge to a fellow-student named Macartney, and the two exchanged shots. The duel resulted from a quarrel in which Ardagh charged Macartney with being the informer who had betrayed him to the college authorities.

Young Macartney was the son of a clergyman-magistrate in County Antrim who was active in discovering and arresting the disaffected in his part of the country. Both the father and son were undoubtedly convinced that they were acting for the salvation of Ireland, but their devotion to the Protestant Ascendancy, which to them represented the country, was in no wise restrained by their expectation that the Government would reward them for it, and that handsomely. Young Macartney fought several duels in an effort to clear his name of the suspicions that now rested on him publicly, but he also continued to keep the Provost of the College well informed of what the rebellious spirits within the college were doing.

In April of 1798 the Chancellor, Fitzgibbon, now the Earl of Clare, conducted a solemn visitation to inquire into the politics of the institution. He was equipped with a list of suspected rebels, furnished mostly by young Macartney and another student who came from Tipperary.

The Chancellor took his place on an elevated platform at one end of the large dining-hall, his face hatchet-sharp, his eyes obliquely hostile. His assessor, Dr. Duignan, equally inimical to anything that yielded an inch to national or Catholic claims, was beside him. Flanking the pair were the Provost and Fellows of the college. The students were ranged below them. To many, the Chancellor's name was already synonymous with the most violent bigotry and cruelty. He was, they found, in his usual form.

He had come, he began frigidly, to inquire whether the disaffection imputed to the college was founded on reality or was a mere rumour or surmise. Appointed to the high office of superintending the conduct and promoting the welfare of the college, he would be neglecting an important duty if he were to suffer it to continue stained with the infamous imputation of disaffection and rebellion, if unfounded, or permit any guilty member thereof to poison and destroy the prospects of the uninfected. His duty, therefore, to what he considered the happiness of the students—without referring to the more general consequences to society, if the lettered portion of the rising generation should cherish and act on those devastating principles that had destroyed the peace and almost annihilated the morals of Europe—indispensably required of him to investigate and suppress any serious disorders. He would remove all those who did not exonerate themselves from the treasonable charges made against the university, and he promised to see to it that they did not contaminate the youth of the several colleges of England and Scotland by representing their principles to the governors of those institutions and so excluding them from admission.

Beginning with the Provost, the roll of the college was then called and each person examined on oath. If the answer did not please Lord Clare, or if any refused to be sworn, he asked

roughly if they were fools or madmen. Any expression of
liberal principles was sure to draw another favourite comment
from the Chancellor, " The young gentleman's reason seems
to be affected."

Young Dr. Whitley Stokes, a great friend of both Wolfe
Tone and Thomas Russell, provided the sessions with a bit
of comic relief. Dr. Stokes had been asked if he knew any
United Irishmen. He answered that he did not. The Chancellor had some information that made him think that he did,
and so he tried another question. Did the Doctor know of
any secret or illegal societies in the college ?

Without hesitation Dr. Stokes admitted that he did. He
was called on to declare what they were.

" The only societies of that description which I am aware
of," said Stokes innocently, " are Orange societies, and I
know some members of them." The reaction of the choleric
Clare was everything that the amused audience expected.

The Chancellor was particularly insistent that each witness
give the names of students he knew to be United Irishmen.
In this way he learned that there were four branches of the
Society in the college, that Robert Emmet acted as secretary
of one, young Corbet of another, and that students named
McLaughlin and Flinn acted in others.

This ensured that Robert Emmet's grilling would be
especially severe, but the Chancellor was denied his sadistic
pleasure. Even for the privilege of remaining in college
Robert Emmet could not reconcile himself to giving information that would endanger others. He wrote a letter to the
Board of Fellows, denouncing the practice of demanding
information on oath that might inculpate others and asking
to have his name removed from the books of the college.
He showed the letter to his father, and it was sent with Dr.
Emmet's consent.

Nevertheless, the name of Robert Emmet was called, and
when he did not respond to it, he was marked down, as a few
others who had not appeared had also been marked, as con-
tumacious. At the close of the proceedings he and eighteen
others were recommended by the Chancellor for expulsion,
and the direction was immediately executed by the Board of
Fellows.

True to his promise, the Chancellor wrote to the heads of universities in England and Scotland, warning them of the dangerous political beliefs of the expelled students, thus barring the doors of those institutions to them.

Dublin talked of nothing, Dr. Drennan wrote Mrs. McTier, but the Chancellor's visitation and the lectures on morality and religion by one " whose conversation is a tissue of obscenity and blasphemy."

CHAPTER NINE

Two Questionable Characters

CURRENTLY another drama was taking place in England, and several of the actors in it were later, because of it, to have influence on Robert Emmet's life to an extent hitherto unsuspected. Early in January, Arthur O'Connor went to London. As McNally immediately reported to the Castle, " he departed much displeased and irritated with even his confidential friends for their disapprobation of his intention to promote an immediate rising of the people." McNally thought that probably O'Connor would go to France and represent to the officials there the state of Ireland to answer his purpose best.

Mr. Wickham, by now expelled from Switzerland, was as busy as ever in London, keeping track of the democrats there and managing delicate matters for the Home Office. O'Connor was of course watched in London, and it was planned to arrest him if he should attempt to go to France.

But for several weeks he lived at Strattan Street, associating with the foremost Whigs and also seeing some less prominent persons with more advanced political ideas. About the middle of February he received from the head committee of the United Irishmen the terms the French were insisting on before they would attempt an Irish invasion.*

* Just what the terms were was revealed to the Government in April when a Frenchman who had been some time in Ireland gave them to the Government. As there had been a lapse of six weeks since they had been sent over to O'Connor, the inference is that the new informer had been arrested during that time. He is mentioned only as A.B. in the deposition which he made to the Irish authorities and which Lord Camden sent over to England. He said he had left France with the Compte D'Artois and had taught French to the son of a prominent United Irishman, Mr. Byrne of Mullinahack, a large estate on the outskirts of Dublin. By the Byrnes he had been introduced to the United Irishmen. He had been a member of the head or secret committee of the Society, which, he said, controlled it.

His deposition shows that the United Irishmen had wanted France to send over only a small force and such a quantity of arms as would enable them to overcome the existing government but not leave them subject to the French. Ten thousand men

The upper Castle Yard of Dublin Castle.   *Malton's Views of Dublin*

Street map of Dublin, 1803

O'Connor must have decided to take the acceptance of the terms to the French Directory himself, for he shortly set off for France. He had met in London a Father James O'Coigley (Anglicised Quigley) who was also on his way there on a political mission. Father Quigley had spent several months in France in 1797 and had been followed back to England by the Irish informer, Samuel Turner. He was acting for both the United Britons, a recently organised association resembling the United Irishmen, and the parent society, and he had visited Ireland briefly after his return to England. Of course, he had been accompanied by secret agents all the way, and when he joined forces with O'Connor, the authorities were able to plan the capture of two prime figures at the same time.

Not suspecting that every move they made was watched and that the Government was quite aware of the nature of their separate missions, O'Connor and Quigley eventually reached Margate and made arrangements to hire a boat to take them to France. They were accompanied by O'Connor's servant Leary and a boisterous individual from Dublin who posed as Father Quigley's servant, one John Allen. All four men were arrested as they were about to set sail and taken to Maidstone gaol. The charge against them was high treason, the chief evidence being a letter found in Quigley's pocket from the United Britons to the French Directory.

Both the English and Irish Governments were determined to convict the men, particularly O'Connor and Quigley. Mr. Wickham, who took charge of the proceedings, wrote to Dublin Castle from Whitehall the middle of April that O'Connor was moving heaven and earth to save himself. " I trust however," he added ominously, " that all their

---

were the force suggested. The French refused this proposal, saying it was calculated to aid the Irish without assuring any advantage to the French. The smallest force they would consider was 25,000 men. For that they wanted the promise of £3,000,000 sterling, and a yearly payment of the same amount for ten years. After conquest they would leave the Irish to form their own government. After long debate the committee had agreed to this and had sent a man to England to notify O'Connor.

A.B.'s deposition ended with a list of important United Irishmen headed by the name of Thomas Addis Emmet : " The most dangerous man in Ireland he considered to be Emmet, from his zeal, his manners and address, his eloquence, his ability and his bloodthirstyness. He considered him to be the bloodiest man in the world." Except for that last questionable statement, everything A.B. said had already been demonstrated to the people at the Castle. A.B. may have been the Frenchman mentioned in the footnote on p. 60.

The deposition is now at the Public Record Office, London.

attempts will be defeated, though it may be necessary to adopt some very vigorous and extraordinary measures before so desirable an object can be fully obtained."

Already one rather extraordinary measure had been put into operation. A young Mr. Leonard H——, described by Mr. Cooke at Dublin Castle as "son to Counsellor McNally *le côté gauche*, an attorney at law," had been sent to Maidstone. "He will make known his address to you," Cooke told Wickham, "and will obey any instructions you shall convey to him as to the mode of communication with you," * Since young Mr. H—— had been active in Ireland as a United Irishman, it seems evident that, like his father, he was a spy posing as a patriot.

When O'Connor sent over to Dublin a London attorney named Wilkenson, he got in touch with McNally, possibly at the suggestion of the son. Wilkenson, of course, trusted McNally implicitly and told him what the prisoners' defence would be. This was relayed to the Castle, together with the names of the prominent Irishmen O'Connor was asking to testify for him. Among them were Mr. Grattan, Dr. Drennan, Mr. James McGucken, an attorney from Belfast, and Mr. William Dowdall, who had been one of the publishers of the *Press*.

It was necessary for the English lawyers to know something of these men, and so Mr. Pollock went over to Maidstone about May 1, much to Mr. Wickham's satisfaction. Pollock was, so Wickham wrote the Castle, "precisely the sort of man we want."†

Pollock not only helped Wickham with the O'Connor case but did a great deal to round up Irish exiles who were infecting the English with ideas of democracy.

When the trial of O'Connor and his companions began, Pollock reported it graphically for the Castle, covering page after page with his easy, effortless writing. "O'Connor is the most altered scoundrel you ever saw," he wrote on May 21. "He looks at this moment like a self-convicted traitor."

Besides his Irish friends O'Connor had had no difficulty in getting some of the most important Whigs in London to appear as witnesses for him. Writing from the courtroom at

* P.R.O.L.   † I.S.P.O.

Maidstone the next day, Pollock listed the people who had gone on the table for O'Connor :

Lord Moira, Mr. Erskine, Mr. Fox, Lord Suffolk, Mr. Sheridan, the Duke of Norfolk, Mr. Grattan, Mr. A. Taylor, Lord John Russell, Lord Thanet, Lord Oxford, Mr. Whitbred, all these persons have sworn to their knowledge of O'Connor's character and principles. . . . The guilt of every one of the Prisoners is manifest and plain, but everything will depend on the Judges' charge. . . .

The next day he described the scene in the court-room when the jury brought in the verdict :

Quigley—Guilty.

O'Connor and all the others Not Guilty. . . . About half past two o'clock A.M. this day, the Jury brought in the verdict as above. A proceeding then took place which never had an equal *in Ireland*. It was supposed that there was a Secretary of State's warrant to detain O'Connor, and the moment Judgment of death was pronounced upon Quigley the Dock was beset and several voices were heard calling out " The other Pris'rs are discharged. Discharge Mr. O'Connor." In an instant he leaped from the Dock, the Crowd was immense, the noise prodigious, the officers of the court calling out to stop him. " Seize O'Connor." " Take O'Connor," " Stop O'Connor." " Let O'Connor out." . . . Swords were drawn, Constables staves, Sticks, Bludgeons, *Knocking Downs*. . . . The Judges frightened to death. In short it is impossible for you to conceive such a scene. O'Connor, however, was brought back, restored to his place in the Dock, and immediately after committed to Jail. I ought to have mentioned that the Secretary's warrant did actually come down, and he (O C) detained under it.*

The Judge's charge and statement of the evidence against O'Connor had been feeble, weak, and defective, Pollock thought.

This point is important, since O'Connor's later actions make it impossible not to suspect that his life had been spared so that he might use his acquaintance among important Whigs and United Irishmen for the advantage of the Government. Even the kindly Lord Holland, nephew of O'Connor's friend Charles J. Fox, called his frantic concern for his own safety " hardly honourable to any man, and quite unpardonable in any one who had involved others as well as himself in very dangerous transactions."†

* Under it, he was sent over to Ireland and confined with the other State prisoners.
† Lord Holland, *Memoirs of the Whig Party*, p. 121.

Whether or not O'Connor became an informer then or
later, the Government was able to get at some of his correspondence through another of those "extraordinary
measures" Mr. Wickham had hinted might be used. The
day before O'Connor left London for Margate, he had given
up his Strattan Street lodgings and gone to stay with Mr.
Hugh Bell of Charterhouse Square, a gentleman with a wide
acquaintance among the democrats of London. After
O'Connor's arrest Mr. Bell had been taken up, too, and
charged with high treason. His correspondence was seized,
of course, but there were other letters that the authorities had
previously "intercepted" that were not found, and the
Government was anxious to get hold of them. Cooke wrote
over to Wickham, suggesting that Mr. Bell be granted a
pardon and induced to produce the intercepted letters.

The charge against Mr. Bell was never pressed, and thereafter
he handed over to the Government letters from O'Connor.

It is of course possible, if not highly probable, that O'Connor
was not aware that his observations on the Irish in France
(where he went following the release of the state prisoners in
1802) and the general intentions and state of preparations of
the French army were reaching the British Government
through Mr. Bell. But the use of an intermediary to pass on
the letters of an unsuspected informer to the Government was
standard practice. As an example, the Government at that
very time was arranging that Turner's letters be sent to the
Castle through a gentleman in Belfast who had once been
intimate with him there.

The boisterous Dubliner, John Allen, must also be an object
of suspicion from this time on. Allen was an extremely
uncouth and vulgar individual, and how he managed to attach
himself to O'Connor's party is something of a mystery. He
dressed in a slovenly manner, his pantaloons always stuffed
carelessly into his boots. He was addicted to swearing and
slang and spoke with an accent as broad as the Liffey at Carlisle
Bridge. "The rale Dooblin," it is called with affectionate
derision, and it indicates an origin in the Coombe district back
of Dublin Castle. A pug nose, dark cropped hair, and hollow
blue eyes complete the picture of this always entertaining
individual.

But while there is no doubt that Allen came from humble circumstances and had a natural affinity for rowdyism, he must have had intelligence as well, and later there is an indication of a more serious side to his character. However, he had no sixth sense to warn him that the well-known Irish patriot, Samuel Turner, who was cultivating Father Quigley so assiduously, was a traitor to his old associates and a mercenary informer. He trusted this new acquaintance so thoroughly that he even told him that he had killed a man just before he left Dublin. Of course, Turner passed the information on to Mr. Wickham.

Wickham also learned of the murder from Mr. Cooke at the Castle. Allen had been employed by a Mr. Shannon, a woollen draper of Castle Street, who thought that the description of one of the men arrested with O'Connor answered that of an apprentice who had suddenly left his employment in January. He went to the Castle and told Mr. Cooke what he knew of Allen : He had been a model apprentice, zealous and honest. About the end of January he had been out all night, and the next day he wrote his employer that from the perfidy of his friends he was forced to fly. But Shannon had heard that he had been concerned with a murder that had taken place because of a riot at Astley's theatre. Some United Irishmen in the audience had opposed the playing of " God Save the King." A man named Kelly was the leader of the loyal party who had insisted that it be played. He had been driven out of the theatre and murdered in Kevin Street. A scene painter, Graves, had seen the murder and had reported it to the coroner, saying that Allen had committed it. The Government had bound Graves to prosecute the case, but he had left the country and was then in Liverpool. Cooke ended his letter to Wickham with the statement that, if he sent for Graves, he could possibly identify Allen.

This letter was written on March 27, 1798, seven weeks before the trial of O'Connor and his party at Maidstone ; thus there was plenty of time for Wickham to investigate the matter.

But writing to Cooke on June 11, when every one but Quigley had been acquitted and all the others except O'Connor had been released, Wickham blandly overlooked that fact.

He told Cooke that Allen was undoubtedly the man who had murdered Kelly, and that " had he had the same information on that point at the trials Allen would certainly have been detained on a charge of murder."

" But even now," he added artlessly, " I have no proof but his own confession, made to a person we cannot ever bring forward."

It was not like Wickham to let a man off from a charge of murder, particularly when a witness who had been hound to prosecute was then in England, unless he was getting something for it. An information lodged against Allen on August 23 of that year, by an Irish informer then in London, seems to indicate that Allen had been used to try to trap two prominent noblemen known to be friendly to the Irish cause. Allen, the informer said, " frequently sees the Dukes of Norfolk and Bedford whom he thinks staunch friends to the Irish cause but he says they act so cunningly that nothing can be laid hold of. Both have given very handsome sums to advance the business and the Duke of Bedford offered Allen £50 which he refused."*

When Allen returned to Dublin early in 1799, another informer told the Castle that "Allen who was tried at Maidstone lives in College Green, is a Woollen Draper there. He will be very active."

Even with all these things against him, Allen was never molested, and in 1803, when Robert Emmet was making preparations for his rising, Allen was one of his associates.

* I.S.P.O. and P.R.O.L.

CHAPTER TEN

The Red Harvest of 1798

THE trial at Maidstone coincided with the breaking out of
the insurrection of 1798 in Ireland. A rising there, even
without the assistance of the French, had become inevitable.
The people had been tortured and goaded until they could
bear no more. The object of the Government had been to
make them rise prematurely, before the French could arrive.
Lord Castlereagh admitted this later on, and it is implicit in
many official letters of the time. In districts where there had
been no indication of disturbance, troops had been sent to
live at free quarters, which meant that soldiers notorious for
their licentiousness were turned loose into the cabins of the
poor, and that plunder and rape were commonplace. They
invaded larger homes in greater numbers, and what provisions
they could not consume themselves they destroyed or sent
away.

The picketings, half hangings, floggings, and other brutali-
ties that were being inflicted on the Irish people moved Lord
Moira to protest in the British House of Lords. "I have
seen, my Lords, a conquered country held down by military
forces, but never did I see, in any conquered country, such a
tone of insult as has been adopted by Great Britain toward
Ireland." A yeomanry officer of the County of Wicklow,
Captain John Edwards, of Oldtown, wrote to the Castle
protesting against the brutal treatment that the people of his
district were receiving from soldiers stationed there. He was
incensed that he, a magistrate and a responsible person, was
not allowed to be responsible for the quiet of his neighbourhood. The dragoons who had been sent there were torment-
ing harmless inhabitants and exasperating people who had
never shown the smallest sign of disturbance.

The High Sheriff of Tipperary, one Thomas Judkins, who

had added Fitzgerald to his name, was earning a reputation for brutality by wholesale and indiscriminate floggings of persons against whom there was no charge whatever, but who he thought might give information about the disaffected. The High Sheriff of King's County was doing the same ; he felt such childish delight at the success he met with that he could not keep the good news to himself. Writing to Lord Castlereagh on May 29, he gleefully explained that, in consequence of finding the good effects of a measure he had adopted in his own neighbourhood, he had been induced to go forward with it through some parts of the country,

. . . and the discoveries that [we] are making on account of it are wonderful. Knowing that almost every one of the Lower orders got pikes made I sent an order to many parts of the county to take the blacksmiths into custody. I whipped such of them as refused giving a list of those they make pikes for and whipped those that got the pikes if they did not inform me who swore them and of what meetings of the United Men they attended. . . .

The Castle did nothing to discourage this sort of thing. In fact, it was exactly what the Government wanted. When the new Commander-in-Chief of the Army, Sir Ralph Abercrombie, learned of the way troops had been terrorising the country, he was horrified and tried to bring them to some sort of discipline. He was not successful, chiefly because most of the officers were inclined to reflect the attitude of the Castle in such matters. There was one articulate exception and probably a few lesser inarticulate ones. General John Moore, later Sir John, the hero of Corunna, had come to Ireland with Sir Ralph Abercrombie, and he set down in his diary just what the Government attitude was :

The Chancellor and those of his party would never explain exactly what they wished, but it was evident that they wished the Commander in Chief with the army to take upon themselves to act with a violence which they did not choose to define, and for which they would give no public authority. Their approbation therefore would depend upon the success. Sir Ralph said he never chose to understand them. . . . Those who have the government of the country seem to have no system but that of terrifying the common people ; they will give you every power to act against them, but the rest of the community are to be indulged in every abuse.*

Diary of Sir John Moore, I, p. 287.

Both Sir Ralph and General Moore asked to be relieved from such obnoxious duty, but it was some time before they were allowed to leave the country. General Moore was sent to disarm part of County Cork. His orders were to treat the people with as much harshness as possible as far as words and manner went. He tried to excite terror, he said, but it was already so great that, the moment a redcoat appeared, everybody fled. The common people had been so mistreated by the local gentry, and so often deceived, that he felt that neither attachment nor confidence any longer existed. Only two, he said, had acted with liberality or manliness. The rest seemed to be actuated by the meanest motives.*

Even young gentlemen whose political convictions had led them to crop their hair were assaulted by the military on the streets of Dublin with impunity. Wickham sent over to Cooke a letter he had intercepted " as proof of how successful your warfare against the Crops has been in Dublin." The letter, which had been written in Dublin on April 10, confessed that the writer was now wearing " a false appendage to the back of his head called a false tail." It went on to explain that

Crops cannot walk the streets without being insulted in the grossest manner by the military. I have twice, and there have been repeated instances of Gentlemen being beaten by these Ruffians and laughed at, on complaint. Government have issued orders not to suffer any of the above description to enter the Castle Yard, and countenance the soldiers in any outrage on their persons. My Father without any positive command on the occasion requested me to procure one, as for so silly a thing it was absurd and imprudent to expose oneself to daily insults, more particularly as you received no redress.†

To make matters worse, the military went around " cropping " every one they suspected of Republican inclinations. Cropping was common practice in Belfast, Mrs. McTier wrote to Dr. Drennan in April. A young gentleman of aristocratic connections had been forced into the guard-house of the town at noon-day by soldiers who thereupon cropped him. " I suppose to serve as another proof of General L[ake]'s system being in force."‡

In Newry the Ancient Britons, a Welsh regiment that was

* *Diary of Sir John Moore*, I, p. 288.   † I.S.P.O.
‡ A correspondent of McNally's wrote him a letter showing that a similar situation existed in Cork.

the terror of the Irish in districts where detachments were stationed because of the wanton way they shot down the poor people, gave a young lady well known for her patriotic outlook what Mr. Pelham admitted was some very rough treatment and then tied her petticoats about her neck and allowed her to go home.

As they expected, Castle officials began to get information from their numerous secret agents that the United Irishmen were about to rise. The arrest of Tom Emmet and his associates in March had thrown the control of the United Irishmen to less patient leaders, and it is probable that even the moderate men would have seen the desperateness of the situation and agreed with Godwin that a time came when only the sword could serve.

On May 1, Francis Higgins sent word to the Castle that Lord Edward Fitzgerald was in town hiding, waiting to take command of the Leinster United Irishmen. The Sheares brothers, two young lawyers who originally came from Cork who had long been ardent Republicans and United Irishmen, would command Munster. The French, it was said, were unquestionably coming. Another Castle informant, a down-at-the-heels gentleman who signed his letters S, wrote a day or two later that Lord Edward, Samuel Neilson [who had been released from prison a few months before], and another not known were the new Executive. Another note from S said that Neilson was pushing on the rising by every earthly means, distressed about arms but determined on the trial.

By promising Francis Magan, an impoverished young United Irishman of good connections, that he would get him a reward of £1,000, Higgins induced him to betray the place where Lord Edward was hiding. He was captured, severely wounded, on May 19, five days before the rising was to commence, and taken to Newgate gaol.*

The day after Lord Edward's arrest, S warned the Castle that Newgate would be attacked that night to rescue Lord Edward. Soldiers were sent to prevent the attempt. Neilson was *mad*, S insisted, in a letter he wrote the next day, to get out Thomas Russell, whom he called a commander and chief leader.

* He died, probably of blood poisoning, on June 4.

That day, Neilson and the Sheares were arrested. The two brothers were secured by a trick devised by Lord Castlereagh himself. When it had become evident that the Sheares would be important figures in the intended rising, Castlereagh arranged with a colonel of a Militia regiment that an officer under his command, Captain John Armstrong, should cultivate their acquaintance, ostensibly as a sympathiser who would be glad to act with them. The Sheares were completely deceived by the suave little person, who passed on to his superior officer everything he learned from them.

The new arrests made the rebels suspect that their plans to rise on May 24 were known, and so they hurriedly moved the date forward.* On the afternoon of May 23 the informer B. Senior, who was now captain in a regiment of the United Irishmen in Dublin, went in frantic haste to a gentleman at the Custom House to have him warn the Castle that a rising would begin that night.

Soon the sound of drums beating to arms rolled ominously through the air. Militia paraded the streets ; cannon were brought up. Soldiers went about arresting suspected persons, who were flogged to make them disclose their secrets. As the news circulated through the great houses of Merrion Square and St. Stephen's Green, the gentry who were dining out hurried home on foot, not waiting for their carriages. Gaming tables in the fashionable clubs were deserted. One gentleman saw a lamplighter being flogged and learned that the lamplighters of Dublin had planned to put water into the street lamps that night so that the rebels could assemble in darkness. With expert timing Lord Castlereagh announced the threatened danger in the House of Commons and the Lord Lieutenant proclaimed martial law.

* " Information given by Col. L'Estrange of the King's County Regiment on Sunday Evening the 20th of May, in presence of the Lord Lieutenant :

" Col. L'Estrange states that Capt. Armstrong saw the Sheares today. They said it was necessary to make an insurrection immediately that their friends in the Country complained that they could hold out no longer if they were not supported by Dublin, that it was intended to make an attempt tomorrow or Tuesday night, that the Executive were to settle it tomorrow.

" The plan was to send five or six men well armed to attack the Houses of the Privy Councillors, that the Chancellor was a Chief Object.

" To attack in force the Castle Gates, to send a body through Houses in Stephen's Green into the Castle Garden, and thus place the Guard between two attacks. To have persons well armed placed on the Quay to intercept communications with the Barrack. To liberate the Prisoners in the jails. . . . He said they had the Country secured for 14 miles round Dublin." P.R.O.L.

These measures kept the city of Dublin from rising, but in the surrounding country men brought out their hidden pikes, fastened green cockades on their hats, and slipped into the darkness. Fires signalled from Kildare and Wicklow hilltops, groups of rebels collected, and a few preliminary skirmishes took place in Kildare.

A thousand men attacked Naas the next morning at two, and smaller groups surprised detachments of soldiers at Prosperous and Clane in Kildare. There was a small engagement at Ballitore, where an ex-officer of the Austrian army, Malachy Delaney, was in command. (He had a reputation, it developed later, for distributing Paine's *Rights of Man*, and he was high in the confidence of the Dublin United Irishmen.) By May 26 the rebels were strong in north and central Kildare. They had more success than the Castle admitted, but it did not last long. The next day the military burned Naas. The high point of the insurrection in Kildare had been reached. Fighting there did not cease for weeks, but separate groups of rebels surrendered from that time on. More than three hundred of them were slaughtered at the Curragh after they had laid down their arms.*

But by now the rebels in Wexford and Wicklow were in great strength and gaining recruits hourly. When martial law had been declared, many of the magistrates there, where Orangeism was in great force, had considered it as equivalent to an open season on Irish peasants. They had gone out with yeomanry corps accompanied by an executioner ready with ropes and cat-o'-nine-tails. The long-brutalised people were so terrified that they left their houses and took refuge in small groups in woods and mountain caves. The men were not inactive long. They went for their hidden pikes, put some wheat into their pockets, and set out to meet the enemy.†

---

* Madden, in *United Irishmen*, I, p. 322, *et seq.*, gives a list, collected from contemporary historians, of the numbers massacred by the magistracy, yeomanry, and King's troops in 1798 in County Wexford alone; thus the massacre at the Curragh is not included. It totals 866.

He also gives a list of the murders committed by the insurgents in Wexford. It amounts to 257. But as it has been admitted, no outrages were committed by rebels until they had been taught innumerable lessons in cruelty by their foes. The *Freeman's Journal* for June 16, 1798, admitted that the rebels had not exercised cruelty upon their prisoners except at Enniscorthy, where they had put several to death.

† The next year the grain in the pockets of those who had been killed sprouted and grew above the places where they had fallen.

Almost overnight an army was born, an army of tall young men dressed in corduroy knee breeches and frieze swallow-tailed coats, felt flower-pot hats upon their heads. Miles Byrne, a handsome young man of eighteen, was one of them. They made tents of winnowing cloths, banners of the petticoats of their wives and sweethearts. Every stray fowl they met was their prey. They wrung their necks and plucked them as they marched. After they had passed, the windward side of the road was white with feathers. But for all that, they fought well, and their engagements were conducted with attention to military principles. Ten thousand were in one encampment in Wexford by June 6, and the number was doubled within a week. To oppose them the Castle could send only 5,000 troops.

But in spite of the growing strength of the rebels, certain individuals at the Castle were quite satisfied with the state of affairs. Soon after the rebellion began, Edward Cooke, an under-secretary, wrote to Wickham that he considered it, however distressing, " as really the salvation of the country. If you took to account that 200,000 are sworn [the number was really much greater] in a conspiracy how could that conspiracy be cleaned up without a burst? Besides it will prove many things necessary for the future settlement of the country when peace arises." * On June 2 he wrote again that he was in good spirits as to the event.

However, as the rebels continued to grow in strength and to win many victories, an anxious note began to creep in. " The rebellion in Wexford has assumed a more serious shape than was to be apprehended for a peasantry, however well organised," Lord Castlereagh had to admit on June 8. . . . " The enemy are in great force at Vinegar Hill, within half a mile of Enniscorthy, and at Carrickburne, near Taghmon. Their numbers consist of the entire male inhabitants of Wexford, and the greatest proportion of those of Wicklow, Kildare, Carlow and Kilkenny. . . . Rely upon it there never was in any country so formidable an effort on the part of the people." † A little later he wrote apologetically to Pelham, the Chief Secretary, then ill in England, " The

* P.R.O.L.
† Sir John T. Gilbert, *Documents Relating to Ireland*, p. 130.

rebellion in Wexford has disappointed all my speculations. I had not a conception that insurgents could remain together and act in such number."

On June 6, two counties of the North, Down and Antrim, took up their arms, but there every intention of the rebels was known to the Government through the informer Maguan, and the Army could place its men at strategic points. Hundreds of rebels were killed, but the Castle could not be sure the danger was over. Army commanders in Connaught and Munster were fearful for their districts ; the rebels in Wexford were winning victory after victory. The Lord Lieutenant wrote frantically to England demanding reinforcements.

That, for Pitt, was the signal that " fermentation " had done its work. The Irish gentry were in consternation. Purposely, Lord Castlereagh had kept from prosecuting any Protestant leaders in order to give the Ascendancy the impression that the rebellion was a religious one.* They believed they could not stand without help from England.

It suited Pitt's plans to send the troops Lord Camden asked for and to accept his resignation. To replace him, he sent over General the Marquis Cornwallis, who assumed both civil and military command of the country. A private note of instruction from the King said that he must not lose " the present moment of terror for frightening the supporters of the Castle into an union with this country." †

* Castlereagh to ———. Dublin Castle, June 6, 1798. Original in the Royal United Services Institution, Whitehall, London. Lord Clare also admitted the policy in a letter to Lord Auckland, June 5. See C. Litton Falkiner, *Studies in Irish History*, p 149. Original in British Museum.
† *Documents Relating to Ireland.* National Library of Ireland.

CHAPTER ELEVEN

The Harvest of 1798, Second Phase

LORD CORNWALLIS went to Ireland as reluctantly as he had gone to fight the American colonists twenty years earlier. He had been dreading this appointment for months. But he had a soldier's concept of the duty of obedience, and Pitt and the King had known how to approach him. They put it that the Union would be for Ireland's own good, and that it was the only way of preserving the Empire. This was the perfect tactic, and Cornwallis was undoubtedly an excellent choice for Pitt to make. The Prime Minister knew that fundamentally the Marquis was an imperialist, a royalist who regarded anything Republican or democratic as the most dreadful evil on earth. He felt sure that the man who had handled Indian princes, English adventurers in the East, and corrupt civil servants as successfully as Cornwallis had when he was Viceroy of India would be able to manage the task of buying out the Irish officeholders and members of Parliament so that they would vote for the Union. It had not taken the blue ribbon of a Garter Knight to give Cornwallis a feeling of competence and authority. If he appeared simple-hearted and informal and a little apt to dispense with unnecessary buckram both literally and figuratively, he did not allow any easing of discipline in essential matters ; and his love of justice and fair play, which crops out time after time in his correspondence, did not operate beyond the point where it interfered with matters of Empire. He never seemed to realise that in buying out the Irish Parliament he himself was as guilty of corruption as the men whose votes he bargained for with titles and pensions and whose ethics he deplored.

Of course, he could not undertake that part of his mission until the rebellion was suppressed ; and when he reached Ireland on June 20, it had reached formidable proportions.

In Wexford even priests who had previously opposed the United Irishmen were now with the rebels, driven to war themselves by the countless atrocities they saw committed upon the poor peasants. Twenty thousand men, armed mostly with pikes and with a few hundred muskets, now opposed the King's troops. But these, reinforced and better armed, won a decisive victory over the rebels at Vinegar Hill the day after Cornwallis landed.

But two days later, thousands of them collected and attacked Hacketstown. They did not retreat until all their ammunition had been fired and after ten hours of stubborn fighting. Michael Dwyer, a sturdy, realistic Wicklow man, one of their captains, was now well launched on the career that would make him one of the most noted rebel chiefs in Ireland, and Robert Emmet's ally in 1803.

On June 30 the new Lord Lieutenant offered amnesty to all who would lay down their arms, but few cared or dared to do so. The "protections" given them were not honoured by the local yeomen, who murdered and mistreated many after they had surrendered. Many of their homes had been burned, anyhow, and their hopes of ultimate success did not die easily. Some still expected the French to come and help them. After the defeat of Hacketstown, Michael Dwyer and a few other mountain captains retreated to the glens with bands of followers that numbered from half a dozen to several hundred. Throughout Ireland thousands of men, singly or in groups, held on to their arms. Some of them kept up their spirits by singing a song that William Allingham was later to transform into a nursery phantasy :

> Up the rocky Mountain
> Down the boggy Glyn
> We'll keep them in commotion
> Till the French come in.

It did not take Cornwallis long to realise that a great deal of the trouble in the country came from the fact that the administration and certain members of Parliament were doing their best to make the rebellion seem a religious war. Easing his dislike of his job (it was his idea of perfect misery) by writing long, complaining letters, he told his friends he found that even at his own table his guests did not try to conceal their joy when there was news that a priest had been put to death.* He also acquired the conviction that the reports of the number of rebels killed did not mean that the men had been killed in battle, but that any man in a brown coat found within miles of a battlefield was murdered as a matter of course. What he saw going on, he said, was less a war than a horrid system of plunder and massacre, with all the leading people as violent as the troops.†

Mr. Fitzgerald, the High Sheriff of Tipperary, was still flogging almost any one he could lay hands on. "If five hundred lashes didn't bring out the truth," he boasted later, "it generally frightened scores of conspirators into voluntary exile." ‡ "You know it was the Cat that brought out the truth and 9500 pikes and 1500 stand of arms," he wrote Lord Castlereagh at one time. Far from discouraging him, Lord Castlereagh had an Act of Indemnity passed protecting "those who had acted for the public service with good intentions, however in the moment of warmth and struggle they may have acted with indiscretion." In 1802 the High Sheriff was made a baronet.

From the cells of Kilmainham and Newgate, Thomas Addis Emmet and other leaders of the United Irishmen could not see enough hope of ultimate success to justify the terrible suffering of the people and the lives being lost. How could they, when the Lord Lieutenant was writing that

. . . except in the instances of the six state trials now going on there is no law either in town or country but martial law, and you know enough of that to see all the horrors of it, even the best administration of it. Judge then how it must be conducted by Irishmen heated with passion and revenge. But all this is trifling compared to the numberless murders that are hourly committed by our people without process or examination whatever. The yeomanry are in the style of the Loyalists in America, only much more numerous and powerful, and a thousand times more ferocious.§

So when young Billy Byrne of Ballymanus, one of the Wicklow leaders who had been arrested and sentenced to be

---

* *Cornwallis Correspondence*, II, p. 358.
† Ibid., p. 355.
‡ I.S.P.O.
§ *Cornwallis Correspondence*, II, p. 369.

hanged even though he was in possession of a protection
issued by Lord Cornwallis, and Oliver Bond and Samuel
Neilson were scheduled to be tried by methods that were a
discredit to the name of justice, Tom Emmet and Dr. McNevin
made a move to stop the bloodshed. They suggested a compact whereby they and other State prisoners, numbering about
seventy, would go into perpetual exile in exchange for stopping the executions entirely and granting amnesty to the
people in general.

The agreement as it was finally worked out exempted any
man guilty of deliberate murder, and the Government made
it a condition that Emmet and McNevin should write a
general account of the history and organisation of the United
Irishmen. At first, the names of people concerned were
demanded, but the State prisoners refused to implicate any
one, either by name or description, and this was finally agreed
to. To the original committee of two, Tom Emmet and
Dr. McNevin, the Government added Arthur O'Connor ;
thus, if he had become a friend to the Government, the Castle
would have been put into possession of the private thoughts
of the important State prisoners and of the men for whom
they were negotiating. In fact, his appointment is an added
cause of suspicion that he had been saved from death in order
to be useful to the Government.

The Government was highly pleased with the whole idea.
It saved them from using a great deal of information they had
obtained from Samuel Turner, whom they considered so
important a spy that they did not want to risk having him
suspected by his colleagues. They also wanted to publish
the facts of the organisation of the United Irishmen as arguments for a Union. And, as Edward Cooke admitted,

. . . we get rid of seventy prisoners, many of the most important of
whom we could not try, and who could not be disposed of without doing
such a violence to the principles of law and evidence as could not be well
justified. Our zealots and yeomen do not relish this compromise, and there
has been a fine buzz on the subject, but it being known that the Chancellor
most highly approves of it, the tone softens.*

While the negotiations were going on, Billy Byrne was
hanged. Cornwallis explained to his chiefs in London that,

* Cornwallis Correspondence, II, p. 376.

while he himself approved the bargain which would have saved the man's life, his political friends would not hear of it, and that " the minds of the people are now in such a state that nothing but blood will satisfy them."

However, the State prisoners renewed the proposal, and the Chancellor backed Cornwallis up in thinking it a fine bargain. The committee of the State prisoners fulfilled their part of the contract and began to plan to exile themselves. But they found to their consternation that Lord Cornwallis (evidently at the suggestion of others *) now planned to keep many of them prisoners until it would be " convenient " to banish them, which, it appeared, would not be until the Anglo-French war was over. Also, to their consternation the Castle published a misleading account of the transaction, obviously with the intention of discrediting the leaders who had signed the memoir.

Tom Emmet's strong remonstrances to the Government at these violations of the agreement did nothing to increase his popularity with the Government, and they made Lord Castlereagh, who was conducting them, his bitter personal enemy. Emmet was singled out for special severity. He was confined in a windowless underground cell, fed on bread and water, and forced to live in the most degrading manner.

On August 22, the hopes of the Irish people were revived for a time by the appearance of three French frigates in Killala Bay. That they were there at all was due to the efforts of Wolfe Tone. The French Directory had almost given up the idea of sending an expedition to Ireland. Their ships were harbour-bound by the British fleet, they really had not enough men for a large expedition, and they would not send a small one. But when Tone, then with the French army at Rouen, heard of the rising in Ireland and of Lord Edward's death, his whole being was flooded with determination to force the

---

* Wickham later overcame the scruples of a British minister who had made certain promises to one of the men arrested in connection with Emmet's rising. The man had been promised that his name would never be mentioned as having given information, and that his life and the lives of two friends would be spared. Wickham, then in Ireland, wanted the prisoner sent over from England and insisted so strongly that he was finally sent, the fact of his giving information disclosed, and his life again put in jeopardy.

At the time of the trial of Thomas Russell in 1803, it was privately admitted by government officials that the terms of agreement with the State prisoners had been broken. P.R.O.L.

French to send some assistance to Ireland. Even a corporal's guard would be better than nothing, he thought. It would keep up the spirits of the Irish until a larger force could be assembled. He went to Paris and stormed the War and Navy Departments.

The new plan of a French invasion that was decided on as a result of Tone's entreaties was that General Humbert should sail from La Rochelle with 1,000 men, some arms for the Irish, and uniforms for the recruits they expected to make when they landed. General Hardy would sail from Brest with 3,000 men, and General Kilmaine (an Irishman whose real name was Jennings) was to follow with 8,000. Tone himself was to sail with General Hardy, and his brother Matthew and young Bartholomew Teeling were to go with General Humbert. Napper Tandy, who expected he could raise a great many men when he landed, was to sail in a fast little corvette from Dunkirk.*

But even after Tone had wrung the promise of this make-shift expedition from the Directory, his enthusiasm had to face not only the normal difficulties of equipping men and ships but the subtle opposition of British agents with connections in the various departments of the French Government.† Like General Hoche two years earlier when he commanded the expedition to Bantry Bay, both General Humbert and General Hardy now experienced strange delays. The money that was needed for their expeditions was promised time after time, but always they got excuses instead of cash. Finally, the impetuous Humbert commandeered the necessary thousands of francs at La Rochelle and sailed for Ireland on August 6. He expected that he would reach Ireland in time to aid the rebels, and that Hardy's men would soon reinforce him from Brest.

---

* The I.S.P.O. has a list of the Irishmen who were in France at this time, and it gives the places to which each was assigned. The young Trinity boy "Jones" was with Tandy and acted as his secretary for part of the voyage. Later he was arrested in England and induced to become an informer. His letters to the Government begin in November, 1799.

† According to Dr. Richard Hayes, a M. Vannelet, employed in the French Ministry of Finance, manipulated the money voted by the French Directory and was largely responsible for the failure of the 1798 expeditions to Ireland. Dr. Hayes quotes the *Memoirs* of M. Larevellière-Lépeaux, one of the French Directory, to the effect that the clerks of the Treasury Department were responsible for the delay in sending the necessary cash to the expeditions, and that the English Government was informed of the plans of the French. *Last Invasion of Ireland*, p. 10.

The Irish welcomed the little force eagerly. They threw themselves on their knees as the French marched into Killala and lifted their arms to heaven, praying for their success. " We shall be masters of Connaught in a few days. Erin Go Bragh," Matthew Tone, with some of his brother's exuberance, wrote to a friend.

Humbert's manoeuvre in not waiting longer for cash from the French Treasury somewhat upset the calculations of the English-Irish officials.

" This expedition came a few days too early. It will take, I fear, four or five days before we can act offensively," Cooke wrote to Wickham on August 24. The official letter accompanying the private one told of the joy with which the French had been welcomed and said that hundreds of Irish were joining the French ranks.*

Two days later, this little army won such a victory over the English-Irish troops that to this day the battle is spoken of as the " Races of Castlebar." But the first success of the invaders did not last for long. Hardy did not appear to reinforce Humbert. Cornwallis himself went west to take command of defensive operations, and on September 8 the French and their Irish allies were finally defeated at the bloody battle of Ballinamuck in County Longford.

In mid-October, Wolfe Tone, on board the *Hoche*, one of the ships carrying General Hardy's army, was again off the coast of Ireland prepared to fight for the freedom of the country. But an English fleet overtook the French squadron and gave it battle. Tone could have escaped in a small vessel that did get away, but he refused. " Shall it be said," he asked Frenchmen who urged him to save his life, " that I fled whilst the French were fighting the battles of my country ? "

The *Hoche*, after a six-hour engagement, had to strike her colours. Only two French frigates escaped the English fleet. The rest were taken and the men on board landed in Ireland as prisoners of war.

Tone was recognised by a quondam friend from Trinity, put into irons, and dispatched to Dublin under heavy escort. He was tried by a court martial on November 10, convicted, and sentenced to be hanged. The King's Bench was sitting,

* P.R.O.I.

and his lawyer, John Philpot Curran, decided to test the legality of Tone's conviction. But even as he appeared in court to stop the execution, Tone's life was dripping away, drop by drop.

The Chancellor wrote to a friend in London on November 15 :

We have got into a little scrape by bringing up Mr. Tone for trial to Dublin, sitting by the side of the King's bench. We shall probably get out of it by the death of Mr. Tone, who was suffered to cut his throat on the day appointed for his execution, and if the vagabond should not die of his wound, we may get out of it if his Majesty's Attorney General will act as he has been advised to proceed.*

Whether he committed suicide or was murdered in his cell is still a debatable question.

The French danger was over, the rebels generally suppressed. Fifty thousand Irishmen had lost their lives, the Government troops less than half that many. Hundreds of men were prisoners ; other hundreds had fled into exile. The Castle, in violation of the terms of its agreement with the State prisoners, was holding Tom Emmet, Thomas Russell, and other important State prisoners for the duration of the Anglo-French war. The country was full of troops. The time had come, Cornwallis decided, when it would be safe to broach the question of the Union. The Irish nation was to be dissolved.

But the quiet of the country was deceptive. The people were held down by force and by fear, but within them there was still the desire to throw off the English yoke. In principle they were democratic. Their aspirations were for an Irish republic. Their intention was to fight again as soon as an opportunity offered. Under the thatch of many a cabin pikes were hopefully concealed. In the Wicklow glens Michael Dwyer still led a little band of political outlaws. Every prison held potential rebels anxious to fight again. The United Irishmen were still organised, and Robert Emmet either was on the Executive (the directing committee) then or was appointed to it early in 1799.

*Journal and Correspondence of Lord Auckland, IV, p. 67. The Attorney General had been advised to bring in legislation making courts martial legal. It was tacitly admitted that Tone's conviction by a court martial was illegal.

CHAPTER TWELVE

Robert Emmet in Office

WHILE there can be no question that Emmet was acting with the leaders of the United Irishmen in Dublin during 1798, there was no direct evidence to show just what his duties were and exactly where he was. From necessity his biographers have had to skip the period. The available correspondence and journals of his friends do not mention him, unless a letter from Mrs. McTier to her brother, written in September, saying that " Nancy wants you to go to Italy with the Emmets," can be stretched to cover Robert, which seems unlikely. No Government informer whose reports have survived has a word to say of him till January of 1799.*

Then the Government, having made a recent addition to its corps of secret agents, began to hear of him almost daily, and from those reports (which seem to have been among the secret papers that were once in the sealed chest or chests in the Tower of Dublin Castle and are now available for research) it is obvious that Emmet must have been active in an important post before the new informer was put on his trail.

The Government's new acquisition, who later played a most important part in Robert Emmet's rising in 1803, was James McGucken, an attorney of Belfast. He had been one of the leaders of the Northern United Irishmen and in 1797 had been on a legal committee of the Society to defend its members who were in gaol. Samuel Turner was on the same committee.

Turner, it will be remembered, had been in England at the time of Arthur O'Connor's trial, giving information about the Irishmen who were there to testify for him and pointing

*All of McNally's informations from July 16 to November 14, 1798, are now missing from the State Paper Office.

out those whose political activities were especially obnoxious to the Governments of both countries. McGucken and his companion William Dowdall had been arrested there at Turner's suggestion. John Pollock, who was also in England at that time to help convict the Irish prisoners, had decided that they might be good material for him to work on, and they had been sent over to Ireland.

Though Dowdall had been politically active both in London and Dublin, there was no evidence that could be brought against him that would not expose Turner, and so he was released. But Pollock, on his return to Ireland, worked up such a case against McGucken that on July 22, 1798, he wrote jubilantly to Wickham :

I have decisive evidence against M'Guichen (sic) who was sole Attorney-General for the Ulster Executive, and joint for the National. He had been a most active and mischievous Rebel, and is a most dangerous man. I will either try him by a Court Martial, or make him give evidence against those whom we have not yet sufficient proof.*

Armed with this intention and the evidence against McGucken, Pollock went to see him in Newgate. Rather than face a court martial (it was just at the time Cornwallis was complaining at the way they were being conducted by men " heated with passion and revenge ") McGucken decided to save his life. But he was not made to come forward against other prisoners. Instead, he was released on condition that he would become a spy on his old associates.†

From that time on, he circulated among them assiduously, picked their brains, and reported what he learned to the Government almost daily. Some of his news was given to Pollock orally, who sent the Castle page after page of information penned in his easy flowing hand. More often McGucken wrote his own reports in a tight difficult scrawl.

" Emmet did not come to Newgate to-day as was expected," Pollock wrote for him on January 3, 1799, which gives the first clue as to what Robert Emmet was then doing. Many of the important State prisoners were still in custody. Tom Emmet, Tom Russell, Arthur O'Connor, Samuel

* *Cornwallis Correspondence*, III, p. 85.
† Ibid.

Neilson, Dr. McNevin, and a dozen others were divided between Kilmainham gaol, Newgate, and the Bridewell. Robert Emmet had access to them all, and he was evidently in contact with the leading United Irishmen who were at liberty. Through him, their ideas and plans were co-ordinated.

Since the Government had violated their part of the compact with the State prisoners, they felt at liberty to go on with plans to free the country. They still hoped for another French invasion. McGucken discovered from them that a French fleet was expected to sail from Brest at the end of January, that the North was making pikes and arms and exercising by night. Women and children carried the intelligence. McGucken recommended to the Castle that the moment a landing was probable all communication between Dublin and the country should be shut off. The same thing, he said, should be done if an insurrection took place in any part of Ireland.

McGucken had evidently gone over to the enemy with his whole heart, for he also had some suggestions about examining a prisoner named Farrell who, he said, was at the head of Dublin and had been a general messenger. Through him, McGucken thought, the Government could find out about the new constitution of the United Irishmen and what the preparations for a new rising were in the counties.

The report ended with the statement that "Russell, McNevin, Sweetman, O'Connor and Emmet are certain that the fleet will sail by the end of the month." This last Emmet was Tom, who was now a prisoner in Kilmainham.

A few days after the foregoing information McGucken recommended to the Castle that the State prisoners be sent away. "They would be in communication with one another with 1000 guarding them," he warned.

The Government had long been considering sending the most important men to one of the Highland forts but had doubted the legality of such a proceeding. Pending a report on the matter, orders were given that no visitors should have access to the State prisoners.

Dr. Emmet could not have known of the latest political activities of his sons, for he saw no need for the stringent ruling. After a time he addressed a request to some one at the Castle for permission to see Tom.   It is still as appealing and pathetic an epistle as a proud father could bring himself to write :

Sir,
    A month has now elapsed since I or any of his family have been permitted to visit my son in his prison ! As there does not I hope exist any necessity for a continuance of the order, may we hope to be readmitted to the painful pleasure of seeing him even in that prison ! Had you, Sir, a Son, like me, you would feel in reading what I feel in writing this letter.
    I am Sir with due respect Your Obed't humble Serv't, etc.
Rob't Emmet

Feb'y 12 1799 *

    Some one at the Castle endorsed the letter with its date and a *résumé* of its contents : " Doctor Emmet desires permission to see his son."   After more than a week another endorsement was added : "Answ'd 22, that no change can at present be made in the Orders given."
    It is hardly fair to introduce the Farrell whom McGucken wanted kept in Newgate as a young man who wore a locket, moreover, a locket that hung from a green ribbon round his neck.†   He was a much more masculine person than that would indicate to modern readers.   Jimmy Farrell was a bit of a lad in some companies, and his particular crony was that lusty and rambunctious individual, John Allen.   But he put on a genteel appearance and made himself agreeable to all sorts of people.   Tom Russell liked him, Robert Emmet liked him, and the Thwaites girls and their clever brother Austin liked him.
    The locket was inscribed, " Remember Wolfe Tone and

---

* I.S.P.O.
  † Originally from Waterford, Farrell had been a confidential clerk to a woollen merchant in Parliament Street, Dublin.   He was looked on as an influential man among the rebels.   When Tom Emmet, McNevin, and O'Connor, in accordance with their agreement with government, were trying to get the rebels to surrender in Wicklow, Farrell went down there with a representative of the Castle, Francis Dobbs, to induce them to come in.   A little later, Major Sirr searched his room, and, finding a dagger and a pamphlet he considered seditious, he arrested Farrell and sent him to Newgate.   McGucken's informations soon showed the Castle how important he was.   He was released in February of 1799, as will be seen, but a petition still in the I.S.P.O., dated 1800, says he was still confined there.   McGucken also submitted such a petition after his release.   The implication is that both men were released for the purpose of watching the rebels.   Letters in the P.R.O.L. definitely prove that Farrell gave information to the Castle in 1803.

Teeling." * The trouble with James Farrell was that his memory later failed him.

But in 1799 Robert Emmet had the utmost confidence in him, as he had in McGucken. When Farrell was released from Newgate in February, he went to live in lodgings at 33 Paradise Row. It was hardly more than an alley leading from Dorset Street, an unfashionable section on the hill north of the Liffey. There he went by the name of Edward Hewson.

The Emmets had now given up their house on St. Stephen's Green and were living at Casino, a lovely little estate of thirteen acres at Milltown, six or seven miles to the south of Dublin. Since Robert was busy visiting the State prisoners, forming a new Executive of the United Irishmen, and reorganising the structure of the Society, he arranged to turn over some of his official correspondence to Jimmy Farrell. Emmet still took care of the messages sent in from Connaught, but delegated to his friend those that came from Ulster. The person who sent the letter containing this news was the new informer, McGucken, who had gone back to the North to pick up his old connections there. Travelling almost constantly between Belfast and Dublin, he was able to learn practically everything of the plans and expectations of the United Irishmen. He even got hold of a copy of the officers' handbook and arranged to distribute it in Ulster.

When the new Executive was complete, he told Pollock (who of course promptly notified the Castle) that Emmet, Junior, O'Hanlon, and George Teeling (the brother of Bartholomew) knew them and had access to them. Later he learned that Emmet was actually on the Executive himself.

McGucken's informations generally recommended that no

---

* The Teeling mentioned on the locket was Bartholomew, brother of Charles Hamilton Teeling who had been arrested in September of 1796 when Russell, Neilson, and other Northern leaders were taken up. He went to France in 1797 and returned in Humbert's expedition as the General's aide-de-camp. He was court-martialled, convicted, and condemned to death, with a recommendation for mercy. However, he was hanged, and the gallantry of his conduct, combined with the cause for which he died, instantly made him a popular hero.

His brother George was in Dublin in 1799 and either on the new Executive himself or close to the members. The father, Luke Teeling, was a State prisoner in the Belfast Provost, in a prison ship in Belfast Bay, and in the bitterly cold Carrickfergus Castle, for four years after his arrest in 1798. The Government, following its policy of clearing the country of all people with nationalistic tendencies, was trying to get him to emigrate.

arrests be made, partly because he was afraid of being discovered and partly because he knew that other men, whose confidence he might not have, would at once be appointed to take their places. But the Government was not making arrests for quite another reason. Its idea always was to "develop" any plot, which actually meant that they watched it grow by means of secret contacts and then made sure, by the same means, that it would be frustrated. Wickham in London was quite in agreement with this plan, and early in March, learning of the new activity among the United Irishmen and the reorganisation going on in Ireland, he wrote over to say that he was far from thinking them an evil. He was persuaded that the seeds of insurrection were lurking in every county, and he felt that the sooner they bore fruit, and the more partially, the better it would be.

Toward the end of March, McGucken was at the Carrickfergus Assizes, where he was handed a letter from Dublin. It seemed to be entirely on business, but a key word, which he had arranged with Emmet, indicated that a message was written in invisible ink. Having no discovery wash with him, he hurried to Belfast and made out Emmet's message :

Any persons that have occasion to come to town send to Farrell at No. 33 Paradise Row.* He has got out since you left this, and is the only person I could get. I would have written you sooner but that he expected to change his lodgings. Send me word by return of post whether this has arrived safe. Direct to Edward Hewson, 33 Paradise Row. There is every expectation of the French coming immediately to the amount of 17,000. Govt. are dreadfully alarmed. Be exceedingly cautious. Everything should be kept as quiet as possible. Fix upon one or two persons to send down communications to in case of anything happening and write this name up.

McGucken was certainly cautious, but not in the way Emmet meant. To make doubly sure that the Government would have the news, he sent two copies of Emmet's letter to Dublin, one direct to Cooke at the Castle, the other to Pollock.

I am certain the within come from young R. Em——tt [he told Pollock] as he was the person with whom I had settled to communicate with before I

---

* This was undoubtedly James Farrell, but it is interesting to know that another Farrell of Paradise Row had helped to arrest some rebels in June of 1798. The Union Star once described a Farrell of Paradise Row as an older man than James would have been and said he was connected with an establishment of unsavoury reputation.

left Dublin, and as he sayd he would get some person to act with me in his place he not having time, and more certain it must be he, the word mentioned, which we settled on as a password is in the letter. The truth of this must be depended on.

Emmet was not mistaken in thinking that the Government was considerably alarmed. They had recently discovered a connection between the disaffected in Ireland and England and had made some arrests in London.* The plot in Ireland had been developed sufficiently for them to know the chief actors. They had already made some arrests of suspected persons in Dublin and the North and were determined by taking up the leaders to bring an end to all nationalistic activity. Warrants were issued for the arrest of Robert Emmet, James Farrell, and other men McGucken had pointed out. Nineteen important State prisoners, including Tom Emmet, Tom Russell, Samuel Neilson, and Arthur O'Connor, were shipped off to Fort George with only a few hours notice.

McGucken came down to Dublin and made out long lists of conspirators with hints as to where they might be found. He also told the Castle where to look for arms. " Search for arms in Antrim and Down, Antrim particularly. Break down the walls next to the kitchen fires, as well on each side as behind, and under them. The arms are concealed there."

Robert Emmet had dinner with O'Hanlon, an ex-officer of the Spanish service, some time in April, and the Castle got the idea that a meeting had taken place at Casino. McGucken, posing, of course, as a sympathetic friend, questioned O'Hanlon about it and decided that no such meeting could have taken place. " The Suspension [of the Habeas Corpus Act] and the entreaties of Emmet's sisters keep him in the Country," he told Pollock.

The Government still did not have the plan of campaign of the United Irishmen or a copy of the military books. McGucken went to work and learned that they were not yet printed. The members of the Executive still had the manuscript. The books had been written by Surgeon Wright,

---

* *Castlereagh Correspondence*, II, pp. 193, 237; also I.S.P.O. and P.R.O.L. McGucken was useful in telling what he knew about the disaffected in London, and through his information young Valentine Lawless, son of Lord Cloncurry, was arrested and confined in the Tower of London. The English Government soon supplemented McGucken's informations with those of a Londoner who gave himself up and turned informer. P.R.O.L.

who had served with the British Army in the American war,
but who had been a United Irishman for years. They had
been amended, McGucken was told, by Quin, Lawson,
O'Hanlon, Delaney (probably Malachy), and Emmet.

In order to get a copy of the book, McGucken slyly told
his unsuspecting friends that the North was ready and impatient to rise, but, unless he could give them the plan of
campaign, the only result would be another failure. He was
operating under instructions from the Castle to keep the
people quiet if possible but, if they were determined to rise,
to take the command himself.

O'Hanlon was arrested toward the end of April and committed to the Tower of Dublin Castle. Pollock thought it
likely that he could be got to peach, but before he could try
the prisoner's integrity he escaped. As soon as he was at
liberty, O'Hanlon wrote to Emmet, Dr. Wright, and three or
four others that they had been informed against and must fly.
McGucken did his best to make it appear that O'Hanlon himself was the informer. He told the Castle that Emmet should
be taken as soon as possible.

An attempt was made to do so, but Emmet escaped. An
undated letter from McGucken that fits in here says that he
had absconded.

Try his friends' houses. Search his father's house most minutely for
papers, particularly all the leaves of the books in the library on the right
hand side of the hall as you go in. . . .
Let the Commanding Officer at Belfast take up every man whose name
he shall receive in any letter signed Americus. . . . McGucken will leave
town at the end of the week. Money. Something permanent during
pleasure.

A footnote says that the military plan for insurrection was
in shorthand and was either with a man named Beard or with
Emmet. A second undated letter suggests some Belfast
arrests. "Young Mr. Brown son of the Banker of Belfast
who was expelled with young Emmet should be cautioned
by the General and will probably leave the country."

The Castle had more luck with Dr. Wright, who was
arrested on April 28. Finding that his protestations of innocence could not be sustained, he burst into tears and asked to
be allowed to leave the Kingdom.* But Castlereagh, having

* P.R.O.L.

lost a possible informer in O'Hanlon, had decided that Wright might be useful. He wrote Wickham that, as it might be of the utmost consequence to depict the whole of the present state of the conspiracy, the Lord Lieutenant felt a disposition to admit the Doctor's making further confession.

A few days later, Dr. Wright's full confession was sent to England.* He seemed inclined to blame religious bigotry for the disaffection then existing in the country, then with perfect inconsistency went on to indicate the importance of Robert Emmet, a Protestant. He had a high regard for his military talents and believed him to be at the head of the young men who had been expelled from Trinity. His advice to the Castle was that they should all be attended to, since they were all fired with military ideas.

Searches and arrests went on. Pollock must have enjoyed those climatic days. There was a buoyancy about everything he wrote. No detail was too small for him. He always had a keen sense of drama and rhythm, and they are evident in page after page of informations and instructions, all flowing easily from his racing quill. He often translated McGucken's rambling recountals into one-act thrillers with plenty of sharp, decisive action. He recorded the end of the 1799 conspiracy with an artistry worthy of a great playwright.

> Take W—— about the end of next week. He will tell all.
> Emmet is concealed and will leave the Kingdom the first opportunity.
> Beard lives in a lane at the end of Paradise Row near to Dorset Street.
> Take up Coyle as soon as possible, and then those that are in custody and those that have fled have for the present broken up the whole.
> Dublin is done.
> The heads of the South are given in.
> I'll answer for the North.

One can almost hear the thump of the falling curtain.

With the most important leaders of the United Irishmen either in prison or in hiding, there was to be a long entr'acte before the curtain rose on the drama of Irish nationalism. When it did, the leading player would be Robert Emmet.

---

* It is now in the P.R.O.I. Lecky, in quoting from it in *Ireland in the Eighteenth Century*, V, p. 255, made an error in transcribing his notes and attributed Emmet's leadership to the shopboys of Dublin.

4
INTERLUDE

CHAPTER THIRTEEN

Robert Emmet in France

AGAIN Robert Emmet slips for a time into obscurity. McGucken heard that he was in England shortly after O'Hanlon was arrested, but there is no other reason to think he went away then. He was probably, for a time at least, in hiding at Casino. To this day, there are secret passages and cubbyholes between floors, and an elaborate arrangement of ropes and pulleys evidently used to raise and lower a person seeking concealment. Wherever he was, his family realised he was in danger, for he was never mentioned in their letters to Tom at Fort George.

He is said to have visited his brother there in 1800. There is also a tradition that he ventured to attend some of the debates on the Union then being held in the Irish Parliament. Having failed to pass the Act of Union the first time it was presented, the Irish Government was trying again. This time, the necessary votes were frankly bought by offers of peerages and pensions. Lord Cornwallis, who grumbled at " trafficking with the most corrupt people on earth," Lord Castlereagh, who went about the business with characteristic cold-bloodedness and efficiency, and Mr. Alexander Marsden, a young Crown lawyer with a natural aptitude for intrigue, were chiefly concerned with the negotiations.

The majority of the people of the country were strongly opposed to the measure, and many members of the House of Commons spoke hotly, though futilely, against it. John Philpot Curran, the famous orator, was one, Peter Burrowes, an old friend of Tom Emmet's, was another, and so was a young barrister named William Conyngham Plunket. This articulate opposition to a Government measure in 1800 was to have an unfortunate effect on Robert Emmet a few years later.

The Castle still considered him a dangerous and active man,

and Major Sirr was armed with a warrant for his arrest made out early that year. A new plan of organisation was being circulated through the North, and McGucken was certain that he was the author of it. Emmet's name appears time after time in the spy's letters of this period. In August, Samuel Turner also wrote over from Hamburg to warn the Castle that young Emmet had been appointed to supersede the envoy of the United Irishmen at Paris, Edward Lewins. The hunt for Emmet was intensified. John Pollock rashly promised the Castle that he would " get young Emmet for them soon " if they would promise to keep him. McNally limped around making casual inquiries, and probably other agents as well were on his trail.

But he was already out of Ireland. With Malachy Delaney, the ex-Austrian officer who had been active in Kildare and Wexford in 1798, he had got as far as Hamburg on his way to Paris. While they waited for passports for France, Samuel Turner again heard of them through another old United Irishman of Dublin, one William St. John.* Naturally, he kept his eye on them from that time on and sent in official reports concerning them.

Delaney had formerly been in the Austrian service and was personally known to General Augereau, who was then in command of Austrian forces on the French frontier. Eventually, Emmet and Delaney made their way to him and told him of their mission. The General considered the matter of so much importance that he personally conducted them to Paris and introduced them to the First Consul. At Buonaparte's suggestion Emmet drew up several memorials showing the political and military situation in Ireland.†

* Until the rising of 1798, St. John, a tall young man with a remarkably round head, smooth face, and thick brown whiskers, had been a clerk in the Dublin Post Office. He was a friend of Lord Edward Fitzgerald and belonged to his body-guard. He used his official connections to open letters that might help the United Irishmen. After Lord Edward's death St. John and two fellow-members of Lord Edward's body-guard, William Putnam McCabe and John Palmer, the son of a hosier in Cut Purse Row, escaped to England and then went to Holland. According to letters now in the P.R.O.L., St. John " rendered some very valuable assistance " to the British there, and later this made the British promise to drop all proceedings against him. His later actions seem to indicate that from that time on he was not entirely loyal to his fellow-patriots. See p. 148.

† In 1803 a young man who seems to have been an intimate friend of Emmet's, wrote three letters for Wickham at the Castle, describing Emmet's trip. They are unsigned ; thus for convenience I refer to him as " Fine Hand." See note, p. 292 and 315.

Robert Emmet had left a country stripped of her last claim to self-government, but he found in France many men willing and anxious to make her a free nation, entirely independent of England. One of the chief men among the exiles was a barrister from Mayo, James J. McDonnell. When General Humbert had landed with his French troops at Killala in 1798, McDonnell had marched 1,000 men to join him and had won the General's praise for his leadership. After the defeat at Ballinamuck, Humbert had been allowed to go back to France. McDonnell had managed to escape the general disaster and had eventually joined his old ally in Paris. They were both anxious to have another try at the English, the French General for the sake of his professional reputation, the Irishman for the sake of his country.

William Hamilton, Thomas Russell's nephew by marriage, had also been with Humbert's expedition, and, not being recognised as an Irishman, he had been exchanged with other Frenchmen for English prisoners of war. He too, was in the General's confidence and sympathetic to his plans for another French invasion, as were many other Irish exiles then in Paris.

Besides the General's clique, Robert Emmet met more Irish nationalists at the home of a former Dublin man, Lyndon Bolton. The young Trinity man known here as " Fine Hand " lodged with Bolton and frequently saw Emmet, Surgeon Lawless, a relative of young Lord Cloncurry and a former teacher of medicine in Dublin, Malachy Delaney, and Patrick Gallagher of Dublin in conference there. The other young Trinity boy " Jones " was also in Paris at times during Emmet's days there ; and, as he was considered one of Emmet's intimates, there can be no doubt that both Whitehall and Dublin Castle knew about his activities there through his reports.

There were of course uncounted thousands of Irishmen on the continent. As a people they had the age-old impulse to travel which had made one continental scholar of the Middle Ages complain that " all Hibernia, a horde of philosophers, had landed on our shores." In past centuries Ireland had given many brilliant teachers to Charlemagne's Palace School, and learned churchmen to countless mediaeval foundations. They had enlivened even monastic gatherings from the Loire to the valleys of the Apennines with drinking songs written by

Irishmen who " did not think the devil should have all the best tunes." After the defeat of the Irish cause at Aughrim and the Boyne, hundreds of Irishmen, under the poetic appellation of the Wild Geese, had left their country to seek adventure and fortune abroad. They not only filled the Irish brigades of half a dozen continental armies but officered them and helped to plan their campaigns. Some of them were as familiar with the scents of boudoirs as they were with the acrid odour of gunpowder. Marie Antoinette had her Beau Dillon, and almost every European court knew Irishmen as polished and gallant. But by far the greater number of Irish exiles were the students and teachers in the various Irish colleges, some transplanted Irish families, and the eternal optimists of politics and the camps.

Among these Robert Emmet was unique in the variety of his connections. His birth and breeding gave him *entrée* to the *salons* of aristocrats and the intelligentsia. His interest in chemistry made him a friend of Vauquelin and other scientists. His devotion to democracy made him welcome among the Polish patriots and with the American colony. He knew the American Ambassador, and in Joel and Ruth Barlow he had Yankee friends whose large and hospitable house in the Rue Vaugirard must have reminded him of St. Stephen's Green.*

In Emmet's day the Barlows had as a permanent house guest another young American, Robert Fulton of " Clermont " fame, who was also Robert Emmet's friend. The young men had two things in common, Utopian ideas about mankind and a love of invention. It is not impossible that Emmet got from Robert Fulton some of his ingenious ideas about the rockets and explosive beams that he was to use in his rising. Already the young American was perfecting an underwater craft that he called a diving boat, the ancestor of the submarine.

* John Dos Passos, in *The Ground We Stand On,* gives a vivid picture of that shrewd and energetic Yankee. He had gone to Europe years before to sell Ohio land to Frenchmen, and, though the scheme was a bit on the shady side and was eventually a failure, Barlow made a satisfactory little fortune by other ventures. He had done innumerable semi-official jobs in the diplomatic line for the United States. He was a liberal and a democrat in the best sense of the word. In 1792, when he was living in London, he had been sent to Paris as a delegate of the British Society of Constitutional Information to pay their respects to the National Convention of France. He had been toasted at the famous dinner at White's Hotel in Paris when Lord Edward Fitzgerald made the speech that cost him his commission in the British Army. He was a friend of Thomas Paine's, and it is quite possible that Emmet may have met Paine under the Barlows' roof.

Emmet also frequented the famous *salon* of Madame de Staël, that vigorous intellect in petticoats who continually irritated Buonaparte by her interest in politics and philosophy. In fact, Emmet made such an impression on her that years later her granddaughter, the Comtesse d'Hausonville, was able to describe him vividly and accurately.

All his movements were rapid, she said, and (unlike most of the portraits painted from memory after his death) not sad in appearance.

His countenance pleasing and distingué, his hair brown and his complexion quite pale, the eyebrows arched and the eyes black and large with dark eyelashes, which gave his looks a remarkable expression of pride, penetration and mildness. His nose aquiline, and his mouth slightly disdainful. Energy, delicacy and tenderness are expressed in his melancholy features. Such was, however, his total absence of affectation, and his simplicity, that nothing seems to have at first attracted attention to Robert Emmet. The modesty of his character, joined to a sort of habitual reserve, hid the working of his mind to the ordinary circumstances of life, but were any subject started which was deeply interesting to him, he appeared quite another man.*

One can guess some of the topics that made Emmet blaze into that charming incandescence before Madame de Staël and her guests. Thomas Jefferson had left too deep an impression on Paris society to have his idea of government by a natural aristocracy, not grounded on wealth or birth but talents and virtue, forgotten in the *salon* of the lady who championed government by the élite of the intelligentsia. Emmet's own ideas were close enough to both of these to make him enter any discussion based on them with the heat and intensity that were so attractive to his audience.

He had an even more intimate friend in the Marquise de Fontenay and her family. They had been in Dublin during the early days of the French Revolution and were now back in Paris, all of them, the Marquise, her husband, and her daughter, obviously devoted to the young man they had known as a boy in Dublin. When Lord Cornwallis was in France toward the end of 1801 negotiating the final treaty terms between England and France, she wrote Emmet to inquire if this were the same Cornwallis who had been Lord Lieutenant of Ireland. Emmet answered that he was, and,

* Quoted by Dr. T. A. Emmet in *Memoir of Thomas Addis and Robert Emmet*, II, p. 7.

after telling her of the expected release of his brother from Fort George, went on to speak of himself. The translation of his letter runs :

I feel also glad to inform you that I had some time ago formed the resolution of not soliciting the interference of this Government, but simply of asking whether they had made any stipulation for us or not. This I did, and having received an evasive answer, I left the place without making any demands, telling them at the same time, that we merited their intervention at least as much as the patriots of Naples.

I have just learned by a letter from London, that the principal motive that influenced the British Government in making the peace was the declaration of Lord Cornwallis, that if ten thousand men landed in Ireland the country would infallibly be lost. I have also been informed by a gentleman coming from London, that it is the intention of the British Government to proclaim a general amnesty, and to provide a system of conciliation in Ireland, so that, if we have not found friends to acknowledge or appreciate our service, we found enemies at least capable of estimating our importance.

I am in want of nothing, my dear Madame. If I were I am quite convinced of the friendly interest you take in me ; apart from the affectionate manner in which you write me, but in this respect my father's generosity has left me in want of nothing. . . .*

When the end of the Anglo-French war made probable Tom Emmet's release from Fort George, Robert began to think of leaving France. In April of 1802 he wrote the Marquise about his plans. Tom had made up his mind to settle in America when he was released, and he wanted Robert to accompany him. But Dr. and Mrs. Emmet would be obliged to stay in Ireland, and Robert was faced with the necessity of choosing between them.

If I thought only of myself [he told the Marquise], if I took into consideration the sorrows that are before me in Ireland, and the advantages I would find in the society of my brother, I would joyfully share his fate, but on the other hand I find that my father and mother have left me perfectly free to make my choice ; and that they have made the sacrifices of their own wishes, and that sacrifice shows me that I must not allow myself to be carried away by personal motives.†

I have therefore determined on returning to Ireland, provided I can do

* Dr. T. A. Emmet, *Memoir of Thomas Addis and Robert Emmet*, II, p. 26.
† In an earlier letter Robert Emmet had told the Marquise that his father planned to sell Casino so that the family could be united in England or Wales, and " enjoy the only happiness that now remains to us, that of looking back on the past in the society of friends who esteem us, with full conviction of the purity of our motives." But Castlereagh, at that same time, was having a law passed which excluded the State prisoners from Great Britain as well as Ireland.

so without contracting any engagement that might compromise my honour. No one better than you, dear Madame, knows how much it has cost me the resolution of returning to a country where, in the presence of all that must awaken the souvenirs of the past, I must forget everything— that I had friends, hopes, tender ties, perhaps. I am not however certain that this can be done and I doubt it myself. I am not, in any case, to leave, until time shall show us more clearly the intention of the British government ; but this uncertainty is still more painful. . . .

Tom Emmet, with the other Irish State prisoners remaining at Fort George, was not released until the end of June ; and then it was only by an act of unofficial generosity on the part of the Lieutenant Governor of the Fort that he was not kept in confinement. When warrants turning over the prisoners to the custody of the captain of the ship that was to carry them to Cuxhaven reached Lieutenant Governor Stuart at the Fort, he discovered that there was none for Tom Emmet. Being one of the most kindhearted and honourable of men alive, he did not suspect that Emmet might be the victim of special antagonism on the part of the Irish Government but interpreted the omission simply as an oversight. Tom was allowed to sail with the other prisoners. Shortly after this, the Lieutenant-Governor was removed from his post, but Tom was safely out of British jurisdiction before the Government knew of his release. Otherwise, Irish history might have been different.

In what is, so far as the author knows, the only signed letter of Robert Emmet's in Ireland, he wrote John Patten about his reunion with his brother. He had gone from Paris to Amsterdam, and his letter is dated from there August 7, 1802.

My dear John,
    Tom, Jane the Children and Myself are at last together after many delays which have been distressing to us and which I fear must have caused a good deal of uneasiness to all of you. However, thank God that we have nothing more to complain of.
    As soon as Jane is a little recovered from the fatigue of a Voyage of 20 days (*sic*) across the Zuider Zee and from all that she suffered previous to it [she had given birth to a child in April] we mean to set out for Bruxelles where we will establish headquarters until the children can come to us *there*.* I think it likely that Tom will remain there to practice the children in French and as it is at the same time both cheap and exceedingly pleasant, we will possibly be stationary for some time.

    * When Jane Patten Emmet had gone to join her husband at Fort George in 1800, she had taken her three oldest children. The three youngest had been left with the family at Casino.

If you come there I need not tell you what pleasure it will give us, and independent of what I know you will receive by the company of Tom and Jane (and myself not excepted) I will introduce you to one of the first chemists of Europe to whom Vauquelin had offered me letters though I set out too suddenly to take advantage of it.   I have got in Paris letters from America from the most respectable persons there, particularly Kosiosko (*sic*), the American Ambassador and Joel Barlow, to Jefferson and most of the principal persons in New York, Pensilvanie (*sic*) and Washington !   A letter which I had written to Tom from Paris never reached him and we might both have been at a loss but that we met by accident at the Post Office where we were looking for letters, and I believe that the Mynheers were a little surprised to see us run up and hug each other a l'Irlandais without going through the formality of taking off our hats.   My delays spared me a good deal anxiety and I would have been here ten days before them if I had been able to set out when I intended.

Though it has I believe been the finale of almost all my letters, it is no less true, my dear John, that the Post is just going out and that I must of course break off my correspondence for the present.   I will not say that I do so with much reluctance, for I will candidly confess that after I have given to my friends the information which I know will give them pleasure my pen feels no inclination to run on, besides at present I have some excuse as it may easily be supposed that I have no inclination to sit still.   God bless you all.   The persons arrived with Tom are Russel (*sic*) Sweeny, Wilson and Cormick, the latter of whom is gone off to America.   They are all well. . . .

R. Emmet.*

Robert stayed for a while in Brussels with Tom and his family and then went back to Paris.   The old group of Irish exiles there who were anxious for another try for Irish freedom was now increased by some of the Fort George prisoners. Tom Russell in particular had ended his six years of confinement with his very soul on fire at the thought of the friends he had lost in Ireland and the sufferings of those who had survived.   Soon he was intimate with General Humbert, who had some vague plans about leading an expedition to Ireland.

It was just at this time that William Pitt, impatient to get into power again, was planning to manoeuvre Addington out of office.   Whether or not he was concerned with Emmet's

---

* When Major Sirr arrested Patten in 1803, he carried off all his correspondence, this letter among them.   Otherwise, there would be no " undisputed " sample of Emmet's handwriting to compare with the unsigned papers he left behind in the depot in Thomas Street the night of the rising.   I am greatly indebted to the late Mr. Albert S. Osborne for having compared these documents and having given his opinion that the unsigned ones were doubtless written by Robert Emmet.

recall to Ireland, as the letter to Marsden, which Sir Bernard Burke is said to have seen had suggested, Robert Emmet did get a message urging him to come home and take part in a rising, the preparations for which were said to be general throughout the country. He was so delighted with the prospect of helping Ireland gain her liberty that in talking to young Lord Cloncurry (who as Valentine Lawless had been an active United Irishman in Dublin and London in 1798 and had been arrested at the suggestion of McGucken) his forehead glistened with perspiration, and his features glowed with animation.

He evidently left Paris in October, so hurriedly that he did not take all his things with him, and they had to be sent after him. He went through Brussels and stopped to see Tom and his family. According to a family tradition, Jane Emmet went down on her knees to implore him to give up the project. (Little Robert Emmet, the ten-year-old son of Tom and Jane Emmet, witnessed the scene, and it made such an impression on his young mind that many years afterward, when he was Judge Emmet of New York, he used to describe it to his granddaughter, Lydia Emmet. Miss Emmet, it is interesting to note, bears a most striking resemblance to the portrait of Robert Emmet that is reproduced in this book.

Characteristically, he did not allow personal considerations to keep him from what he felt was a public duty. He went on to Ireland. With him, so John Patten said later, went Malachy Delaney.

CHAPTER FOURTEEN

The Mystery of the Summons

HAD William Pitt, as Sir Bernard Burke told Dr. Thomas Addis Emmet of New York in the 1880's, really suggested that a messenger be sent to Paris to induce Robert Emmet to return to Ireland and start a new rising ? Besides Sir Bernard's word, several circumstances seem to support that claim. Sir Bernard also told Dr. Emmet that the Government agents in Dublin were informed of every move (of the rebels) and were thoroughly conversant with the whole affair. But he did not tell him, probably because he did not know it himself, that the Lord Lieutenant who was in office at that time, Lord Hardwicke, was kept ignorant of practically all the information concerning the rebels and their plans which was known to Mr. Wickham, the Chief Secretary, and to the Under-Secretary, Mr. Alexander Marsden. It was to Marsden the Pitt letter was said to have been sent. Wickham had been assigned to the Dublin post at Pitt's suggestion and was devoted to him. The Lord Lieutenant's brother, Mr. Charles Yorke, was in the Addington cabinet that Pitt was trying to displace ; thus he could not have been concerned in the intrigue. When the rising was over, and the Irish Government was being criticised for not having prevented it, Wickham and Marsden did their best to prevent an official investigation that would have disclosed how much they had known of the affair before it broke out. Wickham even went to the extent of writing a note as a reminder to certain Irish members of the British Parliament who were pressing for the investigation that " Marsden was the person who conducted the *secret part* of the Union. Ergo, the price of each Unionist, as well as their respective character and conduct is well known to him. . . ."

A high Government official does not resort to such thinly

veiled blackmail unless he has something of great importance that must be kept hidden.

If the Irish Government, or Wickham and Marsden, working privately for their friend Pitt, did send some one to France for Emmet, it would necessarily have been some one supposedly a United Irishman, whose connection with the men at the Castle would not be too strongly suspected. Among the secret papers that were destroyed in the 1880's were probably letters that indicate who that person was. No direct proof of his identity now remains. He may have been some one whose duplicity has never been suspected. It is more likely that he was one of the confidential agents whose activities have recently come to light.

The dark-haired Trinity boy "Jones" is a remote possibility. He seems to have been at Hamburg when the State prisoners arrived there from Fort George ; and on August 29, 1802, he wrote a letter to the Government naming some of the people with whom they dined. "Jones" customarily acted as courier for the United Irishmen and might have gone back to Dublin between then and October, when the summons reached Paris.

It is also possible that "Fine Hand" may have taken the message, though it appears that he did not become an informer until the summer of 1803.

Malachy Delaney may have been one. According to "Fine Hand," he had left Paris for Dublin early in 1802. John Patten told Dr. Madden, many years later, that he was with Robert Emmet when he returned to Ireland. He, too, could have come to Dublin and then returned to Paris. And although Delaney has never been proved an informer, he has been strongly suspected of being one, and there are some very suspicious circumstances connected with clearing his slate at the Castle.

In the spring of 1803, he was tried for "murders" committed in Kildare by men under his command in the rising of 1798. Just before the trial Marsden wrote a Kildare gentleman then in England to inquire about Delaney's activities in that year. The gentleman answered very fully but said he was afraid his information might come too late for the trial. In thanking him, Marsden said the delay was of no importance as the

Government did not expect to convict him. But a Dublin gentleman, who voluntarily offered some information about Delaney so that his conviction would be certain, was rebuffed. He was told that there was no doubt of Delaney's guilt or conviction.

When Delaney was brought into court, the prosecutor announced that the Crown had decided that a prosecution could not effectively be carried on. Then, instead of dismissing the case, a jury was sworn, the prisoner given in charge, and a verdict of " not guilty " ordered. This automatically removed Delaney from all jeopardy. Samuel Turner, now definitely known to have been a spy, was cleared in a Dublin court by an equally ingenious device a few months later.*

Delaney was arrested in September of 1803 on a charge of high treason and discharged without bail four months later. Before he left Dublin, he wrote the Castle asking for an interview with Mr. Wickham.

If he did become a spy, his services can only be guessed at. But even if he did not, everything he knew about Robert Emmet must have become known at the Castle, since his lawyer was Leonard McNally, who never failed to pick his clients' brains.

The most likely candidate for the doubtful honour of having brought Robert Emmet back to Ireland is William Putnam McCabe, who actually did introduce the project to many of the men who followed him, and who went to France from Ireland that summer. McCabe was a self-possessed and handsome six-footer, about twenty-seven years old at that time. On his travels he often posed as a wealthy gentleman, but when he was among poorer people, he made an equally plausible Scotch pedlar or Irish countryman. He could mimic perfectly all sorts of Irish and Scotch accents and had a predilection for melodramatic disguises.

His father was a watchmaker of Belfast noted for his Republican principles and his sense of humour. At the time of the dragoons' attack on Belfast in 1793, his shop had been

---

* Turner claimed that he was not in the country at the time the Fugitive Bill was passed ; therefore, he could not be the Samuel Turner mentioned in it. The Crown officers gravely agreed with him. There had been considerable consultation between Turner and the Government officials both in London and Dublin as to the best means to ensure his future safety, and this had been decided on as the best plan. I.S.P.O.

one of those destroyed. He refused to repair it and put up a sign "An Irish Slave." His son followed in his political foot-steps. When Tom Russell and the other Northern leaders had been arrested in 1796, it had been thought necessary to have some person carry communications to "the higher order" among the United Irishmen, and young McCabe had been chosen. He organised many of the counties around Dublin before the 1798 rising and drew up the rebels' military plans. He was one of Lord Edward Fitzgerald's body-guard, and a great friend of Arthur O'Connor. He was arrested about the time of Lord Edward's capture but made his escape from gaol through the intercession of an Army officer. Since this was a usual means of releasing men who had been won over to the Government service and since he "escaped" many times after that from prisons in England and Ireland, there must be doubt of his integrity from then on. As a matter of fact, his own comrades had had some suspicion of him in 1797, but he had been able to convince them of his loyalty to the cause.*

After the 1798 rising, McCabe went to England and France with William St. John and young Palmer, and in 1802 he established a cotton manufactory in Rouen. But he always travelled a great deal and kept up his contacts with Irish exiles everywhere, in England, Scotland, and France. All this, of course, would make him extremely valuable as a spy. He went to see Napper Tandy twice in four months after that broken-down old Republican was allowed by the British Government to go to Bordeaux. After his last visit, McCabe headed for Ireland by way of England, visiting democrats in many towns along the way.

On his return to England after his Irish visit, McCabe stayed with a man who had long been under the eye of a local informer and, through him, came to the attention of a magis-

---

* There is no documentary proof that McCabe was a Government agent until 1818 when he was in gaol in Dublin and was writing various Government officials as a subsidised employee of long standing. Arthur O'Connor (who is himself suspect) says vaguely in a memoir published by Madden that the French Government dis-covered that McCabe was a double spy, and that he, O'Connor, saved his life by interceding with the French Government. It was O'Connor who for years sent McCabe from France to England and Ireland, well supplied with information, some of which is known to have reached the Castle.

Miles Byrne, the Wexford rebel, who knew McCabe in Paris late in 1803, had very strong suspicions of his loyalty.

trate who managed several spies in that district for officials
at Whitehall and Bow Street. A letter written by this gentleman in July, 1802, recounted the places McCabe had visited
lately and said that he was particularly anxious not to be known
by any of his own countrymen. He was advising the English
citizens not to have anything to do with them. " He says
the citizens are very numerous in Ireland, but little confidence
ought to be placed in them." *

Such sentiments are hardly those of a bona fide rebel but
smack instead of the Government's usual policy of creating
distrust among the disaffected. McCabe's unwillingness to
have his own countrymen know of him suggests that his
missions were not for the United Irishmen but to get information for the British and Irish Governments. And it should not
be forgotten that there is definite proof that in later years he
was a spy.

Always lurking in the background of the 1803 rising was
Arthur O'Connor, who had no connection with the Emmet
party and was most emphatically distrusted by Thomas Addis
Emmet. His actions, as will shortly be seen, were as suspicious
as those of William Putnam McCabe, and their connection
darkens those same suspicions.

* P.R.O.L.

5

EMMET PREPARES FOR
ANOTHER RISING

CHAPTER FIFTEEN

The Castle Watches

THE claim of Sir Bernard Burke that the Government agents in Dublin were informed of every move of Robert Emmet after his return to Ireland is strongly supported by documents, though it is obvious that many others probably even more incriminating have been destroyed. Soon after Emmet reached Dublin, he was invited to dinner at the home of a man who still posed as a patriot, though he had long been in receipt of a secret-service annuity, paid in the most furtive manner.* This was Mr. John Keogh of Mount Jerome, the wealthy silk merchant who had been derided in the House of Commons in 1792 for advocating Catholic emancipation. He had been one of the prime movers in that cause for many years, and he and his sons had also been concerned somewhat less publicly with the United Irishmen. Young Cornelius Keogh had been at Trinity with Emmet and had also associated with him in Paris, when he, too, had been an exile for a time.

All this would make it appear quite natural for the Keoghs to entertain Robert Emmet on his return to Ireland. John Philpot Curran, the famous orator and defender of many United Irishmen, was also a guest at the dinner. Emmet must have thought the company entirely sympathetic, for, when Keogh skilfully turned the conversation to the possibility of a new rising, he spoke freely and with optimism.

"How many counties did he think might be engaged?" Keogh prodded. Nineteen, Robert answered explicitly, but he thought an attempt could be made with even less. Curran thought that two dependable counties would make the matter possible.

Keogh later arranged another dinner at which Emmet,

---

* Secret Service Money Payments include many entries of money paid to John Keogh. Receipts are in the same handwriting as a letter from John Keogh to John Ryan of Marlborough Street, which was dated from Mount Jerome. There is also at the I.S.P.O. a note from one Castle official to another asking him to send a hundred pound note in the usual manner, in a plain envelope, to Mr. Keogh at a small Dublin hotel.

Curran, and James Ryan, a wealthy young man known as the Duke of Marlborough because he lived on Marlborough Street, Dublin, were to be the sole guests. In some way, Keogh's letter to Ryan, saying that he had gone to Milltown to prevail upon R. E. to attend, found its way to the Castle.

It is quite possible that Ryan was one of the wealthy and influential men who urged Emmet to enter a new conspiracy and then deserted him at the last moment.

At any rate, soon after his return, Emmet became convinced that a new insurrection might be successful, and that another effort should be made to win Ireland's freedom. Even though the current Lord Lieutenant, Lord Hardwicke, was a mild and humane man, and his administration marked by none of the ferocity and repressions that had distinguished Lord Camden's, the country was now without a vestige of self-government, a state of affairs unbearable to a person of Emmet's principles and ideals.* The Union had abolished the Irish Parliament, and the Irish members of the British Parliament were now a small and futile minority, as Pitt had planned that they should be. The Catholics of Ireland, whom Lord Cornwallis had contrived to keep from opposing the Union by leading them to believe that it would be of benefit to them, now saw that the purposely vague promises Cornwallis had held out to them would never be fulfilled. They were angry and dissatisfied, which added to their inbred disaffection to the Government.

Everywhere people were again thinking of freedom, appraising its cost, and steeling themselves for sacrifice. So long as there was wood and iron in the country (to make pikes), one Kildare farmer told his labourers, he would never give up the fight. They had only one life to give, he reminded them, and he thought they ought to give it cheerfully in the common cause. Such instances, multiplied over and over again, must have charged the Irish air with an electric quality. Something

---

* Dr. Madden, writing in the middle of the nineteenth century, knew nothing of the reputed Pitt letter, but he learned from Jimmy Hope that Emmet had been tricked into conspiracy. The Doctor had a theory that the Orange faction of Ireland, backed by Lord Castlereagh in England, were angry at Hardwicke's refusal to ally the Government with them, and that they instigated the rising to make Hardwicke feel that they could not be dispensed with. That the deception practised on Emmet did involve the Orange element is indicated by two letters written to leading Orangemen just before Emmet's rising, which carry the implication that they are awaiting some great event. They will be mentioned later. I.S.P.O.

of it still remains. It pervades even official accounts of spies reporting on the feeling of the country. Their point of view made them call it disaffection, sedition, or treason, but the instances they cited testified to love of liberty and devotion to the national cause.

Convinced that the people of Ireland would be behind him, Emmet got in touch with a hard-headed and patriotic weaver from the North, Jimmy Hope. In all probability he had known him before, because Jimmy had long been an active United Irishman, and Emmet soon put him into a position of trust. He asked Hope's opinion as to the prospects of success of a new rising. When Hope said he was for an appeal to arms, that seemed to settle the matter for Emmet. He told Hope at this meeting that " some of the first men of the land had invited him over." (Later Hope told Dr. Madden that " there were persons of distinction in the confidence of our leaders, who kept up communication with them in exile, and were in league with the oligarchy at home, which Russell and Emmet, from the purity of their intentions, never suspected.")

About the first of December, Major Swan, one of Major Sirr's colleagues, went out to Milltown in search of Emmet. He was not a home that day, and Swan told Dr. Emmet he was glad not to find him. No further notice was taken of him officially, and the Government later claimed it had no knowledge of his presence in Ireland until after the rising in July.

There was a great deal of travel that autumn and winter between Ireland, England, and France by men who were interested, in one way or another, in the new rising.* Robert Carty, a red-haired little Wexford man whose pointed beard gave him a fox-like appearance, went from Ireland to France in December. Carty, who had been an important person in

---

* In peace-time emissaries of the disaffected sometimes travelled on the regular packet boats that sailed between Ireland and England and England and France. More often—and always during war-time—for the sake of privacy, they went in vessels whose owner-captains were smugglers. When this was discovered by the Government, many such captains were bought over with secret-service money. They carried on their smuggling operations and the transportation of emissaries as usual but notified officials who their passengers were, and what their business and destination were. A Captain Lewis Mumford (sometimes called Montford) was one such unsuspected spy.

In 1800, Mr. Edward Cooke of Dublin Castle, writing to some one in London about Emmet's mission to France, said : " I am informed the messengers go over to France from Little Hastings, and that the boatmen are in their pay. If this be true they may be as well in your pay." P.R.O.L.

Wexford in the 1798 rebellion, talked to many of the Irish exiles in Paris and was introduced to Humbert. The General was now interested in what was called the Louisiana scheme. Ostensibly this was a colonising expedition to French territory in America, but actually the name masked plans for a new and unofficial invasion of Ireland headed by the General. Thomas Russell, who had become one of the General's most intimate and trusted friends, had heard that old cast arms from the French army could be bought in quantity at 13 livres each. Surgeon Lawless went around trying to raise money to buy them, and a depot was planned for Havre, where Swiney, a Corkman who had been a State prisoner at Fort George, was then living.

Shortly after Carty's arrival in Paris, William Hamilton, Russell's nephew, left for a short visit to Ireland, evidently to consult with Robert Emmet. With him went Edward Carolan, a Louth man who had been in Paris some years and had made frequent trips back to Ireland. Carolan stayed in the country (where Major Sirr soon spotted him and reported his presence to the Castle), but Hamilton returned to France after ten days or so. He had been very short of funds on his way over, but, going back, he had £80 provided by Robert Emmet, some of which was given to Thomas Russell and used for expenses connected with sending back other Irishmen.

Part of Hamilton's instructions from Robert Emmet had been to go to Brussels and get Tom Emmet to take his place at Paris. Arthur O'Connor, though he was looked on with deep suspicion by many of his countrymen, particularly those who had been fellow-prisoners of his at Fort George, was putting out pretentions to that post himself and had a small following, chiefly men to whom some suspicion is attached. One of these was William Putnam McCabe. But though the Castle was later told that McCabe had been employed by Arthur O'Connor to organise the country (for the rising), O'Connor's connection with him could not have been known to Robert Emmet, for it was McCabe who went around ordering certain men back to Ireland to take part in it.*

---

* The person who gave the Government the information was Michael Quigley, after he became an informer at the end of October that year. It is quite possible, even highly probable, that O'Connor was back of McCabe, and that both of them were working under the direction of Wickham and Marsden, perhaps under the supervision of Pitt.

One of them was Michael Quigley, a tall, hollow-eyed man who had been a rebel captain in Kildare in 1798, and who with several other United Irishmen had been released from Kilmainham about the time the more important State prisoners were leaving Fort George. Though he was only a mason by trade, he was exceptionally intelligent, and he knew all the Kildare people likely to be interested in a new rising. This made him, from either Emmet's point of view or that of the Castle, an ideal person to take charge of preparations for that part of the country.

At McCabe's direction, Quigley climbed down from the ladder in Paris where he was setting bricks, got ten guineas from Russell, and set out to join Hamilton and McCabe in Rouen. McCabe stayed in France for a time at least, but Hamilton and Quigley left immediately for Ireland.* They reached Dublin on March 5 on the " Beresford Packet," and two days later Hamilton introduced Quigley to Emmet.

The momentous meeting took place at Corbett's hotel in Capel Street, where Quigley was staying. It lasted from eleven until noon. Emmet treated Quigley cordially and without reserve. He told him that arms and everything for a rising were ready in Dublin, and that he wanted him to organise the County Kildare.

If it did as well as it had in 1798, Hamilton put in, nothing more could be expected. Emmet added the information that there were then in all Ireland no more troops than the Kildare men alone had had to fight in the previous rebellion.

Emmet must already have decided on his policy of keeping secret till the last possible moment the date of the new attempt, for he wanted to know how much notice the Kildare men would need to come into town for the fight. Quigley thought the farthest away could get in on two days' notice.

Apparently pleased with his new lieutenant, Emmet arranged to meet him again that evening at the White Bull tavern in Thomas Street. There he gave him fifteen guineas to go to Kildare, taking with him two other Kildare men McCabe had

* A report from a Bolton-le-Moors magistrate dated March 1, 1803, a copy of which was sent to Marsden from Whitehall, said that McCave (*recte* McCabe. There is no doubt of the identity.) who had lately been in France was then in Ireland. P.R.O.L. and I.S.P.O.

sent back from France, Thomas Wilde and John Mahon. The three accordingly set off the next morning for the country.

Quigley managed to see a great many people on this trip. They were all men with good records from the last rebellion. Thomas Daley, whom he met in Naas, had been appointed a general in 1798 by Lord Edward Fitzgerald himself and had been one of the County Committee of United Irishmen. Michael Dalton, clerk to a miller at Johnstown, was another noted rebel. Quigley also met Michael Flood of Newhall, a well-to-do farmer-miller, whose family, according to Admiral Sir Thomas Pakenham who later was to spend many months hunting them, was one of the chief agents of rebellion in Kildare. One of them, Andrew Flood, had only recently returned home after spending four years at sea, where he had been sent by Lord Carhampton simply for being a Defender. The memory of that alone was probably enough to make him glad to take the pikes that Emmet later sent down to him.

On his way back to Dublin, Quigley stopped at his own home town of Rathcoffey, where there was another meeting of old rebels, and some of them were delegated to go back to Dublin with Quigley and meet Emmet. Michael Dalton was one of these, and so was Thomas Frayne, another prosperous farmer from near Maynooth.

Quigley had told Emmet he thought a thousand men might be got into Dublin without detection. Actually, he himself was watched every step of his journey to Kildare, and information about his movements began to reach the Castle almost as soon as he returned.

A spirited, spendthrift little sportsman, Sir Fenton Aylmer, was a magistrate of the county, and it was his sworn duty to keep an eye on the tranquillity of the district. None of the stigma that attaches itself to a mercenary informer should cloud the reputation of that energetic and merry little man. He is chiefly noted for having founded the Kildare Hunt and for the enthusiastic way he followed his hounds. When news of the arrival of emissaries from the disaffected reached him through a near-by gentleman, he entered into this new kind of chase with characteristic verve and eagerness for the kill.

His first bulletin to the Castle reported that Quigley, Wilde, and Mahon had been at a meeting at Hogestown the Wednesday before (March 9, 1803) and that the men had come over from France to prepare the country for a rising.

That leaving Paris they got no further instructions than that they would receive them when they got to Dublin where they would find French officers. . . . [This was practically word for word what Quigley had been told by Hamilton in Paris.]

That expresses are now going through the country in all Directions. That they are to rise on a French landing. That their dependence is on the old Militia who are not willing to take the small bounty and feel sore at their late disembodiment. . . .

That the intention of the French now is that on their sailing of which they are to get notice those of the party in Dublin and from the country are to rise there. That they then judge the King's forces will be called into and towards Dublin, that the French are then to land in and around another part.

That Quigley went to Naas and Sallins with the expresses together with John Moran of Hogestown.

That they hurried over from Paris to be in time to rise with the people. That the French fleet is ready to sail. . . .*

Other letters from Sir Fenton soon followed, all equally explicit. In one of them he gave the general outline of the rebels' plan and said that the people in general were determined to rise. Another said that he had seen another magistrate in Kildare and had made arrangements relative to Quigley.

The Castle was, of course, getting information from other sources. Whatever went on in the vicinity of Maynooth was reported by the son of the postmaster there, Daniel Collison. Both the Collisons had been active in hunting the rebels in 1798, but the son must have been adept at playing the double game, for he had managed to insinuate himself into the confidence of the current conspirators. At least, he managed to learn all their plans, which he sent to the Castle through Alderman James.†

* The French fleet was far from ready, and as yet Buonaparte had no plans to invade Ireland. Whoever induced Emmet to return must have deceived him deliberately on this score, as the news of French assistance would have been most encouraging to him and to the Irish people generally. It is true that he may have been expecting Humbert at the head of his unofficial expedition, but, if so, he was equally deceived. That venture never got beyond the conversational stage.

†Alderman James was one of the Police Commissioners of Dublin, and, like Major Sirr, part of his activities were conducted in conjunction with the Castle. He had had an office in Dublin in 1798, especially to receive informations, issue passes, etc. A memorial from the elder Collison written later in 1803 says that "The late Mr. Emmet with Quigley was but a few days in this country when Mem't [memorialist] had information thereof which through [Alderman James] was faithfully forwarded with a detail of their conduct and designs, a true account of the state of the County of Kildare, and the conduct of its inhabitants." I.S.P.O. The letter mentioned has not survived.

Francis Magan, Lord Edward's betrayer, got £100 secret-service money on April 2. It was sent to him at Philipstown, and, since Lord Hardwicke later spoke of Magan as " one who had correct intelligence of the proceedings and connections of the Kildare rebels," it was doubtless for services rendered at this time.* Wilde's sister was married to the gaoler of Philips-town, who was himself more or less sympathetic to the rebels, and so it would be quite natural for them to stay there. As Magan had not been suspected of betraying Lord Edward, he would certainly know everything that was going on. The rewards given for information made it worth while for traitors to keep their ears open.

Besides these local sources of information, Major Sirr, whose activities were by no means confined to Dublin, was also on Quigley's scent. He went to the brother of a Kildare man who was about to be transported and, for the promise of the prisoner's release, got the brother to tell what he knew of the plot. The information that Sirr sent to the Castle practically duplicated Sir Fenton's. Sirr learned that Quigley was then at a place about two miles beyond Rathangan and was sure he could be arrested. No effort was made to apprehend him, evidently on Marsden's orders.

Marsden was keeping from Lord Hardwicke much of the information he received and even deceiving the Government officials in England. When he heard late in March from a gentleman at Whitehall that Emmet had come to Ireland some time before, he ingenuously pretended to believe that the Emmet referred to was Tom. Using him as a red herring, he assured his correspondent that Tom was in Brussels. He even mentioned some of the details of the correspondence between John Patten and Tom Emmet which showed he had access to it, probably through the post office. Even if he had not known before of Robert Emmet's presence in Dublin, which he undoubtedly did, he would have learned of it in the letters he quoted in part. However, he did not mention him but kept up the fiction that, as long as Tom Emmet was not in Ireland, there was no cause to worry.

Soon after this, Marsden drew some secret-service money for the case, but whether he paid it out for expenses, gave it

*Vice Roy's Post Bag, p. 366.

to an informer, or handed it over to Quigley himself is not now known. He could have done any of these three things.* Most likely he gave it to some one who was watching Quigley.

The entry in the original Secret Service Money Book now at the Royal Irish Academy reads as follows :

"1803 May 2 Marsden for [a long space] Quigley £40 0 0."

When Russell reached Ireland early in April to join Emmet, his presence was immediately known to the Castle, where, as Wickham privately admitted later, it caused the greatest alarm.† Until after the rising, no search was made for him.

* There is also the possibility that the money was paid to the brother of Father James Quigley (no relation to Michael) who had been executed in England in 1798. He had been an informer for a couple of years, and early in July of 1803 Wickham sent him to Paris for information. P.R.O.L. It is possible that he may have been engaged in the Irish business before this.

† *Diary and Correspondence of Lord Colchester*, I, p. 466.

CHAPTER SIXTEEN

Men and Arms

QUIGLEY came back from his trip to Kildare on March 10 or 11, bringing with him heartening reports as to the enthusiasm of the Kildare people for a new rising, and two men from the county who wanted to meet Emmet.* They were introduced to him and to William Norris, a Corkman who was to be one of the Dublin leaders, at the White Bull in Thomas Street.†

Emmet was so impressed with Quigley's ability and his wide acquaintance among the nationalists of Kildare that he put him in charge of preparations for that county. He was told to find a suitable place for making pikes which would also be convenient as a meeting-place for men coming in from the country.

In those days packet boats on the newly-opened Grand Canal took care of a large part of the traffic between Kildare and Dublin. The Canal Harbour was only a few hundred yards from Thomas Street, and after the long, slow journey many of the travellers called at the taverns of that busy shopping street before going on to dryer matters.‡ The White Bull was very popular with them, so Quigley thought that an empty malt warehouse at the back of the tavern would answer Emmet's purpose exactly. Mrs. Dillon, who ran the inn, had had a young brother hanged in 1798 ; thus she could be depended on to shield the conspirators, and the hostler, John Fleming, was also on their side. He was a Kildare man

---

*According to Quigley's later accounts the men were Thomas Frayne and either Michael Dalton or William Sheridan.

† Norris was managing a tannery at Dolphin's Barn, just outside Dublin, in which John Patten had invested some money a couple of years before. He was a great nationalist and had met Patten through Counsellor Holmes, Mary Anne Emmet's husband. Ostensibly, Robert Emmet was learning the tannery business from him.

‡ Other taverns popular with the Kildare people were the Golden Bottle, a few doors away from the White Bull (it was owned by Bryan O'Rourke, brother of Felix O'Rourke, a Kildare rebel of 1798), the Longford Inn, also close by, and Mrs. Ryan's at 99 Thomas Street. During the quieter hours of business Mrs. Ryan sometimes gossiped with an ironmonger whose shop was in that vicinity. What information he picked up from the unsuspecting woman he passed on to Mr. Pollock, who was even busier than ever watching this new conspiracy.

himself and knew many of the people in the movement. No one, so Quigley and Emmet thought, would notice Kildare men dropping in at the tavern.

Quigley looked up an old acquaintance, Henry Howley, who was still lame from a leg wound he had suffered in the last insurrection, and got him to take a lease for the building in his name. Soon the two men were fitting up the old warehouse with false partitions to hide pike handles and other arms. Ash was difficult to get now, and deal made the next best pike handles, so Howley, a carpenter by trade, bought some deal timber and went to work cutting and planing. Other workers came in one by one : Pat Finnerty, a middle-aged Dublin man ; Edward Condon, a resourceful young person from County Kildare whom Emmet employed as an agent ; and a dark-visaged Northerner, Barney Doogan. Condon and Doogan also scouted around for arms and ammunition, which they carried into the depot and stored away in the secret chambers.

Emmet was so busy with other arrangements and with meeting men who might join the rising that he did not go into the new depot for some time. Through Norris he met Miles Byrne, who had been out in Wexford in 1798, and who had been living more or less secretly in Dublin ever since. He had a genuine and deep-rooted love of liberty which, combined with the tenacious possessiveness that is a large part of Irish nationalism, made him an enthusiastic recruit. He had been eager to meet Emmet ever since he had heard he was back in Ireland. To him, and to many others, the Emmet name was practically a hallowed one. At this time, Tom's halo was a bit the brighter one because of what he had done and suffered for the Irish people, but Robert's efforts had also won him respect and affection. When Norris asked Byrne if he would like to meet Robert Emmet, he was delighted.

Their first meeting took place toward the end of March, and Emmet told Byrne that he wanted to know all the people who had escaped the 1798 rebellion and were still considered good patriots. He felt justified in making another effort for Ireland's freedom, he said, because the Union had deprived the country of the last vestige of self-government, and seven-

eighths of the people had no right to send a representative even
to a foreign parliament. He told Byrne that the French had
promised that if an army did land in Ireland, it would be considered an auxiliary one and received on the same principles
as General Rochambeau and his army had been received by
the Americans in their war of independence. Emmet did not
like the means by which Buonaparte had come into power,
but he was convinced that it would be to Buonaparte's interest
to deal honestly with Ireland.* Finally, Emmet said he was
willing to risk his own life and fortune in getting rid of the
enemy.

These arguments sounded very powerful to Byrne, and
Emmet's earnestness and enthusiasm made it impossible for
the other to refuse to join him. He told Emmet he only
hoped that the poor people of Wicklow and Wexford who
had suffered so much in 1798 would not be called out till
Dublin had taken the lead. But he also said—and Emmet
counted on it from that time on—that there were 300 men
who had escaped from Wexford after the last rising and who
were living in Dublin who would be glad to take part in a
new insurrection.

It was a bit unfortunate for Emmet that, shortly after this,
another Wexford man, Thomas Cloney, six feet four, and a
gentleman in the narrow sense of the word, came back to
Ireland after a short exile in England.† He met Miles Byrne

* This seems to indicate that Emmet was expecting an official French invasion, not
Humbert at the head of an unofficial one. Actually, there was no invasion intended,
a fact which shows that Emmet had been deceived into thinking that one was planned.
    † Unfortunately, there are some circumstances that rather cast a doubt on Cloney's
sincerity, and even before the rising he withdrew himself from all danger. His own
Personal Narrative, published in Dublin in 1832, denies that he had anything to do with
the affair, or that he even knew Emmet and Russell. He also omits other particulars
that would show his connection with the disaffected party.
    The Narrative excuses Cloney's part in the 1798 rising by saying that he had not
taken part until he saw the atrocities committed on his fellow-Catholics. He was
imprisoned many months after it and finally court-martialled and sentenced to death.
Lord Cornwallis commuted the sentence to transportation to America, but he did
not immediately send him off. This so enraged the Wexford Orangemen, always a
most bitter set of men, that, when General Groze, the commander of the district, was
absent, they had Cloney whisked down to New Geneva prison with the intention of
shipping him off to Australia. He was saved by the return of General Groze, who
took a special interest in him. Through the General's intervention Cloney was
allowed to go to England for two years instead of being exiled in America for life.
He was also indulged in other ways. In Liverpool he met many of the Irish patriots
who lived or visited there and was accepted by them as one of themselves. John
Allen, on his way back to Ireland, visited Liverpool, met Cloney, and spoke of him
as a fellow-rebel.

at a dinner given to celebrate his return and asked him if he knew of young Emmet and his plans for a new rising. Cloney wanted to meet him, he said, to dissuade him from what he called his rash scheme.*

Miles Byrne did arrange a meeting, but Emmet either won Cloney over to his side, or the Wexford man, from an ulterior motive, pretended that he did. He was accepted as a conspirator and from this time on was constantly with the rebel leaders.

Acting with Emmet as leaders of the Dublin district were Philip Long, a small, foreign-looking merchant who had often given money to the cause and who was a friend of McCabe's ; Henry Hevey, a heavy-set and florid brewer of Thomas Court, just opposite the White Bull on Thomas Street ; and William Dowdall, an athletic young man who had once been a protégé of Henry Grattan but who had forfeited his favour when he got mixed up in Republican politics. Dowdall had spent some time at Fort George but had been released before the rest of the State prisoners. Other leaders were Henry Hughes, an attorney, and his brother-in-law Nicholas Grey, both of Wexford ; last but certainly not least was John Allen.

His 1798 murder still overlooked by the Castle, Allen was now in business as a woollen merchant in Dame Street, his partner being one Arthur Hinchy. Allen's arrest with Arthur O'Connor in 1798 had made no obvious change in his politics, and his personality was still as exuberantly vulgar as ever. He had been in London on a visit in 1801, and evidently he and Jimmy Farrell had gone in for some high jinks together. He wrote Jimmy on his return :

You mistook my character very much if you supposed I could carry any part of two bottles of liquor 400 miles. I have given your friends a very just idea of them by description, so much so that they feel as great a desire for the reality as I who have tasted them. I stopped at L'pool, where I met and was introduced to Todd Jones, Cloney an Irish rebel and other Irish of great note in their own way.

I felt the nearness to my native land as well by the men I associated with as the distance I had come. None of your damned circumspection or conformity to custom. Nature had fair play here in the circle of my male as well as female companions. . . .

* *Memoir of Miles Byrne.*

The letter had begun with a threat to "that griping old cheat, my ci-divant landlady," and Farrell had been instructed to inform her that she must return at once the waistcoat she had detained, or he would see that she got lodgings at the public expense. But Allen's roughness must have hidden a more complex nature than the world suspected. In another letter written to Farrell in March of 1803, he asked, with considerable profanity it is true, for Farrell to buy and send over to Ireland immediately the second part of Volney's works.*

One of Emmet's most important colleagues was the famous Wicklow leader, Michael Dwyer. Though Dwyer's following had been cut down to a few men, he was still holding out in the Wicklow mountains. His name was so potent that the Government was doing its best to trap him, but the people were glad to shelter him. When he learned that there was a possibility of a new rising, he ventured up to Dublin to get a man named Shaughnessy to drill men for it. Major Sirr learned of the visit through a huxter in the Coombe and got the man to make a formal deposition.† It said that Martin Burke and Arthur Develin ‡ had been with Dwyer.

This Arthur Develin, commonly called Big Arthur to distinguish him from another Arthur, was one of Dwyer's many cousins and, until two years before, had been one of his band. Then going had got too hard for him, and he had enlisted in the British Army. He had been stationed in the south of England when some of the returning Paris exiles went through there, and he learned of the new rising from them. Immediately, he and forty or fifty other Wicklow men in the regiment deserted and came over to Ireland to join up.§

Big Arthur must have got in touch with Emmet very shortly and been put to work getting arms and ammunition as well as entering into communication with the disaffected

---

* After an explosion in the Patrick Street depot in July, a copy of Volney's *Ruin o Empires* was found there by a peace officer.

† It is now in the Sirr Collection at Trinity College Library, Dublin.

‡ The name is now generally spelled Devlin, but the current spelling used an additional *e*.

§ From the "Life of Michael Dwyer," written by Brother Luke Cullen. It is still only in manuscript, which is in the possession of the Very Reverend Myles Ronan, P.P., of Dublin, to whom I am deeply indebted for having been allowed to take copious notes from it.

Michael Dwyer
From the portrait drawn and engraved by Petrie

A room of Emmet's arms depot in Thomas Street, as imagined by an old artist. There was no forge in the depot, but the pikes and firearms shown are all historically accurate

Reproduced by courtesy of the National Museum of Ireland

party in Wicklow. Some time in April he helped Emmet to find a house near the Dublin mountains.* He had some cousins, also named Develin, who lived at Rathfarnham ; and, when Emmet asked about a house where he, Russell, Hamilton, and Dowdall could live, Big Arthur went out to them. The father, Bryan Develin, the patriarch of the family, had been in Wicklow gaol for two-and-a-half years after 1798 for having harboured rebels. The family at that time had been living near Rathdrum in County Wicklow. While the father was lodged in gaol, his young daughter Anne had ridden twice a week over the mountains to Wicklow town to take him provisions. She was a spunky little rebel even then. When her cousin Big Arthur was inquiring about a house for Robert Emmet, the Rathfarnham Develins told him of one on Butterfield Lane. Under the name of Ellis, Emmet rented the house.

Naturally, a housekeeper was needed, and Big Arthur told Emmet that no one would be more suitable than Anne. He must have been thinking of her common sense and her stubborn, sturdy loyalty. Anne was a plain, earthy, realistic person, sharp-tongued when tormented by others, and she had a violent, volcanic temper. But though she was small in body, her heart was big and warm, and all her energies were channelled to serve and protect the people she loved. Soon she was looking after Emmet and Russell with all the fervour of an ardent nature. To the neighbours who were curious to know who the new tenants were, she gave no information. What profession was Mr. Ellis, they asked, or was he an attorney ?

"Aye, is he ? " said Anne, and that was all the satisfaction they got. Her red-haired brother Little Arthur, who drove his father's cart into town to bring supplies when he was not helping Big Arthur get ammunition for the depot, was just as reticent. On being pressed he would lie with equal loyalty.

* Dr. Emmet had died at Casino in December of 1802, and shortly after that Mrs. Emmet, Mary Anne, and her husband, Mr. Robert Holmes, and Tom Emmet's three youngest children had left the pleasant acres and comfortable old house and moved to a new home at Donnybrook, a bit nearer Dublin. At the Doctor's death Robert became heir to a sum of about two or three thousand pounds. Robert did not go to Donnybrook with the rest of the family but went to lodgings with a family named Palmer (no relation to the young Palmer who had been in Lord Edward's bodyguard) who lived at Harold's Cross, on the way to Rathfarnham. He stayed there until the house in Butterfield Lane was taken.

The gentleman was from Connaught, he told one inquirer shortly, and his name was Frazier.

It was small wonder that the nearest neighbours, the Fraynes and Flemings, should think there was something strange about the house, where very little furniture had been brought, but where there were often a dozen or more guests for dinner. But they assumed that Emmet and Russell were in debt or coiners (counterfeiters), and they used to listen at night with their ears to the ground for the sound of presses at work.

When Hamilton and Dowdall came to the house, the attorney who executed the leases, seeing Dowdall, told Michael Frayne that the men were rebels. But no one took that seriously, and in the evening Hamilton used to walk in the Fraynes' garden with the daughters of the house, laughing and flirting mildly. For some reason, Anne looked on this with disapproval and thought he was facetious.

Emmet of course was anxious to meet Michael Dwyer, and he sent Big Arthur Develin and Jimmy Hope down to Wicklow to ask him to come up. But Dwyer had not kept his liberty for five years with half the countryside and a good part of the Army on his track by being too trusting, even with an Emmet. He would make no promise to come. Certainly he would set no time for coming. But he turned up at Butterfield Lane one Sunday evening, accompanied by three of his followers, Martin Burke, Hugh Byrne, and John Mernagh. Immediately, he announced that no one then present could leave till he did.*

Were he and his men, Emmet asked, still willing to fight for Ireland ?

Yes, they said, and glad of the chance.

Suppose Dublin were taken and men of the first rank acting with them. What assistance could they count on from the people of their part of the country ?

Dwyer thought nearly all the Catholics would come out, and that in a few days he would have a third of the loyalists

---

* Cullen's " Life of Michael Dwyer," from which this is taken, says the meeting took place when England and France were on the verge of war. This dates it as sometime previous to May 17, probably about May 1 or a little earlier. Emmet had taken possession of the house on April 23, 1803. Cullen's "Life of Anne Develin," the manuscript of which is also in the possession of Father Myles Ronan, says that some gentlemen, including Mr. Cloney, were present.

with their arms and ammunition. He was asked if he could get some pike handles made if timber for shafts was sent down. He said he could, but he would not bring out the county or create a ferment until a start had been made elsewhere. The Wexford and Wicklow people had made up their minds not to be the first in the field again.*

Afire with eagerness, Emmet urged him to come for the attack on Dublin Castle, which was to start the campaign. He would light fires on the mountain to let Dwyer know when it was to be.

The answer he got from Dwyer was characteristically blunt and realistic. The only signal he would take, he said, would be the sound of cannon.

On the third day of the visit Dwyer looked out a window and saw a girl in the next house watching what went on at Emmet's. At once he became alert and apprehensive, and that very night he went off with his men under cover of darkness. A little later, old Bryan Develin drove a two-horse cart down to Wicklow with a supply of powder and balls hidden under some timber for pike staffs.

By now Emmet had rented several other places that he meant to use as depots for arms and ammunition.† One of them, in Patrick Street, on the way to the Wicklow mountains was intended to serve the Wexford and Wicklow men as the Thomas Street depot would the men from Kildare. Miles Byrne was more or less in charge there and had got a Scottish carpenter, McIntosh, to take the place ostensibly as a workshop. Quigley came over and helped him fit it out with hidden closets and false walls and partitions, like the depot in Thomas Street.

Emmet told Byrne to have seven or eight thousand plain pike handles made, and six hundred jointed ones that could be folded at the middle and carried under a man's great-coat. Arthur Develin got hold of a powder mill, and a man named

* From a copy of Examination of Michael Dwyer, taken at Dublin Castle January 11, 1804, in the possession of Dr. Charles Dickson, who most generously loaned that and several other documents to the author.

† According to Quigley's later information, the depot in Thomas Street was taken first, then one at the Double Inn in Winetavern Street, which was not made use of. Third was the Patrick Street depot, then another unused one in South King Street, and one at No. 4 Strawmarket, where two carloads of timber were sent to make pike handles and enough pike heads to finish them. *Dickson Transcripts.*

George McDaniel began grinding. Soon the place was redolent with the odour of gunpowder and deal shavings.

To keep the depot from being an object of suspicion, very few men were allowed to go there. McIntosh and two young brothers-in-law of his, named Keenan, worked there, and also a young Darby Byrne. Hamilton sometimes went there, experimenting with some rockets Emmet had designed. Big Arthur Develin was continually going in and out. Besides these, only one other person was ordinarily there. Miles Byrne, in his *Memoirs*, said that he went by the name of Johnston, but he was probably William St. John, who had used the name on the continent. He had, it will be remembered, rendered such valuable assistance to the British there, quite unknown to his fellow-exiles, that he had been promised a pardon for his past offences. St. John had seen Russell in London when Russell passed through there at the end of March and had evidently come over himself soon after. He was considered one of the chief rebels, but his past history and his subsequent conduct makes it more than probable that he had been sent over to spy on the rebels.

CHAPTER SEVENTEEN

Emmet's Communications with France

ALL these preparations, of course, cost a great deal of money, and, contrary to what the Government later claimed, Emmet did not provide it all. His legacy from his father was £3,000 at the most. Fifteen thousand, according to one of Emmet's friends, was spent in the preparations for Dublin, and they were much less extensive that had been planned at first. Many of the mysterious " men of rank and fortune " who had promised Emmet their assistance in a widespread general rising failed to keep their word, and he was obliged to abandon the depots in the Strawmarket, Winetavern Street and South King Street.

Walking with Jimmy Hope from Dublin out to the house in Butterfield Lane, Emmet indulged in a bit of irony. Referring to a certain Colonel Plunket * of Roscommon who had thought fit to withdraw his support from the enterprise, he remarked :

There are many who profess to serve a cause with life and fortune, but if called on to redeem their pledge, would contrive to do it with the lives and fortunes of others. For my part, my fortune is now committed ; the promises of many whose fortunes are considerable are committed likewise, but their means have not as yet been forthcoming. If I am defeated by their conduct, the fault is not mine. Even my defeat will not save the system I oppose, but the time will come when even its greatest advocates cannot live under the weight of its iniquity. . . .†

This conversation must have taken place about the middle of May, for it was about this time that Emmet sent a message to his brother Tom in Paris. It was delivered to him by Pat

---

* In 1798 Colonel Plunket was to have had charge of the fighting in Roscommon, which, however, never took up arms. His actions then and in 1803 were such as to arouse the suspicions of Dr. Madden, with some justification. He had been in negotiations with the Castle prior to the 1803 rising, and his encouragement of Emmet and his subsequent desertion of him helped accomplish what Marsden wanted, a frustrated rebellion.

† Madden, *United Irishmen*, III, p. 357.

Gallagher, one of the Paris exiles who was a friend of Arthur O'Connor ; and, as Quigley later heard that Gallagher had been in Ireland and had left it before the war (which was resumed on May 17), it is probable that Emmet sent the message by Gallagher himself.*

Tom Emmet received the message on May 30. Gallagher told him he had been charged to communicate it to no one else, but that Tom was to use his discretion as to what others should know of it.

The message said that an organisation on a new and closer (more secret) plan had been carried to a great extent among the United Irishmen, that there was a close communication established between the North and South, that proper men had come forward, that Kildare, Wicklow, and Dublin were in a forward state. There were depots of arms in Dublin ; one had 2,500 pikes ready handled, and 1,000 more were ready to be handled. Dwyer was pledged to come in and bring the Wicklow men if any depot was attacked—the signal for beginning. Independent of Dwyer's party there were numbers of men from neighbouring counties in town only waiting to defend the depots if attacked. Delegates of the people had been spoken to, who wanted to know when they would be called out.

At present, wrote poor unsuspecting Emmet, there was no suspicion of all the preparations by the Government ; but this state of things could not last for long, and Tom was asked to apply to Buonaparte for arms, ammunition, money, and officers. If he was not willing to supply them, Tom was to raise the money from Irishmen or Americans. The lack of money was the principal difficulty, since any attempt to get more by subscription would inevitably make the matter public. Tom was to send home three men, McP, S, and McD, particularly the last, as communications were worse established with his county than elsewhere.†

* Wickham later spoke of a cypher addressed to R. E. which had been found in the depot on Thomas Street after the rising. It is now in the Irish State Paper Office and gives directions as to what commercial terms are to be used to indicate that ———— (evidently meaning a rising) is to take place or has been postponed, etc. It ends, "Adieu, G." Whose handwriting it is, is unknown. No sample of Gallagher's has survived for comparison.

† This probably refers to McDonnell of Mayo, Sweeney of Cork, and McPhea of Belfast. Sweeney did get to Cork but never reached Dublin.

The Irish and Scots were said to be disgusted with France, and would take her help to secure their independence but no more.*

There was nothing for Tom to do but try to see Buonaparte, but he did so with the greatest misgivings. He himself was under no illusions about the French. Plunderers and looters, he called them, terms that showed how deep his feelings were. Only the day before, he had received an official notification from the French Minister of War, M. Berthier, that the French were thinking of sending an expedition of 25,000 men to Ireland, but not for six months, and that the Irish were not to act in the meantime.

Tom could not get to the French Consul himself, and it was not until July 28, after a long series of disappointments and deferments, that he was promised even a messenger to send to Ireland. Even then the money for the trip was held up.

It is evident from all this that there were no bona fide plans for an official French invasion, nor had General Humbert's Louisiana scheme materialised. But by the end of May some one playing a double part must have come to Dublin and made Emmet and his party think that the French were about to land immediately with 10,000 troops.† Hurriedly, messengers were sent out to summon leaders in other districts to a conference in Dublin.

McGucken, of course, heard of the man who was sent to Belfast. On May 31, he wrote Marsden that one Metcalf had been summoned to go to Dublin without delay. The man who carried the message from Dublin had said that 10,000 French troops were to come immediately. " He speaks of an immediate business, and fears something may take place before he returns." ‡

Metcalf was to go to Jimmy Hope in Dublin, McGucken learned, and he, too, arranged to go there and find out all the plans of the rebels.

---

* *Memoir of Thomas Addis Emmet and Robert Emmet*, II, p. 342.

†As the arrival of the messenger came so soon after the resumption of hostilities with France, it looks very much as though the would-be rebels were being manipulated so that a rising would hurry the Suspension of the Habeas Corpus Act. Mr. Addington was not then willing to ask for the Suspension. The rising, when it did take place, removed all opposition to the measure, and the British Parliament passed Suspension Act on July 29.

‡ *Vice Roy's Post Bag*, p. 274.

McNally also heard later, through Cloney, that an emissary from France had been in Dublin " and still remains here [so he wrote the Castle on July 19], has had conferences with several persons who have come to Dublin especially for that purpose from almost every county. He cannot specify names, but assures me that the fact was communicated to him from a person who had the information from young Emmet." *

* *Vice Roy's Post Bag*, p. 278.

CHAPTER EIGHTEEN

The Disaffected outside Dublin

KERRY, at the southwest corner of Ireland, is a wildly beautiful country of majestic mountains, deeply indented by narrow rocky bays. Even now it is the outpost of Gaelic Ireland. The native language survives there, and the people inherit the tradition of their ancient culture. Remnants of Irish poems written by Pierce Ferriter or Owen Roe O'Sullivan, Owen of the Sweet Mouth, are still recited by old men who learned them from the lips of their fathers.* They have long memories, and the happenings of other days are still alive in their minds. To them Sir Walter Raleigh is not a courtier who laid his cape at a queen's feet. He is an English captain who massacred 700 of their Spanish allies at the Castle of the Golden Rock on their own Kerry coast. They do not know Good Queen Bess of England as a patroness of arts and literature. Elizabeth, to them, was an alien ruler whose soldiers repeatedly scourged and harried the country, destroying men and beasts, corn and cattle, so completely that they boasted they had left neither corn nor horn, nor house unburnt, from one end of Munster to the other. They remember later famines and hangings and people torn from their homes and transported to Botany Bay or sent to slavery in the West Indies.

In 1803, all these memories were nearly a hundred and fifty years clearer and closer to the people of Kerry, and they still suffered under the English rule. They had not fought in 1798, and the thought of their inaction then rankled in their hearts. They were determined to rise now whether any other part

---

* O'Sullivan was one of the most beloved of the peasant poets of the days when schools had been suppressed, and young people were taught surreptitiously at alfresco hedge-schools. He composed poems in Latin, Greek, English, and Irish but earned his living as a *spailpín*, or spade labourer. He once requisitioned a spade in verses that are delightful even in translation. " Crowning all," he added, " let it have the sweetness of a bell."

of the country did or not. In neighbouring Cork and Limerick the feeling was just as intense.

A mysterious figure, known as General Clarke, though his real name was Daniel Cullinane, had been flitting around Munster for the past four years, breathing the spirit of vengeance and revolt and holding out hopes of a new French invasion.* A school-teacher of Limerick, John Noonan, who had great influence with the people, was only recently returned from a few years exile in England (where he had gone when an informer had told the Government of his activities in 1798) and was advising his friends to " take " all the arms they could get, as great things were on foot. Another school-teacher at Ballinagarry in County Limerick, who the Government later thought was connected with the pseudo-General Clarke, was also deep in the business. So was a third teacher, Barrett of Tubberbui (the Yellow Well) near Limerick city.

General Payne, the new military commander of the Limerick district, which included the Counties of Kerry and Clare as well as County Limerick, wanted to buy over both Noonan and Bagot, but he had such an aversion to mixing secret service with soldiering that he bungled the business badly. Eventually, however, he managed to collect " a few scoundrels of the most finished sort " to spy on the disaffected. From a local gentle-

---

* Cullinane was a tall, dark man, about forty years old at this time, with a scar that extended from his left nostril to his lip. He was the son of a farrier of Cashel, County Tipperary, and had studied for a time at an Irish seminary in Paris, then returned to Ireland and taken up the national cause. He was as brave as he was bigoted, and, though his letters show that his education had not put too much of a polish on him, they breathe devotion to the ideal of Irish freedom.

In 1798 he had been sent to Paris to see why the promised French aid had not arrived in Ireland. He stayed for a while in London, where he posed as a gambler, took the name of Thorington, and frequented Mother Nelson's gambling house at 60 Pall Mall. When he returned to Ireland, he was first known as Father Murphy. The Government officials, from Lord Clare to Lord Castlereagh, were anxious to get their hands on him, and informers and spies constantly hounded him, but by moving constantly about and changing his name half a dozen times he managed to elude them. In 1800, as General Clarke, he was in the North, carrying a plan of organisation that McGucken was sure was the work of Robert Emmet. In 1801, he had tried to get in touch with Michael Dwyer so that Dwyer's Wicklow men and his own followers in Munster could consolidate. The man who introduced him to one of Dwyer's friends may have been, according to Dr. Dickson, the Irish historian, Jimmy Hope himself. However, the letter Clarke wrote for Dwyer never reached him. The messenger was arrested soon after Clarke wrote it, and it was found on his person. A little later, the High Sheriff of Tipperary got hold of a letter signed " Erin Go Bragh," which he took up to the Castle. Clarke was said to have written it, though there does not seem to me much of a resemblance between the handwriting and that of the Dwyer letter. It showed that a regular organisation existed in the south, and that the people were preparing for a rising even then.

man who had connections with an informer he learned that letters had come to Limerick from Dublin and from Irish gentlemen in France. By May he was in possession of a strikingly accurate description of the plan of insurrection for Dublin and the rest of the country. In one way or another Payne learned the names of a great many men of wealth and position who were said to be concerned in the new movement, and that arms had lately been landed somewhere in Kerry.*

To show the Castle just what the state of his district was, he sent up a deposition made by an informer known only as A.B. :

A.B. states that he was in Turner's public house near Balls Bridge, Limerick, Tuesday night [April 5, 1803]. There were 16 Recruits of the Lim. City Militia. They were spending their bounty and drinking treasonable toasts and singing treasonable songs in Irish such as The Friends of Ireland, The English Fleet, keels uppermost. Uprise to King George. Downfall says another recruit to him you Rascal. The other replied I mean a Rope and Saddle to him and that he may be guillotined.

There was a gentleman in the room who wore elegant clothes, had a watch and his shirt trimmed, heard the songs and toasts and walked about the room. Afterwards he gave one Murphy a guinea and desired him to spend that amongst the boys worthy to take a share of it. This gentleman afterwards sat down with a man who appeared to be a Tradesman and drank a noggin of Punch. Murphy at the time was singing a song in Irish. Some of the words were " That the Irish with Pikes the Orange Tree tribe will drive afar." †

A little after this, General Payne learned from a very prominent gentleman near the Limerick-Kerry border that there was a report that the whole of the country from Tarbert to Tralee and on southward had been sworn within the last two months.

---

* They included a Counsellor Marshall of Tralee ; Mr. John Collis, " a rich man who keeps two or three ships and it is generally said he conveyed arms into the country very lately " ; Mr. Minor Tate, " a man of fortune living somewhere near Tralee " ; James Hoar of Killarney, a shopkeeper ; Nicholas Sands, an ex-magistrate of Listowel ; Donovan, school-teacher, of Tralee ; Ulysses Fitzmaurice, and Mr. F. Holmes of Croagh in Limerick. Also included was Mr. John Russell, a well-to-do cloth merchant of Limerick city, no relation to Thomas Russell.

† A.B. later tried to get Noonan to give information, but the school-teacher would not be trapped into divulging any incriminating news. He was in Noonan's company one evening when a man said, " It's a long time threatening, and there's no sign yet of the French." Noonan, according to A.B. replied to him hotly : " You fool, do you dispair of God's mercy ? He has decreed that the world would be of one way of thinking and it has been decreed by prophecies many thousands of years back." He added, " When the sword is drawn and the French land it is reported by many of the great ones that the Loyalists will put to death every man who had a hand in the United Business but that there would be a defence made against that before the time came. . . ." I.S.P.O.

He went over to Kerry himself, and, while he discounted many of the rumours that arms were being landed and that the French were coming shortly, he did believe that a great many oaths had been administered to the lower orders in the last few months. He arrested and brought to the Limerick gaol a man who confessed he had been travelling through the North of Ireland and Connaught for the last few months, swearing the people.

The General must have got wind of Emmet's friend Norris, who was in charge of organising Munster, for in June he wrote up to Marsden to ask if Norris was on the Black Books at the Castle and that he (Payne) should be informed the next time Norris left town.

At that time General Payne did not anticipate any immediate trouble, but when Marsden, probably with his tongue in his cheek, gave a glowing account of the peace and quiet of the country, Payne who had a most delightful sense of humour, answered with a touch of sarcasm that he was glad to learn that reports were so favourable of the general disposition of Ireland, but that " in spite of all your information I would recommend you not to be too sanguine of the Province of Munster. By this you are not to conclude that I apprehend any immediate consequences, only do not calculate too much on our dispositions if we have an opportunity of showing them."

The County of Carlow was in expectation of a rising, a regular Castle spy wrote Marsden on May 26. The United Irishmen there had been warned to be quiet so that the Government would not suspect anything. A magistrate of County Tipperary was only one of many from all over Ireland who sent in word of robberies for arms and other indications that the people were preparing to take some sort of action. Lord Massarene of Antrim Castle, County Antrim, replying to the Lord Lieutenant's request that he get up an address of congratulation to the King, said that the state of the country around him was more infernal than could be imagined by any one who had not inhabited it.

Nothing but petty little assemblys or committees, all for the purpose of *uniting*. There are people in correspondence with the French Directory. Report of war has set all heads at work (and bad heads they are heaven knows) and all hearts too, and hideous black ones they are heaven well knows too. . . .

The informer B. Senior, who had followed " Carey and the Frenchman " in 1796 and 1797, and who had managed to give the Government warning of the intended rebellion in Dublin on May 23, 1798, noticed such a stir among the people that he wrote the Castle, suggesting a supply of the needful, so that he could increase his staff. Evidently he got it, for soon his brother John came over from England and began to travel about with a companion who posed as a French emissary. They were cordially received by all the disaffected farmers they called on, mostly in County Kildare and Carlow.

A Dublin lawyer who had been one of the earliest United Irishmen but who had been bought off because of the brilliant pamphlets he wrote for them added himself to the list of Castle correspondents who were reporting on the return of exiles and State prisoners. He had got in touch with a man who was in a position to know what was going on, he wrote Marsden, and though his informant had some scruples about giving names, he provided some general information that corroborated what others were sending in.

"A green coat with a pea-green cape one would think to be a sort of party uniform worn by the people," the lawyer observed, " or by the heads of them. Many men notoriously disaffected appear in that dress."

A few days after this, Marsden was told by this same person that Dwyer had been to town and had been treated with. The people wanted to rise even without an invasion, he said, and he surmised that there must be a council at the head of the disaffected party that was in correspondence with France.

Wickham received a similar warning about this time from Peter Burrowes, a lawyer who had been a great friend of Tom Emmet and also of Wolfe Tone. He was now regretting his opposition to the Union and was anxious to acquire official favour. Probably he also had a sincere dread of any further disturbance in Ireland. Thus, when he learned, toward the end of May, that something unusual was going on among the disaffected, his first thought was how he could communicate the news to the Government without running any risks of discovery.

He solved the problem by writing the Honourable George Knox, another friend, who was then in England. A new

revolutionary government, he told them, was in great for-
wardness and activity and had numerous partisans in the city
of Dublin and all through Leinster, in the city of Limerick,
and in other places. He believed that Arthur O'Connor was
the principal agent between the French Government and the
emissaries in ˙ ˙land. These, he had been told, were all men
of inferior ɪank in life but of boldness and talents who had
taken minor parts in the last rebellion. Several such men had
displayed quantities of gold in Dublin, with which they were
very liberal.*

Knox immediately let Wickham and Marsden know of this
information and arranged to have Burrowes write directly
to the Castle under the name of Junius.† However, neither
Wickham nor Marsden informed the Lord Lieutenant of this
new source of information or let him know what they had
learned from it.

In spite of all this accumulated evidence of the intentions
of the people to make another play for their freedom, Marsden
himself wrote an account of the condition of the country for
one of the Dublin newspapers that was just the opposite of
the truth.‡

If Bonaparte had sent to this country agents on whom he could rely he
would know that Ireland is not the turbulent, disaffected, and insurrectionary land which, doubtless, he believes it to be ; he would know that,
satisfied with our government and loving our rulers, we are tranquil and
happy ; he would know that his own conduct has helped to cure the
revolutionary disease which for a while affected us, and that Liberty and
Bonaparte are terms which the meanest and most uninformed peasant in
Ireland has long since learned to disassociate.

The article was signed Man of Ulster, a pen name Marsden
had used before when presenting bits of propaganda to the
reading public.§

* *Vice Roy's Post Bag*, p. 450.
† The only letters signed Junius that have survived at the State Paper Office are a
couple of notes in a disguised hand, which does bear some resemblance to Burrowes'
natural writing. They are dated after July 23.
‡ The article appeared in the *Dublin Evening Post*, which had been famous as the
organ of Irish nationalism. The illness of its editor put it for some time into the hands
of H. B. Cody. From July, 1801, to January, 1804 (when the available secret service-
money records end), Cody received £900 in secret-service money. W. J. Fitzpatrick
in *The Sham Squire* says that after the family of the owners rescued it from Cody's
hands, the Government gave him a 900-pounds-a-year post in the Revenue. Cody
was in the habit of slipping in and out of the Castle offices, asking for directions as
to the news treatment of critical situations, and even supplying Marsden with minute
scraps of information about men on the newspaper staff.
§ Letters of Cody's now at the State Paper Office indicate the authorship.

CHAPTER NINETEEN

Love and War

FOR months now Robert Emmet had been in love. To all his fine, unselfish, impractical ideas of arming Ireland almost overnight and taking Dublin Castle by surprise, he had added the reasonably selfish hope of having a wife in whose lap he could lay his honours. Some time soon after his return to Ireland he had discovered, with an ecstatic flooding of his heart, that Sarah Curran, daughter of the famous lawyer, was "formed to give happiness to every one about her." The Priory, the Currans' summer home at Rathfarnham, was not half a mile from Emmet's house in Butterfield Lane, which may have been the reason Emmet had wanted one in that vicinity.

Anne Develin, who used to carry messages for the lovers, said that Sarah's look was "the mildest and the softest and the sweetest *you* ever saw." She was twenty-one that spring when Robert Emmet was courting her, her figure girlishly slight, her white skin flecked with freckles. The portrait of her by Corballis shows her hair a burnished auburn, and the gold of a locket that holds a lock of her hair entwined with Robert's is not much lighter than the souvenirs it contains.

Looking down on her soft curls as she sang to him in the drawing-room of the Priory, or perhaps during one of their innocent trysts when she was even closer, he must have touched her hair gently and asked for a bit to carry with him always. She sewed some into his velvet stock.

The little red workbox where she kept her thread and needle still holds a slip of paper with the words *L'Académie de Celbridge*, written in her fine and dainty hand. It was like her to use the French form. She sprinkled French phrases through her letters with almost childlike playfulness.

There was a pensive side to her nature that had undoubtedly been intensified by two family tragedies that had taken place while she was still small. Her sister Gertrude, her father's favourite child, had fallen from a window of the house and been killed. Curran had almost lost his reason with grief. He would not let the body be taken away, and the child's grave had been made in the Priory grounds. Sarah used to stand for hours at the nursery window looking toward it. When she was fourteen, her mother had become involved in a scandal and had left home. After that Curran had become cold and stern.

Recently, he had let his ambition overcome his support of the national cause. It must have been hard for a man of his brilliance and ability to suffer frustration after frustration, simply because he was backing the losing side. All the cleverness of his famous cross-examinations that had made hundreds of Crown witnesses squirm had been worse than useless as far as worldly success went. Political rewards in Ireland did not go to liberals and reformers, much less to those who had opposed the Union as stubbornly as Curran had.

Thus he had begun to cultivate a devotion to the Government and a secret ambition to get into office that hardened him against anything or any one who endangered it, even his own daughter. Robert Emmet, he noticed, was coming to the Priory with surprising frequency, more than his friendship with young Richard Curran would justify. Knowing Emmet's politics and the reason he had come home to Ireland, he told the family to discourage him. But by that time it was too late.

Sarah had not been easily won. Emmet first spoke to her of his attachment at a time when the rebels expected to rise immediately, and, as he wrote to Curran later, when he was " neither expecting nor, in fact, under those circumstances, wishing that there should be a return of attachment, but wishing to judge of her disposition—to know how far they might not be favourable or disengaged. . . ." * She gave him no encouragement, and he stayed away for a time, busy with preparations for insurrection. When the rising was postponed for a while, he went back, drawn by his growing love for her. He could not see any change in her attitude

---

* Probably in February, when there had been some expectation of an insurrection, according to Robert Carty's later statement. P.R.O.L. Sirr later said that he found a great pile of Emmet's letters in Sarah's room, indicating that their engagement must have lasted for some time. *Sirr Mss.*, Trinity College, Dublin.

Sarah Curran, from a portrait painted by Edward
Corballis in 1802. *Courtesy of Mr. John Butler, Dublin*

Anne Develin, Emmet's housekeeper.
Original in the National Library of Ireland

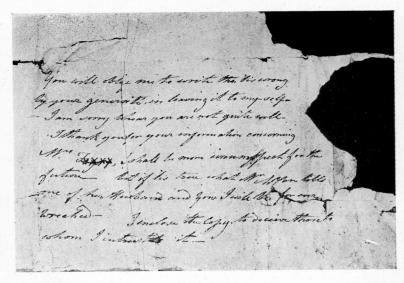

A note written by Sarah Curran to Robert Emmet shortly before the Rising
The original is in the Irish State Paper Office, Dublin

The fly-leaf of Sarah Curran's Music Book : her signature and sketches
See footnote on page xvi

toward him. To all appearances he was merely an ordinary acquaintance.

Afterwards [his letter to her father continues] I had reason to suppose that discoveries were made and that I should be obliged to quit the Kingdom immediately ; and I came to make a renunciation of any approach to friendship that might have been formed. On that very day she spoke to me to discontinue my visits. I told her that it was my intention, and mentioned the reason. I then for the first time found, when I was unfortunate, by the manner in which she was affected, that there was a return of affection, and that it was too late to retreat. My own apprehensions, also, I afterwards found were without cause, and I remained. . . .*

On the flyleaf of her music book where she had sketched some of her family and herself in a long sweeping gown, Sarah added a little profile of Robert Emmet, with his initials underneath. R. E., she wrote, and then, lover-like, she pencilled them again below the others, R. E.

Secretly, Anne Develin brought her the tenderest of love letters. Slipping upstairs to the room she shared with her sister, Sarah answered them ardently. She even sent Robert verses that she signed with her own initials. How both of them were to regret that later, and even the seemingly harmless lock of her hair sewn into his cravat ! Everything that happened now seemed to turn into danger for them later.

Robert was so often busy with plans for the rising that a great deal of their love-affair was carried on by letters. If he wrote Sarah from the house in Butterfield Lane, the messenger was likely to be Anne Develin, but if he were in Dublin, he might send his letter by Biddy Palmer, the sister of young Palmer who had escaped from Ireland in 1798 with McCabe and William St. John.† Her father, old John Palmer, was now living at New Row on the Poddle not far from Thomas Street. Emmet used to stop by there when he wanted to send a letter to Sarah or to meet some of the other leaders. Mr. Palmer

* *Vice Roy's Post Bag*, p. 392.

† Young Palmer was drowned in Holland about 1800, while he was trying to get at the informer Smith. One reason for thinking that the Johnston whom Miles Byrne spoke of as frequenting the Patrick Street depot was really St. John is that in August Mr. Wickham took down a deposition from a man he called Johnston, so short and so restricted as to its field that it was obviously only a supplementary one. It described young Palmer's death, and as St. John had been there at the time, and as the deposition gives information that probably no one but St. John would have, the chances are that they were the same. Even if the Johnston of the depot was not St. John, St. John was named as a leading conspirator in August ; thus he would in all probability have visited the Palmers.

bought most of the household supplies for Butterfield Lane, sending them out in the Develin's cart by Little Arthur. Since McCabe always stopped with the Palmers when he was in town, he would have learned everything about Emmet from them (the Castle heard that he was in Ireland that spring); and so, for that matter, would William St. John, whom they suspected no more than they did McCabe.

Dwyer and his four followers made a second visit to Butterfield Lane about the middle of June, and it was settled that he was not to turn out his part of the country until Dublin was taken. There could not have been any reluctance on Dwyer's part to join the insurrection then, for after the party had left, Russell complimented Anne on her fine cousins.

" They're certainly large enough," she said diffidently, but secretly she was delighted with the praise.

She was so busy keeping house, cooking dinners for the men who came to see Emmet, and helping pack up ammunition and uniforms for some of the leaders that Jimmy Hope's wife Rose came out from Dublin to help her.

About July 9, John Allen, William Norris, Thomas Cloney, Henry Hughes of Wexford, William Dowdall, Tom Russell, Emmet, and Quigley dined there. Matters were coming to a crisis now, and the date of the rising was to be decided the next day.* The conversation at dinner was entirely on the chances of success the rebels might have. A toast was drunk to Nicholas Grey, Hughes' brother-in-law, who was not there but who was to take command of the forces in Kildare.

When dinner was over, Emmet showed Quigley how to fire some horizontal rockets he had invented, and Quigley and Hamilton tried out bombs made of bottles filled with shot, which they had been making in the depot in Patrick Street. Quigley stayed all night, and as he was leaving the house the next day he met Norris and a man from Munster, evidently on their way to the meeting of the leaders at which the date of the rising was to be decided.†

Within the next few days, Emmet somehow became aware that he had been tricked into the conspiracy. Who had

---

* Quigley's informations. *Dickson Transcripts.*

† So Quigley later said. Hope told Dr. Madden years later that a man from Cork was in Emmet's company the day before Hope left for the North with Russell, i.e., about July 14. If the Munster man was from Cork, it might have been David Power,

deserted him ? What informer had he found out ? What had happened to make him, the least suspicious of all persons, realise that he had been deceived ? If he had not been so honourable, so unquestioning a believer in *noblesse oblige*, the answers to those vital questions might be known to-day. But even the bitterness that must have followed the realisation that he had been a pawn moved by some sinister hand could not overcome Emmet's breeding. He put a seal on the lips of the men who knew the secret, or as much of it as was discovered. Years later, Jimmy Hope would speak of what had happened only in general terms. What he told Dr. Madden seems to indicate that Emmet realised that " the men of rank and fortune " who had urged him to head a new rising had had ulterior motives, but that Emmet and Russell, depending on the eagerness of the great mass of the people to rise, had decided to go ahead with their plans without them. Of course, neither Emmet nor Russell had any idea that people at the Castle knew of the conspiracy, and they must have been entirely ignorant of the many sources of information that the Castle had about their movements and intentions.

The conspiracy, Russell said, was the work of the enemy. " We are now in the vortex—if we can swim ashore let it not be through innocent blood ; if the people are true to themselves we have an overwhelming force, if otherwise, we fail, and our lives will be sufficient sacrifice." *

whom Pollock spoke of as travelling about with Norris. But it is interesting to know that a man whose name has never appeared in connection with Emmet's rising, James Wolf, of Limerick, was a great friend of Norris's, and that he was arrested in Kildare in September and confined in Naas gaol. A Black Book got up some years later said Wolf was a friend of all the principal rebels and was a teacher of Irish.

Hope also said that a gentleman from Meath was with Emmet. *United Irishmen*, III, p. 359. Hope also told Madden that he had seen Lord Wycomb, son of the Marquis of Lansdowne, in the depot on Thomas Street. Lord Wycomb was subsequently of the County Meath, and Hope may have been thinking of his later residence when he described him to Madden.

* It is possible that when Russell spoke of " the enemy," he meant Orangemen. Two letters now in the State Paper Office which were sent to prominent Orangemen, one on June 25 and the other on July 7, 1803, seem to suggest that these men were engaged in some conspiracy and were expecting some unusual event. The letter of June 25 was sent to Mr. Thos. King. A magistrate of that name lived near Rathdrum and was one of the most bloodthirsty yeomen of the time. The salutation is to " Dear Friends," which would seem to indicate that King was acting with others. The letter goes on : " To you I direct these few lines hoping that they will find you in as good health as I and all the rest of the party are at present, thanks to God. We arrived safe to our destination port, and things are doing well. We have heard of Arthur's return and are glad of his safe arrival and as the time is approaching be kind enough to send by the bearer every necessary article that is to be sent as he is going down on that

"One great point," said Emmet, "at least is gained. No leading Catholic is committed. We are all Protestants—and their cause will not be compromised." *

So, desperately hopeful and still deceived as to how he was being manipulated and made use of, Emmet set the day for the rising for July 23, then only a little more than a week away. That would give Hamilton, Hope, and Russell time to get to the North, where, it was believed, 50,000 men would turn out almost overnight to answer their call to arms.

purpose. We every hour expect the soldiers to encamp on our plains as Bakers and Butchers are Employed these ten days back on the occasion.

"Therefore we would be very willing to know as near as possible to the time of gathering our Lambs in order to have them in proper order for ———— as the times are likely to be troublesome a supply would be very necessary to compleat our design as we are almost beat out of Cash.

"In like manner we have heard of the arrival of three friends after our departure and we expect that they and ye have agreed in opinion. An answer to this would very much oblige and satisfy your friends.

"Fal de rol with a caper.

"June the 25th, 1803.

"I remember your servant Sir in the Ditch."

The other letter is in the same handwriting and on similar paper. It is addressed to George Grierson, Cork Hill, Dublin, which was the address (Parliament Street) of the King's Printer. Grierson's country house was at Rathfarnham near Emmet's. Ostensibly Big Arthur Develin was working for him but actually was engaged in getting arms and ammunition for Emmet.

The Grierson letter is addressed to "Dear Brothers :

"I write to you these few lines and am happy to hear that you are well and in good health as I and all the family at present are, thanks to God. I am very uneasy about the delays that may attend this matter and if things are put in Execution immediately it would in my humble opinion be much better. For per adventure some evil person might give intelligence of your residence. Let your vigilance be ever so active and by that means our Long wished for blessing would be blasted. (sic).

"Consider, my dear Brethren, consider seriously what a loss the Kingdom at large would sustain by the want of so great and so formidable a leader as any one of your family. Think seriously—but I shall always be ruled by your better judgment as Counsel is no command.

. . . .

"The Leaders of the County Wexford and I have joined our intimacy to such a degree that they say they will leave it to the Cast of a die whether they come and join me or I them. However with the blessing of God our junction will be compleat and both Counties know the strength of each other. As you very well know we are no strangers to hostilities.

"The Bearer of this is the Man I mentioned in your Company by name. [The name given is a common one in the County Wicklow, and the person cannot be identified exactly. However, since his mention here casts some unpleasant shadows on the man, it cannot be given.] If you recollect I told you if you would do anything for any one to do it for him. He is going to town to get some cloathes as you may observe he is quite bare. I have had frequent proofs of his integrity and good conduct ; in Battle he is a Lion and in peace a Lamb. This is his true character upon my word and Honour. Therefore I rely upon your attention to his welfare while he may remain in town. No more at present from

"Round the World for Sport

"This is the man that was thrown over the Bridge at the Boyne, as I was telling you."

* Madden, *United Irishmen*, III, p. 357.

CHAPTER TWENTY

The Explosion in Patrick Street

BEFORE daylight on July 14, and dawn breaks very early in Ireland on a summer morning, Emmet said good-bye to Russell, Hope, and Hamilton as they set out on their journey to the North. Probably Anne Develin and Rose Hope were hovering in the background as the trio started down the driveway on their fateful enterprise. Russell had his green and gold uniform rolled into a bundle, but the decision to go on with a rising had been made so suddenly that Emmet had no money for their expenses, and they had to borrow some in Dublin.

Emmet must have hurried into town soon after them and sent Quigley out to Kildare to bring in three men from near Maynooth. He must also have got in touch with Nicholas Grey, for the next day he introduced the Kildare men, Thomas Frayne, Owen Lyons, and Thomas Keregan, to Grey in the depot in Thomas Street. Grey, he told them, was to be the general of County Kildare, and they were to be officers under him. Quigley was directed to send 2,000 rounds of ammunition to the country for their use.*

That same day Emmet met Robert Carty, the foxy little Wexford man who had gone to Paris at Christmas time. He had only recently returned from France and England, and, the day before, Thomas Cloney had taken him to a meeting of rebel leaders at Philip Long's.† Though Carty had been one

* Quigley's information. *Dickson Transcripts.* Men from Naas and that part of Kildare were to come into Dublin after the attack on the Castle. Others were to act in the county itself.

† Edward Hay, another gentleman from Wexford, was there, John Allen and his partner, Arthur Hickey, Big Arthur Develin, a man from above Newry named Armstrong, and two or three others. The conversation was about the rising, and so unreserved that every one there must have been considered a conspirator, though Carty and Cloney both claimed later that they had not been in sympathy with a rising. While this meeting was going on, Russell and Hamilton came in on their way to the North, and Carty loaned Russell 10 guineas, which Long repaid for him the next day Russell said he was going to raise 50,000 men in the North. P.R.O.L.

of the emissaries of the disaffected who had asked aid of the French, he was not in favour of a rising without some outside assistance, and he was now deftly withdrawing himself from the conspiracy and planning to sell his property so that he could leave the country before the insurrection took place. However, he kept all this to himself, and he let Cloney take him to a second meeting of rebels on July 15. It was held in a timber yard near the Patrick Street depot. Burton, a clerk there, was one of Emmet's friends. Emmet came in while Cloney and Carty were there and made a long speech in which he said, with a bit of bravado, that he would show the people of Ireland that there were men who would put themselves at their head. Carty was urged to rise in Wexford, to " box his corner," as they put it, but whatever promises he made he never expected to keep, and he left Dublin the next day.

On the face of it the incident appears unimportant, but later the names of the men who were at the meeting and their conversation became matters of tremendous importance.

The day after the meeting in the timber yard, a terrific explosion almost wrecked the depot in Patrick Street. Miles Byrne, going there on the morning of Saturday, July 16, found a crowd collected at the door and was told that three men had been taken off to hospital desperately wounded. Going inside, he found John McIntosh, who told him that one of the Keenans, Darby Byrne, and Johnston had been blown through the windows into the street. The other men working in the depot had escaped.

Miles Byrne and McIntosh put the place in what order they could ; then Byrne went over to the Thomas Street depot to tell Emmet of the disaster. Coming on the heels of the other bad news, Emmet could hardly be blamed for thinking that now they had but a forlorn hope of going on with their plans. He was sure the police were watching the Patrick Street depot to see who would go there, as they were indeed. But there was no open move to alarm Emmet, and he decided to try his luck in salvaging whatever he could from the wreckage.* Miles Byrne went off to hunt for a house in which the supplies

* John Fleming, the hostler of the White Bull, had been in the conspiracy for some time, and later he told the Government officials that Emmet, dressed in a loose surtout, " not like a gentleman," had been at the depot with John Palmer of New Row. They asked Fleming for some sacks to carry ammunition, which he loaned them. I.S.P.O.

could be stored. Through Michael Berney, a Wexford man who had been in the conspiracy for some time, he got Berney's cousin, Denis Redmond, to loan Emmet a house on Coal Quay he had just bought for his approaching marriage.*

At dusk that evening some men Miles Byrne and Arthur Develin had rounded up began to shuttle between Patrick Street and the new depot, each carrying as much ammunition, jointed pikes, and blunderbusses as he could conceal under his great coat. By daybreak everything fit for use had been removed from the old depot or hidden in the secret closets there. But one cask of flints and ball cartridges intended for Michael Dwyer was still left.

A husky tailor, Murphy of Bull Alley, hoisted it to his shoulder and with only one companion went up Patrick Street toward the Poddle, where they intended to leave it with John Palmer. Just before they reached Palmer's house, they were accosted by two watchmen who asked where they were going.

" Come along and see," they answered saucily.

At Palmer's house they set the cask down and knocked at the door. Palmer, who was expecting them, came out, but on seeing the watchmen he closed the door behind him and walked off. The men who had been carrying the cask retreated ; the watchmen picked up the prize and started toward the guard-house. They had not got far when Murphy came back with Arthur Develin and other reinforcements and attacked the watchmen. Again the cask changed hands and the watchmen retreated in defeat. The next day, Arthur took the ammunition over the mountains to Dwyer.

The *Dublin Evening Post* carried a soothing paragraph about the explosion, evidently inserted at Marsden's suggestion. It said that various reports had been circulated about it, and that alarmists had not been idle, but that inquiries led one to believe that nothing of a political nature was connected with the transaction. No open move was made by Marsden, and later he consistently minimised the whole affair.

Young Keenan had been so badly injured that he died soon after he and two other men were taken away by the police. To the Lord Lieutenant toward the end of August, when

* In 1798 Redmond had helped organise the County Longford with Hans Denniston, a local rebel. Denniston was arrested after Emmet's rising, and it is possible that both had been in the conspiracy for some time.

blame for the whole conspiracy was pointing toward himself, Marsden explained that

> . . . the explosion on the 16th of July was not sufficiently loud to occasion a very general observation of it : and it appears that even the windows of the room where it took place were not broken by it. To prevent suffocation the persons inside broke the glass and Keenan who is since dead, cut himself so deeply by running his arm through the pane that the effusion of blood principally occasioned his death.*

Actually, the house had been so badly damaged that the police officer who examined it later testified on oath that he was afraid to stay inside the building. The front wall was cracked, the sills blown out, the fire-place torn. But there was no inquiry about the accident, and no search of the neighbourhood was made. Marsden's explanation in August : " The alarm attending it would have been exceedingly great, and the event might not have justified such a very strong measure."

Palmer was arrested that Sunday morning and questioned, but he was released almost immediately. Marsden's explanation : " I thought it best to liberate him as I was certain he would have got a judge to discharge him in the course of the day and that his being liberated in this way would expose our want of powers and be a matter of triumph to the disaffected."

Major Sirr also looked over the house and made a report. Then, on getting some further information (he does not say from whom) he wrote Marsden on Monday that he had found that Arthur Develin was the principal agent in the gunpowder manufactory, and that it was he who headed the party that had attacked the watchmen. The explosion, Sirr said, came from the friction of the mill that had been grinding powder.

> This Arthur Develin is now at work for Grierson [the King's printer, and the gentleman who had received the letter mentioned on page 164] and altho' Mr. Grierson promised me that this Develin should be arrested by tomorrow night I have reason to doubt it as I told Mr. G. long ago the necessity of its being done, yet still he employed him. I therefore think you should without loss of time write to him to desire this arrest should take place, and as I think it probable Develin has a considerable quantity of

* I.S.P.O.

arms concealed it will be necessary to use much precaution on his appre-hension, as search should be diligently made. If Grierson would give me notice what time to attend him on this occasion we might plan it so as to be certain of our capture.*

Arthur Develin was not arrested, and to the Major, baffled and angry, Marsden made no explanation. He did tell the Lord Lieutenant that, though Darby Byrne (in special confine-ment in Steeven's Hospital) would give no account of the depot, " some of his accomplices where known and of course watched."

There was never any official mention of the fact that on July 2 McGucken had sent word to the Castle that James Hope had taken a depot at 26 Patrick Street.

* I.S.P.O.

CHAPTER TWENTY-ONE

"So Little Time"

FROM the time Miles Byrne told him of the explosion, Emmet lived in the depot in Thomas Street. He slept on a pallet on the floor of one of the upper lofts. He ate in carmen's taverns in the neighbourhood or had food sent in from cook shops. As the days went on and nothing happened, his first discouragement gave way to renewed hope. The soothing paragraph in the *Post* accomplished its purpose. The Dublin leaders met and again decided to go on with the rising. Miles Byrne, John Allen, Felix Rourke of Rathcoole, and others who were to command in the city went about notifying the men who were to serve under them when and where to collect. One of the men pledged to John Allen was a belligerent little calendar man of Francis Street, Pat McCabe, no relation to the mysterious William Putnam McCabe.

The date of the rising had been decided on before Russell and Hamilton had left for the North, but a messenger was sent to them to confirm it. Word went to Kildare on the twentieth which made William Andrews, Richard Scott, and some others mount their horses and ride around the country calling on various men, a surprising number of whom turned up in Dublin on the twenty-third.*

Andrews and Scott had been mentioned by General Trench early in March as attending seditious meetings at Pat Dunne's in Naas.

The next day Quigley's lieutenants Wilde and Mahon, who

---

* The Royal Irish Academy in Dublin has a large manuscript volume that is chiefly filled with copies of depositions taken from Kildare men by the Solicitor General, Colonel Wolfe, a magistrate of Kildare, and John Pollock. (Some of the originals are in the I.S.P.O.) It also includes a list headed "Names of Leading Men." The first four men on the list are Daniel Brophy, William Andrews, Benjamin Burchell, and Richard Scott, and each is credited with having ridden out from Naas to raise the country for the twenty-third. They had got their orders, the same list reveals, from the clerks of a Dublin distiller named Grange.

had been working in the depot, also went to Kildare to give notice of the rising, and during the week men from the county came to town to get instructions. Emmet sent a Naas man, James Byrne, out to Ringsend to look over the Pigeon House, an ordnance depot on Dublin Bay. There was no money to send messengers to the more distant counties, but it was expected that they would act when they heard of the Dublin success.

In all this suppressed excitement it did not seem queer to any one that a pair of strangers, speaking broken English with a French accent, arrived at the home of Patrick Carey near Straffan and introduced themselves as " friends of the cause."

Carey was the man B. Senior had trailed assiduously since 1796, and dozens of *his* informations at the State Paper Office mention " Carey and the Frenchman." Carey had the reputation of being a violent democrat, and the Castle knew from the ex-Trinity student, " Jones," that he had been with Napper Tandy's expedition in 1798. Just when he had come back from his political travels and resumed farming in Kildare has not transpired, but B. Senior evidently had his eye on him still. The two strangers who called on Carey on Thursday were not, as they represented themselves to be, " friends of the cause " but just the opposite, paid Castle spies. They were B. Senior's brother John, newly returned from England to join his brother's staff, and an ex-soldier, James G——. Quite evidently it was expected that Carey and his family would be summoned to Dublin to take part in the rising, and the pair of spies had been sent there to accompany them, and perhaps also to act as *agents provocateurs*. Marsden and his agents were as busy that week as were the rebels themselves.

To make up for the loss of the jointed pikes that had been destroyed in the explosion Emmet conceived the idea of making chests of huge pieces of rough timber, which would look so much like solid wood that, filled with pikes from Thomas Street, they could be carried through the town without exciting suspicion.

Besides making these, there were thousands of things to be done, and the depot was more and more crowded and confused. Quigley, Barney Doogan, Ned Condon, and Pat Finnerty had been living there since it had been taken, and it now also harboured Terence Colgan, a tailor from Lucan who was busy making uniforms. Nicholas Stafford, a baker so handsome that Wickham remarked later on his appearance, had lately been enlisted by Quigley and was also staying there, and so were two deserters from the Army. Supplies were constantly being brought in, and men passed in and out getting ammunition and instructions.

Emmet left off writing an Essay on the Art of War and made up a list of things to be done :

> Bore the beams
> Make the hollow beams immediately
> Make the bags for the grenades   100
> Pound the Roisin and make the balls
> Get Nails
> Make 10 ladders, 1 30 feet long and block them
> Send for cramp irons and bars
> Send a Person with the Proclam to Barn : B
> Make the Ladles and Rammers
> Make a small box $\frac{1}{4}$ inch shallower than the tubes.*

Naturally, there was not time to do all those things, and the desperate pressure under which Emmet was working makes one wonder why he went on in the face of so many difficulties. Of course the Castle wanted him to, or they would not have taken such pains not to alarm him. But what motivation was there within himself that kept him true to such a hopeless venture ?

Part of the answer is to be found in a letter to Sarah Curran which he must have written at this time but which was never sent to her. He put it, with other papers, into a slant-top desk that was one of the few pieces of furniture in the Thomas Street depot. Unlike some of those papers, it is not now at the State Paper Office ; but part of it was introduced as evidence at Emmet's trial, and later a writer for the *Dublin Evening Post* made derisive use of it in an article for that paper. In it he quoted one enlightening paragraph :

I have had little time to look at the thousand difficulties which still lie between me and the completion of my wishes : that those difficulties will likewise disappear I have ardent, and, I trust, rational hopes ; but if it is not to be the case, I thank God for having gifted me with a sanguine disposition. To that disposition I run from reflection ; and if my hopes are

* I.S.P.O.

without foundation—if a precipice is opening under my feet from which duty will not suffer me to run back, I am thankful for that sanguine disposition which leads me to the brink and throws me down, while my eyes are still raised to the visions of happiness that my fancy formed in the air.

There was no ostentatious emphasis on the fact that it was duty that made him go ahead with his plans, but elsewhere he said he felt himself too much involved to desert the men who were depending on him. Dublin's rising would be the signal for others throughout the country, and Emmet, knowing how anxious many men were to win their country's freedom, was determined that the key effort should not fail again, as it had in 1798.

Some of the optimism expressed in the letter was probably due to the fact that he was writing to the girl he loved, and he naturally would not want her to worry or to think that he was unhappy. But he had a motive even higher than unselfishness. It is to be found in his Essay on the Art of War, which he also left behind in the slant-top desk.

The manuscript of part of this work, dealing with the technicalities of soldiering, is now at the State Paper Office. It is evidently derived from Templehoff's work.* Another part of the manuscript is missing, but it was copied at some time by Mr. Flint at the Castle. That section, dealing with the ethical aspects of warfare, contains the germ of Emmet's own philosophy and is based on his congenital faith in the decency of mankind and, in part, on his recollection of the address of the United Irishmen that was presented to the Society at the time Tom Emmet became a member, December 15, 1792. That had asserted that " the sacrifice of life in the service of one's country is much too sacred a duty to be entrusted to mercenaries."

The Essay on the Art of War expanded this idea :

Let the exercise of arms be an occasional duty of the citizen, as such let it be common to all. Neither wealth nor interest shall be an exception. At the call of danger the humblest subject in the land shall come forth, strengthened by Labour and Independence, and stand beside the highest. Fighting for the same country he shall find the same dignity. Merit shall conduct him to Honour.

* Emmet's copy of this text, now at the Royal Irish Academy still carries in its margins dozens of notations in his handwriting which corresponds with paragraphs in the Essay.

Emmet proposed a system of rewards and punishments by special pennants to be awarded to battalions that had distinguished themselves on the field of battle. The black standard of disgrace went to cowards. To the brave went a standard that symbolised honour, and it was evident in every line of that essay that Emmet thought any man would be glad to give his life to win it.

CHAPTER TWENTY-TWO

Thomas Russell and the North

> Why vainly do we waste our time
>   Repeating our oppressions?
> Come, rouse to arms, 'tis now the time
>   To punish past transgressions.

Thus had Russell once begun a hymn to liberty, which continued:

> 'Tis said that Kings can do no wrong.
>   Their murderous deeds deny it,
> And since from us their power is sprung
>   We have the right to try it.

Chorus:

> Let each Hibernian prayer then be
>   O give us death or Liberty.

That chorus could not have satisfied him, for he added a couple of alternate ones:

> Then let us sing with 3 times 3
>   The reign of peace and Liberty

or

> Then let us sing with hearts so free
>   Ah, give us death or Liberty.
> Then let our song forever be
>   Our choice is death or Liberty.

When Russell set out to head the rising in the North, the manuscript of the song had been in the Castle for the past seven years, sent there by the Belfast magistrate who had seized his papers at the time of his arrest in 1796. Russell himself had been in prison for six of those seven years, but he was still willing to risk his head for the sake of peace and liberty. Jimmy Hope and Hamilton were with him, his green and gold uniform was carefully rolled into a bundle, and he carried the conviction that his name alone would bring out

50,000 men. In the days when he had worn his boots thin walking the Ulster roads as an emissary of the United Irishmen, he had been welcomed at hundreds of family firesides where the politics of the people were the same as his own. Countless men had drunk his health and toasted Irish freedom at country taverns or met him clandestinely at the " singing societies " or " reading clubs " that camouflaged gatherings of the United Irishmen.

He must have remembered the sympathy and support that had always been given him, the admiration he had won as a writer for the *Northern Star*, the respect in which he was held as a martyr in the cause of democracy. Once, years before, he had been flattered when some young patriots had told him they rated him above the *Northern Star* men, whom they thought too moderate and not ready enough to take the field. When he was in gaol in Dublin in 1797, he had got a letter from some unknown admirer, assuring him that " although he had long been immured within the walls of a loathsome dungeon, suffering for the cause of the people, his name, even among those who never had the pleasure of his acquaintance, was alive and revered." * In spite of poverty and imprisonment he had never given up the fight for Irish freedom, and he expected that every one else was as loyal and unselfish as himself. Both he and Jimmy Hope had made visits to the North that spring and had been warmly received.

But the Castle still kept McGucken there to frustrate any move of the people toward freedom. For years, while he retained the position as leader of the disaffected, the crafty little man had been trying, as hundreds of his letters show and as he once stated explicitly, to remove every political idea from the minds of the old Defenders and United Irishmen and to disgust them with the French.

In spite of what they had suffered, this had not been easy. In June, McGucken had admitted to Mardsen that though his part of the country was quiet, it was anxiously waiting for invasion, and that " the spirit yet continued there to a great extent." When, about July 8, Metcalf and Scott returned from meeting Emmet in Dublin and spread the news of another expected rising, many a man thought of pikes long

* I.S.P.O.

hidden beneath hearthstones, of blunderbusses and muskets concealed in corn or flax, of gunpowder and bullets and the flutter of a green flag, and the old love of liberty leaped up again.

But another image was associated with the longing for liberty, an image deliberately imprinted there by the agents of the Government. It was the picture of a gibbet silhouetted against the sky, its victim slowly twirling or swinging in its chains, the nauseating odour of rotting flesh, and the raucous call of carrion birds circling downward to their loathsome feast. For centuries the policy of the English had been to weed out, by death or transportation or imprisonment, the leaders of the disaffected Irish, and to intimidate the lesser ones. From 1796 on, hundreds of men in the North had been hanged and thousands sent away, some to transportation, some to service in the British or Prussian armies, some to the fleet, some to prison. Only three years before, at a time when the country was supposed to be quiet, a court martial at Ballymena in County Antrim had tried a hundred persons from the surrounding district. They had been charged with acting seditiously, or with being seditious in their sympathies, or with having disarmed local yeomen. Some had been arrested at a meeting of Defenders.

Sixteen of the men tried were hanged, and the bodies of some of them for long afterward had dangled and decayed on the gallows on which they had died. Some had been hanged, cut down, beheaded, and quartered. Then their flesh and bones had been strung up again on the blood-soaked gibbet.

Sixteen other men had been flogged and then transported.*

---

* Transportation did not mean a simple transfer of the place of one's abode. Usually it was a punishment involving the most degrading imprisonment and an existence bordering on the bestial. Men intended for transportation were chained two by two to the floor of the prison at the place of embarkation, a thin layer of straw their only mattress. At Cork, before their ship sailed, they were attended by Dr. Harding, the official physician. His reports are chronicles of disease and misery and physical and spiritual degradation. On ship-board the men were placed in a reeking, crowded hold. They were stifled for air, thirsty and hungry. Disease and vermin were customary, the death rate high. Prisoners sentenced to transportation could not take with them supplies or implements for their future life. Sir Harry Hayes, transported from Ireland in 1802 for having abducted a young lady, was not allowed to take the seeds, farm tools, and implements he had purchased. The condition of the women prisoners was indescribable. For political purposes, Michael Dwyer and his party were given special consideration when they were transported in 1805.

Five hundred lashes, seven hundred lashes, a thousand lashes the sentences had read.* Twenty-three men, intimidated by these examples, had given security to transport themselves rather than be tried. Ten men had been sent to general service in the Fleet or Army. Thirty-two had been liberated on bail. Ten escaped trial only because the person who had informed on them had absconded. They were released on giving security for good behaviour. Only one man had been acquitted.

Some of the men who had been mainstays of the nationalist party in the North had been disposed of by that court or bound by it to keep the peace. Robert and William Simms, who had helped Wolfe Tone and his family financially when they were in America, and who had sent money to Russell on his release from Fort George, had sworn, only the year before, not to engage in any conspiracy under pain of forfeiting £2,000 each of their own money and an equal amount put up by bondsmen.

Even with these measures and memories to help them, the Government could not count on the quiet of the liberty-loving people of the North. It depended more on what its secret agents could do to frustrate their rebellious activities after these had served the purposes of the Castle. Early in July, McGucken, knowing that rebellion would be general in the North, manoeuvred himself into a position where he could control the activities of the rebels in County Down. He was told by Mr. Minis of Saintfield that the people would certainly look to him. This was just what the spy wanted. He told Minis to say that he would take command at some time, but that the people should be kept from acting rashly. Having furnished the Castle with so much information about the rebels in Dublin, McGucken was counting on defeat there and was urging the Northern men not to act until they saw how the rising succeeded in the capital.

* The report of the court martial is at the State Paper Office. At the National Library of Ireland, in one of the volumes that make up the *Kilmainham Papers,* documents from the Headquarters of the Army at Kilmainham, there are entries for almost every one of the men sentenced by the court. They indicate that some of the men sentenced to transportation and flogging had the corporal punishment remitted, but most of them suffered their full punishment.

From the *Kilmainham Papers* it is evident that the court continued beyond the date covered by report at the State Paper Office, so that one may safely assume that many more men than those enumerated suffered the most extreme punishments.

He also sent for a man from Ballymena to work out a plan that he hoped would keep Metcalf and Scott from having much influence with the people. Writing to the Castle, McGucken said that Metcalf gave out that " leaders (experienced officers) would attend, and even turn out with [only] three men, but can't tell what plan is meant to be pursued. Goes entirely on the old system of 1799, formed by young Emmet," etc.*

He asked for instructions as to his own conduct, and said he thought that, if Metcalf were arrested, he would be able to give the magistrates enough information to convict him.

But Metcalf was not arrested, and though Russell and Hamilton, on their journey North, were followed by spies from the Castle, no effort was made to take them up.† However, they began to feel the result of McGucken's mysterious " measures " as soon as they got into his territory. A man from Belfast had been sent to rouse the disaffected in Newry and its vicinity, where George Teeling, brother of the young Bart who had been hanged in 1798, was supposed to take command. Russell expected that recruits would already have turned out, and that a guard of honour would meet him in the town to welcome him.‡ But no one appeared, and after waiting two days and a night Russell and Hope took a carriage to Hillsborough and then walked to Knockbracken, a few miles from Saintfield.

James Witherspoon, a weaver there, was an old friend of the two men. They had known one another for years, and Russell had stopped with Witherspoon when he was on his furtive two-day visit to the North in the spring. His name was well known to the Government officials. It was in the Black Book of the North, and McGucken had mentioned him in his informations from the time in 1800 when the swashbuckling " General Clarke " had left him a copy of organisation written by Emmet.§ Only six weeks before, the spy had written

* *Vice Roy's Post Bag*, p. 277.
† *Colchester Correspondence*, I, p. 459.
‡ Quigley's information. *Dickson Transcripts.*
§ The Black Book of the North was a volume containing the names of Northern United Irishmen. It was compiled by a magistrate from information supplied by the informer Nicholas Maguan. It lists the meetings they attended and the offices held by them. It is now in the McCance Collection, P.R.O.B., a small collection of papers evidently salvaged at the State Papers Office when the sealed chests were opened late in the 1880's.

Marsden that Witherspoon had been in Scotland, sounding the people of that country.

Russell and Hope found the welcome they expected under Witherspoon's roof and arranged that a meeting should be held there. While Witherspoon and his son were summoning the local rebels, Russell and Hope went on to Belfast. There they met their second major disappointment. The Simms brothers, naturally enough, would not risk £8,000 by coming forward. And Belfast was McGucken's home town, and his influence strong enough to counterbalance whatever enthusiasm Russell could arouse. Some rebels did meet him at a public house owned by John Sweeney, but they could not make up for the men who held back.

At Ballymena, too, the men were lacking in some of the old fire, owing probably as much to McGucken's efforts as to the dampening memories of the great court martial.

At Carnmoney, a calico printer, William Farrell, who had been in Dublin in May and had been organising that section since his return, could round up only a dozen or so men to meet Russell, and some of these were strangers. Their presence alone would have been enough to damp the enthusiasm of the others, who probably thought they were spies. It is quite likely that they were. At any rate, next day a gentleman of the neighbourhood heard all about the meeting from some one who had been present. Russell's call for recruits was not answered, and he departed in great indignation.*

At Broughshane fifty men were gathered to meet him, but strangers were present, and the meeting followed the pattern of the Carnmoney one. Local men were not willing to volunteer in the presence of strangers. Next day an account of the meeting was given to a local gentleman by some one who had been present.

But at Kells and Connor, Russell's spirits were revived. A delegation of men called on him to ask for a chance to retrieve the character they had lost by their failute in 1798. Evidently they were still ignorant of the fact that the failure of the North had been due to the betrayal of the rebels' plans by two informers, Nicholas Maguan and John Hughes.

---

* From prison lists at the I.S.P.O. and a letter of the Solicitor General, James McClelland, to Marsden, in *Vice Roy's Post Bag*, p. 416.

When Russell returned to Knockbracken, he met, as the general in charge of that district later recorded, " a very wicked and dangerous set of men," but it may be taken for granted that any meeting at Witherspoon's would be attended by a spy, and later one of the men present did give information to the Government.*

On Friday, July 22, Russell and James Drake, who had been a colonel in the fight at Ballinahinch in 1798, went to the southern part of County Down. Metcalf had preceded him, and so had some spy of McGucken's. There were only a dozen men gathered at Smith's public house at Annadorn, and Patrick Smith got up to tell Russell that only madmen would join him. On Monday, young Henry Smith, whose father owned the pub, told the Sheriff about the meeting, but he had already heard of it and of two other meetings Russell had held in that vicinity.

He was working his way slowly toward Loughlin Island, where Metcalf had preceded him and where he had an old friend, Patrick Lynch. Lynch had given him lessons in the Irish language when he was living in Belfast years before. Through Russell's recommendation Lynch had helped Edward Bunting collect the words of old Irish songs that Bunting then reunited with their ancient airs. Russell had also got Whitley Stokes, a fellow of Trinity College, to employ Lynch on some Irish translations.

Weary and discouraged as he was, Russell must have felt for a moment a pleasant sense of quiet and contentment as he reached the little settlement on Friday afternoon. Father McCartan and his curate were playing quoits in the sunset. He saw the face of his friend Lynch. He put out his hand to greet him. And then McGucken's shadow fell again.

Lynch would not even risk shaking Russell's hand. He had heard there was to be a rising, and he wanted to get away. The rising would not come for two or three days, Russell told him, reassuringly. " Consider me a horse-jockey, and let me pass as such."

Timid as he was, Lynch stayed for the meeting Russell held at Fitzpatrick's little inn that night. He was still there when more men came to see Russell next afternoon. Having been up

* Prison lists. I.S.P.O.

most of the night before, Russell was still in bed when they arrived, and Fitzpatrick took them into his room. Even Lynch went back on him again and tried to get Russell to give up his plans. Another man asked what they would do for arms.

It was well known that some were still concealed from the last rising, and at Annadorn Russell had been told that the yeomen would be disarmed easily. But he was tired and exasperated at his countless frustrations.

" Let them use forks and spades and shovels and pickaxes," he answered crossly.

Pat Ranaghan from Clough said that the priests had told the people to be quiet, and that they would not rise. One by one the men slipped out of Russell's room. Suddenly aware that he was deserted, he asked Fitzpatrick where they had gone.

" I told them to go home," his host answered bluntly. " The people will not rise."

" What will you do ? " one last straggler asked Russell.

" I'll go to the County Antrim where there is fighting," he answered grimly.*

* Newspaper accounts of the trials of Russell and Drake, and Howell's *State Trials*.

6

JULY 23, 1803

Dublin Prelude

EARLY on the morning of July 23, Robert Emmet rode out to Butterfield Lane. There were some directions to be given there, and he was probably hoping to find a letter from Sarah Curran. Also, he needed some clean linen, but when he reached the house, the shirt he expected to take away with him was still drying on a hedge near by.

According to Anne Develin's *Life* as Luke Cullen set it down, Emmet that morning sent Big Arthur Develin and a gentleman described as " Mr. William Kenedy (*sic*) who was half-brother to the late Sir John Kenedy of Johnstown," out toward Hazel Hatch and Rathcoole. Mr. Kenedy, Anne said, had great influence in that quarter, and Big Arthur counted on getting the Doyles of Athgoe and some others in the neighbourhood to come in for the rising.*

As Mr. Kenedy and Big Arthur were setting off, Emmet called to Arthur to send a near-by dairyman, Red Michael Dwyer, down to Wicklow to tell Michael Dwyer to " come in all haste to Dublin with all the forces he could collect." †

Anne remembered that Emmet was calm and composed that morning but that there was an air of anxiety about him. When she spoke to him about some domestic matters, he smiled, started to answer, then left the sentence unfinished. Shortly afterward, when he turned his horse to go back into town, he smiled again and said, " Goodbye, Anne."

* It was probably this pair who took the letter to Patrick Carey near Straffan, which John B., brother of B. Senior, mentions. B. said that about twelve on Saturday, July 23, Carey (to whose house B. and his friend had gone on Thursday) received a letter from Robert Emmet " desiring him and all his friends to repair to Dublin immediately, as there was something going forward." Straffan is in exactly the neighbourhood Anne mentioned. Carey and his two sons, B. said, immediately rode in different directions to notify some of their neighbours and returned about two o'clock. Then, with their strange guests, they set out on horseback for Dublin. I.S.P.O.

† The messenger, tragically laggard, did not find Dwyer till late Sunday.

As he started toward Dublin, with its mounting difficulties and confusion, it must have been an effort for him not to take the turning to the right at Rathfarnham village. The Priory, Sarah Curran, love, comfort, quiet, all the gentle things to which he had been bred were not far away, and he was very much in love. The explosion and its resulting complications had made him miss a rendezvous with his sweetheart, but he had sent her a message, and she had written him a hurried note. The torn and ragged little sheet of paper (found afterward with other papers of Emmet's in Dowdall's trunk) may have been waiting for him when he reached Butterfield Lane that morning. She had begun without salutation :

> You will oblige me to write, tho' 'tis wrong, by your generosité in leaving it to me. I am sorry to hear you are not quite well. I thank you for your information concerning Mrs. Fitz [the name is crossed out but legible]. I shall be more circumspect for the future, but if 'tis true what Mr. McCan tells me of her husband and you I will be forever wreched. (sic).
> I enclose the copy to deceive those to whom I entrust it.

No matter when Emmet composed his reply, writing it either at the slant-top desk in the depot or in one of the Thomas Street taverns or in his mind as he rode into Dublin that summer morning, Emmet's first thought was to relieve Sarah's anxiety.* He began, also without salutation :

> Whatever account you may have heard of my not being well, be assured that I never was in better health or spirits, nor looked forward with greater hopes to the accomplishment of all my wishes. I called two or three times to the same place in hopes of seeing [you] and would have continued but for circumstances of which the bearer can inform you. I fear it would not be right for me to call on you at the time I promised, not on my own account, but on your Father's. But on this head I will do whatever you wish. If however I have life I will see you the day after, and prove to you that however other objects may for a time occupy my mind, the ultimate object to which it looks forward above every other for its own happiness is that which it now seems to neglect.

Emmet passed by the temptation of the Priory, and as soon as he reached Thomas Street, those " other objects " closed

---

* It is possible that Emmet had arranged with Anne to bring him his clean shirt as an excuse for picking up this reply to Sarah's note. Anne went to the depot that afternoon while Emmet was seeing some leaders in a near-by tavern, and afraid of being " pulled and hauled," as she told a Castle official later, she left them and came away. Emmet's note was found in the depot early the next morning. It is now at the I.S.P.O.

in around him. The dim lofts of the warehouse were crammed
with thousands of pikes, brought out from behind the false
partitions and leaned against the walls in preparation for the
attack that night.   McIntosh, young Thomas Keenan, and
George McDaniel, who had survived the Patrick Street
explosion, were trying to go on with their work of finishing
hand grenades, handicapped by the growing confusion and
Quigley's disastrous forgetfulness as to where he had put the
fuses. He had also mixed finished slow matches (fuses made
by dipping hempen cord into a mixture of saltpetre or wine
dregs) with unfinished ones, making the entire lot useless.
The makeshift cannon had been left without rammers or fuses
when Quigley sent Wilde and Mahon out to Kildare on
Thursday, and they had to be supplied at the last moment.

Henry Howley, Pat Finnerty, and Edward Condon were
still making hollow beams for carrying pikes through the
city.   Sometimes they had the grudging assistance of Pat
Farrell, an inquisitive individual who had been found by some
of the rebels the night before, listening at the door of the depot.
He had been brought in and kept a prisoner ever since.*

The smiths who had been making the cramp irons for the
scaling ladders did not send them until late. There was only
one scaling ladder finished that day, instead of the ten Emmet
wanted for attacking the Castle.

The depot was increasingly noisy and confused.   More
and more men wedged their way into it.   The clatter of cart-
wheels and horses' hooves on the cobbles of the laneway, the
thud of paving stones and beams being unloaded, the metallic
beat of hammers on nailheads, the sound of saws and planes
ripping and tearing through wood and of men's voices pitched
higher and higher clashed and reverberated in a deafening
discord. It was most unusual activity for a place that had been
a malt storehouse, and Sirr's men who were watching it could

* The men who found him were sure he was a spy sent by his master, Philip
Ormsby, a grocer of 127 Thomas Street. Some of them wanted to "drop him"
immediately, probably meaning that they would have killed him. It was decided,
however, to wait for Emmet's orders. When he came in, he said that the man was
merely to be kept a prisoner in the depot until the rising was over.

Farrell repaid Emmet's humanity by revealing everything he knew of the rebels
and their plans. From his various examinations at the Castle came many of the details
of what was going on in the depot that day. He also wrote later, in his own unformed
hand, a supplementary account which will be mentioned later.

not have failed to report that fact to the impatient but still leashed and muzzled Major.

Since early the day before, half of Kildare had been emptying itself into Dublin. The people came, as one countryman put it, like swarms of bees. They travelled by canal and by turnpike, in hackney coaches, on horseback, and on foot. They came to hire an apprentice, to buy hops or groceries or delf, to consult a doctor, or to see a man about a gamecock. At least, those were the excuses they gave Pollock later on when they were arrested.

The early canal boat brought Patrick Dunne of Naas, at whose house had been held some secret meetings that General Trench had reported to Marsden in March. Richard Scott, whom the General had named as attending them, was in the state cabin with him. Daniel Brophy and William Andrews, who had also attended the Naas meetings, came in a hired coach, with Mrs. Andrews along with them to give the party a domestic appearance.

All these men had been busy since Wednesday riding about Kildare. All had been rebels in the past and were rebels still. Dunne's father and the father of the Scott brothers had both been hanged in 1798, which added a personal feeling to their sons' ingrained enmity to the English. Felix Rourke, on whom Thomas Reynolds had tried to pin the blame for the arrest of the United Irishmen meeting at Oliver Bond's in 1798, was in from Rathcoole, ready to take command of a party of pikemen. From Palmerstown many of the workmen employed by Mr. Edward Clarke were coming in along the river road that led by Phoenix Park.

At nine that Saturday morning Andrews, Dunne, Scott, Wilde, Mahon, Felix Rourke, and a few others met Quigley at the White Bull. Wilde and Mahon had just returned from Kildare with the news that Nicholas Grey did not want more than three hundred Kildare men to come into Dublin for the fighting there. While they were still talking in the tavern, Quigley was called out by Fleming the hostler, who said he was wanted at the Golden Bottle, a few doors down the street. There he found Rourke again, and some Tallaght men. Rourke wanted to see Emmet.

Some time that morning, Emmet did see a few of these men

at Dillon's. Dissatisfaction with the arms provided for the
rising, genuine or fomented for the purpose of crippling his
efforts, had begun to appear. Some of the leaders wanted to
see what preparations had been made. Emmet took them
into the crowded depot and showed them the thousands of
pikes stacked against the walls, bushels of musket balls, and
hundreds of bottle bombs made by Hamilton and Quigley.
Pat Farrell, resentful but observing, saw the meeting of the
leaders in this revealing light :

> The people that seemingly had the command was at this time forming
> their plans, and indeed they seemed to differ very much in their opinion.
> Some would have the Castel their first object, and more of them the
> barracks and others the Auld House [the old Custom House, then used as
> a barracks] as there was a great deal of arms that would be easy taken but
> the first man in command [Emmet] said that there was a Privie Councell
> at the Castle and he'd be very happy to shake hands with Mr. Beresford
> and upon his word he'd not do him the least hurt for really I thought that
> all Dublin would be in one commotion that night at the way I heard them
> speak. They expected it would not stan (sic) two hours till all would be
> over and that without much slaughter or bloodshed. The Lord Lieutenant
> was in the Park that day and indeed I heard it said that he was to be made
> fast by his own gards that night that they would have no trouble in getting
> threw there. . . .

But to the discontented Kildare men who wanted firearms
Emmet could show only about a dozen blunderbusses and
twelve cases of pistols. Money had been scarce for some time,
and he had not been able to buy as many arms as he had
expected.* The men demanded more, and Emmet promised
to send out to buy some. He dispatched a messenger to Long's
for £500. According to Miles Byrne, the leaders had been
satisfied on Saturday morning that they could arm with pikes
and fire-arms the men who had promised to meet them that
night.
  At seven that morning, Pat McCabe, the calender man of
Francis Street, who had long been pledged to serve under
John Allen, went to his shop on College Green to get instructions. Ever since preparations for a rising had begun, the

---

* In all probability other arms had been bought which were not at that time
available to Emmet. In writing Tom in August, Emmet said that the pikes and
ammunition had been lost on July 23, but that the arms were safe. Quigley later
said that arms had been sent to the depot in the Strawmarket and to Brangan at
Ringsend. Quigley's examinations at the I.S.P.O. and *Dickson Transcripts*.

shop had been used as a rendezvous for the leaders, so that if Allen was really in contact with the Government, he was in a position to know the plans of the rebels. McCabe found Allen with a full-coloured, smartish young man dressed in a blue coat, who he later learned was Dowdall.

The three went to Denis Redmond's new house on Coal Quay, where part of the arms from Patrick Street had been taken and where some of the beams filled with pikes were sent from Thomas Street that day and picked up Redmond. Then the four men walked to the second lock of the Grand Canal. Allen pointed out to McCabe a near-by field where, he said, many of the people were to assemble that evening for the rising. From that point, some would attack the Artillery Barracks at Island Bridge, others the magazine in Phoenix Park. While those attacks were going on, other men who had gathered elsewhere would attack the Castle. Some would come from the depot on Thomas Street, some from Redmond's on Coal Quay.*

A great many men would assemble at the Canal Harbour, Allen said, and plenty of arms were near by. Allen and Redmond were to lead the attack on the barracks. Allen, according to Pat McCabe, said that he had but one life to lose and he would be the first in at the artillery gate. Redmond said he would be the second. Dowdall was silent.

After some time spent in discussing their plans, the four warriors went to a public house near Island Bridge for breakfast. Pat McCabe said later that Dowdall was not for carrying on the attack, but that Allen and Redmond were very peremptory. Dowdall said he thought it was too soon for a rising, but Allen and Redmond were for it immediately as the people from the country were to meet and act that night. This conversation was overheard by the proprietor of the

* The plan for attacking the Castle, detailed by both Emmet and Miles Byrne, was for Byrne to have several hundred men from Wexford and Wicklow who were then living in Dublin assemble in front of Redmond's early in the evening. Pikes, arms, and ammunition were to be distributed to them. Emmet was to leave the depot on Thomas Street about dusk (roughly nine-thirty or a little later) with some hackney coaches, in each of which were to be six men, armed with pointed pikes and blunderbuses. Other men would walk behind them. The carriages were to drive into the Castle Yard as though the occupants were guests arriving for a party. As the coaches passed the point on Thomas Street nearest to Redmond's, Byrne's men were to fall in behind them, and they were all to assist in the attack on the Castle. Emmet had had other elaborate plans, which he had abandoned when resources began to fail. See Madden, III, p. 398 and p. 316 of this book.

house, Mr. Nason Browne, who immediately hurried to the Castle and reported it.*

If it is true that Marsden, on Pitt's instructions, had sent for Emmet to start a rising so that the public reaction to it would be useful in one way or another, then things were working out very well. There was a new Commander-in-Chief of the Army in Ireland who was completely ignorant of the real state of the country—that it was on the verge of insurrection. Marsden and Wickham had kept many of the informations concerning the rebels from the Lord Lieutenant and had interpreted others in such a way as not to alarm him or let him know the extent of rebel plans and how widespread disaffection was in the country. Sirr had been prevented from arresting Arthur Develin after the explosion at the depot in Patrick Street, and John Palmer had been released soon after being taken up, all at Marsden's orders, and all for the same purpose : that the rebels would not put off their plans but go on with the rising. The paragraph that the *Dublin Evening Post* printed about the explosion had probably been written at Marsden's suggestion and had quieted the fears of the leaders that their intentions were known to the Government. Whatever Emmet had learned in the middle of July that made him realise that he had been trapped into the conspiracy had not been enough to make him suspect that the Castle itself was concerned. The rising, he thought, would take it completely by surprise.

Marsden reached his office in the upper Castle Yard about eleven-thirty on the morning of July 23. Wickham was in London attending Parliament, and the Lord Lieutenant was at his residence in Phoenix Park ; thus he could manage things to suit himself. Mr. Nason Browne, who had overheard the breakfast conversation of Allen and his companions, must have arrived soon after Marsden did, with the first-hand news that the rebels would rise that night. A one-eared man from Barrack Street, who enjoyed a small pension from the Government (probably he was an informer of long standing, as the pension was given for the loss of his ear, which had been cut

* Mr. Browne later sent a memorial to the Castle claiming some recompense for this service and for having testified against Redmond at his trial. Other details are from Pat McCabe's examinations. All are at the I.S.P.O.

off by Defenders) also called that morning with word of the
intended insurrection. Wanting to make doubly sure that
his news reached the proper authorities, the one-eared man
also notified Brigadier-General Dunne at the Royal Barracks,
who passed the word along to Marsden.

A man whom Marsden later identified only as " one who
was in the secrets of the disaffected and with whom he often
communicated " went to the Castle in great alarm soon after
the under-secretary reached there to warn him that the danger
was imminent.*   Alderman Manders came with similar
news, which he had heard from a priest.

Another morning caller of great importance was Mr.
Edward Clarke of Palmerstown, a few miles up the Liffey from
Dublin.   Mr. Clarke employed a great many men at his
factory there, and on Thursday, hearing from a friend that
something seditious was going on in which his workmen were
concerned, he had come to the Castle to tell Marsden about
it. Marsden had got rid of him by pretending scepticism and
Clarke, an ingenuous soul if there ever was one, had gone
home and asked his men point-blank what they were up to.

With perfectly straight faces they had assured him that they
were all loyal, satisfied subjects of the King, with no thought
whatever of going against his Government.   On Friday
Mr. Clarke had again come to the Castle to give Marsden the
good news.   But that morning the workmen had alarmed
him by asking to be paid at once, and his friend Mr. Willcock
had informed him that they were going to Dublin to take
part in the rising.   The two men had ridden into town to tell
Marsden, but the timid Willcock had let Mr. Clark go to the
Castle alone.

* Marsden's account of the proceedings, written for the Lord Lieutenant in August,
admits that on coming to the Castle that day he received " several communications,
some of them secret, others from persons who had come to some knowledge of the
intentions and in some instances of the actual movements of the disaffected, which
made it manifest that the peace of the city must be very seriously disturbed in the
course of the ensuing night."

Marsden's account also said that it could not be imagined that the Castle or the
public offices in his neighbourhood were to be attacked.   This was the most bare-
faced falsehood.   The attack on the Castle was the key to all the Dublin plans, and
Marsden could not have failed to know it from some of his many sources of information.   But by neglecting to send additional guards to the Castle he probably hoped
to deceive the rebels.   The Castle gates were left open and all was as usual there until
nine or a little later that evening.   Miles Byrne had three men watching the old
custom-house barracks and the Castle, and at a quarter of nine a man passed through
the Castle Yard and saw no signs of activity.

"You have changed your mind very suddenly," the annoyed Marsden had told him when he heard the story, but, to keep Clarke quiet, he said he would notify the Lord Lieutenant and the Privy Council and would call Clarke to tell them what he knew. At least, that was the impression Mr. Clarke took away with him. He went to his Dublin warehouse to await the summons. But the Privy Council was not notified of what was going on or that any danger existed, and Marsden's first notes to the Lord Lieutenant at the Park were of the soothing sort. One said that General Sir Charles Asgill, in charge of the Dublin District, had returned from Kildare and was quite satisfied with what he saw there. Another reported that a priest from Dunboyne (into whom Marsden had put the fear of God a couple of years before by telling him that, if his neighbourhood became disorderly, he would be the first to be punished) had said that nothing wrong had taken place there.

These assurances by no means represented the true picture as Marsden knew it. He must have received many informations that have not survived : from Pollock, who had at least one contact with the rebels through the ironmonger who frequented Mrs. Ryan's pub on Thomas Street, and who was also on the track of Norris and others who were concerned with the rising ; from B. Senior, whose brother had been sent to Carey's in Kildare ; from McNally, all of whose informations for the months preceding the rising are now missing ; and from other known and unknown spies.*

The informations telling of the rebels' plans and the time they meant to take up arms which have survived were sufficient for Marsden to have stopped the whole proceedings before a pike was thrust or a blunderbuss fired, or a single life lost, either of rebel or loyalist. From McGucken he had known since Wednesday that both Belfast and Dublin were going to rise on Saturday, and that morning a Belfast gentleman, Mr. Atkinson, came down from the North with the

---

* In 1805 Mr. Pollock was interested in getting some money for the ironmonger, whose business had been completely ruined when it was learned that he had given information to the Government. Pollock said he had given information in 1803. Lord Norbury made a representation of services (no details given), and £300 was granted him, £200 of which was reward for having taken up Felix Rourke ; the other hundred therefore was for secret information. In February, 1804, Pollock had got £100 secret-service money for him. The memorials are in I.S.P.O.

same news. McGucken had told Marsden that Emmet was
to be the leader of all, and later Marsden admitted to the Lord
Lieutenant that the principal conspirators were known and
" everything except the extent of their plans."   But that last
statement, though it was accepted for a time by the credulous
Lord Hardwicke, can hardly be credited now. It was merely
a feeble excuse Marsden made to defend himself when he was
being criticised for not having stopped the insurrection. He
had heard that day from Colonel Wolfe and Lieutenant-
Colonel Aylmer of Kildare that many Naas men had already
reached Dublin, and that the town had been deserted since
the day before.

Major Sirr must have communicated with the Castle many
times that day. He had men watching the depot on Thomas
Street, and they saw Barney Doogan leave it both in the
morning and afternoon.* Some time during the day the
Major sent a note across the Castle Yard to Marsden :

Richard Knight a Carpenter who is in the Employment of Govt. says that
he employs 26 men that one of them told him that the rest of the workmen
had confidence in him and supposed him to be a Catholic, that the[y] were
to turn out this night to attack the Castle and Barracks and that there were
to be outposts about Dublin : Says that the men were particular in wanting
to be paid early this night. Mr. Knight has a contract from the Barrack
Board and lives in Baggot Court, Baggot Street.

H. C. Sirr.

But the Major was not allowed to move, and no effort was
made to stop the insurrection. Years later, still disgruntled at
the way in which he had been held in check till the fighting
began, Sirr noted on a letter relating to the day that

Government had frequent information given them the 23rd, and on that day
paid no attention to it. Major Sirr and Edward Wilson, the chief constable,
were the only two officials that were au fait. This accounts for the great
attention since paid by government to the most trifling threatening disturbance.†

It was not until two that afternoon that Marsden felt the

* In 1805 Mr. Clarke wrote Marsden a letter about Barney Duggan in which he
said that Sirr had men watching the depot on the twenty-third. This of course gives
the lie to Marsden's assertion that the Government could not stop the rising because
it was not known where the rebels were to assemble. Marsden also claimed that
Emmet never went to the Thomas Street depot until July 16, but both Jimmy Hope
and Barney Duggan said that he did.

† Sirr Mss. Trinity College Library.

time had come to take some defensive measures. Knowing that the new Commander of the Forces, General Fox, would be with the Lord Lieutenant at the Vice Regal Lodge in Phoenix Park that afternoon, he sent a note to Lord Hardwicke :

My Lord,

On coming to town I find a considerable degree of alarm in the apprehension of a rising this night or tomorrow morning in Dublin. I have reason to think that something serious is intended. I wish Your Excellency would come to town with General Fox in your carriage, which I would not request upon any light grounds.

A. Marsden

To His Excellency the Lord Lieutenant.

About that time John Cox, a turfman from Kildare, a little under the weather for having been up all night coming into town for the rising and for having stopped at half a dozen pubs on the way, was being pushed about by the crowds on Thomas Street. At ten the night before, he had been sitting in Margaret Costello's public house at Bourney's Bridge when Big Peter Haley of Allen and some other men had come in and told him they had been sent for by Matthew Donnelly to come into Dublin and join in an attack on the Castle.

Cox had been in the secret of the rising since March, and evidently was in sympathy with the rebels. He and his friends made the journey to Dublin, pub by pub, and arrived at the Canal Harbour about noon on the twenty-third. There they met, at another pub, the man who had sent Big Peter notice that the attack was to take place that night. Somehow, Cox became detached from his party and wandered into Thomas Street. He was accosted by Barney Doogan, whom he had known in Kildare, and steered into a room at the Yellow Bottle, a pub kept by the brother of Felix Rourke.* For about an hour Cox sat there smoking his pipe, during which time he noticed a dozen or more decently-dressed men going into an inner room to speak to a young gentleman who sat

---

* Cox was certain that it was at the Yellow Bottle that he had seen Emmet, but Quigley's later accounts said that Emmet met the Kildare leaders at Dillon's.

there writing. He had a long visage, Cox noted, powdered hair that seemed to be fair, and he was then wearing a surtout. Later Cox was told that the young gentleman was Robert Emmet.

Every time the door opened, Emmet looked up at the turfman. There was no waiter woman attending, but a man dressed like a servant with two tassels on his shoulders came in to bring him something. Cox overheard one of the visitors tell Emmet that he would not bring his men forward until there was a landing of the French.*

The turfman drifted out to Thomas Street again, and Emmet went back to the depot and told Quigley that the generals had deserted him, but since he was pledged to Munster and the North he felt obliged to go on with the rising.

Again the suspicion of treachery crops up. Emmet himself, in a long letter he later wrote his brother, said that "The Kildare men who were to act (particularly with me) came in and at five went off again, from the Canal Harbour, on a report of two of their officers that Dublin would not act. In Dublin itself it was given out by some treacherous or cowardly persons, that it was postponed till Wednesday." †

Since Emmet had seen the Kildare leaders in the morning, most of them had dined either at Martin Madden's of Bridge Street, or at Mrs. Ryan's on Thomas Street. Mrs. Ryan's niece, Mrs. Andrews, had dinner there with her husband and various other kinsmen and friends from Kildare. Mr. Madden also had a relative from the country, an uncle who had come in from Naas the day before. According to the book of Kildare depositions at the Royal Irish Academy, Mr. Madden's uncle " counselled the Naas men that evening." The depositions of some of these men say that Madden's uncle dropped in at Mrs. Ryan's after leaving his nephew's place and chatted with them there.

Whether the uncle was responsible for the change of heart of the Kildare leaders is only a matter of conjecture, but the depo-

---

* From examinations of Cox now at the I.S.P.O.
† P.R.O.L., and also printed in Madden, *United Irishmen*, III, p. 398. Quigley's examination of November 1, 1803, said that " the Kildare men had been told that there were arms and men of talents and property to command them, and finding to the contrary, they refused to act, but E said he was pledged to Munster and the North, and must go on." *Dickson Transcripts.*

sition that Mr. Pollock took from him later disclosed that he had come into town the day before, having been summoned on Friday by Captain Pattison, an officer of the 21st Regiment. The Captain, it turned out, wanted to give him some money, which was paid over by the Captain's agent on Saturday morning. Mr. Pollock, who sometimes put down such minute details as that a man had supped on cockles, did not mention why the money was paid.*

Certainly, word that the leaders had refused to act was flying through Dublin that day and out to the country. A book of suspects, made up at the Castle a couple of years later and concerned largely with Kildare people, lists scores of men who came to Dublin and went home when they heard of it. The book of Kildare depositions speaks of people being turned back by carmen and carters on the Dublin road. One in particular was stationed at the Red Cow about five miles from Dublin. The dampening news with which he greeted travellers going toward town was that soldiers were firing on the people at the Black Horse Bridge.

When Lord Lieutenant Hardwicke and General Fox, the Commander-in-Chief, reached the Castle a little before four that afternoon, Marsden faced one of the most delicate situations of his career. He knew definitely that an armed insurrection was to take place that night. Locked in his mind was a great deal of knowledge about the plans of the rebels which he had not communicated to his superiors. He wanted a rising to take place, and yet he must so manage matters that he would not be blamed for having failed to take precautions to ensure peace and quiet.

He did this by admitting to Hardwicke and Fox that there was a possibility that a disturbance might take place in Dublin that evening. But his visitors were given no idea of the extent of the preparations of the rebels, nor were they told how widespread the insurrection might be. Marsden mentioned McGucken's information that Belfast and Dublin were expected to rise simultaneously, but he contrived to cast discredit on it. He minimised Mr. Atkinson's confirming report by saying that the gentleman had his information at second or

* In 1805 the uncle addressed a memorial to Marsden from gaol, implying that he deserved special consideration.

third hand. The impression Marsden conveyed was that a riot in Dublin was the worst that was to be feared.

Marsden also impressed Hardwicke and the General with the idea that no alarm must be given. He meant that the rebels must not know that their plans had been discovered, and that measures were being taken to frustrate their efforts. This is obvious in the account of the rising he wrote for the Lord Lieutenant in August : " To have prevented altogether the consequence of their secret preparations was impossible," he said then, and he went on to point out how much better it was to have allowed the rebels to rise then, without French aid, than later, " when the mischief must have been greater." *

General Fox said later that the wish to avoid creating alarm had been strongly urged to him. He was not only to wait until dusk (nine-thirty or a little later) before ordering small reinforcements to the Bank, the Castle, Kilmainham gaol, and the Lord Lieutenant's lodge in the Park, but he was even to defer communicating with the officers under him regarding measures to be taken that night.

Mr. Clarke of Palmerstown, tired of waiting at his warehouse for Marsden's promised summons to the Castle to tell the Lord Lieutenant and (as he supposed) the Privy Council what he had learned about the insurrection, went back uninvited while the conference between the Lord Lieutenant and General Fox was going on. He got a promise of a detachment of troops to stop the progress of the Palmerstown rebels toward Dublin, but even this was detained till long after the men had reached the city.

When Emmet returned to the depot after seeing the leaders at the Yellow Bottle and told Quigley that he had been deserted by them, he found other troubles waiting him. Anne Develin had been there with his clean shirt, a pair of hose,

---

* From Marsden's rough draft of the account. It was printed in Lord Castlereagh's *Correspondence,* but several paragraphs, including this significant one, were omitted there. The draft ends with this ingenuous appeal (also omitted from the Castlereagh volume) : " Many persons must naturally be of the opinion that the calamities of the occasion might have been prevented, or more easily defeated. How far persons in situations of responsibility might individually have contributed to this must be decided by others than myself, but should Your Excellency think it expedient to order any inquiry to be made I trust that the blame, if any be due, will not fall upon one of the most zealous of your Excellency's Servants." I.S.P.O.

Marsden's intention of not alarming the rebels is also admitted in the speech Lord Castlereagh made in the British House of Commons on March 7, 1804.

and a cravat ; but, afraid of being " pulled and hauled " by the men in the depot, she had left them and gone back to Butterfield Lane. He must have been disappointed at not seeing her, for it is very likely that the two love letters found in his desk would have been given her to deliver to Sarah Curran.

His other messenger had not brought the money from Philip Long ; but, having made a promise to buy more blunderbusses, Emmet sent George McDaniel with a few pounds to get as many as possible.*

Barney Doogan, who was supposed to be watching the Castle that day (but who had been on Thomas Street at two), came in with news that Mr. Clarke had been at the Castle warning Marsden about the rising.

Emmet's natural conclusion was that the Army would immediately be called out and an attack on the depot ordered. His defence was to send men to guard the roads between the Royal Barracks and Army Headquarters at Kilmainham and the Castle, and to intercept any messengers coming from the Castle. Sentinels were also placed around the depot, and a few of the explosive beams distributed where they would best impede the advance of enemy men and horses.

These details attended to, Emmet, Quigley, Wilde, and Mahon went to the White Bull for some supper. John Fleming, the hostler, saw them there about seven, testing the new slow matches. Hevey, the brewer, who was entertaining sixteen Dublin leaders, including Dowdall and Allen, at his

---

* Long's nephew, young David Fitzgerald, told Madden that Long advanced £1,400 to Emmet, all of which was lost. When Emmet's messenger reached Long's place on Crow Street on the morning of the twenty-third, Long was not there but came in at twelve-thirty. Long sent Fitzgerald to a merchant who owed money to him, and the merchant eventually gave Fitzgerald a draft for the £500 Emmet wanted. By that time the banks were closed, but Fitzgerald got the money from some of the bank runners. He was leaving the bank at six that evening when he was told that news of an intended rising had reached the Castle and that the guards were doubled. In consequence of this the money was not taken to Emmet, and he never received it. Madden, III, p. 372.

The examination of J—— T——, a carpenter who lived at 3 Christ Church Yard, says that McDaniel came to him at eight that evening (it must have been earlier) and said he wanted T—— to buy blunderbusses for him. McDaniel gave him a five-pound note. T—— bought two blunderbusses at 2 guineas each from Tomlinson of Chapel Street. McDaniel wanted him to get more, saying it was for an insurrection. T—— claimed that, instead of trying to get them, he went to his master in Abbey Street and told him of the rising. The master went to the Castle and told Sirr. T—— then went to McDaniel and told him the shops were closed. I.S.P.O.

home in Thomas Court, came in and asked Emmet if the attack was to go on that night.*

Emmet said it was. Hevey had heard the rumours that it was to be postponed and told him so.

" You have heard an untruth," Emmet replied, and he added something to the effect that the Castle of Dublin would know that he would turn out that night.

" Well, your orders I must obey," Hevey said, and immediately left the room.

The Lord Lieutenant left the conference at the Castle about five and returned to Phoenix Park not at all disturbed at what might happen that night. General Fox, also calm and unalarmed, went back to the Army Headquarters at the Royal Hospital at Kilmainham. There his aide-de-camp sent out several notes to subordinates, none of which implies that there is any great danger impending. All of them, however, mention the necessity for not giving alarm. To the officer in charge of the ordnance depot at the Pigeon House he added a second warning : " His Excellency desires me to repeat the necessity of being very cautious in not giving alarm."

To Sir Charles Asgill, the officer in command of the Dublin district, General Fox wrote :

There is a degree of alarm, which altho' not to be entirely believed, came from such Authority that ought not totally to be disregarded. I shall be glad to see you here about Nine O'Clock this night, and am to beg you to say nothing about this, and to come up here as privately as possible. Should this not reach you in time, you will have the goodness to come here tomorrow morning by 6 O'clock. It is of the greatest moment that no alarm should be given on our part, and I will myself give the necessary directions for the Night. [To this the General added a postscript :] Since writing your

---

*Allen could not have been one of the leaders who deserted Emmet that afternoon, for at three o'clock Pat McCabe had been at his shop to get a guinea from him instead of the pay he would miss by being in the rising. At six, McCabe had gone back to get a blunderbuss that Allen gave him. On both occasions there was no suggestion that Allen was holding back. He urged Pat McCabe to bring out as many men as he could. I.S.P.O.

Dowdall could hardly have been one of the deserters, since Miles Byrne, in his *Memoirs*, criticised him for having been carousing at Hevey's when he should have been with Emmet. As Emmet saw Byrne after the rising and gave him many details of the day, he would have known if Dowdall had been one of those who saw Emmet at the Golden Bottle.

A Mr. William Connor, who lived with the Stockdales in Abbey Street, heard a great commotion in the house the evening of the twenty-third and learned later that Dowdall had been there taking leave of Miss Sally Stockdale, to whom he had been paying his addresses. Madden, III, p. 334.

Dragoon is come to me. I will send this by him, and shall of course have the pleasure of seeing you this Night.*

Sir Charles was engaged to dine out that evening and was already in his dress uniform when he received General Fox's note. He immediately went off in a hackney coach to Head-quarters. The Commander told him what he had learned at the Castle and then sent him back to Marsden for any news that might have arrived since he left there. It was after six when Sir Charles reached the Castle, and both he and Marsden were aware that no orders to act generally against the rebels had been sent to the troops. But throughout the evening Marsden restrained every one who called on him urging him to act immediately with the excuse that the troops would soon be on the streets.

He told this to Major Swan, who came in with fresh accounts of the impending trouble while Sir Charles was still there. Next, Alderman Darley, a magistrate, came in to warn Marsden of what he had heard of the rebels' intentions. He was told that the Government had received similar in-formation, and that every precautionary step had been taken. He saw other magistrates who were also peace officers, but, instead of sending them to attend at the various barracks, he seems to have sent them home.† At any rate, only one magistrate did turn up at barracks, and he held the troops in check as long as he could.

Yeomen captains who came to the Castle offering their services received polite refusals from Marsden. Marsden's excuse to the Lord Lieutenant was :

It was thought prudent to restrain the Yeomen from assembling their men, and by their so doing increase the alarm, as well because it was known that few of the Yeomen had arms, and none of them ammunition (no general delivery to the Corps having been made to the Corps) (sic) as because it was conceived that the troops in the barracks of Dublin and at the several posts had received orders to hold themselves in readiness, and were probably at the instant engaged.

Between seven and eight Marsden sent a note to General

---

* P.R.O.L. Copies of the defence of his conduct which General Fox prepared that winter have been printed in An-t-Oglach, July-September, 1928, p. 82 et seq.

† Except under martial law, troops could act only on the defensive, unless under the direction of a civil magistrate. If Marsden had really wanted to defend the city, he would have had magistrates at every barracks.

Fox suggesting that the reinforcements for the Castle guard
be increased to a Captain and fifty men, instead of the thirty
that had been agreed upon, but again he cautioned the General
not to have them leave the barracks till after dark.

Marsden and Sir Charles had supper at the Castle, and then
the General went back to Army Headquarters. Before going
there, however, he returned to his home and changed from
his dress uniform into mufti. (In his account of the proceedings of the day now at the Public Record Office in London
he says he did so because of the request contained in General
Fox's letter, but no mention of uniform is made in that
document. Probably Marsden suggested the change.)

It was nearly nine when Sir Charles arrived at the Army
Headquarters on his second visit. Soon after the hour had
struck, the other officers General Fox had sent for came in :
Brigadier-General Dunne, Colonel Cotton, the officer of the
day, and Lieutenant-Colonel Vassal. Still ignorant of the
seriousness of the situation, Fox merely told them that an idea
of a rising prevailed at the Castle, but that he could not believe
it. The general opinion seemed to be that there was no cause
for apprehension. Sir Charles said he was not alarmed (which
speaks volumes as to the impression he had received from
Marsden) but that extraordinary things could happen in
Ireland, and that it was their business to be prepared and on
the alert.* It was agreed that officers commanding regiments
should be put on their guard, but no mention was made of
magistrates to go out with them.

For the second time General Fox asked Sir Charles to go
to the Castle and see if any more news had been received there.
At Thomas Street he ran into fighting.

* It should not be forgotten that the one-eared man who went to the Castle to warn
Marsden that morning also notified Brigadier-General Dunne. Dunne had also been
told of the intended rising by a young yeoman officer, Captain Coultman. At five-
thirty that afternoon young David Fitzgerald, Philip Long's nephew, had been at the
old custom-house barracks and had seen General Dunne apparently engaged in taking
precautions. He heard him ordering some soldiers to put the women out of the
barracks and to allow no men in. He then galloped off. Very possibly he had
received General Fox's note by that time. But in view of all the turmoil in the city
and the repeated informations he had received, it is strange that he made no mention
of them at this conference.

CHAPTER TWENTY-FOUR

Action

WHEN Emmet went back to the depot from the White Bull some time after seven, huge bundles of the proclamations he had prepared for the people were waiting for him still wet from the press and redolent of printer's ink. The shorter one, addressed to the Citizens of Dublin, exhorted them to rally to the national standard, " the sacred, though long degraded green." The longer one to the people of Ireland was even more rhetorical, but compressed into its finely printed columns was Emmet's political philosophy. It was like him that even in the turmoil of that crowded arms depot, with danger and reality pressing closer and closer upon him, he should employ the last moments before he took up arms in reading some of this proclamation to the men assembled there. He himself was acting on principle, as a disciple of Christianity and democracy, and he wanted the men who were to fight with him to share his views and to follow the precepts of charity and generosity that the paper laid down.

Still in his civilian surtout, he picked up a copy of the large proclamation and held it close to a lighted candle :

The Provisional Government to the People of Ireland :
You are now called upon to show the world that you are competent to take your place among nations ; that you have a right to claim their recognizance of you as an independent country, by the only satisfactory proof you can furnish of your capability of maintaining your independence —your wresting it from England with your own hands. . . . Our object is to establish a free and independent republic in Ireland. . . . We war not against property, we war against no religious sect, we war not against past opinions or prejudices, we war against English dominion.

They would, he went on, enter into no detail of the atrocities and oppressions under which Ireland had laboured during the six hundred years of its connection with England but would

justify their determination to separate from that country on
the broad historical statement that during that time she had
been unable to conciliate the affections of the people of Ireland,
that during that time five rebellions had been entered into
to shake off the yoke, that England had been obliged to enter
into a system of unexampled torture in her defence, that by
the Act of the Union passed by a Parliament notoriously
bribed and not representing the will of the people she had
taken even the name of independence from Ireland.

With characteristic generosity and lack of political realities
the English were advised, in the most high-flown language
possible, how they should treat the rebels in case the fight
should fail. The rebels themselves were advised what their
attitude should be if necessity forced them to measures of
retaliation. They were told to bury their resentment on the
field of battle.

> Fully impressed with the justice of our cause, which we now put to the
> issue, we make our last and solemn appeal to the sword and to heaven ; and
> as the cause of Ireland deserves to prosper, may God give us the Victory.

As Emmet put the paper down, the men were murmuring
among themselves that it was very good. They may not have
appreciated it as an outline of democratic thought—in that
sense it was beyond the understanding of most of them—but
to the men who heard his voice and to all the others he was
addressing there was nothing academic in his reference to
brutality and oppression. Most of them had known both,
intimately and not long past.

Patrick Dunne and the Scott brothers would think of their
fathers hanged in 1798, of the massacre of disarmed men at
the gibbet rath of Kildare. Michael Flood would take up
pikes Emmet had sent him to avenge the long years he had
spent at sea, taken from his farms by Lord Carhampton and
shipped away without trial. Emmet himself was doubtless
thinking of Wolfe Tone, of his own exiled brother, of Tom
Russell, imprisoned for seven years without trial but still
ready to risk everything for the chance of liberating his
country. Across the court-yard at the White Bull, Mrs. Dillon
could think of her sixteen-year-old brother who had been
hanged in an earlier rebellion because he would not betray
his friends.

Thus, with his own rhetoric ringing in his ears and with his eyes impractically fixed on a vision of happiness his imagination had evoked, Emmet prepared to put the cause of Ireland to the test. The abyss he would not acknowledge or shrink from lay just ahead. Reality in all its ugliest forms pressed closer with every passing moment. Treachery, intrigue, incompetence, even his own too-elaborate and unfinished preparations were waiting to plunge him into disaster. Emmet's idealism ignored them. He was so convinced that the cause of Ireland deserved to prosper that he never doubted that God would give him victory. The pikes for the people were ready. A green and gold uniform, with breeches of creamy-white cashmere, was in his slant-top desk. He put it on, and the image of Sarah Curran must have flashed into his mind as his hand touched his velvet stock with the lock of her hair sewed inside. The love letters he had written her were still in the desk. It was too late to send them now. His feathered hat and his sword were on the table. He picked them up. There was the smell of hot candle grease and of twenty dozen loaves of bread fresh from the ovens to feed the men before they went out.

Ned Condon had gone out to get the hackney coaches for the attack on the Castle. He came running back with news. He had been stopped by an officer on horseback who wanted to know where he was going with so many carriages. He had shot at the man with his pistol. The coachman had taken fright, and all of them had driven off.

Emmet asked if the beams filled with pikes had got to Redmond's on Coal Quay. Condon said they had. That meant that there were arms for Miles Byrne's men assembling there.

With the coaches gone the plan for attacking the Castle would have to be altered. He and the men who would have ridden with him would have to go on foot. But reinforced by the men from Wexford and Kildare, they might still take the Castle, and that was the key to Dublin. Then Michael Dwyer would come with his Wicklow men. Russell, Emmet had no doubt, was raising his army in the North. Kerry and Limerick would surely rise when they heard that Dublin was up.

" Who's the general ? " Pat Farrell asked, eyeing Emmet's uniform.

" How bad you are for knowledge," was the only answer he received.

And then, a little after eight, too late to put the rising off and just too soon to begin the attack with success, Quigley rushed in, crying that the Army was coming, and that they would all be taken.

But no army detachments were then on the streets. Quigley must have been tricked into thinking that. Denis Redmond later heard that men acting on orders from the Castle were in Thomas Street and even in the depot that night for the purpose of precipitating the rising and causing confusion that would detach Emmet from his followers. These men had been instructed to go to the depot dressed as country labourers,

then to take up arms and join the standard of liberty that was to be raised that night at a certain appointed hour.

But I am credibly informed [Redmond wrote in an account of the rising, which, in spite of the fact that he was then a prisoner, flaunted his devotion to Irish independence and his adoration of Emmet] their instructions was (sic) when they were armed to rush forward and create confusion by calling out to whatever men were then armed Corner Boys, do not be delaying all night. This had its desirable effect for the people were not regularly arranged which I must say did not proceed from any want of courage or zeal but the appointed hour not been (sic) arrived, some thought their orders proceeded from the gen'l who was then in the depot busily employed in arranging matters for the attack and on hearing that some of the people had rushed forward without orders he then ordered the arms to be speedily distributed.

This was exactly what happened. Hurriedly men were put to work throwing pikes from the windows of the upper loft. Quigley and Stafford got into their regimentals. Emmet gave an order to disarm the sentries at the Marshalsea, " to kill none but to take them prisoner." * He sent a detail to make a

* Pat Farrell heard this order given, but probably it was not executed, as the Marshall, Mr. Henry Ormsby, did not mention any attempt to disarm the guards at this time. He later sent to the Castle a very detailed account of the happenings of that night in the immediate vicinity of the Marshalsea prison where debtors were kept, which was within twenty-five yards of the depot, and immediately off the elbow of Mass, or Marshalsea Lane.

" On Saturday evening the 23rd of July last about the hour of nine o'clock from some circumstances which occured (sic) the Marshal had reason to apprehend that an insurrection was immediately to take place. The Serg't of the guard was sent for by me to enquire into the state of the ammunition of the guard in case of an attack, and

prisoner of Mr. Sylvester Costigan, the proprietor of a large distillery farther down Thomas Street so that the rebels could use his yard to assemble in.* Fleming was told to go to nearby taverns to see that no more drink was served because the rising was about to begin.

" It's beginning too soon," said more than one man, putting down his porter.

On the Quays Lord Moira's bell rang for nine o'clock. A single rocket flared over the roof tops. Emmet drew his sword and called on the men to follow him, and Quigley and Stafford and Condon and all the others who were in the depot went out after him into the crowded alley.†

Already there had been a little skirmish between some of the rebels and a police officer, Mr. Edward Wilson. If Mr.

was informed by him that they had but six rounds a man. The Corpl was then sent for by the Marshal to send him to the Barracks for more ammunition, when on his way from the Hatch door (or entrance to the Marshalsea) to the Marshal's house, about 11 yards distant he saw a vast number of men armed with guns blunderbusses and pikes, rushing down the lane toward him, on which he attempted to regain the Hatch door, but just as he got to the entrance of the door, and before he could close it, a blunderbuss was fired at him the contents of which lodged in his body, and he expired in a few minutes afterwards, in the Guard House. The Marshal on the first alarm got the Guard under arms, and posted them opposite to the doors, where for several hours he every minute expected an attack as numbers of the rebels kept passing back and forward until towards morning, when he was relieved of his anxiety about 2 o oclock by the arrival of a party of the 38th Reg't, that was patrolling the streets, and was challenged from the Marshalsea.

" He cannot here pass over unnoticed the assistance offered and accepted of by him for the defence of the Marshalsea in case of an attack, from a number of the loyal inmates of the place, but particularly from Lieut. John Harney, Royal Meath Militia, who took arms and put himself under the command of the Serg't of the Guard and continued so the whole night. A Gentleman who had the privilege of going in and out, on his return to the Marshalsea that night, was taken prisoner by the Rebels in Bridgefoot Street and compelled, with a pistol at his head, to take a pike and go with them, but on his telling how he was situate, and that he'd loose the privilege allowed him by the Marshal if they detained him, he was instantly let go, and accompanied by one of them to the Marshal's door, and was told by a Rebel, that every prisoner within the walls would in a very short time be set at liberty ; the door of the Marshalsea was opened his voice being known, and on his getting into the Marshalsea he reported what had happened to him, and that he had seen several heaps of pikes in Bridgefoot Street, and a remarkable large heap in a dirty bye-lane leading towards the Marshalsea. . . . ." I.S.P.O.

* There are several depositions at the I.S.P.O. describing how Mr. Costigan was taken prisoner by two men with blunderbusses, who then let in three or four other men. These posted themselves at the doors and gates of the distillery yard and let in seventy or more men, who stayed there nearly an hour, but hearing some shots fired, they all ran out.

† John Cox, the turfman from Kildare who had seen Emmet in the Yellow Bottle that afternoon, was one of those waiting in Mass Lane when Emmet came out. He saw Emmet and Quigley at the head of the party and heard them order the men to step out. Cox armed himself with one of the pikes that had been thrown out of the depot and joined the rebel army. I.S.P.O.

Wilson's account can be relied on, one rebel leader had been shot dead. But Mr. Wilson had retreated by the time Emmet came out of the depot, and the orderliness with which Wilson claimed the rebels had been arming had changed to chaos. Fleming, who went out before Emmet, turned and saw men "fall off from the body in any way they could." He heard them say they were not going to lose their lives for *them*.

As Emmet saw his followers dwindle, he realised he could not possibly expect to take the Castle. His only hope was to march as many men as he could to the country to join Dwyer. It was a forlorn one. "The great body, being Dublin men, refused to follow him," Quigley said later. According to both Quigley and Stafford, Emmet had two or three hundred men when he left the depot. Only forty or fifty went as far as Thomas Street, and even these were not all steadfast.

But Emmet still had faith in the Irish people. Richard Wornall, a Patrick Street victualler, saw a young man most superbly dressed in a white jacket faced with green, with a pair of large gold epaulettes, and wearing a cocked hat with a long green feather, turn into Patrick Street from Plunket Street. He was at the head of fourteen or fifteen men armed with long white poles or pikes (actually blunderbusses).

"When he entered Patrick (Street) he halted," Mr. Wornall later told a magistrate, Mr. Bell, "and addressed the people in the street saying 'Turn out, my boys, now is your time for liberty. Liberty, my boys. Turn out, turn out.'"

To that entreaty there was no response. Emmet fired his pistol into the air, then marched his men toward Kevin Street.

A few minutes later a much larger party, about three hundred men, Mr. Wornall thought, all armed with pikes, came along the same way. They were shouting and breaking street lamps and asking which way the first party had gone. But this band of rebels, probably the Canal Harbour corps that John Allen should have been commanding, never overtook Emmet.

Somewhere on Patrick Street, probably under the great dark walls of St. Patrick's Cathedral, where the bitter brooding spirit of Jonathan Swift seems to linger still, Emmet crashed into the abyss.*

It was still twilight when a lad of fourteen, leaning over a half door in Freestone Alley, saw a little band of men going toward the mountains, carrying what he thought were pikes. It was not in Emmet simply to save his own life, but for the time being that was all he could do. His image of victory and happiness completely shattered, Emmet was on his way to Butterfield Lane.

Besides the men in the depot and the surrounding pubs and the seventy or eighty who gathered in Costigan's brewery yard, several hundred potential rebels had been loitering around Dublin that evening. Along Coal Quay two or three hundred men collected. There was a large crowd near the Cork Street Barracks and another near the third lock of the Canal. Thomas Street, James's Street, and all the side streets around the Canal Harbour were filling up as dusk came on.† They stood about casually in groups of three or four, but with an air of expectancy.

About eight-thirty Mr. Edward Wilson, the Chief Peace Officer of the Workhouse Division of Dublin, having got word from the Chief Magistrate, Mr. Alexander, that a mob might assemble that evening, collected half a dozen men to help him keep the peace, but he could arm them only with five pistols and some swords that were in the watch house.

About the time that the pikes were being thrown from the depot windows to the alley below, Mr. Wilson came along Thomas Street from Vicar Street and ordered the clustered men to disperse, threatening to take them into custody. Thereupon, they all went into the part of Mass Lane that opened off

---

* " There was failure in all, plan, preparation and men," Emmet wrote Tom just before his trial. " I would have given it the respectability of insurrection, but I did not wish uselessly to shed blood. I gave no signal for the rest, and they all escaped. I arrived time enough in the country, to prevent that part of it which had already gone out with one of my men—to dissuade the neighborhood from proceeding." (Quigley later said this referred to Arthur Develin, but Anne said Big Arthur was in the Coombe that night.)   Madden, III, p. 403.

† Somewhere in the crowd on Thomas Street was the informer, John B, who had reached Dublin with Carey and his two sons about six o'clock. With them was the other fake emissary James G——.   Their proximity to Lord Kilwarden's carriage when he was murdered later that night makes one wonder if they were not *agents provocateurs*.

Thomas Street. They had scarcely got as far as the Marshalsea prison, when Mr. Wilson heard firing. Thinking that the rebels were attacking the Marshalsea, he marched his little party to the Bridgefoot end of Mass Lane, stopping a moment on the way to order a public house to close up. When he got to the Bridgefoot Street entrance of Mass Lane, he found himself at the head of a column of men with pikes on their shoulders, moving slowly toward him. The lane was quite full of men, three or four hundred, he thought, and they were moving regularly, as though they were waiting for the men at the rear to get arms.

Mr. Wilson brandished his pistol and ordered them to lay down their arms. They seemed to hesitate and to look where the order came from, but one of the men at their head, better dressed than the others and muffled in a great-coat, stepped forward and gave a thrust of his pike at the peace officer. Mr. Wilson, so he said, placed his pistol at his attacker's breast and fired. The man fell instantly dead.* The mob then divided to left and right, and the party in the rear fired at Mr. Wilson and his men. One of the watchmen was killed, and Mr. Wilson and the rest of the party retreated toward Thomas Street, exchanging fire with the rebels. The mob did not then come out of Bridgefoot Street.

Mr. Wilson made his way through Meath Street to Newmarket watch house on the Coombe and told the story to the officers there. One of them went to the Coombe and Cork Street Barracks to tell the Army officers what had happened. Mr. Wilson then continued to his home in New Street and later joined his neighbour, Mr. John Bell, the magistrate, who had a corporal's guard of soldiers. They placed sentries and patrolled down the road to Harold's Cross.

That, Mr. Wilson said, was about ten o'clock, but it was probably later. Emmet's party must either have emerged from the depot very shortly after Mr. Wilson had left Thomas Street, or Mr. Wilson must have done his patrolling after

---

*Quigley said later that he was in the depot when he heard the shots that Wilson's party fired. When he passed that way with Emmet and his party, he saw the man Wilson had killed but did not know who he was. Wickham later claimed in a letter to Mr. Abbot, that the man Wilson fired at was Emmet. He did not try to reconcile the fact that Wilson had testified under oath that the man was killed by his shot.

Emmet had passed through Harold's Cross, for nowhere does Mr. Wilson mention having met Emmet's party.*

In spite of his wound and profuse bleeding Mr. Wilson said he stayed on duty the whole night, " not wishing to be taken in bed." He and Mr. Bell and his party were firing and taking prisoners the whole night.

Word of Mr. Wilson's little skirmish, and that the rebels were assembling in all directions, reached Major Robertson, the commanding officer at Cork Street Barracks, via the Newmarket watch house, at about nine-thirty that night. Immediately, he ordered the drums to beat to arms and delegated a detachment of forty or fifty men under Lieutenant Brady to march to the home of their Colonel, at Usher's Island.† The Lieutenant had instructions to escort Colonel Browne to the barracks or receive orders from him for the regiment that night.

This little party entered Thomas from James's Street, proceeding very cautiously in the heavy darkness that had now fallen, their bayonets fixed and arms supported. Lieutenant Brady was at the left of the leading division. Suddenly, he found himself confronted by a man in the middle of the street, holding what appeared to be a white pole in his hands. The officer seized him and demanded to know what he was about.

The man did not answer but struggled hard to keep his weapon and the soldiers who came to the Lieutenant's aid made a great deal of noise. A window opened in a near-by house, and a bottle came hurtling down among the soldiers. From the right a shot was fired.

* Miles Byrne and his men also passed up Patrick Street some time after nine that night, hunting for Emmet and his party. Byrne and Denis Redmond had been waiting on the Quay with two or three hundred men, expecting to get a message when Emmet left the depot. When no word came, Byrne sent messengers to Thomas Street to learn the reason for the delay. The first never came back. The second returned with news that pikes were strewn about in the vicinity of the depot and that there were other signs of combat near the Market-house. Leaving the Quay, Byrne, Redmond, and their men set out in search of Emmet and spent nearly the whole night marching and countermarching through the streets of the neighbourhood, meeting no opposition but watchmen whom they easily thrust aside.

† Colonel Browne had already learned of the rising and, coming up Bridgefoot Street on his way to the barracks, had been fired on by one of the rebel sentries and killed.

Lieutenant Brady realised that he had run into a detachment of the rebels. He ordered his men to form subdivisions and to prime and load. From in front of him came a great huzza and a noise of many feet marching forward on the pavement, but the forms of the men were hidden in the dark of the unlighted night.

When he judged that the rebels were quite close, Lieutenant Brady ordered the leading subdivisions of soldiers to fire a volley. By the flashing of the pans he could see he was surrounded by men armed with what appeared to be white staves, but which were of course pikes. The soldiers kept up independent firing, and the rebels (according to the account the Lieutenant gave at the various state trials) fled in all directions, leaving six men dead and one man dying. But there were enough hand-to-hand skirmishes for the soldiers to capture several prisoners and for some of the rebels to dye their pikes with blood before they flung them down. Also, though Lieutenant Brady's orders had been to go to Colonel Browne's house at Usher's Island, he seems to have abandoned that attempt and to have taken his company without loss of time to the James's Street Barracks.

His testimony on the trial of Edward Kearney, one of the prisoners taken in that encounter, stated that he went there to assist a wounded soldier, but Major Robertson's report to the Government says that it was on the Lieutenant's hearing that about a thousand rebels were assembling near Thomas Street. As he would have to make an about-face to get to the barracks, perhaps the word " retreat " is the proper one to use. An account of the proceedings written by General Fox says that Lieutenant Brady " deemed it prudent " to do so, because he understood that the insurgents were in greater force in Thomas Street, and because, having no civil magistrate with him, he did not feel authorised to go in quest of them, although he had already been obliged to act in his own defence.

In the meantime, Sir Charles Asgill and Colonel Cotton, returning to town from the conference with General Fox at the Army Headquarters at Kilmainham, ran into Lieutenant Brady's battle in James's Street, at about ten minutes to ten and, " not knowing the extent of the business, returned to the

Royal Hospital." * Another official account said they had to flee for their lives, and elsewhere it was said that the James's Street Barracks was attacked by the rebels. Thus the engagement seems to have lasted longer and been more vigorous than Lieutenant Brady's account suggested.†

Just at this time Pat McCabe, armed with the blunderbuss he had got from John Allen at six that evening, appeared on Thomas Street with another group of rebels. According to the promise he had given Allen, he had gone to the rendezvous near the Canal Harbour at nine. But Allen did not appear, and, after waiting an hour or so, McCabe went into a public house to get a drink of porter. When he came out, a quarter of an hour later, he met a multitude of people, many of whom had pikes, running toward Thomas Street from the Canal and Somerset Street. (Probably they were the men appointed to assemble there, who were attracted by the sound of firing made by Lieutenant Brady's party.)

McCabe went with them, getting ball cartridges from some one in the crowd. But many of the men were without weapons of any sort, and a voice called out, " Where are the arms ? "

A man McCabe did not know answered to come along with him, and they would get plenty. By this time, they had got as far as the entrance to Mass Lane on Thomas Street ; they turned in there, and to the right at the elbow and so came to the depot. There was still a great pile of pikes outside it, and every man took one up and went on through Bridgefoot Street to Thomas Street again.

Just then a coach came along. The mob stopped it and took out two trunks, but McCabe called out that it was liberty they were after and not plunder, and the trunks were put back.

The mob was now breaking up into sections. McCabe's party continued eastward, breaking street lamps as they went. At Vicar Street they attacked the watch house and seized the constables' poles. From there they went through Francis

---

* This indicates that the Lieutenant must have been pursued by the rebels into James's Street, a continuation westward of Thomas Street, as the Crown made a great point of the fact that one of the prisoners was taken on Thomas Street, not James's Street, and the fighting was still going on in James's Street when Sir Charles reached that part of the city.

† Next day General Fox, asking for certain defences to be erected in the city, included a request for a stronger door for the James's Street Barracks. I.S.P.O.

Street, Plunkett Street, Patrick Street, and back across the Poddle to Francis Street.*

Here a detachment of the 21st Fusiliers under the command of Lieutenant Douglas was drawn up in front of the Coombe Barracks, and as the rebels attacked, they were given three volleys. Whereupon McCabe ran up Francis Street, " as smart as he could," his bit of soldiering over. Unfortunately for him and for Emmet, he was taken prisoner at his own door about one that morning.†

* If this was the large party of men Mr. Wornall saw in Patrick Street, it must have reached there much longer after Emmet's party had passed than he stated. He had been able to see every detail of Emmet's uniform in the twilight. It was very dark by the time McCabe's party reached there.

† General Fox's account of the proceedings of that night include a description of this engagement, which seems to indicate that the rebels moved with some regularity and in formation. According to that account " about half past nine Oclock Mr. Drury, a Magistrate, called upon Lieutenant Douglas at the Coombe, where he commanded the Light Company of the 21st Regiment, consisting of about 57 Rank and File. Mr. Drury informed him that disturbances were apprehended, and that it was his intention to patrol the streets every two hours—at ten, twelve, and so on during the night. He further cautioned Lieut. Douglas to be alert ; and especially to take care of the Barracks. This officer in consequence gave the necessary orders to his Centinels, and the magistrate had hardly left him with his patrole when he received instructions from the sentry which induced him to turn out the company and make them put on their accoutrements and prime and load. He now received intelligence that Mr. Drury with his patrols were at the head of Meath Street, surrounded by the rioters. This led him to move with his men toward the spot, and he there met the magistrate.

" On opening Meath Street, he found the rebels regularly formed across the street, armed with pikes. He then requested orders to fire upon them. This was refused by Mr. Drury, he alledging that this part of town was not in his jurisdiction, tho' in this case it certainly would be difficult to account for his patrolling in it. The lieutenant upon this wished to return to his Barracks, but the Justice would not allow it, and stated the necessity of the whole company moving down Meath Street. It is to be remarked that the whole of this conversation was overheard by the insurgents, whose leader, walking in their front, was distinctly encouraging them, and desiring them to be steady.

" The part of the 21st then moved forward, when the rebels, wheeling back from their center, with their backs to the houses, formed a lane or defile for the soldiers to pass : Lieutenant Douglas observing this, gave orders distinctly and loudly to his men to fire, if the least attempt was made upon them. The instant this was heard by the opposite party, a number of them threw down their pikes and fled ; whilst in the confusion caused by this circumstance the party of the 21st moved on rapidly. Their steadiness was more than the insurgents found themselves equal to oppose, and they ran away in all directions leaving the street quite clear in a few minutes except one old wretch, who had the audacity to attempt piking a soldier. He knocked him down with the butt end of his firelock, and then proceeded down Meath Street, along Thomas Street, where they drove a party armed with pikes out of the Market House, and returned to the Coombe through Francis Street. It had scarcely arrived at Barrack when it was attacked. The magistrate now gave Mr. Douglas authority to fire, when two rounds completely terminated the affair ; and although subsequent information proved that repeated attempts were made to induce these wretches to renew the attack, they could never be brought again to show themselves. . . ." P.R.O.I., National Library of Ireland, and published in An t-Oglach, Vol. 1, No. 4, 1928.

Testifying at the State trials, Lieutenant Douglas said that the rebels, who numbered,

A gentleman from Tipperary, Mr. Donough McCreath, arrived at the Canal Harbour at nineteen minutes before ten that night. As he went toward Thomas Street, he became part of the mob Pat McCabe was with and was swept along toward Bridgefoot Street. He saw pikes thrown out of houses and saw people stoop to pick them up. Some of the men had swords and blunderbusses and muskets, but eventually most of them were armed with pikes. He himself, he testified on the state trials, was forced to take one and was pushed to the front of his particular party. He had on military boots, which may have mislead his neighbours in the crowd into thinking he was a leader ; and on being asked if he were a friend, he diplomatically said that he was.

The mob pushed on as far as the Cornmarket and Cutpurse Row and then stopped. It was here that McCabe's section separated from the remainder and went up Francis Street. Mr. McCreath's portion, though it was repeatedly urged by a soldier in a red uniform to keep together, broke off and surged back to Bridgefoot Street.* No one appeared intoxicated, but the men were very violent. Several of them wanted to attack the Castle.

as nearly as he could estimate, from three to four hundred, having charged his party with a great shout, got three volleys from the guard drawn up outside the barracks. On his being asked if any of the rebels had been killed he said he did not like to advance his men in the dark for fear of being surrounded ; for, if he had gone up Francis Street, the rebels might have come on his rear from the Poddle and another small street near it. At daylight, however, he found four men lying dead within a few yards of his station, and he was told by a gentleman that he had seen fourteen or fifteen dead bodies being carried through Francis Street.

The rebel menace was evidently not considered as dissipated by that time, because Major Robertson's report says that, after the rebels had been repulsed at the Coombe Barracks, a reinforcement of a company from the Cork Street Barracks was sent there.

Anne Develin's " Life " says that many of the deserters Arthur Develin had brought with him from England fell in Francis Street and the Coombe, and that " they kept together the whole night." Arthur himself did not return to Butterfield Lane till next morning.

" I think," Anne continued, " that there were more soldiers fell that night than the public knew of. I am well informed that no person was allowed to go through Francis Street that morning until after the dead soldiers were carted off from it."

* " The man in the red coat who appears on Felix Rourke's Trial," Mr. Wickham wrote Mr. Abbott in November, " was one Bannon, who had been a common soldier. The Generals in green had fled before this man came forward." *Colchester Correspondence*, I, p. 451. This was quite true, but in one of the official accounts sent out by Wickham he said that Lord Kilwarden was murdered before Lieutenant Brady had his encounter with the rebels. This distortion of the truth was evidently made to connect Emmet with the murder, which happened at least an hour after Emmet left Thomas Street.

"Damn the Army," they were saying. "We're not afraid of them. The town will be ours in half an hour."

Mr. McCreath, so he said, tried to get away, but every time he made an effort to do so he was forced back and not allowed to put down his pike. When Lord Kilwarden, the Chief Justice, driving into town from his country seat from Clondalkin with his daughter and nephew, encountered the rebels in Thomas Street, Mr. McCreath was just opposite the carriage. (So, as it happened, were the two fake French emissaries who had come in with Carey and his sons from Kildare.) None of the accounts Mr. McCreath gave later goes into details of the murders of Lord Kilwarden and his nephew ; how they were dragged from the carriage and piked to death, and Miss Wolfe allowed to go unharmed. He did not say that he tried to help them. He did not describe the men who pulled the two victims from the carriage.

On the State trials he said that, when the attention of the mob was on the carriage, he gave a young man who had continually prevented him from leaving the mob some money, and that he was then allowed to escape and drop his pike. The counsel for the Crown made quite a point of this and even re-examined Mr. McCreath to bring it out.

The witness dramatised his relations with this person very vividly.

There was one man more violent than the rest at the beginning, and he was going to pike me several times. I offered some money to befriend me ; I told him the money would be of no use to him if the others took it ; he then seemed inclined to assist me, but he would not allow me to speak to him, and he cried out "Damn you, don't speak to me." When the attention of the people was drawn toward the carriage, I said to the man, "This is the time, if you have a mind to serve me." He took hold of the pike, and I gave him what money I had in my pocket, twenty shillings in silver, and a guinea, and guinea and a half note. He kept the pike and the money and I got off.

But in an account in Mr. McCreath's handwriting, now with some examinations at the State Paper Office and evidently written before the State trials, the young man who befriended Mr. McCreath appears in a very different light. On Mr. McCreath's offering him money he replied, "Hold your peace, perhaps I may give you an opportunity."

About this time [McCreath wrote] a carriage drew up. I was nearly opposite to the carriage when it stopped. Drivers very confused. They [the rebels] presented pistols into the carriage. Saw two people taken out of the carriage but could not tell who they were. The young man took my pike and allowed me to escape. I offered him a pocket book and he declined it. . . .

I went to the Castle and told Major Sirr about what had happened. He said he could not bring dead men to life. . . .

CHAPTER TWENTY-FIVE

Immediate Aftermath

BY nine that evening the appearance of calm and placid indifference that Marsden had so carefully preserved at the Castle all day had been shattered, but since the rebels had finally broken out there was no longer any need to maintain it. Indeed, a certain amount of alarm and the sense of danger now suited Marsden's purpose. The huge iron gates that barred entrance to the lower and upper court-yards were closed ; cannon were rolled up to repel any rebel attack. The exciting red of military uniforms predominated over civilian cloth as the guard was at last strongly reinforced. News of the insurrection and details of related disturbances kept pouring in. Magistrates and yeomen officers still besieged Marsden's office asking to be allowed to act. Some terrified gentlemen from the country sent word to Major Sirr in his office in the lower Yard that the Dublin insurgents would be joined that night by men from Prosperous and other near-by Kildare towns. Sirr relayed the warning to Marsden in writing whose irregularity betrayed his own extreme agitation.

About nine-thirty Mr. Clarke returned to the Castle dripping with blood to tell of having been fired on at the Quays as he was returning home to Palmerstown.* Shortly after this Miss Wolfe, Lord Kilwarden's daughter, hysterical with fright, found her way to Marsden's office in the upper Yard. A mounted dragoon who had also witnessed the murder of her father and cousin clattered in about the same time. Mr. McCreath gave his own account of the gory transaction. The Lord Mayor of Dublin added to the excitement by rushing in to say that a party of men had stormed the Mansion House

---

* It was Barney Doogan who had shot Mr. Clarke, and that circumstance and the fact that Sirr's men watching the depot in Thomas Street had seen him leaving it twice on July 23 later had a most important effect on Irish history. See p. 394.

and robbed it of all its arms. A slater from Naas, riding into town to warn Colonel Wolfe of the intentions of the rebels, had noticed many men marching along the line of the canal. He hurried on to notify Marsden of the danger.

In the midst of this confusion and consternation Marsden remained perfectly calm and in control of the situation. He now gave permission to the anxious magistrates to take out detachments of troops ; he sent on to General Fox the warning about the Kildare men coming along the canal. He wrote notes to the various barracks urging that parties of soldiers be sent to the streets where there was fighting. (Later, he claimed that he was not responsible for the insurrection because it was not his duty to give orders to the military.) Then he sat down to send official notification of Ireland's latest rebellion to the English Government.

The letter was a masterpiece of carefully selected facts mixed with prevarication. Given the benefit of hindsight, the impression he meant to convey and the use he intended to make of the rising are obvious in every line. Addressing himself to Lord Pelham, he wrote that he was much afflicted to inform his Lordship that a very serious degree of insurrection had broken out in Dublin and its vicinity. (Intended impression : alarm. Ultimate object : repeal of the Habeas Corpus Act. When it suited his purpose, the " serious insurrection " became a brief rioting by a handful of rabble.) He gave no indication of the extent of the information he had received of the rebels' widespread plans, or of how long he had known of their intentions ; he merely said that for some days past they had heard that a rising was talked of, and that it was asserted by many that it would take place.

Such precautions were taken as the circumstances appeared to warrant, but the mischievous disposition which prevails at present is beyond what was calculated upon. [Object : to prevent blame from falling upon himself.]

Early this day we heard from the neighbourhood of the capital particularly on the Kildare side, that the country people had forsaken their labour under an idea of marching to Dublin. The sensation excited by this in Dublin and in the country encreased in that degree during the day that the mobs in the street toward evening assumed a very formidable appearance. [True, but not the whole truth.]

General Fox and Sir Chas. Asgill concerted measures with the Lord Lieutenant to make the best disposition of the forces of the garrison that circumstances would permit of, and the Yeomanry collected and their services were made use of. [Both assertions false. Some yeomanry officers did take independent action later that night but they had not been allowed to collect or to arm and they had no ammunition.]

As yet order is in no degree restored, and I am distressed beyond measure to acquaint your Lordship that I heard Lord Kilwarden has been stopped in his carriage in Thomas Street, and has been put to death, and I believe his son has shared the same fate. [It was Lord Kilwarden's nephew who had been killed.] A magistrate of the name of Clarke has also been shot at in the street, and is badly wounded. [Exaggerated.]

I write this to your Lordship without being able to communicate with the Lord Lieutenant in the Park. [False.] I shall send another messenger in the morning to inform your Lordship of what further occurs in this most distressing business. . . .

Miss Wolfe was in the carriage with her father and brother, and she says they were both killed. It may not be a fact, but the tide will have fallen if I detain the messenger.*

Two hours later, writing to the Lord Lieutenant in the Park, Marsden made his first mention of how useful the rising might be.

"This has been a most unfortunate business, but however severe in its present circumstance it will excite a feeling which may materially serve us hereafter."

He also made the important revelation that he was in communication with spies placed among the rebel leaders. "I am told that the heads of the parties remained at home, blaming what has been done."

Most important of all was a concluding paragraph that indicated that Marsden was the directing force at the Castle, and not the Lord Lieutenant, at least, while Wickham was away. "It will be necessary to-morrow to take some strong measures in the way of Proclamations and Instructions to Magistrates. We need not now wait for the Suspension of the Habeas Corpus Act." †

In spite of the fact that Mr. Wilson, the peace officer, had known before nine on Saturday evening that the rebels were being armed at the depot on Thomas Street, it was not till after midnight that any attempt was made to investigate the place, and then its discovery had the appearance of being quite accidental.

A detachment of troops taken out by Alderman Darley

* *Vice Roy's Post Bag*, p. 294.
† P.R.O.L.

late in the evening included some regulars of the 38th Regiment and a heterogeneous party commanded by Lieutenant Coultman of the 9th. Lieutenant Coultman had heard of the intended rising during the day and had duly reported it to Brigadier-General Dunne at the Royal Barracks. He had then taken a carriage out to Finglas, four or five miles to the north-west of Dublin, where his uncle, Captain Woodward, was visiting a friend. The two officers returned to the city, where, according to Lieutenant Coultman's testimony on the State trials, he met a party who had taken a rebel with a pike. The Lieutenant took these exhibits to General Dunne and said that the business had begun.

What instructions the General gave the young officer did not develop on the trials, but they certainly did not cause him to take any action at that time. He said he tried to get some yeomen of the Barrack Division together, but that they had no arms and could get none.

He went to his own lodgings on Arran Quay, not five minutes walk from Bridgefoot Street, and quite near those of his uncle, and remained for some time. The insurrection was going on all this time, and the sounds of firing from Thomas Street must have been heard on the Quays.

About midnight some roving yeomen found a box of cartridges on a cart in Bridgefoot Street, near Bonham Street, which was between Thomas Street and the Quays, and took them to Captain Woodward. They wanted the Captain and his nephew to go out with them, and though they could muster no more than a couple of blunderbusses, three firelocks, some swords and pistols, the officers did not again refuse to lead them.

Their party consisted of a sergeant and eleven privates of the Barrack Division of Yeomen, a sergeant and two men of the 9th Regiment, and eight or ten volunteers in coloured clothes but wearing cross-belts. They evidently headed straight for the place where the cartridges had been found and became part of Alderman Darley's party. (The Alderman, who had gone to Marsden early in the day to ask permission to act, had first been refused, but on his second visit to the Castle just as Miss Wolfe arrived there he had been given leave to take out some troops.)

As Lieutenant Coultman's party came up Bridgefoot Street from the Quays, a man ran down Bonham Street and tried to hide in a timber yard. He was pulled out and handed to Major Gordon, who was patrolling with a detachment of the 32nd Foot. Lieutenant Coultman's party then went up an alley that leads to the Marshalsea from the north, and there they were hailed by the Marshal.

The Marshalsea guard had been under arms for hours with only six rounds of ammunition per man, in constant dread of an attack by the rebels. The Marshal wanted to borrow some shells from Lieutenant Coultman, but his detachment was short, too, and could spare only a few cartridges. While the Lieutenant was sharing these with the Marshal, Sergeant Jeff of the 38th Regiment came up to say that he was sure the lane (meaning Mass Lane) was full of rebels, but, having only twelve men, he was unwilling to attack them.

The two little forces united and went forward cautiously, the lieutenant lighting the way with a flambeau.

They met no rebels, but at the depot they came upon great piles of pikes that blocked the lane for anything larger than a man on foot. Just beyond the pikes a deserted hackney coach was standing, the horses hot and breathing heavily as though they had just driven up. Inside the coach were some things that Alderman Darley spoke of as " articles of treasonable appearance." *

The pikes the patrol found were piled against the wall, with the blunt ends down, as if dropped out of a window of the warehouse. Two yeomen climbed up on them to get into the depot. Then a lamplighter's ladder was brought, and the Lieutenant mounted to the deserted lofts.

There were the printed proclamations, drying but still damp, tied in bundles nearly two feet thick. There were flints and more pikes and great numbers of hand-grenades lying on the floor, and hundreds of bundles of ball cartridges.

" There's enough ammunition here for ten thousand men," exclaimed the astonished soldier.

The men explored the depot by the light of a lantern. They

---

* Who the occupant of the coach had been has not transpired. He was probably one of Emmet's fellow-officers who had arrived too late to take part in the rising. When the driver of the coach called at the depot for his pay, he was taken up, detained and, questioned, but the results of his examination are not now available.

found the false partitions Quigley and Howley had built, and
even more pikes behind them, and more packages of proclamations.   They found sky-rockets and pitch and eight of
Emmet's explosive beams, besides musket balls, a scaling
ladder (the only one of ten that Emmet had wanted for the
attack on the castle), some chains, and grappling irons.

It was through a window in the second loft that the men
had entered the warehouse.   Lieutenant Coultman now took
the lantern and went down a sort of ship's ladder to the loft
below.   This was where Emmet had had his headquarters,
and his desk was still standing in the middle of the floor.   A
French trunk was there, too, with a French shirt inside it.

In one corner were mattresses where men had been sleeping.
Near by were scraps of white cashmere, left from the uniform
breeches Colgan the tailor had been making earlier in the week.
A green coat heavily laced with gold was there, too, and a
military cocked hat to go with it.   (It was Dowdall's uniform,
Quigley said later.)   And there were banners of green with
white edging as befitted an Irish army.   Cooling but still
pungently fresh were the forgotten baskets of bread that were
to have fed the men before they went out, mute evidence of
the prematurity of the rising.

The floor of this loft, the Lieutenant discovered, was covered
with loose powder so thick that, when he stepped in it, his
shoes were covered nearly to the ankles.   The whole place, he
realised, was liable to explode at any minute if a spark should
reach the powder.   He ordered the men with him to go
outside and sent for a reinforcement.   Major Gordon and his
party were there for a while, then one of the 38th under Major
Greville took over.

Day was breaking now, and all that section of Dublin was
swarming with soldiers and civil magistrates searching houses,
ransacking for papers, and making arrests wholesale.   Alderman
Darley had already done some investigating of the premises
surrounding the depot and was then in the depot himself,
helping in the search that was still going on there.

He found the manuscript of Emmet's treatise on the art
of war, and a letter addressed to Robert Ellis, Butterfield.
He gave them to Lieutenant Evelyn of the 38th, who had
gathered up the manuscript of the long proclamation, a bill

from a Rathfarnham grocer, a chemistry note-book, and a table of logarithms. With them were the two letters Emmet had written Sarah Curran.

When Colonel Vassal, the Officer of the Day, was brought to the depot by Major Greville, he, too, noticed the danger of explosion from the loose powder. In fact, he was surprised that the depot had not exploded long before. He lifted the lid of Emmet's desk, saw bundles of ball cartridges and other combustibles, and shut it quickly, overlooking some letters of Emmet's that lay underneath. He had Major Greville send for carts to transfer the military stores to the Royal Barracks, took over from Lieutenant Evelyn all the papers he had collected, ordered every one outside, and left the place himself within a quarter of an hour of his entering it.

It was broad daylight when Emmet's desk was handed down from a window in the first loft to soldiers on sentry duty outside and put on a blue artillery cart. Load after load of pikes and other military stores went creaking down the hill to the Quays, over Queen's Bridge, and up the river to the Royal Barracks. Each load was accompanied by an officer's guard, and at the barracks they were put in charge of the Quartermaster Sergeant.*

* Colonel Vassal later furnished the Castle with a list of the military stores taken from the depot, and the *Dublin Evening Post* on August 27 printed a list that tallies with it in most respects. As it is more detailed in some of its descriptions, it is quoted here rather than Colonel Vassal's :

" 11 deal boxes fill with powder and made-up ammunition.

14 bundles of Cannon Powder, No. 1, about 140 lbs.

246 Hand Grenades, formed of ink bottles, filled with powder and encircled with buckshot.

104 Champaign Bottles, filled with powder, enveloped with musket balls, and covered with canvas.

42,000 rounds of musket ball cartridges, tied up in parcels of 20 each, and 4 flints attached to each parcels. [Vassal's account said 36,400.]

1 scaling ladder complete.

156 grappling irons for scaling ladders.

2½ bushels of musket balls (about 150,000) tied up in four each being charges for blunderbusses.

14 quires of cartridge paper.

2 deal cases of skyrockets and other signals [Serpents, etc., according to Vassal's list.]

1 box of tin tubes for the hand grenades.

496 hooks, chisels, etc.

48 quires of the Proclamation of the Provisional Government.

1 large bench vice.

108 cartridge formers.

8 pieces de Sauciesse 78 yards in length (Gunpowder made up in a long roll like a sausage.)

One piece of Green cloth.

2 saws, 2 planes, an old desk with several interesting memorandums in it.

Automatically, they had become evidence of Emmet's treason and were now weapons, not against the Government, but against Emmet himself.

" The above is an exact return of what was delivered to his Majesty's stores at the Royal Barracks, of course does not include the vast quantity of pikes which were broken up, nor the rebel standards, uniforms, bread newly baked, porter, etc.

" The pikes amounted to upward of seventeen thousand. They were of simple form and workmanship, and were broken up by the soldiery, not being deemed necessary to deposit them in the stores."

Vassal's account said 5,000 pikes. Probably more were found later behind the secret panels. Vassal's account also included " 8 logs of deal about ten feet long and one foot square each, bored in the center nearly from end to end, the tube cavity about two and half inches Diameter, charged with gunpowder, the Logs cased round with a Wooden Frame, filled with stones about a pound each. Also 8 single S Iron chains, 9 yards long each."

This inventory confirms the account that Miles Byrne gave Thomas Addis Emmet in September (see p. 301) that a great deal of ammunition and many pikes were lost on the twenty-third, but that the arms were safe. The inevitable implication is that the arms were not under Emmet's control that night but in charge of some of the men who had deserted him. He could not have suspected these men, as he was evidently expecting to be able to use the arms later on. However, their not being available on the twenty-third ensured that the rebels would be easily disposed of when they finally met opposition.

CHAPTER TWENTY-SIX

The Rising Elsewhere

KILDARE

BESIDES the men it sent into Dublin, the County of Kildare had its own action and excitements that Saturday night. It was fitting and also inevitable that they should centre around Maynooth, where the memory of Lord Edward Fitzgerald was still cherished as warmly as that much-beloved person had been in life, and where his influence was still strongly felt.*

Lord Edward's brother, the Duke of Leinster, whose family seat, Carton, was close to the ruins of the ancient Fitzgerald castle of Maynooth, was also, quite unconsciously on his part, responsible for a great deal of suppressed excitement as the eve of the rising approached. In some way the idea that the Duke was friendly to the rebels had become prevalent, and it was even whispered about that he was going to lead them in person. As the Geraldines had always been in sympathy with the native Irish, and some of them had even gone so far as to revolt against the English Government—Silken Thomas and the Earl of Desmond in Elizabeth's time, Lord Edward Fitzgerald only five years back—this did not seem fantastic to the ardent nationalists of the county.

Naturally, Robert Emmet did not know how the Duke of Leinster was figuring in the expectations of the Kildare people, but he did realise how strong love of liberty was in that part of the country. That was why he had counted so heavily on support from it, and why, even though many Kildare men were to come into Dublin for the attack there, he had expected

* " There is a more general and rooted spirit of disaffection in [Kildare] than in any other part of Ireland," Lord Hardwicke wrote to his brother in August. " This circumstance . . . is in a great measure, if not entirely, to be attributed to the industry with which Lord Edward Fitzgerald corrupted the whole of the county." *Vice Roy's Post Bag*, p. 386. This is only one of many illustrations of the way in which Lord Edward's devotion to the idea of Irish liberty and independence lived after him.

that many others would assemble at various places in the county, and that some local engagements would take place. Nicholas Grey, whom he had designated as General of the county, had taken a house near Athy in order to lead a contingent of Kildare men into Dublin after the main attack had been made. (Emmet had purposely limited the number of men to be sent into the city so that it would not appear to be more crowded than usual for a Saturday night.)

About the middle of July, Emmet had introduced Grey to three men from Maynooth who were to head local engagements at Maynooth and Celbridge and then join the main Kildare rebels near Rathcoole. They were Thomas Kereghan, Thomas Frayne, a well-to-do farmer, and Owen Lyons. Lyons had been in the depot in Thomas Street many times, particularly the week before the rising, and had once taken a box of 1,500 rounds of ball cartridges home with him. All these men had been provided with green uniforms faced with white and trimmed with gold epaulettes. Carter Connolly, a teacher in the lay college attached to Maynooth seminary, also had a uniform and was designated a captain.

Rumours that a rising was going to take place that Saturday night were as prevalent in Maynooth as they were in Dublin, and there, too, many more people than usual appeared on the streets. Among them, of course, was a secret agent of the Government, Daniel Collison, son of the postmaster of the place. Since March he had been sending information of the rebels plans to Alderman James in Dublin, who had it sent on to the Castle.

About eight that evening, Lyons, Connolly, and Kereghan, all wearing their green uniforms, assembled more than a hundred excited men in the main street of the town of Maynooth. Some had brought pikes and blunderbusses carefullly saved since 1798 ; the leaders armed others with an assortment of muskets, carbines, pistols, and swords that had been gathered from a variety of sources. The head of the lay college where Connolly taught had donated two muskets and a dozen foils. Collison accepted a pistol, and as far as any one could see, he was as enthusiastic a rebel as any one there.

The first martial act of the little army was to make prisoners of two dragoons who had accompanied the mail coach from

Dublin the night before. Then, all the men not yet being provided with arms, small detachments raided the houses of near-by loyalists for more weapons. Meanwhile, the main body, unopposed by any one, marched up and down the main street, practising military exercises.

They made so much noise that a local exciseman who had slipped away to Carton to warn the Duke of Leinster of the rising was able to overcome his doubts by having the Duke walk to the front of the house to listen to the martial sounds coming from the town. But instead of doing anything to stop the rebels, the Duke sent a servant to Lyons to say that his arms were ready to be taken, and that the men would find refreshments laid out for them.* Lyons, however, decided not to take the arms at that time but sent word to the Duke that he would get them the next night.

About midnight the rebels prepared to attack the mail coach on its arrival from Dublin. They were divided into three parties and placed at intervals of about a hundred yards apart. The first division, headed by Lyons, was armed with muskets, carbines, and blunderbusses. Kereghan's party came next armed with pistols, and the third under Connolly was placed on the bridge. A barricade had been made by drawing up some cars, and it was expected that, if the coach should get through the first two lines, it would be slowed down enough by the barricade to allow Connolly's men to kill the coach horses with pikes.

As the coach, accompanied by a pair of dragoons, loomed up out of the darkness, the first party fired wildly in their direction. The coachman whipped up his horses, the dragoons spurred their mounts, and all dashed forward. The second party of rebels gave a volley that turned the dragoons back to Dublin, but the coach kept on ; and as it approached the bridge, Connolly's men threw down their pikes and let it pass.

Lyons and Kereghan then marched their parties to Celbridge, a few miles to the south, where they expected to be joined by a large party under the command of Thomas Frayne. That leader, however, was already showing a certain timidity that was later to have unfortunate results. He told the Maynooth

---

* He had fourteen stand of arms, enough, as the exciseman pointed out, to arm the servants and make a stand against the rebels. The Duke, however, ignored the suggestion. P.R.O.L.

men that his followers would not be ready till the next night.

The rebels then separated into small groups. Some went on raiding for arms. Lyons left for Rathcoole, where he expected to find General Grey and a large army.

Near the Ten Mile House on the Naas Road, Kereghan's raiding party encountered Colonel Aylmer, who was returning from his day in Dublin. The rebel vedette ordered the postillion to stop, but the driver whipped up his horses and drove on. Other rebels, however, were all along the road, armed and menacing. The Colonel and the clergyman who was with him took to the fields as their only hope of escape, pursued (so the Colonel later asserted) by hundreds of rebels.

Dozens of Kildare householders were wakened that night by parties of rebels demanding arms. The loyal gentlemen gave them fearfully and reluctantly. Others handed them over with more grace. Mr. Timothy Daly of Griffinrath, half-way between Maynooth and Celbridge, gave the party that called on him the flints and powder that they asked for, and also invited them in for a breakfast of bread, beer, tea, and eggs.

Early Sunday morning, Lyons came back from his mission to Rathcoole with the news that he had not been able to see Grey, and that the rising in Dublin had been a failure. He said, however, that there would be an attack again that night, and on that supposition the men were kept together. There were more raids for arms in the vicinity of Rathcoole. That being Quigley's home neighbourhood, all four leaders, with Collison, who had attached himself to them, paid a visit to his family and dined there.

The main body of rebels spent Sunday night on Windgate Hill, expecting to march into Dublin the next day.

Meanwhile, the Duke of Leinster, acting on his own initiative, and with more sympathy for the rebels than realisation of how serious a matter it is to take part in an insurrection, had sent word that, if the rebels would return home, there would be no inquiry into the business. Collison shrewdly urged them to accept the offer and acted as their intermediary.

Monday morning a few tired and discouraged Maynooth men handed over their arms. Connolly turned in a blunderbuss. The other leaders did not appear, and most of the rebels held on to their weapons hoping to use them later. The town put on the appearance of tranquillity, but, like all Kildare, the spirit of disaffection still prevailed there.

Collison, having learned as much as he could about the men responsible for the rising and those who had taken part in it, slipped away to Dublin, and by Tuesday his account of it was at the Castle. Thereafter, he was kept busy for some time providing lists of the men who had been in arms and helping to identify prisoners as they were brought in by yeomen and regular soldiers.

THE NORTH

On the morning of July 23, while Thomas Russell was still at Loughin Island trying to raise men for a rebel army, Brigadier-General Colin Campbell, the military officer in charge at Belfast, received an anonymous letter warning him that a rising was to take place in the city that night. Already rumours of an impending revolt were circulating through the North, and the General knew enough of the temper of the people not to dismiss the warning lightly. Soon detachments of cavalry came galloping back to the garrison from outlying districts, and it was put in readiness to repel an attack.

The warning letter had been sent by McGucken, doubtless on orders from Mr. Marsden.* The little spy also sent a similar message to Mr. Whinnery, the postmaster of the city. Ten years before, Whinnery had helped create a mass hysteria among the loyalists of Belfast by circulating a rumour that Sam McTier was arranging for a French invasion. He now did the same thing by talking of rebels assembled by the thousand in the outskirts of the city.

McGucken was almost as busy as Marsden that day. He had to keep in contact with as many of the disaffected as possible in order to learn all their plans and be able to frustrate them. He was expecting to be called on to lead the Belfast men himself, but he learned that afternoon that the would-be rebels now considered him as too cautious a person. They

---

* Officially, Marsden was not admitting any knowledge of possible trouble in the North, and this was a convenient way of giving the General all the information Marsden thought necessary for him to have. McGucken's connection with the Castle was not then known to officials in Belfast. He certainly would not have taken such a step except by authority, and he was in constant communication with Marsden.

wanted some one " more desperate " for the attack. However, the Belfast company, though it was obviously anxious to fight, came under the same frustrating influence which Russell had met as soon as he reached the North, and which continued to operate wherever groups of rebels gathered. When Hamilton, who was in the country above Belfast, sent into town that evening to ask what the Belfast men intended to do, he got back a blunt answer from one Stephen Wall : " Let the people mind their work. Belfast will not rise."

Still hopeful, Hamilton and Jimmy Hope went to Kells where they found some young men in high spirits and eager to act. Others of the same disposition met him at Craigvally. But that night, as Hamilton waited outside Ballymena to take command of forces there, word came to an apothecary whom McGucken had often mentioned as a local leader that Russell had gone to Dublin to prevent a rising there. McGucken's hand seems apparent in the false report, which stripped Hamilton of all his followers except Jimmy Hope and one other and left the trio in an empty field.

At that time Thomas Russell, disappointed at not receiving the support he had expected at Loughin Island, was making his way toward Belfast in the hope of finding men mustered there.* As a member of the proposed provisional Government of Ireland and General of the Northern District, Russell had written a provocative proclamation :

Men of Ireland, once more in arms to assert the rights of mankind and liberate your country, you see by the secrecy with which this effort has been conducted, and by the multitudes who in all parts of Ireland are engaged in executing this great object, that your Provisional Government has acted wisely. You will see that in Dublin, in the West, in the North and in the South, the blow has been struck at the same moment. . . .

He had not intended to publish the proclamation until after the rising had begun, but already copies of it were being handed about in the places where he had visited. In

---

* He went to John Green's, near Cave Hill, a few miles outside Belfast. After learning of the Belfast failure he went back to James Witherspoon's at Knockbracken for a day or two, and then, as the yeomanry were combing the countryside and Witherspoon's was often searched, he went into hiding elsewhere. At his trial no evidence was brought forward to indicate where he was after he left Fitzpatrick's at Loughin Island, and the prosecution rested its charge of high treason on his activities in trying to get men to take part in an insurrection.

Carnmoney, Andrew Hunter read it to men drinking their
Saturday-night rum in the local pubs before posting it on the
meeting-house door. Then he went to the Widow Gardiner's to
wait for recruits to assemble. Over their rum a few men talked
hopefully of the great turnouts of rebels that would take place
in all parts of Ireland that night. But time went on, and only
a score of men had volunteered. Eventually, armed with old
pikes and muskets, and with Hunter in a borrowed jacket at
their head, they set off for Broughshane, where they expected
to find an encampment.

At Downpatrick candles burned late in many cottages as
men waited up to join the rebels when they marched into town
from a near-by rendezvous. But only a few volunteers
appeared at the appointed place, and the signal fire that they
expected to see lighted at Seaford was never kindled. At two
in the morning they went back to their homes.

McGucken had managed to get his younger brother
appointed as captain of the Malone men. He was out all
night with the rebels there, but as they had received no general
orders and none came to them, they, too, disbanded and went
to their homes early Sunday morning.

Other groups of rebels assembled at Cave Hill, at Cumber,
and in the vicinity of Shane's Castle. At Larne, four or five
hundred men armed with pikes went through military
exercises in a field near the town.

At one o'clock on Sunday morning the drums of the
Belfast garrison beat to arms. Rumours spread through town
that the rebels were approaching. The fears of the citizens
almost reached hysteria, but the attack never materialised.

Later that day, General Campbell received a second anonymous letter. Belfast would surely be attacked that night, it
said. As several messages had reached him telling of assemblies
of armed men throughout the near-by counties, he thought it
prudent to bring to Belfast a detachment of dragoons then
stationed at Lisburn, a few miles away. The troops dashed
into town at three the next morning, giving the Belfast people
their second spectacular alarm and leaving Lisburn quaking
with terror. On Tuesday a detachment of the 50th Regiment
left Ballymena for Belfast, again alarming both towns. The
consternation at Ballymena, which every hour was expecting

to be attacked, was so great that many of the ladies left town with the Army and took refuge in Belfast.

Russell's proclamation had already caused great consternation among loyalists at Lisburn, and the new rumours that were afloat excited considerable consternation. The Reverend Samuel Cupples, who had long taken an unsympathetic interest in Russell, wrote to a friend in Dublin that the withdrawal of the troops left them without even a military guard, and that most of the people of the town were sitting up all night.

Mr. Whinney gave some idea of the degree of consternation in the North when he wrote his superior in Dublin that a renewed disposition to insurrection had been discovered there. Three thousand rebels, he claimed, had been assembled at the rear of Cave Hill. This was the wildest exaggeration ; the postmaster had characteristically added a cypher where it did the most good.

Mr. Marsden received several accounts of the consternation in the North. One of his correspondents, writing from Dungannon, ventured to suggest something that doubtless was already in Marsden's mind.

The sensation produced by the accounts of the 23rd ought to be made good use of by encreasing the strength of the yeomanry. If any good squibs against the French appear . . . pray send them to my brother or me, that they may be printed or circulated. You can't conceive with what avidity they are read when bought, but in the North nothing is valued that does not cost something.

Whether he got the squibs against the French has not transpired, but the yeomen were increased and were most active in searching out the disaffected.*

For months McGucken had been sending Marsden the names of men who should be taken up " when the arrests begin." All restraints were now automatically removed. On July 24, a detachment of the Newtown Yeomanry took up Archibald McClean, who had met Russell at James Witherspoon's. One by one others who had been at the meetings were apprehended and lodged in gaol.

* The middle of November, when every known rebel had been put into gaol, Marsden was still stirring up Northern yeomanry officers to find out who had attended a meeting at Crevilly on July 24, where Jimmy Hope had endeavoured to raise recruits.

The Carnmoney men most noted for their disaffection were also taken up. Among them was a man who had been in Dublin in May and had returned full of enthusiasm for a new rising. He had been one of the most active in that part of the country in stirring up rebellion. Another prisoner for whom officials had a certain reluctant respect was John Vint. They called him a bold, daring man. His nephew, fourteen-year-old William Rodgers, was also arrested and kept in gaol for years. He had been caught red-handed distributing Russell's proclamation at Carnmoney, but he refused, then and later, to tell from whom he had got it.

Wednesday, July 27, a troop of the Lower Iveagh Yeomanry went to Castlereagh Hill to look for some men who had been reported drilling in a field to the tune of a fife. The yeomen did not find the drilling men, and when they searched houses in the neighbourhood, including James Witherspoon's (which Russell had just left), they found no male persons at home.

" This is the usual case," said the troop's lieutenant in making his report, " though in some instances there are three or five looms in the houses.

" General Russell has issued a second proclamation in which, not withstanding the apparent failure in Dublin, he promises ultimate success to the cause in which his followers are engaged."

LIMERICK AND KERRY

For a few seconds that famous Saturday night rockets lighted the Limerick sky. They were signals of the disaffected, evidence that the darkness covered secret activities of hopeful men. They spoke figuratively of school-teachers with democratic ideas, of shop-owners who had smuggled arms into the district, of the men who had toasted Irish liberty in Turner's tavern, of dozens of smiths who had risked their lives making pikes of a new style that looked like pitchforks, of hundreds upon hundreds of simple, stubborn people determined to fight that their country might be free.

But who actually touched off the signals, what message they conveyed, and to whom, are still only matters of conjecture. The night that closed in after their brief flares had faded is illuminated by only a few gleams of actual knowledge, but they are enough to show that in this section, as elsewhere, the activity of the disaffected was being subtly counteracted by secret agents, and that the same pattern of practice that first encouraged and then frustrated the rebels in Dublin and Kildare and the North also kept these belligerent counties from having a dangerous success.

Two local gentlemen warned General Payne that day that a rising was to take place Saturday or Sunday. From still another source he was given a general outline of the insurrection that showed that the disaffected in Limerick and Kerry were in contact with the leaders in Dublin, that they knew of the depot in Thomas Street and the part it was to play in the Dublin attack, and that the southern counties expected to act as soon as they learned of the success of the Dublin rising. Five rebel captains had been in town waiting for the news from Dublin and had left it on Sunday only when a wealthy cloth merchant, whose motives appear extremely suspicious, warned them to quit. However, they left men who were to take them the news when it arrived in Limerick.*

The Counties of Limerick, Kerry, and Clare had been visited by organisers who had administered an oath known as " the finisher." It probably pledged those who took it to take part in the fight.

Even the news of the Dublin defeat did not affect the determination of the southern counties to rise. On Wednesday, July 27, one of General Payne's gentlemen correspondents wrote him that several hundred men had met at the Shannon side that evening to take lighters that were to carry them to a meeting in County Clare. He had moved nonchalantly among them and had overheard men saying that they did not know when the rising was to take place but that they would be informed just before it. They were to rise by signals, probably the next night, on seeing lights on surrounding hills. They were going to attack whether the Leinster people succeeded or not, because they had been thought cowards for not rising in 1798, and they blamed themselves for it. They were not counting on the French but would " shake off the yoke without the assistance of any other nation."

However, there had long been reports of many French

---

* Emmet sent no messenger because of lack of funds.

" delegates " in the district, and one of them, so General
Payne learned, was to act as general of the rebel forces of
Kerry. His name was David Fitzgerald, the son of a gentle-
man living in County Kerry, and said to be a relative of the
Knight of Kerry.*

In sending this information up to Marsden, General Payne
could not have known that he was carrying coals to Newcastle.
The so-called French delegate was actually a British agent
whose history was well known at the Castle.† There can be
little doubt that he had been sent to Kerry to keep the rising
there under control and to learn who were the people involved.
He landed near Bantry Bay soon after the middle of July and
then went to his father's home near the Kerry-Limerick border.

On July 28 a Protestant clergyman of Kerry heard (as did
a Catholic priest) that an attack on the city of Limerick was
to be made within a few days. The Kerry forces, it was said,
were to be commanded by " General Fitzgerald." General

* Burke's *Landed Gentry* does not substantiate the claim. It is possible that a young
man named Fitzgerald whom Jimmy Hope saw in the depot in Thomas Street with
Emmet a week or ten days before the rising and was told was brother of the Knight
of Glyn, was this spy. Both the Knight of Kerry and the Knight of Glyn were
members of the Fitzgerald family and were much intermarried. They were extremely
loyal.

† David Fitzgerald had packed a great deal of adventure into his young life, most
of which was spent abroad. He had acted as a pilot in the Bay of Biscay, as a private
under General Hoche at La Vendée, as a seaman on a French privateer. While on
board this vessel he had been taken prisoner by the British, sent ashore, and confined
at Porchester gaol. He escaped from there and embarked on a London trader bound
for Gibralter. At the Rock the press gang picked him up and sent him to sea again,
this time as an English sailor.

Lord Keith, on whose ship he was serving, suspected that such a rampant democrat
as he had become might be giving information to the French and sent him to London
to be interrogated by police officials. They could find nothing against him but, to
be on the safe side, recommended to the Home Office that he be detained under the
Suspension of the Habeas Corpus Act. Untried and uncharged, he was sent to the
Tothill Fields Bridewell. Some of the leading members of the London Corresponding
Society, an organisation formed in the interest of democracy, were also being held
there, and the young adventurer became friendly with them. A very important
French prisoner on whom the English officials wanted to spy was one of his intimates.

The inevitable offer was made : Fitzgerald was promised his liberty provided he
would become a secret agent. He was told to insinuate himself in to all parties and
companies of the disaffected everywhere and to let Mr. Pelham and Mr. Flint know
what went on.

In 1801 he went to Ireland to visit his father, a moderately well-to-do gentleman.
In Limerick he tried out the feelings of the people by pretending to be in the French
service. This caused him to be arrested by the police officers of Limerick city, but he
explained his real position in a long letter that he sent up to the Castle. Fitzgerald
himself was soon sent there as a prisoner ; and, as the Castle people were careful to
treat him as a dangerous enemy, his value as a spy was enormously increased. From
this time on, he was regarded by the Irish people as a French delegate, some one who
was working with the French to get foreign aid for the Irish cause. P.R.O.L.

Payne, to whom this news was communicated, was naturally greatly alarmed. At first, he had discounted stories of an insurrection, but the spies he had stationed in outlying districts all insisted that the people meant to rise, and he had received other disturbing letters from various county gentlemen giving the names of some wealthy and influential men who were to act as leaders. Some very respectable gentlemen were said to have received smuggled arms intended for the rebels. However, the General was soon relieved to hear that Fitzgerald and four other French delegates had sailed for France.

Whatever excuse " General Fitzgerald " had given his men for leaving them had evidently been accepted without question. Chiefly because of his son's standing, Fitzgerald's father was now approached by two different emissaries of the disaffected.* Both of them offered him command of rebel forces. The first was told, a bit pettishly, that even if 100,000 men were collected they would have no effect against the armed body that would be brought against them. The emissary was advised to have nothing to do with such desperate persons as he was engaged with.

Bagot, one of the democratic schoolteachers General Payne had tried unsuccessfully to buy over, was told by the elder Fitzgerald that " as they did not succeed in Dublin he thought it more prudent for them to delay the rising a little longer, but if it was a thing they were determined upon he would take command of it."†

This followed so exactly the pattern of practice McGucken used in the North that it is impossible not to suspect that the elder Fitzgerald was now playing a part in Kerry similar to McGucken's in Belfast.

The concluding paragraph of this information, particular though it was as to names, also displayed a pattern or principle, this time of the disaffected.

" I know," the informer who sent the report to General

* The documents that show how the younger Fitzgerald became a spy are in the Public Record Office in London, where no restrictions are placed on their use. Those that seem to implicate the father are in the Irish State Paper Office, which does not allow the name of a hitherto unknown informer to be made public ; thus his first name is not given here, or the place of his residence. There are so many Fitzgeralds in Kerry that he cannot readily be identified without them.

† I.S.P.O. He also discouraged a group of local hot-heads, who wanted to raid the houses of some loyal gentlemen and take their arms, and kept them from acting.

Payne ended it, " that the people are all willing to rise, and that though ——— Fitzgerald should refuse to take command of them that it was supposed that Bagot had some other person to take the command." *

CORK

Up to a very short time before the twenty-third, Emmet had expected that Cork would be in arms that day as well as Dublin, Limerick, the North, and Carrick-on-Suir.† For more than ten years, in spite of the most repressive measures the Government could bring against them, the people of Cork had been exuberantly democratic. Thousands of copies of Thomas Paine's works had been printed and distributed there gratis by the same wealthy men who printed a nationalist newspaper called the *Cork Gazette*. In 1795 McNally had warned the Castle that the books were in the hands of almost every schoolmaster in the county and Paine's principles were on the tongue of every schoolboy capable of articulation. Elsewhere in an analysis of the political situation in Ireland that McNally drew up soon after he became an informer, he said that the south and west, particularly in the Counties of Cork and Kerry, " though they were young politicians . . . they would not be less prompt, if occasion offered, in attempting to annihilate the present form of government than [the Northern dissenters]."

The Cork people lost none of their love of liberty through the years. The coercive measures against the Dublin " Crops " for which Mr. Wickham complimented Mr. Cooke at the Castle in 1798 were carried on just as harshly at Cork and confirmed the people in their hatred of the alien Government. The soldiers became so insolent and overbearing that one of McNally's correspondents there wrote him that no man out of a red coat dared venture into the streets. One very respectable gentleman had been grossly mistreated and beaten. Another had had an eye cut out.

* I.S.P.O.

† Quigley later told the Government that one Mahon, of Carrick-on-Suir, was to have been the general there. No other information about him or the activities of the town of Carrick-on-Suir has survived. There was a general raiding for arms in that section of the country in June and July, and several loyal gentlemen wrote up to the Castle expressing their apprehensions that something was afoot. I.S.P.O.

The officers encourage the men and act like savages, stigmatising the whole body of the people as traitors. Should the French land now they would find a great body of friends, for the ill-conduct of the soldiery has completely alienated even the minds of the dispassionate from government, who . . . are cursed and reprobated by men, women and children.

Several young men from Cork were expelled from Trinity about that time ; John Sweeney or Swiney, one of the most influential of the United Irishmen in the city, was sent up to Dublin as a State prisoner (and then to Fort George and exile in France) ; and William Norris, later the friend of Robert Emmet and John Patten, had to leave home, all because of their devotion to the ideal of liberty. Daniel Cullinane of Cashel, who called himself General Clarke after he came back from his mission to France, travelled through Ireland as a fiery apostle of independence and found Cork as disaffected as ever. In 1801, General Myers, in command there, who was trying unsuccessfully to catch the elusive firebrand, admitted to the Castle that Clarke had had two meetings in the city recently, and that the people were ripe for rebellion and would welcome the French. " If the French land they will find more followers than they can dispose of," he wrote in another letter only a few weeks later.

In 1803, neither Clarke nor the Cork people had changed, and Emmet naturally counted on their willingness to take arms.* He wrote to Tom in Paris to have Sweeney sent home from France. In the meantime, Norris was put in charge of communications between the leaders in Dublin and the members of the provisional Government in Munster.† He visited the south himself on organising trips, and on one occasion Pollock wrote the castle that " Norris and Powers are on their way to Cork."

Again it was a case of carrying coals to Newcastle. Powers

* That spring Clarke made another of his narrow escapes from the authorities who were continually on his trail. He was in touch with one Timothy Conway of Cork, a watchmaker. Conway was supposed to be head of the disaffected in the city, but he had been an informer for some years, and through him General Myers heard of Clarke's presence in the city just too late to catch him. Conway's death on May 4 may have had some effect on the intended rising in Cork.

† Quigley did not know who they were. Later he told the Government that, as he was leaving the house at Butterfield Lane the morning after the important meeting there about the middle of July, he met Norris " and his friend from Munster " going to Emmet's. Jimmy Hope told Dr. Madden that the day before he left Dublin with Russell to raise the North, a gentleman from Cork and one from the County Meath were in the depot in Thomas Street with Emmet.

had been one of the Trinity students expelled for patriotism in 1798, but his principles had not been able to withstand the pressures put upon him soon after. He had secretly given information to Government officials and had then gone to England. He came back to Ireland in May of 1803 and, not being suspected of having deserted the national cause, was evidently admitted into the new conspiracy.

At the same time one John Fitzgerald, who a Castle correspondent thought was a Kildare man, but who may have been David Fitzgerald the British spy, was in the western part of the County Cork " preparing " the people.

Sweeney did not get back to Ireland in time to lead a rising in Cork, and for some reason now unknown Norris was in Dublin that day. Cork remained quiet, but Marsden was well informed from many sources who the dangerous men there were, and as soon as the Habeas Corpus Act was suspended he sent down to have them arrested. One by one some forty men were lodged in the gaols of the city and County of Cork. They were charged with having been concerned in the rebellion or with having acted in furtherance of it, or both. A few were charged with treasonable practices. One man was taken up for having expressed a determination that was shared by many of his country-people, that he would join the French with a pike.

THE WEST

Connemara gets its name, Country of the Sea, from the thousands of inlets and bays which penetrate the rocky shores of Galway and Mayo. Like Kerry, smuggling ships slipped easily into its hidden harbours. In 1803 their captains often brought letters from exiles in France to leaders of the rebels who had been on their keeping in the mountains since 1798. Caves and hillsides sheltered these outlaws. The sympathetic people of the district fed them.

This state of affairs was well known to the great landlords of Connemara and caused them the greatest uneasiness. On the very day of the rising in Dublin, Mr. Richard Martin, who had an estate of 200,000 acres in County Galway, wrote a letter to Marsden warning him that there were many indications that even people he had thought loyal were meditating revolt. Arms, it was said, had recently been landed by smuggling vessels that came from Guernsey. He had also heard that two noted rebel leaders in that district had recently received letters from McDonnell, the Mayo barrister who had been in France since 1798.

For Marsden's benefit Mr. Martin listed the rebel leaders who were then in the mountains : Valentine Jordan, formerly a well-to-do shopkeeper, young John Gibbons, known affectionately as Johnny the Outlaw, and most important of all, Father Myles Prendergast. The priest, Mr. Martin complained, was misleading the people from their loyalty. He even said Mass twice a month at the home of a Protestant tenant of his, Mr. Walter Corey.

Lord Sligo of Mayo was also disturbed about these same men.* He was sure that they were carrying on communications with the Irish exiles in France, and he was desperately worried lest the exiles might return. He had recently got Mardsen to send him £50 as a reward for the yeomen who had captured Thomas Gibbons, uncle of Johnny the Outlaw, who had come back from France a little time before.

" I am anxious that the reward should be paid, not only because [the yeomen] risked their lives in taking him, but because there are many of the same class [as Gibbons] over on the coast of France that can not be kept out of the country but by the zeal of the inhabitants." †

McDonnell was undoubtedly in communication with his friends in Connemara, but he did not come back, as Emmet had wanted him to do, to lead a rising there. However, emissaries had been through the district telling the people of what was planned in Dublin, and had that affair been a

---

* Both Lord Sligo and his brother the Honourable Denis Browne, had worked so long to rid the country of its native patriots that a poem in Irish was written about Mr. Browne. Dr. Douglas Hyde has translated it into English, and, as it compresses into its eight lines so much of the feeling of the time, it is inserted here :

" If I got your hand it is I would take it
    But not to shake it, O Denis Browne.
But to hang you high with a hempen cable
    And your feet unable to reach the ground.
For it's many a boy who was strong and able
    You sent in chains with your tyrant frown
But they'll come again with the French flag flying
    And the French drums raving to strike you down."

When Johnny the Outlaw was finally captured, it was Denis Browne, his godfather, who adjusted the hempen cable about the boy's neck.

† I.S.P.O.

success there would have been plenty of recruits for a rebel
army.

When news of the rising in Dublin did reach the west, it
was accompanied by many completely false reports about
conspiracies, massacres, and mutinies so much nearer home
that the already apprehensive loyalists were completely
nerve-shattered. Lord Sligo was certain that the French had
only to land and they would be supplied with everything.
The Bishop of Elphin, whose see was in Mayo, told the Lord
Lieutenant personally that as soon as a French army of sufficient force to maintain itself landed in the country the people
would universally rise. The appearance of quiet was only a
blind, he said. The people would act the fox as long as they
had to, but whenever the opportunity offered the tiger would
break out. Their disposition was Republican, and their object
was to get possession of the country and effect a separation
from England.

That summer an unusually large number of visitors, some
ten or fifteen thousand persons, made their way to a famous
mountain near the Mayo coast. It was Croagh Patrick,
where the great Irish ecclesiastic for whom it was named
had kept a six-week vigil fifteen centuries before. The people
who climbed its steep sides to the barren peak, many of them
barefoot and fasting, were pilgrims doing honour to the
national saint.

7
THE HUNT

CHAPTER TWENTY-SEVEN

Emmet in the Mountains

AFTER she came back from taking Emmet's clean linen to the depot on Saturday afternoon, Anne Develin had a lonely time. There was no one in the house in Butterfield Lane but herself. Jimmy Hope's wife, who had been staying with her for a fortnight, had left that morning. Once or twice, Anne got out some powder and arms for a Wexford man who was still transferring supplies to Thomas Street, and she was reminded how close she and her family were to this new war. Between his visits Anne's thoughts became so gloomy that she finally sent for a little sister to keep her company.

About eleven that night she was in the yard, helping the Wexford man load some sacks of powder and bottle bombs on his horse. He had left Thomas Street about ten, and he was in a hurry to get back. Suddenly, Anne heard voices. Her first thought was that soldiers were coming, and that the man in his light jacket would surely be captured.

Sharply she told him to put on something dark and to get away. But the men who came out of the night were not redcoats. Anxiously Anne looked them over—Mr. Emmet, Quigley, Stafford, Wilde, Mahon, and a few others. But Big Arthur was not there, or Little Arthur either, or any of the Wexford men she knew.

"O what have you done?" she stormed at them. "Bad welcome to you. Have you destroyed the whole kingdom and all belonging to me, you set of cowards? I don't know what my brother would do but I don't think Arthur would run away . And what's become of your preparations? Are they all gone and lost?"

"Don't blame me, Anne," Emmet said wearily. "The fault was not mine."

The shock of the defeat, so complete and so utterly unexpected, had numbed them all, especially Emmet. Since he had said good-bye to Anne in the morning, everything had changed for him. Now all his plans were frustrated, his preparations lost, his hopes of freeing his country shattered. He spent the night in an interval of emptiness almost like the evening at the Historical Society when his oratory had faltered and failed.

Quigley was silent, too. Though every one attributed the failure of the rising to him, because of his false alarm, no one charged him with it. Anne learned of it privately from Emmet and Stafford. They did not think of suspecting that he might have been tricked into it, or that he might have betrayed them.

Big Arthur Develin joined the party during the night or early the next morning, and so did Hevey the brewer.

For the time being Emmet had no plans except to escape capture. It was decided, with Anne's common sense to help them, that the party would be safer at her father's house. Before leaving Butterfield Lane Emmet collected a few papers and burned them. What arms and ammunition were left were hidden in the fields near by. Then in the early dawn the party slipped down the road to old Bryan Develin's house and spent the day in hiding.

In Dublin red-coated soldiers and yeomen were swarming angrily about the section where fighting had taken place the night before. In their search for rebels and arms they gutted houses and smashed and burned furniture in huge bonfires in the streets. The smoke and flames and the violence of the soldiers were as terrifying as the insurrection itself, and the whole city quaked with fear.

The news of Lord Kilwarden's death was the bloody centre around which revolved all the reports of what had happened the night before. The Privy Council met at the Castle that afternoon and framed a proclamation offering a reward of £1,000 for the arrest of the persons who had murdered him and his nephew. The insurrection was mentioned only incidentally as " treasonable and daring " and as " a daring and rebellious outrage."

At the same time, the bodies of the dead men were being removed from the Vicar Street watch-house, and the Liberty Rangers, led by the Earl of Meath and Alderman Sir William Worthington, were parading through the section where most of the action had taken place, " to the terror of the disaffected and the very great and hearty approbation of the loyal inhabitants of that vicinity," as one of the newspapers reported next day. All this added considerably to the general alarm.

Skilfully Marsden played on the feelings of the people. On Monday, Mr. Cody of the *Dublin Evening Post* slipped into the Castle to ask for instructions as to how he was to treat the rising editorially. What Marsden wanted was soon evident in the *Post* and every other paper in Dublin. It was to play up the horror of the murders of Lord Kilwarden and Colonel Browne, to spread the terror the events of Saturday had created, and to picture the rebels as an unreasoning and irresponsible rabble. Robert Emmet's part in the proceedings was to be ignored as long as possible. No mention was made of him or any of the leaders until the impression was firmly imprinted on the public mind that the outbreak had been caused by villains who killed only for blood and plunder.

" Never was a more wretched rabble of desperate insurgents than those which appeared in arms on Saturday night," the *Freeman's Journal* said in its first issue after the rising. "A person who passed one of the videts on that night said he was a sweep and armed with a large holster pistol."

Quite inaccurately it was reported that the proprietor of the depot in Dirty Lane [a name sometimes given to Bridgefoot Street] where pikes and uniforms had been found concealed had given himself up. A number of manifestos had also been found in the depot, the report continued, and a plan of a new constitution. " The stile was sanguinary and blood-thirsty." The *Dublin Evening Post* called Emmet's proclamation (without any mention of the author) "a diabolical and insurrectionary proclamation " and referred to the rebels as hell-dog reformers. Out of whole cloth the *Freeman's Journal* claimed that the Maynooth rebels, disappointed at not finding a man they wanted, had murdered his helpless infant in its cradle.

The insurrection was also described as

. . . a tissue of art and deception on the part of French agents. A few of the disaffected peasantry of the adjoining countries, the incorrigible remnants of the former rebellion, and we have the assurance, the Robber Dwyer and his gang, were induced by money in hand, or the prospect of plunder to repair to the capital in the belief that the strength of its population would cooperate with them.

On Tuesday Dublin papers printed an announcement that the Lord Mayor and Board of Magistrates felt it necessary from the recent disturbances that had disgraced the city to put the Insurrection Act into effect. This practically gave authorities carte blanche in dealing with the disaffected in Dublin ; and as soon as news of the rising reached London, the British Parliament was asked to suspend the Habeas Corpus Act and to proclaim martial law in Ireland. As the unofficial reports of the events of July 23 had been lurid in the extreme, giving the impression that all Ireland was up in arms and that Dublin was in flames, and as Marsden's official letter to Lord Pelham had said that a " very serious degree of insurrection had broken out in Dublin and its vicinity," both Houses passed the measures asked for immediately, and they became law on July 29.

Meanwhile, Emmet was still in hiding, though there is indication that his whereabouts was not exactly unknown at the Castle. The activities of the soldiers had made it impossible for the rebel party to think of going back to the city. On Monday afternoon most of them had been sitting around the kitchen of the Develin farmhouse. Hevey, the brewer, an apron tied about his fat waist, was splashing away at Mrs. Develin's churn. Suddenly, without even a warning knock the latch of the kitchen door was lifted and a neighbour woman walked in. She was the wife of a local yeoman, and she realised at once that the strangers were rebels. Without seeming to notice them she made an excuse for her visit and left within a few minutes.

Less than half a mile away was the country house of Mr. George Grierson, the King's Printer.* The woman hurried there and broke in on a dinner party with the news that fifty French officers were sheltering at Develins'.

But Mr. Grierson and his guests were in much too jovial a mood for interruption. The rebels, they decided could hardly leave the neighbourhood before nightfall. There was plenty of time for notifying the Castle. The butler, however,

---

* This was the man who had received the mysteriously worded letter mentioned on p. 164, which seems to indicate that he and other Orangemen had been expecting something to happen. At the time of the explosion in Patrick Street depot he had promised Major Sirr that Big Arthur Develin would be arrested. Evidently both of them had been restrained by Marsden.

overheard their talk, and, being a friend of Big Arthur's, he sent word to Develins' of the new danger.

There was only one thing for Emmet's party to do. They must find refuge somewhere farther up the mountains. James Commons, who had often been at the depot, and who had worked in that neighbourhood for years, was now with the fugitives. He offered to lead them to the house of John Doyle of Ballynameece.

Emmet made a last visit to the house in Butterfield Lane, and between five and six that evening he and another man mounted his black mare and rode away from the house toward the mountains.

Some hours later, young John Doyle opened the door of his father's house to James Commons' knock and let the party in. By the light of a candle he could see that three of the men were dressed in green uniforms laced with gold, and that every man carried a weapon. Commons introduced Emmet and Quigley as French officers and asked young Doyle to let them have a bed to sleep in.

But the farmhouse boasted no spare room, and the young man could think of nothing better than to have the strangers share his father's bed. Old John Doyle, known to his neighbours as Silky Jock, opened one cautious bleary eye, saw strange men in green uniforms in the room, and promptly shut it again. He pretended to be so drunk (and his breath added plausibility to the sham) that he even ignored Commons' invitation to share some of the whiskey he was carrying in a jar. He had to be lifted to the middle of the big bed to make room for Quigley and Emmet.

But Old Jock wakened early next morning, and while his unwelcome guests were still asleep he slipped out of the room to look around. He found there were more strange men sleeping in his kitchen, and others in the barn. A pair of rebels were doing sentry duty at his gate. Between them all Doyle found he was host to fourteen men, and that there was a musket or blunderbuss for each man.

At breakfast he counted them again and noted as carefully as Richard Wornall had done every detail of their dress : the dark green uniforms of the three officers, the gold lace, the large cocked hats. He knew now that they were not French, for, slipping up behind them unawares, he had heard Quigley speaking in a simple Irish accent.

Most of the rebels stayed at John Doyle's till nine that night, then left for a place even farther up the mountains. After they had gone, their host found one of Emmet's small proclamations under the table, and though he could not read he put it away. Next morning he showed it to two people. One was Richard Jones, a gentleman who lived on a farm near by owned by Mr. Finlay, the banker. The other was Mr. Robinson, the Barony Constable.

By Tuesday afternoon the news that a party of rebels was at Doyle's had penetrated even to the remote recess in the mountains known as the Breaks of Ballinascorney, a mile above Ballynameece. At five, Mrs. Rose Bagnell, the mistress of a comfortable farmhouse there, had a caller. He was Patrick Loughlin, a carpenter who lived near by, and he had come to break the news to her that some of the rebels intended to stay with her that night.

" What kind of people are they ? " she asked.

" Gentlemen, or dressed so," said Loughlin reassuringly. Some of them were French, he told the widow, and they meant to visit her that night if she would invite them. Otherwise, they would not trouble her.

" Sure I have nothing in the house for them," Mrs. Bagnell protested, " nor even for my own children, unless I can get some from town."

" Then send for provisions directly," Loughlin told her, " for I don't think you'll be able to procure any from Dublin on Friday or Saturday."

" Why, what are they about ? " she asked fearfully.

" They'll get what they want," she was told, and she assumed from that that the rebels were still hoping to go on with their insurrection. Loughlin then asked if her tenant Michael McDonough was at home.

" *He* could well afford to give them supper," he added somewhat sarcastically, as the widow was well-to-do and McDonough much less comfortably fixed. He went off to the McDonoughs', and Mrs. Bagnell followed almost on his heels.

" Oh, Mrs. Bagnell, what a dismal story this is I heard from

Loughlin," Mrs. McDonough greeted her. "How bewitched I was not to say I would not let them in." But when the rebels reached there after dark, McDonough greeted them warmly enough. Some other mountain men were with them, and Commons was still acting as their guide. He still had a jar of whiskey, evidently replenished, from which he poured out drinks for every one, including McDonough. The rebels had brought their own tea and sugar, but their host gave them a late supper of bread, bacon, and milk.

While they were still at the table, young John Doyle appeared with two more men, and later seven others joined them.*

About midnight, evidently at Quigley's suggestion that Mrs. Bagnell's house would be a much safer place, they went over there. Once Emmet had spoken to the widow, she was completely reassured and made the party welcome. She said she had but three beds, but they were welcome to them. While Emmet and some others were asleep in the upper rooms, the rest of the party stayed below and put on a bit of a hooley. Tom Duffy, Mrs. Bagnell's servant, and three local men who had attached themselves to the rebels killed two sheep and boiled some of the meat over the kitchen fire, and Commons provided whiskey from his jar.

Emmet, Quigley, and Stafford managed to get other coats next day, and Emmet, now less conspicuous, took some one with him and went into Dublin on his black mare.†

* The pair had appeared at John Doyle's after Emmet's party had left and had asked young Doyle to show them the way to Mrs. Bagnell's. They must have been known to Emmet, as they were received without question, but there is a strong possibility that they were spies who had been sent to keep an eye on the rebels. Some one was supplying Mr. Bell the magistrate with information about the party, which he was sending on to the Castle. That day on Bell's suggestion a search had been made by a military party at Fox and Geese, a place a few miles from Ballinascorney. The report of the officer in command went to the Castle together with a note from Colonel Beckwith. The Colonel had evidently heard about some informer he called C. "If C is really with us, of which I have no doubt, it will be necessary merely to prevent his own side from suspecting him, not to be so public in his appearance, besides that, by so doing he will force Govt. to notice him or give its reasons to the contrary, and then he is of no further use."
Who C was, has not transpired.
Young John Doyle stayed with the party that night, and the possibility that he, too, was there as an informer is also great.
† Mr. Bell heard of Emmet's ride before the day was out and immediately notified the Castle :
"There are 9 Field Officers from France. Two of them with 12 others at Pennybog beyond Ballinascorney, one of them a *Gentleman* of the County of Kildare, and a man who kept a public house in Dublin, but who was sent out of the country, came some

Between four and five that afternoon, while Emmet was away, a ragged-looking man went up to one of the sentries standing watch in a field near Mrs. Bagnell's house and asked to have James Develin sent out to him. [Probably the message was for Big Arthur Develin, who was upstairs in Mrs. Bagnell's at the time, but one of the depositions Mr. Bell later took down from the widow uses the name James.] He wanted to warn the rebels that the Army had received intelligence they were there.

Poor Mrs. Bagnell heard this with dismay. Any one found sheltering rebels was apt to have his house wrecked as a warning to others. She begged the party to go away at once, and although they seemed strangely undisturbed by the news, they did move over to McDonough's about nine.

Sitting by his kitchen fire that night McDonough heard some of them in the next room curse the Dublin people as a lot of tea-drinkers. If they had assisted them, the rebels said, they could have taken the Castle of Dublin.

Whoever was directing the search for the rebels in the mountains evidently felt that there was no great need for hurry. It was not until Thursday morning that the Rathfarnham Cavalry, lead by Captain La Touche and Mr. Robert Shaw, rode out to Mrs. Bagnell's.* By that time Emmet and his followers had disappeared.

Captain La Touche turned his men around and started back toward Rathfarnham, searching houses on the way. At Bohernabreena, two-and-a-half miles from Ballinascorney,

---

time ago from Hamburgh. The French men wear large Epaulets and Gold Lace. The party distributing papers about the size of a ballet (*sic*) in great plenty. They all lay last night at the Widow Bagnell's and Donough's her tenants.

"J. Commons has joined them. One of the Frenchmen came into town this morning. One of them, a very able man, writes English but can't speak to be understood. The other speaks it tolerably well. Either came in by P'bello [Portobello] or New Street. They were in town Saturday night. He *rode* into town this morning. . . . They wear brown nap coats for disguise. They tell the people that *the business* of the whole Kingdom could be done in 2 hours. Seven men went from Dublin to them last night. They and the 14 men slept last night and the night before at the Widow Bagnell's and her tenants, the Donoughs who live in her yard at Pennybog near Ballinascorney.

"Hall Smith a Yeoman in the Rathfarnham Cavalry, and his brother John will act as guides and cannot fail to surround them.

"N.B. The seven men returned to town this morning.

"It is said the commander of the forces has some information on the subject. . . ."

* The Barony Constable, Mr. Robinson, on information supplied by old John Doyle, was also searching for the rebels with a little party of his own.

Captain La Touche surrounded the public house of a man named Kearney, and then he and Mr. Shaw went inside.

They asked Kearney if he had seen any rebels about. Mr. Robinson had already been there searching, and so the publican had his answer ready.

" It's a small house," he offered. " You can see through it easily enough."

"Any one upstairs ? "

"Ah, no," said Kearney carelessly. " The floor isn't able to bear any weight. We only throw light lumber there."

Mr. Shaw started up, nevertheless.

" You'll be killed," Kearney warned him. " You'll fall straight through the floor and be killed."

Above in the loft Emmet and fifteen other men fingered their weapons.* Arthur Develin knelt in the middle of the room, the muzzle of his blunderbuss pointing at the door. The voices of Kearney and the officer came up distinctly to the anxious men. But after that one step on the stairs there was a silence, and soon the troop went clattering away.

* Thanks to Brother Luke Cullen, there is a list of the men who were there with Emmet : Quigley, Hevey, Stafford, Mahon, Wilde, Commons, two young men from Kildare named Parrot, one Pepper from the same place (actually Peppard) Arthur Develin, John O'Neill, brother-in-law to Dwyer, a soldier named Byrne who had deserted from the Castle Guard the night of the twenty-third, and a person under an assumed name, who Cullen thought was one of the Aylmers of Kildare.

This may have been the man Mr. Bell had referred to as a *Gentleman* of the County of Kildare. The Aylmers did include one William Aylmer of Painestown who had become a nationalist in 1796. In 1798 he had been a rebel leader in Kildare. The Government, aware that he would take an active part in the county, had sent one of its most notorious women spies, Belle Martin of Belfast, to act as a servant in the house of young Aylmer's father. When she had procured enough evidence of his activity as a rebel officer to hang him, she made her report to a near-by magistrate. In July, Lord Castlereagh sent instructions to Kildare that, if Aylmer did not surrender in twenty-four hours, a reward of £1,000 was to be offered for him. The terms of surrender that he accepted provided that he was to leave the country.

He was in England in March of 1799, and Mr. Wogan Brown, a wealthy Kildare gentleman, took him to see Mr. Wickham.

In 1801, the informer "Jones" mentioned an Aylmer, "known by the name of the General of Kildare," as having gone to Paris with communications for the French government and to the Irish exiles in Paris.

The Aylmer family history makes no mention of young William at this time. He served in the French army with Buonaparte, and in 1814 he was in the escort that conducted the Empress Marie Louise from Paris to Austria. He was also on the staff of the Emperor of Austria when he went to England. After the royal party had left, Aylmer stayed in England to instruct the 10th Dragoons in some sword exercises. It was presumably for this service that he was finally pardoned for his part in the Irish rebellion of 1798.

There is no other mention of him in connection with Emmet's rising, but he may very well have been one of those gentlemen of wealth and distinction whom Emmet was counting on, and who managed to keep their part in the rising secret.

But there was no certainty that the yeomen might not return, or that still other parties might not be in the neighbourhood. Emmet and the others went back up the mountains. That evening they were disconsolately sitting by the roadside above Mrs. Bagnell's when Anne Devlin and Wilde's sister came riding up in a jingle with some letters for Emmet.*

By now the party had decided to separate. Quigley and the other Kildare men went back to their home county. Emmet was still hoping that something could be done to free the country. After his failure he did not like to face Dwyer in the Wicklow mountains, and, besides that, his love for Sarah made him want to be near her. After dividing some money with the others Emmet got into the jingle with Anne and Miss Wilde and drove nearly to Rathfarnham with them.

Where he was for the next forty odd hours no one now knows. At five on Saturday he appeared at Mrs. Palmer's at Harold's Cross. He looked very tired and asked for tea. He was still wearing the white cashmere breeches of his uniform and his Hessian boots, but he had on a brown coat belonging to Philip Long. His stock was of black velvet, the one into which Sarah Curran had sewn a lock of her hair.

Mrs. Palmer knew, of course, that he was a fugitive, but her affection for him made her overlook the danger he brought with him into her house.

Emmet did not know—or, if he did, he would have attached no importance to the fact—that the proprietor of the Half-Moon public house near by was Simon Doyle, son of Silky Jock of Ballynameece.

---

* Since Emmet and the others had left Butterfield Lane, Anne had had a hard time, but it had not lessened her loyalty to Emmet. Early on Tuesday morning a magistrate, probably Bell, and some troops had gone to Butterfield Lane. Three or four yeomen kept Anne a prisoner with the points of their bayonets touching her breasts and shoulders. The others, accompanied by the magistrate, ransacked the house and practically tore it to pieces. Then Anne was questioned about " Mr. Ellis." When she would not answer, she was prodded and stabbed, then half-hanged from the shaft of an up-tilted cart. When the magistrate realised that even though he kept on torturing her she would never give information, he left. When Anne had recovered somewhat, she went to her father's house.

But there was no security there, and it was decided that Anne had better hide in the city. She went to Newmarket in the Coombe, where the John O'Neill who was in the mountains with Emmet had his home. On Thursday evening she and Miss Wilde set out from this house to find Emmet and give him some letters.

CHAPTER TWENTY-EIGHT

Man Hunt in Kildare

QUIGLEY and the Kildare men who had been with Emmet in the mountains went back to their home neighbourhood after separating from him that Thursday. They counted on being concealed by their friend, and they were, but it was still as hazardous a place as they could have chosen. Already many of the Naas people who had been in Dublin, including William Andrews, William McDermott, Pat Dunne, and Richard Scott, had been arrested and were undergoing preliminary examination by Pollock, Colonel Wolfe, and Colonel Aylmer. Nicholas Flood of Kilcullen had been arrested July 24. Others from Naas, Maynooth, and Celbridge, from every part of Kildare, in fact, were in hiding, and all the thoroughly frightened loyalist element of the countryside was in pursuit of them.

Sir Fenton Aylmer, the famous fox-hunter who had been so hot on Quigley's trail as soon as he had reached Ireland, was now in England. His office as M.F.H. of the Kildare man-hunt went almost by magnetic attraction to a man with one of the most vivid and uninhibited vocabularies ever met with in historical research. After a blast of his language one can hardly help guessing that he was a sailor.

This was Admiral Sir Thomas Pakenham, still salty though no longer at sea, and now Master-General of the Ordnance in Ireland. He could be correct on occasion, but his natural inclination was toward an almost abrasive heartiness.

The Admiral, operating from Celbridge with a party of the North Down Light Company, soon had one of the Maynooth rebels in custody and had prevailed upon him to turn informer.*

---

*A man of his name had been with Emmet in the mountains. Since his treachery to his former comrades has never been known before, he cannot be identified here, and his initial only is used.

" You be damned and your Dear Sir. Prithee why so
formal to me," the Admiral roared amiably at Marsden in
telling him that he was taking the man to Maynooth to assist
in the search. " I sent up the names of some choice spirits,
friends of P——, to Mr. Wickham. The dragoons will swear
to them all.* P—— will make a famous stag and will tell all
he knows."

A few days later, the Admiral announced another capture,
that of

. . . Mr. John Walsh of Celbridge who is the most ungovernable
barbarous croppy I have the Honour to be acquainted with.
They intend to have a touch at us here the first convenient opportunity
as they killed all the dogs for miles around last night. Whenever they do
we'll not trouble you or any other hangman about them. The harvest is
going on without the least obstruction which the number of troops moving
about in this country has not a little contributed. I'll trouble you to let me
know the caracter (sic) of Mr. Wm. Carey who says he is nephew of
Alderman Pemberton and who was taken up yesterday by me in very
suspicious company.†

Walsh refused to give information, and the Admiral thought
it well to send him to Dublin. When the escort he asked for
the purpose did not arrive promptly, the Admiral reminded
Marsden that Walsh was

. . . the greatest ruffian in Ireland. . . . He is a desperate dog of whom
the people who informed upon P—— (against whom he has sworn
vengeance) and indeed every creature in the country are most excessively
afraid. He is a bloody able Rascal and was either in the Rebel camp or
Naas gaol for the whole time since the beginning of the Rebellion [of
1798] to the Peace of Amiens. Weir's sister says he was killed in Thomas
Street but she is a lying bitch and he and Quigley and Frane were at old
Weir's house on the 15th [of August] at night.

The Admiral and many other loyalists throughout Ireland
were beginning to find that the country was far from subdued.
In fact, it was more and more evident that the people had only

---

*An earlier letter of the Admiral's had spoken of two disabled dragoons of the 16th
Regiment who had been taken by the rebels " and were at this house [the letter is
dated from Rockfield] for ten days after." These were the two dragoons who had
been made prisoners by the rebels early on the evening of July 23 at Maynooth. They
later identified many of the Maynooth men who had been in arms that night. So
did the secret agent, young Daniel Collison.

† This Carey was probably some relation to the Carey on whom B. Senior's brother
John and his colleague, another fake emissary, had gone to visit on July 21 and had
accompanied to Dublin.

needed a signal and a rallying point, and that Emmet had provided them. The day after the rising, some Rathfarnham boys who knew nothing about it except that Irishmen had been up in arms in Dublin decided that they would join the war. They had been at a funeral at Kilgobbin, a few miles east of Rathfarnham, and on their way home they stopped at the Grange to refresh themselves. Patrick Fitzharris heard the men say, " between one and the other," that there was a great insurrection in Dublin.

" They seemed glad of it," he said after his arrest. " They said they wished the French would come over and there would not be so much insurrection." *

The Castle lawyer who examined Fitzharris added a note at the side of the paper : " Witness understood by their speeches that they were greatly rejoiced and would join the French if they should come, and would join the rebels."

In the examination proper Fitzharris is reported to have said that the only thing the men wanted was arms. Two gentleman of the neighbourhood, Mr. Foote and Mr. Fry, were thought to have some, so the would-be rebels paid them a visit and stole all their weapons.

In Longford the spirit of insurrection had been evident before the news of the Dublin outbreak reached there. Mr. R. Fowler, a visitor to the county, was writing Sir Edward Littlehales that he had not found one gentleman there who did not believe that the great body of people were as ripe for rebellion as ever when he heard of the rising in Dublin the day before. Evidently, the disaffected there had hoped to join the successful Dublin men later, for accounts had been received of rebels meeting near Granard for the purpose of drilling.

" By the post which has this moment arrived," Mr. Fowler continued his letter, " we are informed that at Maynooth the mail was attacked by a very large body of men, and that there was a rising in and about Dublin last night. If the latter part be true there will be other risings and a speedy attempt at invasion."

Colonel Aylmer, in reporting on the examination of Naas men who had been arrested, said that the people in that

* I.S.P.O

neighbourhood were at work, but he did not trust them. As to the "extreme readiness and rapidity with which the lower orders of this country obey any call to sedition," he knew the Government had plenty of information.

Even the county of Meath, generally accounted a peaceable one, was showing signs of disquiet. Pollock, who had many confidential contacts there, wrote Marsden on August 1 that he had heard of emissaries being there, and that after what had happened he did not know what to believe.

> I will go down this morning with the arms to the [yeomanry] Corps, and if I find it necessary will employ 2 or 3 Ten Pounds as Secret Service. I and I believe you, have been baffled by the astonishing secret organization of the rebels. All therefore that I can say is that I will leave nothing undone in order to get at the fact in my part of the country. Would not the offer of rewards by Government and a pardon (short of the principals) for discovery of the Rebels be a good measure? You can only get at them by money and flogging.

That very day Pollock wrote that the Privy Council, still without mentioning Emmet, was proclaiming martial law and offering rewards for the apprehension of the rebels. "Whereas for the restoration of the public peace, and to deter evil-minded persons from a repetition of those crimes and atrocities which so lately brought down on the people of Ireland the calamities of famine and civil war, it was thought expedient to offer rewards as hereinafter stated." Fifty pounds was to be given for the discovery and apprehension of the first hundred rebels.

The same issue of the *Dublin Evening Post* carried a paragraph to the effect that everything wore the aspect of restored tranquillity and safety.

The effect of the assuring little note was diminished somewhat by an article that appeared a bit later. On August 16, Mr. Bell, who appears to have been active in the vicinity of Harold's Cross, had arrested two men there whom he committed to the Provost prison. He charged them with "wishing the Tree of Liberty to be planted at the Castle gate, the Magazine to be blown up, and many other expressions of an inflammatory and treasonable nature."

Mr. Wilson, the peace officer, had taken up four persons in a public house in Mill Street in the Liberty [a slum section of

Dublin], whom he had heard toasting "The boys of Prosperous, Rathangan," etc.

"These boys it will be observed," the newspaper continued, "were the rebels who committed atrocities in those places during the last rebellion."

On August 23, the Government felt it necessary to proclaim the Counties of Meath and Kildare as being out of the King's peace.

CHAPTER TWENTY-NINE

Harold's Cross

THERE is a popular tradition that Emmet and Sarah Curran had a rendezvous after the rising. She is said to have slipped out of the Priory under cover of darkness and to have met her lover somewhere near the house. Emmet urged her to marry him, the story goes, and escape with him to America. She refused, on the ground that she could not leave her father ; and Emmet, not wanting to go without her, stayed on to meet his death.

This melancholy romance, however, fades upon investigation, and a story replaces it which is even more stirring and much more in keeping with Emmet's code of ethics. He had always placed his duty and honour above his own happiness and safety. He did so now.

Both John Patten and Philip Long had tried to persuade him to go to France. Emmet had answered that " it should never be said of him that he abandoned the brave people implicated through his means." * However, he wanted some to go immediately to France to urge the French Government to send help to Ireland. He was quite certain that, when they knew how eager the people were to rise they would not hesitate to send an expedition. Tom Emmet, who was then in Paris, would act as his spokesman.

He chose Miles Byrne to carry his message to France, and, two days after his arrival at Harold's Cross, Byrne, delighted with the mission, visited him there to get his instructions. (It was Monday, August 1, 1803.) Byrne was to tell Tom Emmet that the provisional government still maintained its connections and correspondence with the country, and that the Government really knew little or nothing. None of the fire-arms had been lost, but a good deal of ammunition and

* *Memoir of Miles Byrne*, I, p. 284, 1906 ed.

pikes. The rising of July 23 had been forced on by the explosion in Patrick Street, and the country in general had not been expected to rise unless Dublin had been taken.

Tom was to urge the French to send an expedition with the utmost speed. If a speedy landing was made, the people, who were in excellent spirits, would receive them better than they would have before the rising. Robert Emmet himself, Byrne was instructed to say, was in no danger.

Such a message was much too dangerous to be committed to paper. Emmet even hesitated to implicate Byrne with a letter of introduction. But he must have credentials of some sort. Thus Emmet heated sealing wax in a candle's flame, dropped some on a sheet of paper, and pressed it with his seal. The impression of an Irish harp became Byrne's simple wordless token of introduction.

During his interview with Emmet, Byrne noticed that he seemed much affected and cast down. When he talked about the failure of the rising he was obviously overwhelmed with sorrow, but he did not utter a word of blame against any of the leaders who had been dining with Hevey that night, and whose desertion, so he believed, had contributed to the disaster.*

* Byrne was unable to get a ship for France till the end of August, when Emmet had been arrested. Long before that, Tom Emmet had heard of the rising from newspaper accounts, but did not know of its complete failure. On August 5, he saw Robert Fulton, the young American inventor who was living with Joel Barlow and his wife in Paris, and they discussed the possibility of using Fulton's underwater torpedo if the rising should become serious enough for him to go to Ireland. Fulton was anxious to try it.

When Tom Emmet consulted the French Minister of War M. Berthier, on August 6, to ask if the French government meant to send help to Ireland, he met with evasions. A decision would have to wait till Buonaparte's return to Paris, he was told.

Buonaparte himself heard of Emmet's rising and on August 8 wrote from Sedan to Admiral Decrès that the affairs of Ireland had become of sufficient importance to warrant a conference with the chiefs of the United Irishmen in Paris. The Admiral was authorized to offer 25,000 men, 40,000 muskets, and all the ammunition necessary ; the French government would engage not to make a peace with England that did not recognize the independence of Ireland. All this was contingent only on 20,000 United Irishmen joining the French army when it reached Ireland.

But when Buonaparte reached Paris a few days later, he refused to see Tom until he could recognize him officially, and the Irish provisional Government as well. Tom was told practically the same terms Buonaparte had sent Decrès with the additional dampening detail that an expedition would probably not leave for at least two months.

However, the French fleet was in no condition to warrant plans for an Irish invasion and would not be in condition for some time. It is probable that Buonaparte told Tom Emmet the terms, knowing that word would reach the ears of the English sooner or later. This talk of an Irish invasion was largely tactical.

Arthur O'Connor was in Paris at this time but estranged from Tom Emmet and

However, within a few days Emmet had the consolation of a letter from Sarah Curran. He had written to Anne Develin soon after his arrival at Mrs. Palmer's, asking her to come to see him. But poor Anne had had another hard time, and it was Thursday or Friday before she could come to him.* Then he must have given her a letter for Sarah, who poured out her heart in a long reply.

I have been intending these many days past to write you a few lines, but was really incapable of conveying anything like consolation, and altho' I felt that there might have been a momentary gratification in hearing from me, I feared that the communication of my own feelings would only serve to irritate and embitter your own. Besides this, I felt a degree of reluctance in writing, which, after what has passed, may be rather inconsistent, but which is increased by considering the extent of the risque I run, as well as by the breach of propriety it occasions.

She was still worrying, it is evident, about a promise she must have made her father not to correspond with Emmet.

many of the other Irish exiles. He now made overtures to Tom and tried to find out what communication he had had with the French government. Tom distrusted O'Connor greatly and refused to be drawn out. What O'Connor had asked of him was so exactly the kind of information that a spy would want that the incident must be added to all the other suspicious circumstances that marked O'Connor's conduct from the time of his trial in London in 1798. His obvious fear for his own life made him exactly the sort of material Wickham could best work with. When Tom Emmet and Dr. McNevin had been trying to save the lives of State prisoners in 1798, the Government had added O'Connor to their committee. At Fort George he had enjoyed unusual privileges, and many of his fellow-prisoners, including Tom Emmet, had come to suspect him.

Quigley said later that McCabe had organized the country for O'Connor, but McCabe certainly did not let Robert Emmet know that O'Connor was concerned in any way.

The fact that weighs most heavily against O'Connor, taken in connection with all others of a suspicious nature, is his connection with McCabe and his attitude toward him when his double-spying was discovered by the French Government. Instead of severing his friendship with McCabe, O'Connor interceded for him with the French Government and thereby saved his life.

* When she left Emmet at Rathfarnham on Thursday, July 28, Anne went back to the home of John O'Neill in the Coombe. On Sunday a party of Liberty Rangers went to the house looking for strangers. They might not have noticed Anne, but she had just received a letter from the two Parrots who had been with Emmet in the mountains, and who were then hiding at Landenstown. Rather than let the soldiers get the letter Anne threw it on the fire.

She was arrested, and taken with O'Neill's wife to the Coombe guard-house. Captain Wilson searched and examined her but could get nothing from her. The people there did not even know who she was. Major Sirr came in and looked at her casually, but, not knowing who she was, he paid no attention to her. After three or four days in the guardhouse Anne was released. This would have been about Wednesday, August 3.

Back at O'Neill's again, Anne found more letters from some of the leaders, and a message from Robert Emmet asking her to call at Mrs. Palmer's at Harold's Cross. He gave her a letter from Sarah Curran. Brother Luke Cullen's manuscript, "Life of Anne Devlin."

(Remember the opening sentence of her short note : " You will oblige me to write, tho' 'tis wrong, by your generosité in leaving it to me.") She ended a quaintly moralising paragraph with the confession that every departure from duty on her part had been attended by the self-approach that is generally attached to the first breach of it, and that those sentiments alone interrupted the satisfaction she felt in sharing every anxiety with him.

"And such is the perfect confidence that I feel subsists between us that I have no fear of misconstruction on your part of any uneasiness I feel. On the contrary, I know you share it, and cannot think it blameable." Lover-like, she wants him to know her exactly as she is. She cannot bear to conceal anything from him, and she wants to atone to him for everything he had lost. She wanted to see him, but not unless they could meet with safety, which she admitted seemed impossible. "At any rate, in the present circumstances is it not wiser to limit myself to the gratification of knowing you are safe and well ? "

Sarah had had a letter from one of the men who had been involved with Emmet in the rising, and who was now despondent and cynical. Little did she think, as she relayed to Emmet the man's opinion of " the late transaction " and his mention of a French invasion, that she was tightening the noose about her lover's neck. She prattled on of a warning letter she had written Emmet to tell him " of the honour intended your country residence by his Majesty's troops, which I suspected the day before it happened." The messenger had not been able to deliver the message.

As he approached the bridge, [Sarah wrote, evidently trying to be as gay as possible] seeing what was going forward, about nineteen persons whose pockets were searching [being searched] he committed the precious deposit to his heel, and marched up to the gate like another Achilles, vulnerable only in his heel. His pockets were soon turned inside out, where, to use an elegant phrase, the devil might have danced a hornpipe without kicking his shins against a half-penny. His Horace was taken for the inspection of Government, and he was sent back in disgrace. . . .

I hope you are not angry with me for writing so much about him : but you ought to be obliged to me for making you laugh, malgre vous. I believe you will find that I began and ended this letter in very different moods. I began it in the morning, and it is now near two oclock at night.

I passed the house you are in twice this day, but did not see you. If I thought you were in safety I would be comparatively happy at least. . . .

I cannot tell you how uneasy I shall be until I know if you have got this. *I request you to burn it instantly.* I shall expect a letter from you to tell me if you are well and in spirits. Try and forget the past and fancy everything is to be attempted for the first time. I long to know how your wife and *ten small children are.* [Perhaps a reference to Quigley and the men who had been with Emmet on the mountain.] Goodbye, my dear friend, but not forever. Again I must bid you burn this.*

But Emmet could not bear to do that. He put the letter into a coat pocket over his heart.

Expecting that the French would soon send some assistance to Ireland, Emmet's spirits gradually revived. Mrs. Palmer thought him quite playful and happy. It was only when he spoke of July 23 and remembered the horrible death Lord Kilwarden had met, as well as the failure of his plans, that he was at all sorrowful. The mention of that always made him sad.

Emmet never ventured outside the walled garden at Harold's Cross. He passed, as he had on the first visit there, by the name of Hewitt. That was how his few callers asked for him ; that was how he was known to the other lodgers, a brother and sister named Murphy. He seldom saw these people, for they dined above in their own apartments.

Soon after his arrival he had thought out a plan of escape in case the house was searched. He would slip out of the window of the parlour of the first floor, where he slept in a press bed, climb the garden wall, and hide in the cornfield that adjoined it.

Gradually, his life settled into a more or less comfortable pattern. He breakfasted about nine, alone or with Mrs. Palmer. Sometimes he played with Joe Palmer's child or napped in a chair in the parlour or talked chemistry with Mrs. Palmer's brother, Mr. George White, who lived a bit up the road. He dined alone with Mrs. Palmer, and Jemima Palmer, the daughter of the house, served them herself.

For reading he had some unidentified French book and Samuel Richardson's edifying novel, *Sir Charles Grandison.* The hero was described as " that man of honour, who acted uniformly well through a variety of trying scenes, because

* *Vice Roy's Post Bag*, p. 342.

all his actions were regulated by one steady principle ; a man of religion and virtue, of liveliness and spirits, accomplished and agreeable, happy in himself and a blessing to others."

John Patten and Philip Long visited Emmet several times during the first part of his stay, and Miles Byrne was there at least once. Anne Develin was his most constant visitor. She came and went with messages and letters all during his days at Harold's Cross. Probably it was Anne who brought Emmet a second letter from Sarah. Under the conventional phrases her love glowed warm and ardent.

> . . . I feel myself cheered even by the sight of your handwriting, and find more consolations from your letters than any effort of reason on my mind. Your last, particularly, made me quite happy when I received it. You know I can laugh at the worst of times.

But the shadow of her father's return from England was hanging over her, and she was faced with two equally unpleasant alternatives. The first was to abide by the consequences of the course she had chosen. The second was to trust to her father's former confidence in her and let him assume a candour on her part that she did not possess.

> I long to hear from you [she almost pleaded] and hope the messenger will have a letter if she comes this day. I hate to desire you to destroy my letters as I know I should find some difficulty in complying with such a request from you : but I think it very unsafe for you to keep it. . . . I would not give up your last letter for all the others. . . .
>
> Adieu, my dearest friend. I hope you will forgive my folly, and believe me always the same as you would wish. I am quite well, except that I sleep badly. My thoughts are running almost equally on the past and future. . . .

Suddenly Sarah must have remembered that her lover was a fugitive and that the law had penalties for anyone who gave him comfort of any kind or kept his whereabouts a secret.

" I am very uneasy about the poems I wrote for you," she added on the cover of the letter. " There were initials under them all. Tell me if there is any danger of the writer." *

Much as he was to regret it later, Emmet still could not bear to destroy anything that came from Sarah. He put the letter into his pocket with the other.

* *Vice Roy's Post Bag,* p. 346.

CHAPTER THIRTY

Reinforcements and Arrests

MODEST as he was Emmet would certainly have felt some satis-faction had he known how skilfully his rising, officially derided though it was, had shown up the weak points in the military defences of Dublin. Immediately, General Fox had his military secretary, Colonel Beckwith, write Wickham asking that barriers be established on Arbour Hill to secure free communications between the Royal Barracks and the new Provost, that the Cornmarket on Thomas Street should be taken and strengthened as a post for a guard, that the gate of the James's Street Barracks should be strengthened, and that a ferry boat should be fitted up to pass cavalry between the lower Hospital Field of Kilmainham and the barracks. He also suggested that temporary wooden guard-houses and some sheds for videttes be put up.*

Whether the ferry was ever provided cannot now be dis-covered, but the Government followed all General Fox's other suggestions. The Market House in Thomas Street was made into a more or less substantial fort, with cannon pointing westward on Thomas Street. It was also fitted up as a barracks, and the 93rd Highlanders were brought down from Dundalk and billeted there. The Royal Exchange next to the Castle was made into a fort-barracks with guns pointing down Parliament Street. Barriers were put up on all the principal streets in the Coombe where fighting had taken place, and gates were erected at all the principal entrances to the city. The Parliament House in College Green, useless since the Union, was made into temporary barracks, and so was an academy on Grafton Street. The *Dublin Evening Post* publicly congratulated one of the city magistrates for his efforts in finding quarters for all the new troops and for finding cars

---

* *Kilmainham Papers.* National Library of Ireland.

to convey ammunition, arms, etc. But there was no publicity for the fact that the Government began to acquire all the property adjacent to Dublin Castle and within a year had spent £90,000 for real estate there.

But the other results of the rising, new plans and preparations to defeat a possible French invasion, and the arrest of hundreds of Irish nationalists, outweighed overwhelmingly any tiny personal triumph for Emmet. His brother-in-law, Mr. Robert Holmes, had been arrested July 26. John Palmer of New Row had been taken up before the rebels had left the mountains and was in Kilmainham, charged with high treason. John Stockdale, suspected of having printed the rebel proclamation, had given himself up on July 29 when he heard that a warrant had been issued against him. He, too, was in Kilmainham on the same charge. John Hart, whom the attorney Pollock had pointed out months before as being concerned with the Hurling Club, had also surrendered and had been similarly committed to Newgate.

Emmet's cousin, St. John Mason, a barrister, had been apprehended at Nenagh August 9 while on his way to Kerry and brought back to Dublin. He was now in solitary confinement in Kilmainham.* Denis Redmond had been captured at Newry as he was about to escape from the country in a sailing vessel. He was in the Tower of Dublin Castle, being urged to give information.

* These state prisoners lived under conditions that were so bad, even judged by contemporary notions of health and sanitation, that eventually they became a matter of official investigation. Some lived in cells only seven feet square. Everywhere the odour of human excrement was overwhelming. The vessels provided were inadequate and frequently overflowed. The water was tainted, the food of bad quality. It was poorly cooked and taken to the prisoners by a dirty attendant.

Prisoners were divided into two classes according to their stations in life. Those of the " first quality " were supposed to receive the value of 5/5 per day for subsistence, but that summer Dr. Trevor got this reduced to 3/3. Even then much of the money was diverted to pay for attendants and for the customary "profits" of the keeper, cook, etc. The allowance for the second-class prisoners became 1/7½ per day at that time, from which the prisoners got less than a shilling's value. In the Provost the allowance for state prisoners was only a shilling a day.

None of the prisoners received enough fuel to keep them warm and were frequently without candles.

In country gaols conditions varied according to the gaolers. Naas prisoners received many indulgences because of their sympathetic keeper. They lived a more or less jolly communal life, with frequent visitors who brought in supplies. They usually managed to keep themselves in liquor by lowering a glove by a string so that passers-by could drop in coins. This, however, was the brightest spot in the prison picture. The life of the usual prisoner was one of misery and mental torture.

A low-comedy pair of pedlars, Ryan and Mahaffy, who claimed they had been forced to take pikes on Thomas Street on July 23, were in Kilmainham, only too glad of the chance to buy their way out by swearing, in the most picturesque vernacular, against any other prisoners who had been in Thomas Street that night. The long list included Felix Rourke, who had been committed to the Provost August 10.

Many of the Kildare leaders were in gaol in Naas or had been released from it on bail.

McIntosh, the Scots carpenter in whose name the depot in Patrick Street had been taken, and his brother-in-law Thomas Keenan, who had survived the explosion there which had killed his brother, were in the Provost. More than a hundred men had been sent to that unspeakable place within forty-eight hours of the rising. By August 1 more than two hundred people charged with being rebels were breathing its putrid air. At the end of the month 462 had been committed to that one prison alone. By autumn more than six hundred entries were on its register as a result of the rising.

As the cells of all these gaols filled up and arrests continued, the overflow had to be sent to prison hulks and tenders in Dublin Bay. If the misery and unhappiness of the men confined there had any specific gravity, the ships must have ridden low in the water. Some of the prisoners had been arrested on the slightest suspicion, some on a mere similarity of names to suspected persons.

It was common knowledge that every prisoner was pressed to give information that might lead to the arrest of others. Philip Long was particularly worried about Pat McCabe, who had been arrested on the night of July 23 with a blunderbuss in his hands. Long arranged to send Mrs. McCabe some money, and a message was dispatched to her husband to say that she would be taken care of. Long had a genuine sympathy for the poor people who were suffering because of the rising, and he also hoped, by relieving McCabe's anxiety about his wife, that his morale would be strengthened. Whether it was that or his stubborn belief in liberty and justice, McCabe held out against the pressure the Government put on him for seven or eight days and even then was a most unwilling and taciturn witness.

They had more luck with Walter Clare, who had been taken up by some soldiers on the twenty-third, hiding in a lumber yard near the Thomas Street depot. But unlike Pat McCabe, who appeared openly, if reluctantly, on the table as a Crown witness against his former comrades, the Government did not let it be known that Clare was giving information.

Many of these prisoners chose Leonard McNally as their counsel, which automatically opened their minds to the Castle lawyers. What McNally did not get from them, Dr. Thomas Wright, also posing as a friend, did. It sealed their own fate and accomplished the even more valuable purpose of " developing the conspiracy."

Early in August the Government began to hear that Russell's friends in the North, who had been hoodwinked by McGucken into keeping quiet on the twenty-third, were thinking of making another attempt. The news first came to the Castle through an attorney in Dundalk, who, hoping for a situation " military or otherwise," decided to get in touch with the Government. Since he originally came from Fermanagh, Hamilton's home town, where Russell also had many friends, and knew many of the leaders of the disaffected people in the surrounding countries, he was sent there to hunt out the local rebels and to try to get on the track of Russell and Hamilton.

Another spy, William Ainslie Houlton, was sent to Belfast to learn more about Russell's friends there. Houlton, a jaundiced, pock-marked little man, a sailor by trade, seems to have got the job for himself by learning about the intended second rising from some friends of Russell who lived at the Hill of Howth. Houlton was well known to the Castle, being the son of a journalist who wrote for the Government and having given information to Lord Carhampton and Sirr since 1797.

At the time of Emmet's rising Houlton had re-established himself in the confidence of the rebels of Howth Hill and was giving information to Major Sirr about their activities.

The Hill of Howth, a promontory at the northeast tip of Dublin Bay, looks across a strip of water to the ordnance depot called the Pigeon House on the Southern Wall. The wily Houlton, hearing that Russell's followers in the North were in contact with some of the rebels on the Hill, pried his way into their plans by proposing that the Pigeon House be attacked for arms. Two local men rose to the bait and gave Houlton the name of a Belfast man who would introduce him to others in the North who might join in the attack. Armed with this strategic bit of information, Houlton called on Major Sirr at the Castle.

There the plan was recognised as an excellent way of trapping some of the Northern rebels who were still undetected and was given the highest official blessing. Major Sirr provided Houlton with expense money, and on August 15 he took the midnight mail-coach for the North.

The next evening at nine he went, as instructed, to a coffee house in the centre of Belfast and inquired for Mr. Hart. The gentleman, he was informed, would be there in half an hour. Soon a tall, genteel-looking man about forty years of age appeared, and Houlton introduced himself. He said he came from the people of Howth " as a person capable of undertaking the business with which he was acquainted, as he had been an officer in the Navy."

Houlton gave him no secret sign, but the man (who was probably John Shaw, a Belfast woollen draper) must have been convinced. He told Houlton that he was not the person to find the ship (evidently one wanted for the attack on the Pigeon House) but that he would take him to one who could help him. Houlton was then escorted to the home of Miss Isabella Shaw, John Shaw's sister, who lived on the main street of the town.*

That kindhearted and equally credulous individual gave the little impostor food and told him to sleep for a few hours. He was awakened about one, and Miss Shaw drove him in a chaise and four to a house some six miles from the town. There he was introduced to a handsome young man about twenty-five years of age who turned out to be Mr. Patrick Byrne, formerly

*A return of the political prisoners in Carrickfergus and Belfast gaols at the end of November, 1803, lists Isabella Shaw and her brother John, 36, woollen draper, as having been implicated with Houlton. The Shaws had long been important among the Belfast people who still clung to their Republican ideals. McGucken had mentioned Shaw several times during the little crisis of 1799 and in February of that year had said that Shaw had been on the Belfast committee when the French had landed at Killala in 1798. In May of 1799, after reporting that Robert Emmet was probably in England, McGucken had suggested to the Castle that John Shaw, woollen draper, of Belfast, ought to be taken up.

of Union Hall, near Dundalk.* Byrne, so Houlton was shortly writing to Major Sirr, was only a month returned from France, and his brothers John and Henry (who the Government well knew were very active on the continent) would come over with the French to Lough Swilly.

Byrne asked Houlton several questions, which were answered plausibly enough to induce the young gentleman to hand over thirty guineas in gold for the Pigeon House project. He also gave Houlton some letters of introduction. One was to Nicholas Goossens, near Jonesborough, the other to Terence Flanagan, a publican in Dundalk.

There, before he met the people to whom he had introductions, he finished a letter to Major Sirr that he had started in Belfast. It recounted his meeting with Miss Shaw and his interview with Pat Byrne and decorated to the last detail the attack on the Pigeon House as he now designed it. One can almost see the ego of the little man expanding as he pictured himself a hero. He was to be made " cournell," he proudly claimed. Partly out of a sense of the importance of the rank, partly from caution, he had dreamed up an outfit he wanted the Major to send him for the occasion.

A flat cocked hat and a sword with a basket hand-guard were supplementary items to a rebel officer's uniform " made slender." The chief feature was a very broad belt made of white leather " for both the shoulder and to go across the waste (sic) like a small coller (sic) which I am to bring in my hand to the landen (sic) at the Pigeon House. By that means I will be so conspicuous that in case of any shots that mite be fired I can be signaled out from the rest."

He planned to have a revenue cutter opposite the Pigeon House the night of the attack, and when everything was

* The Byrnes of Dundalk, John, Henry, and Patrick, belonged to a well-to-do Catholic family that had long been connected with the United Irishmen and the old Catholic Committee. Patrick and John were credited by a local informer with having done much to help the Society get arms in 1797-98. In 1797 John attended some meetings in Dublin as a member of the Northern Provincial Committee of United Irishmen. Samuel Turner, who had probably turned informer at the time, was with him. Later John Byrne and his brother Patrick both escaped to the continent and were much concerned with Wolfe Tone while there. Both brothers had been in the French expedition of 1798 to Ireland but were returned to France as French prisoners of war, their identity never having been discovered. One of the first reports that Major Sirr got of the state of County Louth in the spring of 1803 said that Pat and John Byrne were active in the new scheme.

prepared it was to let fly three rockets. Then the mock battle was to begin. The cutter would fire several blank shots, the fort would return it with some small arms, the people in the wherries would see their gallant, white-belted "cournell" being pursued. Then Captain Vernon of the Fingal Cavalry was to go down to Howth and arrest Houlton. That touch would "carry the fear of things to my men when the (*sic*) find I am pursoode." (*sic*)

He wanted to come to Dublin before the attack, he told Major Sirr in his atrocious scrawl, both to talk with the people at the Castle and to put his men on the Hill in order.

The lovely plan was disregarded. The Castle was by now in trouble enough over one insurrection that had been allowed to come to a head. Sirr wrote Houlton ordering him back to Dublin. Between writing Sirr, however, and the time he received the Major's reply, Houlton met several of the Dundalk people and told them of his plan, which, in his imagination, was growing with lush extravagance. The new friends included a soldier of the 67th Regiment, Private Frederick Kohen, and the matron in charge of the court-house, Miss Jenny Reilly, on whom he made a great impression.

He told his listeners he had four or five ships in Dublin ready to attack the fort, that five artillerymen had been paid £475 each to spike the guns there. He, Houlton, would go in a flat-bottomed boat to within hailing distance of the fort and then call out that the guns were spiked. At that, so he predicted, all the soldiers would stream from the fort ; and when they were gone, he would hoist a signal to his own followers in Dublin to come to him. Then he would level the city with cannon. Or if he could not do that, he would blow the fort up, because there was a train (fuse) from it that he would light. Or if he could not do that, he would sail away to France that night, which would be the next Friday sennight.

Every one seemed delighted with this sailor's phantasmagoria and much disappointed when Houlton told them later that he had to go back to Dublin. Glibly he explained that he had been informed against and had to escape.

He reached Dublin August 22 and told his story to Mr.

Wickham, Major Sirr, and probably the Privy Council.*
Mr. Wickham and Major Sirr wrote it down in detail. But
the Government officials were more sceptical of Houlton's
story of his great success with the would-be rebels than those
unsuspecting people had been of the plan of attack. Besides,
the plan would bear further " development " both in Dundalk
and Belfast and perhaps bring out the names of even more
rebels, which was what the Castle was after. Thus the next
day a friend of Houlton's named Green was sent to Dundalk,
ostensibly as Houlton's servant. He carried a note to Jenny
Reilly (which she kissed before reading) and a gift of green
cloth to the soldier. This in itself was a stroke of genius, for,
made up into a uniform, it would be enough to hang its
owner.

Green was received as cordially as Houlton had been and
was introduced to a dozen or more people. Prior to meeting
some others, including one said to be a leader, Green and his
escort, a man named Bernard Haley or Healy, were walking
through the town. They were seen by Major Stratton, Lord
Roden's brother, and, since Haley was a notorious rebel, the
Major had both men arrested. A crowd gathered to look at
the prisoners, and a yeoman acquaintance of Green's (not
knowing the nature of his mission) hailed him familiarly.
This was done in so open a manner as to leave no hope of
re-establishing Green's credit with the disaffected, to the chief
of whom he was to have been introduced that night.†

However, the Castle was not completely frustrated by any
means. The house of a tailor of suspicious character was
searched, and a green uniform found. The tailor admitted
making it for the soldier and identified the one to whom
Houlton had said he had sent the cloth. The soldier, Kohen,
was arrested and to save his life disclosed what he knew of the

---

*All this is based on documents at the I.S.P.O. Plowden's *Post Union History* says
that Houlton was taken before the Privy Council by Marsden, and that the Chancellor
ordered a magnificent uniform and unlimited means and rewards. However, that
account is unreliable in many ways. It condenses into one two different trips Houlton
made to the North and probably only reflects the gossip current at the time. But it is
probable that Houlton did appear before the Privy Council on his return from his first
trip to the North. Wickham's account of it, taken down on August 22, may very
well have been the notes made at a Privy Council meeting where Houlton was
questioned.

† *Vice Roy's Post Bag*, p. 330.

disaffected in Dundalk, particularly the men in his regiment.*
Later arrests brought about even more information.

Meanwhile, Houlton had been given his rebel uniform
(whether he got the broad white collar is not mentioned),
£68 5s. secret-service money, and orders to go back to
Belfast.

Arrived there, Houlton was befriended by David Thompson,
a young merchant with a consistently Republican history, who
probably introduced him to more of the disaffected there.†
But again Houlton's career was cut short by arrest. Unfortunately, he had reached Belfast before a letter that the
Castle had written to the military officer in charge of the
district. As Houlton was openly carrying on his pseudo-
seditious activities in a tavern, the military, not being warned
of the real object of his visit, took him into custody. The
Shaws, Thompson, and some others who had been in his
company were also taken up, including Miss Margaret Munro,
sister of a rebel general who had been hanged in 1798.‡

They were lodged in the Prevot and refused bail, and Miss
Munro at least was sent off to Carrickfergus gaol on a common
car. Mrs. McTier, who was now somewhat more sympathetic
to the rebels than she had been at first, wrote Dr. Drennan
that there was something too like France in that.

* The record of Kohen's examination, as conducted by the regimental commander,
Colonel Wale, is particularly full and detailed and includes the arguments used to
make the prisoner divulge all he knew of the disaffected in the regiment. Since these
are not often set down so fully, it will be enlightening to give one paragraph entire :
   " Q. You are aware that according to your solemn oath taken before Col'l Wale,
you have most sacredly pledged yourself to declare the full truth of all you really know
concerning Houlton, or his plans, and accomplices, and that if by confronting your
depositions with the confession of any other implicated persons, you are found either
to have prevaricated or withheld anything you know you will virtually forfeit every
least claim to his interference on your behalf, and with that probably every hope of
life. You are now finally called upon to consider deliberately your awful situation,
and as you value your existence or dread the terrors and consequences of an untimely
and ignominious end, to make a full voluntary confession of any and every circumstance that has ever by any means come to your knowledge relative to Houlton, his
schemes, views, and confederates." I.S.P.O.
   † The returns of the political prisoners at Carrickfergus and Belfast gaols at the end
of November, 1803, include among others David Thompson, a hosier, charged with
having procured lodgings for the rebel General Houlton. " This man," the return
states, " in 1798 lived at Lisadalyon near Saintfield, was a rebel leader there and is
included as such in Gen'l Nugent's procl'n in July 1798." Much later Quigley
reported on Thompson's movements and said that he (Thompson) knew all about
Hamilton's and Russell's proceedings in the North in 1803. I.S.P.O.
   ‡ McGucken wrote the Castle at this time that John Shaw and his brother William
had been arrested and should be detained. "John has said that McG is a bad man.
He evidently saw Russell." I.S.P.O.

As for Houlton, though he was now widely suspected by the Belfast people of being a spy, he was made to dress in his rebel uniform and was paraded through the town. General Campbell, whose dramatic effects had made a great impression in his district ever since July 23, then sent him down to Dublin escorted by a brigade major, a sergeant, and eighteen men. The major was ordered to march Houlton into Dublin in his uniform, and manacled.

Meanwhile, arrests in Dublin had been coming closer and closer to Robert Emmet. On August 16 the *Dublin Evening Post* carried an announcement that " on Saturday Mr. Philip Long, a merchant of respectable character, was arrested in the Commercial Buildings and committed a State Prisoner to Newgate."

The *Post* was wrong about one thing. Long was confined in Kilmainham gaol, not Newgate. After five days he was taken to the Castle for a full-dress examination before the new Chancellor, Lord Redesdale, and the Attorney-General, with Mr. Townsend taking notes in a tireless, easy hand. The examination lasted two days, during which Long was questioned about many of the leaders of the rising including Emmet and Dowdall. He broke down on some of his first denials when he saw the evidence gathered against him, and he ended the ordeal by admitting that he could see that there was cause for suspicion about himself, and that he was sorry he had lived so much among improper persons. Yet he did not betray Robert Emmet or admit having seen him since a week before July 23.

Long did admit knowing a Hamburg exile who had returned to Ireland about the time Emmet had, thoroughly cured of any former disaffection but careful to conceal the change. This person, who may be called " Brown " for convenience, had evidently attended some of the Donnybrook hurling sessions, though he does not appear to have been otherwise engaged with the rebels. Perhaps he had gone to Donnybrook to keep an eye on what Mr. Pollock called the " other things than mere play that went on there." At any rate, he seems to have been on very cordial terms with Major Sirr. When the Major, the second day of Long's examination, went to find " Brown," the man was not at home ; but as soon as he returned, he went to the Castle and was taken into custody.*

The next day another man who had known Emmet on the continent, and " Brown " as well, called at the Castle. It was no one less than Samuel Turner.† Probably he had been at the Castle before this, for the conversation he had was too short to have been the first one of a spy of such importance and connections. He recalled, among other things, that Emmet and " Brown " had had dinner at a Hamburg garden called Schlaffenhoff.

Up to now, no reward had been offered for Emmet's arrest ; but shortly after Philip Long was taken up, a proclamation appeared offering £300 each for the arrest of Robert Emmet, William Dowdall, John Allen, and William St. John. Mrs. Palmer was now so worried by Emmet's presence in her house that, when John Patten called on him on Friday, August 19 (the day " Brown " was at the Castle), she begged him to take his friend away. Patten must have promised to do so, and arrangements may have been made, because the next Wednesday, when the Palmers saw the notice requiring a list of all occupants of houses to be posted on the outside door, Emmet asked to have his name omitted " because he was leaving so soon."‡

That day John Doyle's son Simon, who kept the Half-Moon House at Harold's Cross, was seen to ride with extraordinary haste to his father's at Ballynameece.

Comfortably oblivious to all these dangers, Emmet was composing a communication to the Castle. It was evidently

---

* The name of " Brown " does not appear on any of the prison lists now available, but in October his wife was petitioning the Government for his release, saying he had been long a prisoner. Probably he was detained at the Royal Exchange or in the custody of a King's messenger. This was usual practice in the case of a very helpful and useful witness.

† On this occasion Turner was using the name of Roberts, which was one he sometimes used on the continent. His letters to the Government were signed Richardson, and he also used the alias of Furness.

Turner was now under some suspicion by the Irish in Paris and had come back to Dublin in June from his long residence in Hamburg, openly avowing himself a loyal citizen. He had stopped in London on his way to see about his pension and to have his name cleared of all treasonable charges. He had been disinherited by his nationalist father for calling Lord Castlereagh the titular saint of Ireland.

‡ This was from Mrs. Palmer's examination. On Emmet's trial, Joe Palmer, testifying with the greatest reluctance, said that he left Emmet's name off the list at Emmet's request because he was afraid of being taken up. All the Palmers' examinations used here are now at the I.S.P.O.

intended as a warning to the Government that the rebels had not given up the idea of getting their liberty, and that, under certain circumstances, they might feel justified in making another try for it.   No one but an utter idealist like Emmet would have thought for an instant that the Government would be moved by argument, but he evidently felt it his duty to give them this notification before taking any further steps.

Whenever he started it, by Thursday, August 25, he had got to the point of telling the Castle that they knew nothing, comparatively speaking, of the present conspiracy, and of implying that the merciless punishment of the prisoners then in custody would do no more to bring real peace to the country than such treatment had in the past.

Is it only now [he asked rhetorically] that we are to learn that entering into conspiracy exposes us to be hanged ?   Are the scattered instances to be brought forward, necessary to exemplify the statute, if the numerous striking examples which have already preceded were insufficient ?   If government can neither by the novelty of the punishment, nor the multitude of its victims, impress us with terror, can it hope to injure the body of a conspiracy impenetrably woven as the present by cutting off a few threads at the end of it ?

He broke off his writing here.   Perhaps it was to see a caller who came about four that afternoon.   Or perhaps the interruption was the announcement of dinner.*   He left the fatal paper on a chair and went to the room below.   He and Mrs. Palmer had only begun their meal when there was a knock at the door.   Jemima Palmer went to open it, and in rushed Major Sirr.

* While Anne Develin was a prisoner at Kilmainham, she heard a conversation in which it was stated that the man who betrayed Emmet had called on him that morning.   Dr. Madden thought this person was named Lacy.   Some one calling himself Lacy did call upon Emmet while he was in hiding, but that was probably an assumed name.   There is stronger evidence that the real informer was another person.

8

EMMET'S CAPTURE AND ORDEAL

CHAPTER THIRTY-ONE

Arrest and Examination

MAJOR SIRR had got word, probably through Silky Jock Doyle of Ballynameece, that there was a suspicious stranger at Mrs. Palmer's.* Whenever there was a question of reward, the

---

* From the time of Emmet's arrest there has been a tradition that the person who betrayed him received £1,000 reward, besides the £300 paid to Major Sirr for his arrest. Who collected the blood money was not known for thirty or forty years, till the Royal Irish Academy acquired a Secret Service account book covering the period. Under date of November 4, 1803, was the item : " Finlay and Co. Acc. of Richard Jones (to be replaced to the account hereafter) £1 000 00." It was known that Finlay and Co. were bankers, but Jones had been forgotten, and Anne Develin's " Life," by Luke Cullen, was unpublished. It still is, but the manuscript of it is available, and what Anne has to say of Jones does something to solve the mystery.

" Old Doyle of Ballinameece and an idiot son of his was in Kilmainham at this time [Anne was speaking of the end of September, 1803] It has been observed that it was at this man's house Mr. Emmet and his staff stopt the night they left my father's. At this time there was a warrant issued for the apprehension of another son of Doyle's who was accused of robbing a Mr. Ormsby of near Tallaght. A Mr. Richard Jones from that quarter used to visit Doyle in prison and I was informed by Wm. Kearney's wife that it was through Jones' influence that Doyle was not proceeded against. But Doyle had another son Simon who kept a public house at Harold's Cross and used to go of (sic) messages and supplied Mr. Emmet with butter and eggs while he was at Mrs. Palmer's. [Probably Anne meant that Simon went on messages during Emmet's first stay at the Palmer's. He would have known Emmet from those transactions. There is a local tradition that Doyle was delivering some supplies at the Palmer's door the day of Emmet's capture and caught sight of him inside.] On the day previous to the arrest of Mr. Emmet this Simon Doyle rode to his father's at a very unusual and rapid rate. He was very much noticed by his old neighbors who justly held him in very low estimation. . . .

" He rode back at the same rate and his old neighbors did not hesitate to say there was something in the wind. Rich'd Jones, who used to visit Doyle in prison was a tenant to Mr. Finlay the banker. He was in a very respectable station in life (a gentleman farmer) and as silky a fellow as old Doyle, who was called Silky Jock for his insinuating disposition. But if Simon Doyle or his father were the persons by whom Mr. Emmet was betrayed it is certain that they never received the £1000. Jones went to reside in the County Kildare soon after."

That branch of the Doyle family became known as the Stag Doyles, Stag meaning informer ; but whether their neighbours gave them the name because of Silky Jock's information to the Barony Constable in July that Emmet and his party had been at his place, or whether they believed that Simon and his father had betrayed Emmet's hiding-place at Harold's Cross is still a moot point.

It is quite possible, of course, that Richard Jones made his thousand-pound discovery by some other means. But if it was through the Doyles, they were wretchedly paid. Beyond a secret-service money payment of £22 15s. for old John's lodging and subsistence, made in September of 1803, there are only two other dispersals that seem to have been for him. In November he was given £25 for loss of time on trials, and in December £22 15s. was drawn from the secret-service account for him.

Major always made sure that he would be in a position to collect it himself, and so he took only one man with him to the house at Harold's Cross. Previously, however, he had warned the military post at New Street that a detachment of soldiers might be needed and that they should be ready if called upon. Then he sent his man to give a single knock at the Palmer's door while he rode slowly past the house.

Jemima Palmer opened the door, whereupon the Major galloped back to the house and dashed in. The startled girl tried to get to the dining-room to warn Emmet, but the Major was there ahead of her. Breathless and excited as he was, he still had enough professional aplomb to tell Mrs. Palmer and her daughter to leave the room before he asked Emmet his name.

"Cunningham," Emmet said, "from the County Wicklow."

Sirr left his man to watch Emmet and went to the next room to question Mrs. Palmer, taking from a chair near the door the paper Emmet had been writing to the Government.

Laconic as Sirr's official account of this is, it carries its own sense of drama and desperation.

Asked her his name. She said Hewitt, and that he had been lodging there about a month. W [Witness, Sirr] returned to Em. and asked him how long he had been in that house. He said he had only come that morning. Never lodged there before. He was then bleeding in the forehead. Asked the cause in his presence. The man said he had atttempted to escape and had been knocked down with the pistol. Witness said he was sorry but that the man had only done his duty and Em said it could not be helped.

W then searched him, and found other papers in his pocket (the letters from the lady). Asked if the room was his and if that paper on the chair was his. He admitted the room was his but denied the paper. He said he frequented a room upstairs (nothing found there). W then went out and called the guard. They came. W surrounded the house and garden and placed a centinel in the room with Em.

W then went to examine Mrs. Palmer and heard a noise as if an attempt to escape. Then ran thro the hall to the rear of the house and saw Em. running up the garden. The window of the room was open and he must have gone out that way. W ordered the soldiers to fire but still kept pursuing, and got so close to him that he stopt and surrendered. One of the men snapped his pistol but it did not go off. W said he was sorry for the necessity of using restraint. Oh ! says Em, all's fair in time of war. W marched him to the Castle, examined him particularly and sent for some gentlemen who identified him and then he confessed his true name.

The Major neglected to add that he left Mr. Bell the

magistrate in charge at Mrs. Palmer's, busy as usual in pursuit of Emmet's life.

At the Castle the prisoner soon found that the Government wanted more of him than that. They wanted to deprive him of his reputation, his influence, and his honour. That phase of the pursuit of Robert Emmet now began in earnest.

Emmet's formal examination at the Castle was put off for a few days till John Patten and Mrs. Palmer and her son could be questioned. Patten refused to say anything at all, and the Palmers, though confronted by the Chancellor, the Attorney-General, the Solicitor-General, Mr. Wickham, and Mr. Marsden, lied valiantly for hours. They denied knowing their lodger's real name, why he was hiding, or anything whatever about him. For once, Townsend's hand faltered with weariness as he took down their statements, and the Solicitor-General substituted as secretary for a while.

But the probing was searching, skilful, and prolonged. At the end the truth was forced reluctantly from the unhappy pair. Whereupon, shorter versions were made of their examinations, and each was bound in £500 to prosecute Emmet on his trial. Joseph Palmer was questioned again the next day and kept in custody. With what Mrs. Palmer's brother George White, Jemima Palmer, and Emmet's fellow-lodgers the Murphys could tell, the Government now had a complete picture of Emmet's life at Harold's Cross and dangerous admissions about his connection with the rising.*

* Wickham wrote two letters to London on August 28 outlining the case against Robert Emmet as it then stood. The first admitted that there might be difficulty in proving Emmet's handwriting, since he used two or three different styles, and that " as he was much beloved in private life, all the friends of the family, even those who abhorred his treason," would be glad of any pretext to avoid appearing against him. However, they had the draft of the proclamation found in the desk in the depot, the two love letters taken there, the cypher addressed to R. E., and the letter he had been writing to government the day he was arrested.

Wickham's second letter implies that government had only just learned that Emmet had leased the house in Butterfield Lane. " Since my letter of the morning was written, some very material information affecting Mr. Emmet has been procured.

" In the Depot a letter was found addressed to Robert Ellis, Butterfield.

" It has been discovered that Emmet hired a house at Butterfield last spring, and from the lease which I have in my possession to which Dowdall is a witness, it appears that he took it under the name of Robert Ellis.

" The Attorney who prepared the leases and who witnessed it together with Dowdall, has been to see Emmet in prison today, and has declared that he is the man who called himself Robert Ellis, to whom the lease was made. . . ." P.R.O.L.

But it is significant that a magistrate, probably Mr. Bell, and some soldiers had

While this material was being put into shape for the Home Office in London, Wickham sent them a letter outlining the programme then being carried out. It has been used over and over to suppress nationalist movements in Ireland and other countries under British rule whose ambitions have conflicted with England or the Imperial interest. It is the classic pattern of imperialism in action against anything that endangers its own life or prosperity. It appeals to fear, distrust, and avarice. It rewards those qualities and punishes devotion to principle. Expediency, no matter how well disguised, is its only criterion. Nothing is too fine to be sacrificed to it. It devours wholesale the youth of a nation and callously corrupts its idealism. This was the weapon, terrible and sinister, that Wickham was using to destroy the cause for which Robert Emmet had risked his life.

We must give the enemy no breathing time [he wrote on August 27]. Every day will produce new discoveries, and, I hope, give new reason to the disaffected to mistrust each other. These advantages must be followed up throughout Ireland. The fugitives must be pursued into every corner, rewards offered for apprehending them whenever they escape ; so that the leaders, if not taken, shall find nowhere any resting place. Insurrection, wherever it shows itself, must be instantly beat down and most severely punished by military execution ; and above all things those who harbour traitors and facilitate their escape must be most severely punished. Let this system be but steadily and unremittingly pursued for twelve months, and large rewards and open protection and encouragement to all who shall discover [betray, in other words. " To make discoveries " was a euphemism for giving information.] and apprehend known traitors and I think Lord Hardwicke may safely answer for the peace of Ireland for some years to come against all attempts to disturb it by the leaders of the late rebellion or their late abettors and successors.*

Into that one paragraph, written with icy abstraction, Wickham compressed the general plan of campaign against the rebels. But he had too keen an understanding of human nature not to know the value of dramatising a cause in the

visited the house in Butterfield Lane three days after the rising and had tortured Anne Develin to make her reveal where " Mr. Ellis " had gone. Mr. Bell had a spy with Emmet's party in the mountains ; thus it is inconceivable that the Government did not know until August 28 of the house in Butterfield Lane, and that Emmet had used the name Ellis. The withholding of this information is an indication that Wickham was not being candid with his official correspondent in London and adds to the possibility that Wickham was concerned with Marsden in directing the conspiracy for some ulterior motive.

* *Vice Roy's Post Bag*, p. 328.

career of an individual. Robert Emmet, it becomes increasingly obvious, had been selected—perhaps months before and very possibly by Pitt—as the symbol of Irish nationalism. He, who had aroused the hopes of his fellow-countrymen and had appealed to their patriotism, was now marked not only for death but for dishonour. He was pre-sentenced to lose his life among circumstances that would be humiliating to the last degree, banded with tatterdemalions and accused of deserting even them. He was to be charged with personal ambition, with having tried to buy place and honour with the blood of others. He was to be urged to forsake his principles and thus encourage others to denounce them. He was to be kept from martyrdom by dying in disgrace, branded as an informer, to an Irishman the deepest nadir of degradation.

The first indication that Robert Emmet was to be made the scapegoat of the rising slipped into a letter Wickham wrote the next day, when sending over to London the copies of the Palmers' examinations. Next to keeping the French out of the country, he said, the conviction of Emmet was the event that would contribute most to the internal tranquillity of the whole island.* Thereafter, official accounts repeatedly referred to Emmet as " the very life and soul of the insurrection." He alone, according to Castle publicity, was responsible for the rising. But in a private letter written in September Wickham named Russell, Hamilton, Long, Allen, Murphy, and Byrne as well as Emmet as being " the very life and soul of the treason." †

The first objective in the campaign to degrade Robert Emmet was to make him give information against his fellow-rebels. In Sarah Curran's letters which Sirr had taken from him the Government had their cruellest means of bringing him to terms. How he was tortured by the thought of them in the possession of his enemies, not that they were evidence against himself, but that they might bring harm to Sarah. He had five nights and nearly five days to agonise over the danger he had brought to her before he was taken to his inquisition at the Castle.

* He attributed the idea to Lord Hardwicke, but Hardwicke had no part in this new coercion of Ireland. Whoever had originated the policy, Wickham and Marsden carried it out.
† P.R.O.I.

At three-thirty on the afternoon of August 30 Robert Emmet faced Lord Redesdale the new Lord Chancellor, Mr. Standish O'Grady the Attorney-General, and Mr. Wickham in a room in Dublin Castle. Marsden sat with a pile of draft paper before him, ready to record the desperately important questions and answers.

The Attorney-General began by asking the prisoner his name.

" Robert Emmet," he replied, and made it clear that he would decline answering any questions that went further than that.

He was told that he had been sent for to have an opportunity of explaining what might appear suspicious in his late conduct. He thanked his questioners but declined anything further than that.

"At the same time," he added, " I wish it to be understood that there is nothing which could come within the limits of this society to ask which I could not answer with pride."

" Then why not answer ? "

" It might be a breach of confidence," he explained. He made it a point of honour with himself not to do that. A limit had to be set. If he answered some questions and not others, he would draw an invidious distinction that he would not wish to draw.

Had he been in France for two years ? they pressed him. When had he first heard of the insurrection ? Had he any previous knowledge of it ? Was he in Dublin that night ? Had he corresponded with any persons in France ? . . . Was he acquainted with a person of the name of Howley ?

" It would be an infringement of the rule already laid down to go any further," Emmet replied to every question.

Had he gone by the name of Hewitt ? of Ellis ? of Cunningham ? He was silent. Was he inclined to answer as to his handwriting ?

" No."

Had he ever seen a proclamation purporting to be a proclamation of the provisional government ? Had he seen a manuscript of it ? Had he seen it in his own handwriting ?

He must have thought, when they mentioned that, of the desk in the depot, and of the letters to Sarah he had left there.

Then it came, the question he had been dreading.

" By whom were the letters written which were found on your person ? "

Eagerly he answered that. "As to the letters taken out of my possession by Major Sirr, how can I avoid their being brought forward ? "

Now it was their turn not to answer. Discerning that Emmet must attach importance to them, they probed as to whether they were his own or merely committed to his care. Perhaps they had been left with him. Then again, what was the name of the writer ?

" May I know by what means those letters might be prevented from coming forward ? "

If they answered him, Marsden did not put it down. He did put down the question Emmet's love forced from him : " Has anything been done in consequence of those letters being taken ? May I know what means [were used] or what has been done upon them ? "

He could not be answered as to that, he was told.

" You must, gentlemen," Emmet implored them, crediting them with the same qualities of compassion and the same high code of ethics that he himself possessed, " be sensible how disagreeable it would be to one of yourselves to have a delicate and virtuous female brought into notice."

There was evidence in those letters, they implied, which could legitimately be used against him.

" Could the evidence be brought forward without the name ? " Emmet asked.

The evasive answer was that there were evidences of high treason in the letters, and therefore their production was necessary.

Could not those points be produced, Emmet pleaded, and not the name of the writer ?

" Producing some points and withholding others never was done."

" May I be told the utmost limit necessary to go to prevent the exposure ? "

Again Marsden put nothing down, but the shameful terms may be surmised in Emmet's reply : " Then nothing remains to be done. I would rather give up my own life than be the means of injuring another person."

"Knew before you came into the room that this was the line you would take," Marsden recorded, his usually precise hand distorted by haste, but he put down every syllable of Emmet's courtly answer : "I am glad you have had that opinion of me."

The duel went on, but now, to discover his weakness, they were letting Emmet make the thrusts.

"Have any proceedings been taken upon those letters ? "

No answer was given, but again it can be read in Emmet's next statement : "I have mentioned as nearly as I can the line I mean to adopt.

"I will go as far as this : If I have assurance that nothing has been done and nothing will be done upon those letters I will do everything consistent with honour to prevent their production. Now may I know whether anything has been done ? "

Still they did not answer him. Emmet asked for counsel and must have been refused. He was evidently told that he would be brought up for arraignment.

"Might I then make one request, that until my arraignment nothing has and nothing will be done ? "

He was at liberty to make the request, he was told, but it could not be answered immediately.

Even in the laconic reporting that Marsden gave Emmet's answer, his anguish is evident. "Can only repeat what he has already said that he would do anything to prevent the production of those letters.

"Personal safety he knows out of the question.

"With notions of honour in common, persons may have different principles.

"But all might be agreed as to what a person might own to a female.

"Personal safety should weigh nothing if the production of those letters c'd be prevented."

A longer, sharper rapier came darting out, straight for Emmet's heart. "Are you aware that they form evidence against the person who wrote them ? "

Feebly he parried that : "As to that I do not know how far there can be proof as to who wrote them. However, there may be opinions and he was not aware how far similarity of handwriting might be evidence. But if the person who is primarily concerned does all that in him lies it is very unnecessary and very cruel to proceed against the writer. I feel the more acutely on this point because it is the only act of my life within these five months with which I have to accuse myself."

Marsden must have fallen behind here and missed an argument to clear the still unnamed writer of treasonable intentions, for some one asked if the female who wrote the letters had only opinion.

"I say it on my honour," Emmet answered. "I say that a woman's sentiments are only opinions, and that they are not reality. When a man gives opinion it is supposed he has actions [i.e. that he acts] accordingly. But a woman, the utmost limit is opinion."

Thinking that perhaps Emmet's resolve not to answer might be softened by now, they began to question him again. Any depot of arms? of ammunition? He held firm.

"Perhaps," he was asked, "you consider the disclosure of names as inconsistent with your notions of honour?"

"I will purchase honour with personal safety," he said, meaning that he would give up his personal safety as the price of honour.

Now they began to tempt him, not with the promise that his life would be spared, because it was evident that life was not the thing that Emmet held dearest, but with this woman's safety.

"You cannot expect to draw forth any compromise on the part of the Government," they insinuated. . . . "However, if you could render a service to government by making a disclosure which may entitle this person to some favour it might be attended to as far as respects that person, altho' not extending to yourself."

Even after that he would not answer a question about concealed arms. A trace of sarcasm creeps into the record.

"Is disclosing concealed arms dishonourable?"

"I must adhere to my former rule."

"As a matter of curiosity I put to you a question why government should indulge you with consenting to a partial disclosure of these letters, when you decline on your part to make any satisfactory answer."

Again, it was Emmet the generous idealist who answered that. "It is not as an indulgence. I only ask it as if I was in a situation of power I would grant a like favour. I wish every one in Ireland was as innocent as she is."

They fought over the old ground again. Still Emmet held out. He would never make a full disclosure. They must have pressed him here (later he wrote Sarah that they did) to make disclosures without mentioning names.

"I am not asking you where Mr. Dowdall may be appre-hended," some one teased. "I am not asking you who visited you two hours before you were taken." (They had learned of this call from Jemima Palmer's examination.)

They got no reply and went back to the letters again.

"May I not ask," Emmet entreated, "altho' I am not told what I am to do, or how far I am to go, whether these letters lie there to be used or not, whether any disclosure has been made by them or any arrest has taken place ? "

"Would it answer your purpose to have the writer brought into the room with you ? "

Emmet rose from his chair at the terrible thought. "It might answer yours better," he burst out bitterly.

But when they began to question him about the Palmers, instead of placating his tormentors, he tried to excuse the people who had sheltered him. "The lady [Mrs. Palmer] was under personal obligations to a part of my family. Her sentiments were not the same as mine."

They were connected perhaps, he was questioned, with a person named Palmer on the Coombe, the person who had the gunpowder ?

"I do not mention the gunpowder."

"Some one under obligation to you or Mr. Patten ? "

Few people had obligations, said Emmet, ignoring Patten's name.

They told him he might be given a further opportunity for a further communication. Again he asked for counsel, a Mr. Burton. He was refused.

He asked, too, if anything had been done to the Palmers and replied to their answer that there were circumstances in which the gentlemen might not think it criminal in him to shelter any of them.

"Are you aware that the persons in '98, among whom was your brother, made disclosures, concealing only the names of persons ? " he was asked.

" I believe that they of '98 were differently situated. The object for which they spoke was to save the lives of others, their own never having been in danger."

Here he smiled, and the fact was noted, perhaps later, by Mr. Flint, on the margin of the sheet.

" I know the comparison you are going to draw and that it will be taken down."

" There was no intimate circumstance relating to the plot which they did not disclose," he was told. But Emmet knew quite well that this was not so,

For the third time he asked for counsel and when he would be arraigned. To be allowed counsel was an unusual indulgence, he was told.

The Chancellor made an observation. " Mr. E's feelings are a good deal affected."

" I wish they were at an end," said Emmet sadly, but he also wished the gentlemen a courteous good morning. Either the session had lasted through the night, or it had been adjourned and resumed the next day.*

Emmet was taken back to Kilmainham, and the problem of how much a man might with honour tell to save his sweetheart went to his cell with him.

* When Miles Byrne got to Paris, he told Tom Emmet that Robert had been three times before the Privy Council.

CHAPTER THIRTY-TWO

Building the Case against Emmet

WHILE this covert pursuit of Robert Emmet's integrity was going on and informers gave secret information against him, scores of persons were openly seeking his life. Mr. Bell was one of the most active magistrates gathering evidence to be used on his trial. He was still getting depositions from Crown witnesses and then swearing them, under penalty of heavy fines, to appear on the witness table against Emmet. John Doyle, after his story had been taken down, was bound by a thousand-pound fine, then taken to Kilmainham and shown Emmet. The next day he swore before Bell that the man he had seen in gaol was one of the French generals who had come to his house soon after the rising. Other people who had seen Emmet in uniform were taken to Kilmainham by Mr. Bell for a surreptitious look at the prisoner. All were bound to prosecute.

The informer " Fine Hand " was telling Mr. Wickham about Emmet's friends in Paris in 1802, when many of the Irish exiles used to meet in the house where " Fine Hand " lodged.*

* I have never been able to identify " Fine Hand " definitely. His letters are unsigned and bear no indorsement, but circumstantial evidence points strongly to a young man who had been in Trinity with Emmet and in Paris while he was there. He had known William St. John and William Putnam McCabe on the continent, and St. John seems to have been the one who mentioned his name to Wickham. He was evidently taken to the Castle at this time, questioned about Emmet, and induced to give information against him. There is a strong possibility that he was the same young man who wrote the letter mentioned on p. 315, and who, posing as a patriot still, was allowed to visit Emmet in prison in order to pick his brains for the benefit of the Government. It is interesting to note that if " Fine Hand " was this person, he was the second of his family to be a secret informer. His father, a person of wealth and influence but a bit on the timid side, had long been in receipt of a secret-service allowance paid in a furtive manner.

Whoever he was, " Fine Hand " wrote three letters for Mr. Wickham at this time in the beautiful script that is the reason for his pseudonym. One was written August 31, the second September 3, and the third October 6. In the last the writer promised to make the connection Mr. Wickham had desired him to ; thus it is evident that he continued to help the Castle " develop " the conspiracy. His later letters, however, have not survived.

From England "Jones" was sending over long detailed accounts of all Emmet's associates both in Ireland and France. (He must have written one about Emmet, too, but that is no longer available.)   Robert Carty, who had been arrested almost by accident in London, had been induced to become an informer for the usual price, his life.*

By now, John Fleming, the hostler at the White Bull, Pat McCabe, and Pat Farrell, all of whom had been in the depot in Thomas Street and had seen Emmet there, had agreed to prosecute him and had given the Government page after page of information.   Denis Redmond was still being tempted to save his life by disclosing what he knew about the insurrection.

But most important of all, so the Government evidently felt, was the fact that they now had the entire Develin family of Rathfarnham in custody and were using both threats and bribes to get Anne to save their lives and her own by telling what she knew of Robert Emmet.   The Develins had been arrested the night of August 29, only a few hours after Anne had returned home from the O'Neills' on the Coombe.   They were taken to the Castle under a heavy guard, the men with their hands tied behind them and their trousers cut in the back. Anne was put into a room in the Tower, and a little brother, ill of the smallpox, was left with her.   All the others were separated and next day, after being identified by Thomas Halpin, an old Wicklow neighbour who was now in the Government's service, they were examined separately.   They showed a common willingness to defend "Mr. Ellis" and Big Arthur Develin and evidently rated loyalty a much

---

* Wickham was now carrying on a battle by letter to get Carty sent over from London so that he could give information on the spot.   Carty's bargain with the British Government had been that he was to have a pardon, that he would not be required to come forward as a witness, and that Thomas Cloney and Nicholas Grey, his friends, who had both saved his life at various times, should also escape punishment for their part in the conspiracy.

Carty had been examined in London on August 26, and a copy of the examination sent to the Castle.   However, Wickham wanted the English officials to let him have Carty for further questioning.   When Mr. Charles Yorke, the Home Secretary, a most honourable man, thought that the terms made with Carty precluded that, Wickham tried to evade his scruples by pretending that Carty had not kept his part of the bargain.   He assumed that the engagement had been made either on the direct or implied condition on Carty's part that he was to tell the *whole* truth, and that he would conceal nothing that he knew.   This had not been the case, and Mr. Yorke refused to send Carty to Dublin without his consent.   However, after a deluge of letters from Wickham, all of them more and more insistent, he gave in and sent Carty over.   Not hindered by scruples, Wickham let it be known that Carty was giving information, so that other rebels would be terrified.

greater virtue than veracity. They lied even more sturdily than the Palmers had. They refused to admit they had even seen either Ellis or Big Arthur since the rising.

Anne of course was the one officials worked on hardest. She was questioned both by Major Sirr and Mr. Townsend. The Major told her briskly that she would have to tell where the leaders were if she wanted to save her family.

"I know nothing about them," Anne retorted. "I had enough to do to earn my bread and mind my own business." She persisted in calling her master Mr. Ellis, and about the only thing Sirr could draw from her was that Mr. Ellis had a small black trunk, and that she had taken some clean linen to him at a warehouse off Thomas Street.

The next morning about eleven (August 31, the day after Emmet's first examination) Anne was taken to Marsden's office and questioned again. Mr. Wickham was present. If these men thought they could deal easily with a simple country girl, and that they would soon have her as a Crown witness, they were quickly disillusioned. Anne said she knew nothing about Mr. Ellis or his visitors, and she adhered to that line in spite of every persuasion and pressure.

Marsden lectured her on the sufferings a prisoner underwent (of which she had already had a foretaste at the hands of Hanlon, the keeper of the Tower) and hinted at a shameful execution. He spoke, too, of the disgrace to aged parents, all without making any change in Anne's attitude. She was often asked about Russell, but she was almost as devoted to him as to Emmet, and they got nothing from her.

"You are a most incorrigible girl," Marsden scolded her, "dead to all the kind and noble feelings that adorn the character of a woman."

Anne made a disrespectful remark about informers and what she thought of them, and the interview ended.

Mrs. Hanlon, the keeper's wife, a very decent and kind-hearted woman, told Anne that every one was trying to get information for the Lord Lieutenant and the Privy Council. Anne's experience bears the story out. Fleming was the next one to work on her. With the Major as a witness, and urging him on, Fleming reneged handsomely on his former adherence to the rebels, excusing himself on the ground of his youth and his need of employment. He told Anne that " he knew what to do after."

" You villain," Anne flared, seizing him by the cravat. " You're some one wanting to swear my life away, but I'll have yours first."

The Major ran to pull the bell, and some of his men came in. The little rebel, her captors were beginning to find, was not only stubborn, but she had a temper hot as any hell-cat's and a picturesque vocabulary of profanity that she used as an escape valve. (She told Dr. Madden later that it eased her mind when Dr. Trevor tormented her.)

It was about this time that the Doctor had his first try at her. He was medical attendant and deputy governor of Kilmainham gaol and an inspector of prisons, and he used his office as an excuse to interrogate prisoners. He had all sorts of ways of inducing them to give information, and he was a great help to the Castle in getting prisoners to become informers.

At first, Trevor was gentle and insinuating with Anne, and she was inclined to like him. But when she would not break down and give information, he put off this pose for his more usual sadism.

Then Major Sirr tried again. This time he offered Anne £500 for information about Emmet's movements after July 23. He told her that the leaders did not care about the poor people they deluded.

" Don't be a fool, Anne," he urged. " Just tell what you know. Five hundred pounds will be a very handsome fortune [dowry] for a young woman like you. Be your own friend and don't refuse it."

" If I never get a fortune till I get one of blood money I'll be without one all the days of my life," Anne retorted, and though Brother Luke Cullen did not record it, she probably added something from her stock of invectives.

" What do you mean by blood money ? " Sirr asked.

" I suppose you want me to be like Bid Dolan," Anne retorted, referring to a notorious character who had sworn away the lives of dozens of Wicklow men.

" Who is Bid Dolan ? " he countered.

" I'm sure you don't know her."

"No," the Major lied gruffly.

"Perhaps you might know Croppy Biddy better?"

This was too much for the touchy Major. He said he had sent her father and mother home, but that he would keep Anne in gaol for the rest of her days as a pattern for other women.

Actually, Anne's father, mother, two sisters, and a brother had been sent to Kilmainham, a brother John to the guard-house in Ship Street, and her cousin Edward to the Provost. Kilmainham was now so crowded that Anne herself was kept some time in the Tower before she was sent there.

When she was transferred to the prison, they put beside her name in the Kilmainham register the hopeful comment, "To prosecute." Never was there more groundless wishful thinking. Anne would gladly have died before she betrayed Emmet by even a single word.

Four days after his examination Emmet was still unwilling to go beyond his own ideas of honour even to shield Sarah Curran. He wrote Wickham on September 3 that he had weighed well the proposal that had been made to him when he was before the Privy Council : he knew how much he owed to one whose peace of mind he had already too deeply injured, but that every way he turned he found obstacles almost insurmountable. Between the case held out to him (that of the State prisoners in 1798) and the present he could find no parallel.

What was done then was neither done by one, nor for one, nor to spare their own personal feelings, nor to obtain an object of a private nature, totally unconnected with the public act that was done. Give me the same advantages. Let me have free communication with some friends, let the lives of others be spared ; the documents affecting another person be suppressed, and I will try how far in my conscience, and according to *my* notions of duty, I ought to go. But I will stand my trial, for I will not purchase my own safety. If this proposal can be agreed to I request that the gentleman I mentioned [Mr. Burton, a young lawyer associated with Sarah's father] may be permitted to wait on me.*

But Emmet had already demonstrated how inflexible his ideas of honour were. To frighten him into a less ethical mood Dr. Trevor was entrusted next day with a message to

---

* *Vice Roy's Post Bag*, p. 354.

Emmet which concealed, in its rejection of Emmet's limited offer, a further threat to Sarah.

Dr. Trevor carefully wrote down what he was to tell Emmet :

When he came up for examination on Tuesday last he expressed very considerable anxiety to prevent any proceeding being taken against *a particular person*, and that to protect *that Person*, he would sacrifice his own personal safety. He was told that no such sacrifice was desired, that he was not required to furnish any evidence against himself. But as he expressed such considerable anxiety for *that person*, it was suggested to him to consider how far his Notions of honour, as he explained them, would permit him to make such communications to Government respecting the late Insurrection, further depots of Arms, Ammunition, etc., etc., as might justify the Government in acting towards *that person* with the Delicacy he required. So far the Government may be induced to go upon receiving information equivalent to the indulgence ; But it never entertained any ideas of receiving any information from Mr. Emmet which could extend to protect him or any of the persons engaged with him, further than that particular person.

This communication was considered so important that a copy of it was sent to the Home Office in London. Dr. Trevor's memorandum, after being used, was taken back to the Castle. Across its back a Castle clerk had written an endorsement : " Note to be communicated to Mr. Robert Emmet by Dr. Trevor : Sept. 4, 1803."

If he was up to his usual form, the Doctor did an expert job of trying to get Emmet to turn informer.

CHAPTER THIRTY-THREE

Emmet Plans to Escape

AMONG the menaces surrounding Robert Emmet in prison was the usual one of a seemingly sympathetic turnkey. This man, one George Dunn, so thoroughly deceived Emmet that the unsuspecting prisoner conceived the idea of bribing him to help him escape. He sent a note by Dunn to his cousin St. John Mason, also a prisoner in Kilmainham, suggesting that money offered to Dunn might procure an escape for several persons.

Accordingly, Mason did promise the man £500 and an additional reward of £500 more if Emmet should get out of the country. Dunn agreed, but he immediately reported the offer to Dr. Trevor. He was told to allow the prisoners to develop their plan but to keep the Doctor informed of everything that passed between them. When Mason gave Dunn a letter intended for Emmet, both Trevor and Wickham read it before it was delivered.

It was Mason's idea that the turnkey should get the key from the Governor of the prison while he was at dinner, and that Emmet should slip out unnoticed. He would be wearing a coat which he hoped a friend would bring in the next day. This was about September 5.

Emmet's plan was not only to escape himself but to take four other persons with him. In one of the notes that passed through Dunn's hands Emmet wrote Mason to have Dunn the turnkey find out when the Governor, Mr. John Dunn (no relation to the turnkey), dined, and if he left any one at the door then.

Though it might be a little early [Emmet added], yet as he is away longer then than at any other time, it would better enable us all to go out, and with the change of dress would not be noticed. If it cannot be done then, then G. must watch the first opportunity after dinner that Mr. D. goes down to the house, and let me out immediately. I will be ready at the moment. Don't let him wait until the guards are doubled, if he can avoid it, but if he cannot do it before let me be on the watch then, as D. will probably go to give them instructions when placing them in the yards, as he did last night.

I am anxious not to defer it till tomorrow, as I heard the officer who came the rounds consulting with him about placing the sentries for better security, and I think I heard them mention me in the *hall*. D. also came in at one oclock last night, under pretence that he thought he heard me calling. If it is delayed till tomorrow it must be done at dinner time. If sentries are placed in the hall by day the only way will be, whenever D. goes down let G. whistle *God Save the King* in the passage, and I will immediately ask to go to the necessary, and will change my clothes there instantly, but in this case, G. must previously convey them there. Send for a pair of spectacles (No. 5 fits my sight) which will facilitate the disguise. After I am gone G. must convey the clothes I wore away.*

Mason was against taking any one with Emmet, and wrote him so emphatically :

You must relinquish every idea of not going alone, or nothing can be done. . . . I have a friend at Booterstown [it was a Dr. Twomey] who will be here tomorrow. If he can I know he will procure a blue coat that will do, but it cannot be brought here. . . . You say if you could all be safe for two nights : Suppose I grant you all but the If. But I say the difficulties of concealment, even afterwards, would be ten fold for each person. Once more, I conjure you not to think of it.†

The next day Mason gave Dunn some things to take to Emmet which he did only after showing them to Dr. Trevor, who extracted some he did not think it wise to let the prisoner have.

But almost immediately this bit of mouse-baiting stopped. The turnkey told both Emmet and Mason that he could do nothing more for them, since the Governor's suspicions had been aroused, and he had moved his own quarters to that side of the goal. Unfortunately, Emmet's suspicions were not aroused, and he continued to think the turnkey was his friend.

That day Emmet had been taken to Green Street courthouse, where he was put to the bar.‡ He named Mr. Curran, Sarah's father, and Mr. Ponsonby as his counsel. Being told that Mr. Ponsonby had gone to Tipperary, he named Mr. Burton,

---

* Madden *United Irishmen*, III, p. 434.

† Ibid., p. 433.

‡ That same day Felix Rourke was being urged to tell what he knew about the rising. Wickham instructed Major Sirr that he was not to commit the Government to anything, but to let the offer come from Rourke. "All that you and Captain Clinch must do will be this—ask him whether he is prepared to go to the *full length* of a full

with the understanding that Mr. Ponsonby could be substituted at any reasonable time. McNally, who had probably been hoping for the assignment, was named as Emmet's agent.

Lord Norbury appointed the next Wednesday for the prisoner to plead and stand his trial.*

and unreserved disclosure both as to the fact and persons from the year 1796 downward. If so inform him you will represent his intentions to government and solicit their further consideration of the case. Press him to do so but promise nothing. In the meantime he will be put off his being brought up for Judgment until Emmet's fate shall be decided." *Sirr Papers.* Trinity College, Dublin.

Rourke refused to give any information that might injure others and was immediately tried and hanged at Rathcoole.

* The trial was later postponed to September 19th.

CHAPTER THIRTY-FOUR

More Trickery

THE next day, September 8, Robert Emmet saw Anne
Develin for the last time. It was a meeting arranged by
the Government as a means of tricking Anne Develin into
admitting that she knew him. After every State trial and
its subsequent execution (and they were now taking place
almost daily) or on the eve of one, Dr. Trevor would come
to Anne and threaten her with the same fate if she did not
make disclosures about the men she had known at Butterfield
Lane. Felix Rourke had been tried the day before and was
then waiting execution. So were two other men who had
been taken in Thomas Street, Killen and McCann. Anne
therefore was not surprised when the Doctor appeared at her
cell door.

But instead of speaking of death and disgrace, as he usually
did on these occasions, the Doctor was in one of his ingratiating
moods. He asked Anne if she would not like some fresh air
and exercise, a major indulgence to a person in solitary confinement. She was conducted, not to the usual exercise
yard for women prisoners, but to the place where male
prisoners sometimes took the air. On her way there she
passed some persons standing by a window, and, recollecting
that she had seen them at the Castle, she was immediately
on her guard.

Anne had only entered the yard, and the door had not yet
been shut behind her when she saw Emmet. He was some
distance from her, and fortunately he was not looking in her
direction. All her life Anne was to remember the feeling of
dismay and consternation that swept over her, but she had
learned some prison lessons, and she kept her alarm from
being apparent.

The closing of the door startled Emmet. Turning his head,
his eyes met Anne's. She was afraid he would speak or salute

her in some way, so she put on a stern appearance and frowned. Then she looked significantly toward the window, where the Castle gentlemen were watching.

Emmet realised at once that something was wrong. He had a racquet and ball in his hand, and as if by accident he struck the ball in Anne's direction. As he followed it, a smile, unforgettable to Anne, though it was half suppressed, lighted his face. Stooping over the ball, he said softly, "Anne dear, confess what you know of me, so you and your family can be free."

Anne made no answer then but walked on. As she came back, she limped a little, as though something were hurting her. When she was near Emmet, she stopped and took off one of her shoes and shook out a bit of imaginary gravel.

"I thought, sir," she said under her breath, "that you would be the last man in the world to encourage me to become an informer."

"I didn't mean that," Emmet said. "Tell of no one but me. But I am a dead man already, though you see me walking here."

Again they had to pass on. Anne was racking her brains for some other excuse to stop. She could think of nothing but to pull up her stockings.

"There will be plenty of people to swear against me," Emmet said as they met again. She warned him that some one was watching at the window.

"Do it for my sake, Anne. I can't die easy while you and your family are in such danger through my means."

"Not for a thousand pounds," Anne swore vehemently. "Not for the whole world, would I swear one *syllable* against you!"

It was her last word with Robert Emmet. (Recalling the scene for Luke Cullen many years later, when her body was twisted and worn with the disease her years of imprisonment had given her, she, like Miles Byrne, could speak of Emmet only with love and respect. "That generous soul," "that noble-minded young man," she called him.) They continued their walks a little longer but seemed to take no further notice of one another.

Anne went back to her cell and Trevor's abuse for the

failure of his plan. Emmet, in his, poured out his heart in a letter to Sarah Curran.

Castle officials had not yet discovered who the *particular person* really was, whose safety was so precious to Robert Emmet. They learned it when George Dunn made him an offer to deliver a letter to any one outside the prison with whom Emmet wanted to communicate. Unfortunately, Emmet still trusted the man implicitly, and he gladly took advantage of the offer by writing to Sarah :

My Dearest Love,

I don't know how to write you. I never felt so oppressed in my life as at the cruel injury I have done to you. I was seized and searched with a pistol over me before I could destroy your letters. They have been compared with those found before. I was threatened with having them brought forward against me in Court. I offered to plead guilty if they would suppress them. This was refused. Information (without mentioning names) was required. I refused, but offered since, if I would be permitted to consult others, and that they would consent to enter into any accommodation of that nature to save the lives of those condemned, that I would only require for my part of it to have those letters suppressed, and that I would stand my trial. It has been refused. My love, can you forgive me ?

He told her how, on his examination, they had shown him her letters and suggested bringing the writer of them into the room.

I was sure you were arrested, and I could not stand the idea of seeing you in that situation. When I found however, that this was not the case, I began to think they only meant to alarm me ; but their refusal [to the answer he had given Trevor] has only come this moment, and my fears are renewed. Not that they can do anything to you even if they would be base enough to attempt it, for they can have no proof who wrote them, nor did I let your name escape me, nor even acknowledge that they were written directly to myself. But I fear that they may suspect from the stile, and from the hair, for they took the stock from me, and I have not been able to get it back from them, and that they may think of bringing you forward.

I have written to your father to come to me tomorrow. Had you not better speak to himself (*sic*) tonight ? Destroy my letters, that there may be nothing against yourself, and deny having any knowledge of me further than seeing me once or twice. For God's sake, write to me by the bearer one line to tell me how you are in spirits. I have no anxiety, no care, about myself ; but I am terribly oppressed about you. My dearest love, I would with joy lay down my life, but ought I to do more? Do not be alarmed ; they may try to frighten you, but they cannot do more. God bless you, my dearest love.

I send this off at once : I have written it in the dark. My dearest Sarah, forgive me.*

* *Vice Roy's Post Bag*, p. 358.

Openly writing " Miss Sarah Curran " on the cover, Emmet gave the letter to Dunn. Within an hour it was at the Castle.

This was what Wickham had been working for, but once he learned that the writer of the letters Emmet prized so highly was Sarah Curran, he was under a bit of a difficulty. Sarah's father, the famous John Philpot Curran, so long in opposition to the Government and a champion of nationalism, had just shown by an open overture that he was ready to reverse his position. Acting as a defence counsel on one of the minor State trials, Curran had made a speech praising the Government, congratulating the court on the loyalty of the great majority of the people, and professing his own loyalty. He abused Buonaparte for having caused the late rebellion and advised the people, as an old friend, against their " present folly." Then, forgetting all he had said, he spent an hour proving to the court that no rebellion existed and that Ireland was a contented and happy nation. Having thus demonstrated his complete political about-face, he sat down ; he had completely ignored his client in the transaction.

Government had been only too ready to welcome this new convert. Naturally, Wickham did not want to damp his ardour by an abrupt intrusion on his family's privacy. Still, Emmet's letters to Sarah had to be seized, and Sarah herself examined. Major Sirr was given a velvet glove in the shape of a most polite and considerate letter to Mr. Curran from Mr. Wickham. The Secretary regretted that the Lord Lieutenant was obliged to direct a search be made in Mr. Curran's house for papers connected with the late treasonable conspiracy, which he was persuaded had been concealed without Mr. Curran's knowledge, etc. Also, since the circumstance leading to that investigation particularly affected Miss Sarah Curran, it was necessary that she be examined immediately. If Mr. Curran preferred to have the examination take place at his town house rather than at the Castle, he was to take his daughter there without delay and notify the Lord Lieutenant.

By the time these delicate adjustments had been made, it was too late to go to Rathfarnham that night. Early next morning Major Sirr and his men set out for the Priory.

CHAPTER THIRTY-FIVE

Major Sirr Raids the Priory

MR. CURRAN was not at home when Major Sirr and his aides arrived at his country house. Sarah's brother Richard and her sisters Amelia and Jane were downstairs at breakfast, but Sarah was still abed. The Major insisted on being taken up to the room she shared with Amelia, and his sudden entrance demanding Emmet's letters threw the poor girl into hysterics. But the shock to her nervous system had one good effect. It diverted the attention of the Major while Amelia with great presence of mind quietly fed the letters to the fire. By the time the Major became aware of this, only a few scraps were left.

As Mr. Curran did not return immediately, and Sirr had no authority to arrest Sarah, he sent into town for instructions. Mr. Wickham, to whom he applied, was dining with the Lord Chancellor when Sirr's note finally reached him. He ordered him to come away without Sarah and professed himself much distressed to hear of the state of her mind.

Her father's concern, when he did reach the Priory, was not for Sarah but for his own career. He hurried into town to call on the Attorney-General and Mr. Wickham. He protested that this was the first he had known of Emmet's connection with his daughter. He denounced her, he denounced Emmet, he pleaded to have the Attorney-General come out to the Priory and examine his papers. He even asked to be taken before the Privy Council to prove to them that he had no knowledge of the conspiracy. He neglected nothing to prove his innocence, his loyalty, and by implication his perfect suitability for a Government position and advancement at the bar.

When told of the matter, the Lord Lieutenant thought the love affair of Emmet and Sarah a most extraordinary story, and that the letters strengthened the case against Emmet. He ruled, however, that no action should be taken against Sarah, and that Mr. Curran should withdraw as Emmet's counsel.

Curran was only too glad to do this, and in a note dated September 10 he curtly notified Emmet of the fact. He also suggested that Emmet should not mention to his new counsel the reason why Curran had withdrawn. Mr. Burton also withdrew from the case, "from a motive of delicacy." He happened to be Curran's clerk.

To Curran's brief and chilly letter Emmet replied passionately and at great length. It was not Curran's refusal to act as his counsel that bothered him. He dismissed that in a few lines, not blaming Curran at all. But he was most anxious that Sarah should be held blameless for their love. It was he, he protested, who had done the injury, an injury much greater than he could atone for with his life.

That atonement I did offer to make before the Privy Council, by pleading guilty if those documents were suppressed. . . . My intention was not to leave the suppression of those documents to possibility, but to render it unnecessary for anyone to plead for me, by pleading guilty to the charges myself.

He went on to tell Curran how he had first spoken of his love to Sarah and how, after some time, they had finally become engaged.

There has been much culpability on my part in all this, but there has also been a great deal of that misfortune which seems uniformly to have accompanied me.

That I have written to your daughter since an unfortunate event has taken place was an additional breach of propriety for which I have suffered well. But I will candidly confess that I not only do not feel it to have been of the same extent, but that I consider it to have been unavoidable after what had passed ; for though I will not attempt to justify in the smallest degree my former conduct, yet, when an attachment was once formed—and a sincerer one never did exist—I feel that, peculiarly circumstanced as I then was, to have left her uncertain of my situation would neither have weaned her affections nor lessened her anxiety, and looking upon her as one whom, if I had lived, I hoped to have had my partner for life, I did hold the removing of her anxiety above every other consideration. I would rather have had the affections of your daughter in the back settlements of America than the first situation this country could afford without them.

I know not whether this will be any extenuation of my offence. I know not whether it will be any extenuation of it to know that if I had that situation in my power at this moment, I would relinquish it to devote my life to her happiness. I know not whether success would have blotted out the recollection of what I have done. But I know that a man with the coldness of death upon him need not be made to feel any other coldness, and that he may be spared any addition to the misery he feels not for himself, but for those to whom he has left nothing but sorrow.*

It probably eased Emmet's anguish to write the letter. If it did not, it was a waste of time and paper. Curran had set himself coldly against his daughter and Emmet, and his attitude was not changed in the slightest degree by that heart-broken confession.

* *Vice Roy's Post Bag,* p. 391.

CHAPTER THIRTY-SIX

Russell Comes to Help Emmet

MEANWHILE, unknown to Emmet, Thomas Russell had ventured down to Dublin in the hope of helping his friend escape. Careless of his own safety as always, Russell had begun the dangerous journey as soon as he could after hearing of Emmet's arrest. Mary McCracken, sister of Henry Joy McCracken of Belfast who had been hanged in 1798, and who cherished an ardent but secret love for Russell, gladly provided the money for the journey.

When he reached Dublin, Russell got in touch with Biddy Palmer of New Row, and doubtless with her father as well.* Biddy took a message from him to Philip Long's clerk, young David Fitzgerald, evidently asking for more funds for the hazardous undertaking, and also that the boy should come to see him.

About eight o'clock in the evening on that September day when the Kilmainham turnkey Dunn had put an end to Emmet's own plan for escape, Russell, using the name of Harris, had taken up lodgings in Parliament Street, in the very shadow of Dublin Castle.

Earlier in the day a man whose identity is still unknown had called on Daniel Muley at 29 Parliament Street and engaged some rooms for a Mr. and Mrs. Harris who he said would arrive that evening. Muley was a gunsmith Russell had known as far back as 1798 when he was in Newgate gaol. Muley had made pistols and blunderbusses for the rising in July which he gave to the rebels gratis. However, he was far from being well off and not only shared his shop with a

---

* Young David Fitzgerald of Dublin later told Dr. Madden that " when Russell was concealed, she [Biddy Palmer] came to him and said that Russell wished to see him, that he wanted money to take him off. Fitzgerald sent forty guineas to him by Miss Palmer, and either that day or the next, Russell was arrested, but in the meantime, Russell sent a gentleman to Fitzgerald, and that gentleman said that Russell had received neither message nor money from him." Madden, *United Irishmen*, III, p. 373.

shoemaker but let out the rooms of his upper floors to lodgers. It was quite natural, then, for Russell to have thought of him when looking for a place of concealment while he made plans to get Emmet out of Kilmainham.

When Russell, accompanied by the man who had engaged the rooms, arrived that Wednesday evening, Muley himself showed the new guest upstairs and thereafter took the most unusual precautions not to let him be seen, even by members of his own family. It was given out, to explain Russell's lack of luggage, that " Mrs. Harris " would arrive the next day, bringing bags with her. On the street door, as required by law, Muley added the name of " Mr. Harris " to the list of the occupants of the house.

The day after his arrival Russell, evidently waiting for Biddy Palmer and young Fitzgerald to come to him, did not stir from his shabby quarters. He passed the time reading some old magazines of Muley's or turning the pages of Josephus and a copy of Paine's *Geography*. Muley took him up a dinner of beef-steak, but aside from his host he saw no one that day.

On Friday the man who had engaged the rooms visited him briefly ; then Russell was left alone again.

The establishment of Grierson, the King's Printer, adjoined the house where Russell was hiding, a guard-house was in the same street, and Sirr and his myrmidons had their headquarters within a stone's throw of Muley's doorway. But Russell, armed with a pair of pistols, probably wasted little time worrying about capture. He trusted his friends implicitly, and he probably did not know that Watty Cox, the weather-vane patriot-informer, was separated from him only by the thickness of a single wall. Already he had been betrayed to the Castle.

In some way, perhaps through Cox, Mr. John Emerson, an examiner in one of the Crown law offices, had been told that a suspicious stranger was staying at Muley's. He immediately tried to find Major Sirr, so that the man could be taken up. But the Major was at Rathfarnham that morning, raiding the Priory. Emerson told his suspicions to Marsden, then wrote a note to Sirr, expecting that he would make the arrest as soon as he returned to the Castle.

As I could not see you this morning, I called on Mr. Marsden and informed him of the following particulars. I have the strongest reason to believe that there is a Traitor concealed in Mr. Muley's (Gunsmith) house in Parliament Street next door to Mr. Grierson. You know (I dare say) the disaffected Character of *Muley*. He conducted the man I suspect two nights ago to the Room immediately *over* the Drawing room which lies over *his* shop : so particular is he, as to bring the man his breakfast every Morning himself, and does not allow even his wife to go into the apartment to adjust it until he has previously *in the Dark* conducted the Stranger to a Room in the 3d story. Take care in the search to secure the Top of the house to prevent any Escape, the Stranger is there *now*. The window shutters of his apartment is kept generally closed. *It is well worth the* Search at any rate.

Emerson added a postscript to his letter : " The Stranger's Room is next to Waddy's house and the *second room* over Muley's own shop. I say his *own* as a Shoe maker occupies half the Shop."

But when Sirr got back to his office at the Castle, he was tired and disgruntled. He had not been allowed to arrest Sarah, he had waited hours for the return of her father and to hear from Wickham, and her sister had been able to destroy most of Robert Emmet's letters. He did not relish the idea of walking even the short distance down Parliament Street to Muley's on the chance of catching some anonymous rebel. Russell's name had not been mentioned ; thus the thousand-pound reward offered for his arrest did not spur him to make any effort.

But Emerson was sure the mystery man at Muley's must be some one of importance. He called on Sirr later in the evening and insisted that something be done. The Major somewhat crossly collected his brother-in-law Humphrey Minchen and a few of his burly assistants and sallied forth. Muley was not at home, but Sirr and Minchen gained an entrance to the house. They cautiously climbed the stairs, leaving Emerson and the others outside, then burst into the room where Russell was sitting. The Major was no stranger to him, and his hand went to his holster. But when he saw that Sirr was unarmed, the over-ethical Russell would not fire.* He was overpowered and taken prisoner.

---

* Newspaper accounts of the arrest said that Sirr barely escaped with his life, as Russell was about to shoot the Major when he was overpowered. But two letters still in the I.S.P.O. tell the true story. In October of that year Marsden wrote Baron Smith, in whose office Emerson was engaged that " there is reason to think his [Sirr's] life was saved by the accident of his going into the room unarmed. I believe Russell

Up the street he was marched and into the Castle. It was a great ending for the Major's day, a wonderful bit of luck for Wickham and Marsden, who rightly considered Russell a prize of great worth, and a disastrous end of the attempt to rescue Emmet. For Russell himself it meant inevitably trial and execution. Knowing this, he announced that he was as ready to die on the scaffold as on the field.

But Wickham had no idea of letting Russell be hanged until he, too, if possible had been deprived of his honour and made to give information. He was too dangerously devoted to the idea of democracy to be allowed to live, and so the Government would not tempt him with the offer of his life. He had no sweetheart whose safety they could hold over his head as a threat, but they soon found what they believed was a sure way of forcing information from him.

The lodgings of a sister in Dublin were searched. From letters found there the Castle learned that John Russell, who had visited his brother in Paris, was then in London. John was arrested and examined, and the papers sent over to Dublin Castle. Though even Wickham had to admit that there was no reason to think that John Russell had been concerned in the rising, the threat of danger to him and to Miss Margaret Russell was used to try to induce Tom to give information to the Government.*

Before he was taken to Downpatrick to stand his trial, he wrote a friend, " I mean to make my trial, and the last of my life, if it is to close now, as serviceable to the cause of Liberty as I can."

who drew a pistol, said he would have shot at Sirr had the Major been armed. . . ."

The Bishop of Derry wrote to Sirr in May of 1804 : " I cannot exactly recollect the whole of Mr. Emerson's conversation as to the arrest of Russell, but I know in talking of him he said he would always consider him as a man of humanity as he certainly had the lives of two people in his power but would not make use of pistols against unarmed men."

The pistols, which had Russell's name engraved upon them, were probably a pair Muley had made for Russell.

* Belying the official attitude that Emmet was alone responsible for the rising, and its " very heart and soul," Wickham wrote to an English official : " Thomas Russell is, I am persuaded, the man who had the most direct communication with the French Govt. in the course of the last Spring, and it is in his power to make on that subject the most important discoveries, and his Temper of mind and natural character are such that nothing would be so likely to induce him to take such a step as kindness to his relatives *when you have it in your power to do them mischief.*"

Wickham's idea was that Russell should give information regarding the French, depots of arms, etc., and that in return his brother and sister would not be harmed, and that the Government would make some provision for them to secure them from distress and want. P.R.O.L.

CHAPTER THIRTY-SEVEN

Into the Depths

THE day of Russell's arrest was triply tragic for Robert Emmet. Besides the frustration of his friend's plan to help him escape, Major Sirr had raided the Priory, thus bringing Sarah Curran's name into public notice and making her father his bitter enemy. Also on that Friday, September 9, Elizabeth Emmet died, probably of a broken heart.

For some reason, Robert was not told of his bereavement for several days. When his sister Mary Anne wrote to the Lord Lieutenant asking permission to see him if only for a few minutes and in the presence of another person, she was refused.

To the already overwhelming load of sorrows and disasters that had descended upon Emmet, he himself added more in his choice of lawyers to replace Curran and Burton. For Curran he substituted Leonard McNally, for whom it was almost second nature to betray his clients.* In place of Burton he acquired Peter Burrowes, who had been giving the Castle information about the rebels since May and who was almost as anxious to please the Government as McNally was.

McNally immediately went to see Emmet in Kilmainham and found him terribly worried about Sarah Curran. " On this subject his mind seems wholly bent, and cruelly afflicted," the informer wrote Wickham. " For his own personal safety he appears not to entertain an idea. He does not intend to call a single witness, nor to trouble any witness for the Crown with a cross examination unless they misrepresent facts." †

This would seem to leave Emmet in a sufficiently helpless condition so that the Government could hang him and let it go at that. But this did not fit in with the policy concerning

---

* McNally had just got £100 secret-service money through Mr. Pollock, and two days after his appointment he was given another hundred.

† *Vice Roy's Post Bag*, p. 390.   Originals are in P.R.O.L.

him which had been decided upon, and which was being developed day by day. From the hundreds of prisoners who had been taken up since July 23 for their part in the rising, less than twenty had been selected for trial. They had been chosen not on the basis of their importance, but because of their very unimportance and poverty. The idea was to identify Emmet with persons from the very lowest class of society— an old-clothes man, a baker, a slater, some labourers—and to make it appear that it was only from people of this kind that the rising had had support.*

Besides degrading Emmet (and the utterances of the Attorney-General on Emmet's trial make it obvious that this was the Government's object) this deliberate distortion of the truth served another purpose. In every trial of these poor men the officers of the Crown made it appear that the prisoner in the dock had been tricked into the conspiracy, that he had not acted from any genuine desire for a political change, but that he had been victimised to satisfy the personal ambition of a few men. The ultimate effect of this, it was hoped, would be to dampen the national ardour of the common people and keep them from entering another conspiracy.

With candour quite unusual for him Wickham admitted this explicitly in a letter to London. " We are endeavouring here as much as possible to make the leaders contemptible and to represent them to the people as traitors to the cause and sacrificing the lower orders to their own interests." †

The trial of Emmet, on whom all the calumny was to focus, was now set for September 19, which gave the Government only a week more to work on him. In that time they hoped to make him renounce his principles, to get from him through informers whose intentions he did not suspect every last detail of the rising, and to make him regard the gallows as a disgrace.

This last, in a country where so many national heroes had lost their lives by hanging, was an essential part of the

* Every one of the Crown officers who prosecuted Emmet emphasised this point, and it was reiterated in newspaper articles for months. The *Dublin Evening Post* printed a typical one in October, listing the occupations of the persons who had been tried by the Special Commission . " Such," it concluded after naming twenty-one persons including Emmet, " are the description of persons, who, with a few others equally contemptible, and of the lowest order of society, one or two excepted, presumed upon overturning the Government of the Country."

† P.R.O.L. The letter was written September 11, 1803.

Government's programme, not only as far as Emmet was concerned, but with the lesser State prisoners who were brought to trial. It kept them from becoming martyrs. Every pressure was exerted by the Castle to try to get men who had been sentenced to death make a public repentance.

Edward Kearney, who had been taken by Lieutenant Brady's party on Thomas Street, and who was the first of the prisoners to be executed, won a posthumous commendation from the Lord Lieutenant for telling the mob at the foot of the gallows, "This is a bad business, boys. I advise you to have nothing more to do with it."

Maxwell Roche, a slater, said much the same. James Byrne, the Naas baker Emmet had sent to look over the Pigeon House a few days before the rising, warned the men who had come to see him die against the crime that had brought him there. At least, that was what the *Dublin Evening Post* reported, but it may not have been the fact. In some cases newspaper accounts were given the lie by official private correspondence.

Whatever expressions of repentance were actually pressed from the prisoners were obtained partly by appeals made by the Government officials who were in contact with them, Dr. Trevor, Major Sirr, Marsden, and Wickham ; partly by means of Irish clergymen who had been under pressure from Castle officials to force the men they ministered to to make reparation for their crimes against the Government, partly through Leonard McNally acting ostensibly as their friend as well as their counsel.*

All these forces were now brought to bear upon Robert Emmet.

In his case, of course, the clergymen were Protestants, and their part had to be played with some finesse. McNally unctuously acted the part of an elderly friend offering personal advice. Peter Burrowes spent hours with his client under the pretext of preparing his defence. Some unidentified informer,

* Without the Lord Lieutenant's knowledge, Kearney and Roche had been denied a priest to attend them at their last moments, and even denied a confessor to give them absolution. When he heard of the omission, Lord Hardwicke ordered that priests be admitted to other condemned men. But what the Lord Lieutenant had granted out of humanity and generosity of spirit Wickham tried to make use of to get information and to have the prisoners make public recantations.

a friend of Emmet's who may have been " Fine Hand," was visiting Kilmainham and having long conversations with him, to whom Emmet made many disclosures that were passed on to the Castle and from there sent to London.* It is more than likely that he carried out the Castle's wishes along this line as well as getting Emmet to talk about the rising.

Emmet had no idea of the attack being made on his integrity and thus could not combat it consciously. It was his character, his habits of thought and action, which would help him in this crisis. He was young, but for more than half his life he had entertained the idea of dying for his country. He had put himself in danger as far back as his Trinity days, when Tom Emmet had sworn him a United Irishman. He had given up all hope of a professional career in Ireland when he had withdrawn from college rather than name the students who had shared his political views. He had renounced the possibility of a new life in America, which the letters of introduction to Washington and Jefferson and " the principal people of New York and Pensilvanie " would have made possible, when he had been summoned back to Ireland from Paris. He had given the word of command to open the door of the depot in Thomas Street. The responsibility for that act rested on him like a garment. He had worn the epaulettes of a general and had drawn a general's sword. And inextricably entwined with all these memories, never dominant perhaps but in the background of them all, must have been the polished sheen of a silver salver and his family's motto *Constans*. The weapon defending Robert Emmet in this tremendously sinister struggle in which he had been chosen by his enemies to be the symbol of Irish nationalism was his honour.

In one way it was a handicap to him. In honour he could not betray the men who had been acting with him and who had escaped detection. But his idealism had been abraded

* On September 10 the Castle forwarded to London a copy of a note transmitted by " a confidential friend of Emmet's." On September 15 they sent another, which was to be destroyed after being read by Mr. Yorke and any person he thought proper. As the covering letter announced the arrest of a young gentleman named Burke who had been in Trinity with Emmet and expelled at the time of Lord Clare's visitation in 1798, the possibility of the informer being " Fine Hand " seems to be increased. Emmet might well have told one Trinity friend about the political activity of another. Emmet, of course, would look on " Fine Hand " as a fellow-conspirator. No suspicion rests on Burke.

Nicholas Grey and his brother-in-law Henry Hughes were also arrested at this time.

to the point where he realised that he would be allowed to bear the burden of blame for the failure of the rising. He wanted his brother at least to know the truth of the matter. His life was not precious to him, but his reputation was.

Carefully, explicitly, during the last few days of his life he wrote "Account of the Late Plan of Insurrection in Dublin, and the Cause of its Failure."

The Plan was comprised of three heads : *Points of Attack, Points of Check, and Lines of Defence.*

The Points of attack were three, the Pigeon House, the Castle, and the Artillery Barracks at Island Bridge.

The attack was to begin with the Pigeon House ; number of men, 200, the place of assembly, the Strand, between Irishtown and Sandymount, the time, low water. . . .

Lines of Defence. Beresford Street has six issues from Church Street, viz, Coleraine Street, King Street, Stirrup lane, Mary's lane, Pill lane and the Quay. These to be chained in the first instance by a body of chainmen, double chains and padlocks were deposited and the sills of the doors marked. [Here he stopped to sketch the double chains.] The blockade to be afterwards filled up; that on the quay by bringing up the coaches from the stand, and oversetting them, together with the butchers' blocks from Ormond market. . . .

The whole of this plan was given up by me for want of means, except the Castle and lines of defence ; for I expected three hundred Wexford, four hundred Kildare, and two hundred Wicklow men, all of whom had fought before. . . .

Had I another week, had I one thousand pounds, had I one thousand men, I would have feared nothing. There was redundancy enough in any one part to have made up, if complete, for deficiency in the rest, but there was failure in all, plan, preparation and men.

I would have given it the respectability of insurrection, but I did not wish uselessly to shed blood. I gave no signal for the rest, and they all escaped. . . .

I know how men without candour will pronounce on this failure, without knowing one of the circumstances that occasioned it ; they will consider only that they predicted it. Whether its failure was caused by chance, or by any of the grounds on which they made their prediction, they will not care ; they will make no distinction between a prediction fulfilled and justified—they will make no compromise of errors ; they will not recollect that they predicted also that no system could be formed—that no secrecy nor confidence could be restored, that no preparations could be made—that no plan could be arranged—that no day could be fixed without being instantly known at the Castle—that government only waited to let the conspiracy ripen, and crush it at their pleasure, and that on these grounds only did they predict the miscarriage.

The very same men that after success would have flattered, will now calumniate. The very same men that would have made an offering of unlimited sagacity at the shrine of victory, will not now be content to take back that portion that belongs of right to themselves, but would violate the sanctuary of misfortune and strip her of that covering that candour would have left her.

R. E.*

That last sentence shows how he was suffering within himself. It was his second, and last, use of the word misfortune as applicable to himself. Already he had assumed the manner currently described as unostentatious fortitude, which so impressed the people who saw him. But beneath the brave show and the easy air, Emmet's heart and soul were aching and torn with anguish.

* P.R.O.L.

CHAPTER THIRTY-EIGHT

Miles Byrne Reaches Paris

MILES BYRNE, with his message from Robert to the French Government to be transmitted by way of Tom, did not reach Paris till September 15. Emmet's trial was then only four days away. Byrne had been on his journey since August 31, all the time in an agony of fear that he would be too late to save his friend. He had not reached Bordeaux until September 6 and had been held up for several days by official investigations and the short-sighted hospitality of the Irish exiles there. His peace of mind was not improved by the fact that his only token of credential, the waxen impression of Robert Emmet's seal, had been taken from him by French officials there.

Hugh Wilson, one of the old Fort George prisoners, immediately wrote Tom Emmet in Paris of Byrne's arrival and sent him other news from Ireland. Meticulously Tom entered all this in his diary :

> A messenger is arrived in Bordeaux from Ireland and is on his way to me. I can learn that he has some not unfavourable and some very bad and to me distressing news. My brother Robert is arrested, and has been three times before the Privy Council, but has declined answering anything. My brother-in-law John Patten was arrested and liberated and is arrested again, so that now every male relative I have in Ireland that I know or love is in prison or perhaps in danger. God protect them to their friends, their families and country. . . .*

Byrne's journey from Bordeaux to Paris took four nights and five days, and to Byrne every minute was an hour. He was thinking of the assistance that Tom might be able to get from the French.† Would it be in time to save Robert Emmet ?

---

* *Memoir of Thomas Addis and Robert Emmet*, I, p. 367.
† In some way, perhaps, through " Fine Hand " Wickham had learned that Byrne was instructed to use every means in his power to prevail upon the French Government to constitute the English prisoners then in France hostages for State prisoners in Ireland. *Vice Roy's Post Bag*, p. 389. The effect of this would be to hurry Emmet's trial and execution.

At three o'clock on Thursday, September 15, the coach in which Byrne was travelling drew up at the diligence office in Rue Montmartre. Dr. McNevin, who had been one of Tom Emmet's companions at Kilmainham and Fort George, was there to receive him, accompanied by Adjutant-General Dalton of the French Ministry of War. Transferring to General Dalton's coach, Byrne was driven without delay to the Grand Judge Régnier's hotel in the Place Vendôme. In the Grand Judge's study Tom Emmet was waiting anxiously.

" Do you know this man ? " the Grand Judge asked Tom when Byrne was ushered in.

" I have never seen him before in my life," Tom had to answer.

Two hearts at least must have been very low at that moment. But on Tom's answer, the Grand Judge handed him the paper with the wax impression, which had been forwarded to Paris by the officer who had taken it from Byrne in Bordeaux.

As soon as he had compared the impression with his seal ring, Tom crossed the room, took the other Irishman in his arms, and embraced him with affection. That satisfied the Grand Judge of Byrne's identity, and he told Emmet that the First Consul wanted, as soon as possible, a detailed report of the state of Ireland. A *carte de sûreté* was given Byrne, and the official welcome was over.*

Tom took Byrne to his lodgings in the Rue du Cherche-Midi and presented him to Jane and their children. After dinner, with Dr. McNevin to help them, the men sat down to write the memorial for Buonaparte.

Miles explained the Irish situation ; Tom and Dr. McNevin asked questions and took notes. It was late before they retired, but by that time a rough draft of a memorial for Buonaparte had been prepared, which they copied in the morning.

Byrne's account of the state of Ireland as Tom recorded it in his diary the next day was that the provisional government still maintained its connection and correspondence with the country, and that the English Government knew little or nothing. (In this, of course, both Robert Emmet and Miles Byrne were wrong. The Government knew a great deal, but not everything.) The people, he reported quite correctly, were

* *Memoir of Miles Byrne*, I, p. 300.

in excellent spirits. None of the fire-arms but a great deal of ammunition and pikes had been lost.

The Insurrection of the 23rd Inst (*sic*) was forced on by the explosion of the powder manufactory in Patrick Street and a slight battle for recovering some ammunition a few nights before, but the country in general was not called upon or expected by the Provisional Government to act unless Dublin had been taken.

Russell's proclamation was not intended by him to be published till Dublin was taken, but it transpired from the over-zeal of some friends. In the same way the Proclamation of the Provisional Government was not to have been published till the next day, and was therefore not signed by the members.

If no persecutions are permitted the people will be quiet till the French come, and the instructions to me were to urge an expedition with the utmost speed. But as to arms, if they come they could be concealed, but not used before a landing, and that therefore it was useless to run the risk of sending them.

My brother says he is not in danger, but I doubt that. John Patten expected to be let out the day after Byrne came away. [Patten would not give information about Robert Emmet and the people who had helped him before and after the rising, and so was kept in confinement till the Habeas Corpus Act went into effect again, early in 1806.] He says the people's spirits have received a spring by the effort and that if a speedy landing takes place they will act much better than they would have done.*

The next morning Dalton called on Tom very early to inquire, for the Minister of War, what news the messenger had brought. Tom told him the substance of what he had written in his diary and said he would not press for arms at that time. In his turn, Tom asked what the French intended to do for Ireland. The General gave the strongest assurances that all the activity and preparations at Brest and the western ports of France, which people thought were for an English invasion, were actually intended for Ireland.†

Not knowing that Robert's trial would take place in Dublin the next Monday, Tom must have enjoyed an interval of comparative peace.

* *Memoir of Thomas Addis and Robert Emmet*, I, p. 368.
† The French navy was still unprepared to transport an invading army, but Buonaparte, for the benefit of English spies, was talking as though an invasion were imminent.

9
THE TRIAL OF ROBERT EMMET

CHAPTER THIRTY-NINE

The Crown's Case in General

"IT would be difficult for a stranger to form any idea of the degree of general interest and expectation that the approaching trial of Emmett (*sic*) begins to excite in this city," Wickham had written to London on September 15.

By the day of the trial, Monday, September 19, 1803, Dublin was seething with excitement. Emmet was more than just another prisoner to stand in the dock and be sentenced, for all practical purposes, for the murder of Lord Kilwarden. He was Robert Emmet of St. Stephen's Green, son of Dr. Emmet, born with a silver spoon in his aristocratic mouth. He was Robert Emmet of Trinity, Robert Emmet who had been in France and seen Buonaparte, Robert Emmet who had filled Dublin storehouses with pikes and blunderbuses and thousands of rounds of ammunition, Robert Emmet who had been on his keeping in the mountains, Robert Emmet who had been captured by that villain Major Sirr. He was the youth who had stirred the imagination of thousands by wearing a gold-laced uniform of emerald green. He was the crystallisation of the hopes of the mass of the Irish people, the symbol of their burning nationalism. Spontaneously, he had been elevated to the level of a national hero, companion of Wolfe Tone and Lord Edward Fitzgerald. He had been chosen because of his gallantry, because of his love of Ireland, because he had done what thousands of Irishmen had secretly wished to do—he had drawn a sword for Ireland.

Who could work while his fate was in the balance ? Who could stay indoors and be occupied with ordinary affairs ? Excited men crowded into taverns and public houses ; they gathered in groups on the streets, venting their emotion in conversation and scraps of song. Thousands of them became consolidated into a mob which pressed toward the court-house in Green Street, hoping for a glimpse of Emmet as he came from his cell in Kilmainham.

Even outside Dublin, Irishmen thought of little else that day but Emmet and what he stood for. The Hacketstown fair brought together a burly set of young men who jostled against soldiers and yeomen and flaunted their disloyalty by singing " The Green Flag " and other seditious songs. As far away as London, groups of Irish people congregated to speculate on what was happening in Dublin. They toasted " the poor young man," " the dear young man " so enthusiastically and so often that some got themselves arrested, thus making their devotion to Emmet and the cause he stood for a matter of court record.

Even men who disapproved of Emmet's politics joined his friends and sympathisers in trying to get a seat in the court-room. One who had betrayed him while he was in Trinity was among the spectators of the trial. So were a future consul of His Majesty's diplomatic service, some clergymen of the Established Church, an embryo judge of the Irish High Court, and other attorneys of steadfast loyalty.

Young William Henry Fitten of the Trinity Yeomanry Corps was there dressed in the King's uniform, as were a few others of the college corps, more sympathetic to Emmet than one might imagine. So was George Petrie the artist, with pencil and paper in his pocket ready to make furtive sketches of the historic scene. So were scores of other friends, discreetly undistinguished and anonymous.

The Castle was taking no chances that Emmet might be rescued. Enough red-coated soldiers were on the streets to keep the enormous crowds in order and prevent any mishaps. They surrounded the court-house in Green Street and coloured all its corridors. They stood almost shoulder to shoulder around the dock, their bayonets fixed and ready.

The slender young man who was the centre of all this interest was probably the calmest person in Dublin. In a brief and furtive conversation he had snatched with St. John Mason just before he had left Kilmainham, he had told his cousin he was prepared for anything. He had even been collected enough to use the Latin phrase, *Utrumque paratus*.

Surrounded by an escort of mounted soldiers, he had been

driven to the court-house a little before nine and had entered
it, as all prisoners did, by a laneway from Halston Street.
Until it was time for him to appear at the bar of justice, he
was kept waiting in a brick-walled cell below the courtroom.
Its arched ceiling was so low that he could hardly stand erect.
It was so narrow that a single iron gate easily barred one end.
At the other a flight of stone steps led to the room above.

As he waited there, witnesses who were to testify against
him occupied other basement cells or sat in apartments off
the courtroom. Some had come from Kilmainham, some
from Newgate next door, and some were soldiers who had
been at the depot early on the morning of July 24.

Joseph Palmer was there, reluctant to do anything to harm
his friend but bound by his oath to prosecute, and himself
now in danger of the law for having harboured Emmet.
Under cover of night Mr. Bell had fetched Mrs. Bagnell in a
coach from the mountains. In their pleasant book-lined
chamber just back of the bench the three judges were robing
and adjusting their wigs. The men called for jury duty
crowded against one another on wooden seats high up at the
back of the courtroom.

A little after nine the Attorney-General, Mr. O'Grady, came
in and settled himself with a handful of papers at the Crown
side of the court-room, under the sombre walnut dignity of
the judges' bench. The Solicitor-General joined him. The
attorneys for the Crown, Mr. Townsend, Mr. Mayne, Mr.
Plunket, and Mr. Ridgeway filed in and added themselves to
the wigged and black-gowned assembly on the prosecution
side of the room.

Opposite them, Leonard McNally and Peter Burrowes put
in their appearances as defence lawyers, but both were traitors
to their client and would covertly help to tighten the noose
around his neck. No witnesses had been summoned to testify
for the prisoner. In spite of the sympathy of the majority of
the spectators, there was no one in the court-house to speak
for Robert Emmet but himself.

He was kept waiting in his basement cell till the judges had
entered the courtroom and seated themselves on the bench.
Then guards came for him. He was led up the narrow stair-
way and ushered into the dock. Looking up at the judges'

bench across the room, he met the cold and hostile eyes of John Toler, Lord Norbury, the Chief Justice.

Slowly a jury was chosen and sworn. One by one they took their places in the balcony-like jury-box to the left of the judges' bench. The prisoner was put to the bar of justice. It was a round iron rod an inch or so in diameter which topped the partition of the dock. As Emmet stood there, facing the judges and jury, the clerk of the Crown, from his desk near the bench, read the indictment against him :

You, Robert Emmet, stand indicted that, not having the fear of God in your heart, nor weighing the duty of your allegiance but being moved and seduced by the instigation of the devil as a false traitor against our lord the king . . . on the said twenty-third day of July in the forty-third year of the reign of our said lord the king at Thomas Street aforesaid in the city and county of Dublin aforesaid with force and arms falsely, maliciously, and traitorously did meet consult combine conspire confederate and agree to and with divers other false traitors whose names are to the [Grand] jurors aforesaid unknown to raise levy and make a public and cruel insurrection rebellion and war against our said sovereign lord the king within this kingdom and to procure great quantities of arms and ammunition guns swords pistols gunpowder and shot for the purpose of said rebellion and to alter subvert and overturn the constitution of this kingdom and the government of our said lord the king of and in this realm. . . .

To this indictment you have heretofore pleaded not guilty, and for trial hath put yourself on God and your country. . . .

Gentlemen of the Jury, your issue is to try to discover and enquire whether the prisoner at the bar is guilty of the offence in manner and form aforesaid or not.

The clerk of the Crown sat down, and the Attorney-General, bowing solemnly to the bench and the jury-box, opened the case for the Crown.

My lord judges and gentlemen of the jury : It is my duty to state, as concisely as I can, the nature of the charge which has been preferred against the prisoner at the bar ; and also, gentlemen, the nature of the evidence which will be produced to substantiate that charge. It will require upon your part the most deliberate consideration ; because it is not only the highest of crimes of which at all times the subject can be guilty ; but it receives, if possible, additional aggravation, when we consider the state of Europe, and the lamentable consequences which the French revolution has already brought forward.

The prisoner was indicted, Mr. O'Grady explained, on a very ancient statute, that of the twenty-fifth of Edward the Third ; and the indictment was grounded on three clauses, the first, that of compassing and imagining the death of the King ; the second, of adhering to his enemies ; and the third, of compassing to levy war against him. Quickly clearing away the legal verbiage, Mr. O'Grady explained that the matter reduced itself to two distinct points : the first " whether there has or has not existed a traitorous conspiracy and rebellion for the purpose of altering the law, the constitution and the Government of the country by force, and secondly, whether the prisoner has in any, and what degree, participated in that conspiracy and rebellion."

It soon became evident that the Attorney-General had more than these two questions on his mind. Wherever the conspiracy may have originated, and for what purpose, the Government now intended to use it as the means of preparing the country for a possible French invasion and of crushing, as far as it was possible, all seditious activity. The rebellion, therefore, must be represented as dangerous enough to merit the severe measures being taken, but, at the same time, the disaffected were not to be encouraged by a public acknowledgement of the seriousness of the situation. The loyal had to be encouraged to act as yeomen ; their fears that the nationalists were concerting measures with France had to be quieted. It was a task of rhetorical delicacy and mental juggling, but Mr. O'Grady entered upon it with the benefit of sixteen other such trials behind him.

Gentlemen [he began], I was happy upon the opening of this commission to have stated to the public through the jury I had the honour to address, that this rebellion, dark as it was in its object, and mischievous in its design, was in truth, in point of numbers, contemptible in the extreme, and that it was prepared and put forward by those only who had been distinguished for their former treasons. I am happy to state with more confidence, that during the investigation which has taken place here, that what I then stated has turned out to be precisely the fact. I then also congratulated the public on the tranquillity of the country ; and I am happy at this period to be able to renew those congratulations, and to state, that notwithstanding the cruel and dastardly efforts of that rebellion, peace and tranquillity now reign throughout the land. [The Government admitted later that the boasted peace and tranquillity of the country were due to the presence of large numbers of troops.] . . .

We live under a constitution we love, free, affluent and happy. Rebellion can find no incentive in our present condition. We feel the happy effects of beneficial laws. Of the just administration of them there is no colour of complaint.

Mr. Emmet, he said, was the head and soul of a conspiracy that would have destroyed this state of affairs. As was his duty, the Attorney-General outlined the case against him : the proclamation in his handwriting, his living at Harold's Cross under an assumed name, the leasing of depots in various parts of Dublin. He spoke of the house at Rathfarnham and the explosion in Patrick Street. He pictured Emmet as sleeping on a mattress in the depot in Thomas Street. He made derisive use of the enthusiasm Emmet had expressed in his long love-letter to Sarah. Ill-fated and delirious passion, Mr. O'Grady called it.

Mr. Wickham's principle that the rising must be made to appear contemptible sounded through the next part of the speech. Mr. O'Grady accomplished this by the use of sarcasm, waxing more and more scornful as he proceeded.

If the people of Ireland, who are not insensible to the influence of rank and character, could but take one glance at the precious materials of which this Provisional Government is formed, I think it would forever cure them of revolutionary speculations.

He held up to ridicule this " highly vaunted " provisional government, made up, so he implied, but quite incorrectly, of one Stafford, a baker, a man of no superior distinction, Quigley, formerly an eminent bricklayer, and Dowdall, a bankrupt clerk " sitting on the second floor of a malt house, meditating without means and marshalling armies they never enlisted."

But the appointed hour arrives. The prisoner puts himself at the head of his motley banditti. He marches out with his pistols on either side, his sword glistening in the air. But the people took a moment for reflection. They saw the misery to which they were devoting the country, and the immediate destruction to which they were involving themselves. . . . On that fateful evening the infatuated few who composed the mob came forward only to fly, and the rebellion which was to have taken the Castle, annihilated the government and dethroned the King, fled precipitately in every direction, and I am at a loss to say whether the general led the way or became a follower in the flight.

With the same expert distortion of the truth the Attorney-General mentioned the taking of the depot as having been carried out by the assault of a single private soldier with a pistol in his hand. He listed the contents of the desk found there, including "a song" addressed to him under the name of Robert Ellis, Butterfield.

Here Emmet's fears for Sarah must have begun to torture him again, since he could not have known that her father's change of principles had saved her from being brought forward. But the Attorney-General, without comment, went on to list the other contents of the desk. He spent some time ridiculing the manuscript of the proclamation :

> It begins, a band of Patriots mindful of their oath, and faithful to their engagements as UNITED IRISHMEN, have determined *to give freedom to their country* and a period to the long career of ENGLISH OPPRESSION. And what is the oppression which is exercised over us ? We live under the same king, we enjoy the same constitution, we are governed by the same laws, we speak the same language.

Blithely ignoring the fact that to a people proud of the antiquity of their language and the richness of its old literature this common tongue that had been forced upon them was the very badge of subjection, Mr. O'Grady went on with his exercise in ridicule. When he came to Emmet's sojourn in the mountains, he treated it as a farce.

> . . . The generals went to bed with their host [Doyle] leaving their followers in the true spirit of equality to shift for themselves. . . . Finally having remained in concealment a month, Major Sirr, to whose activity and intrepidity the loyal citizens of Dublin were under so much obligation, conferred an additional one by . . . going to the place where, he had learned, the prisoner was in concealment.

As the Attorney-General described the events of that evening, Emmet must again have been thinking of Sarah. A variety of papers had been found on the prisoner's person, Mr. O'Grady said, but it would only be necessary to call attention to a paragraph or two of one of them.

"The first paper I allude to appears to have been written by a brother conspirator, acquainted with his schemes, and participating in his crimes. . . ."

"*A brother conspirator!*" Emmet must have heard those words with relief. Then they were not bringing Sarah forward. At least, not now ! The worst had not happened. By keeping her letters he had done her harm, but not the dreadful danger and disgrace he had been fearing.

He could listen, it is probable, without rancour as his letter

to the Government was held up to ridicule.   At least he could
listen up to a certain point.   But when Mr. O'Grady came
to the concluding paragraph, he used Emmet's plea for the
poor men who had been arrested since the rising in a way
which must have stirred Emmet's anger, but which accomplished the very useful purpose, so far as the Government was
concerned, of dampening the ardour of future patriots.

Here, in a very feeling, pathetic address, the government is called upon
not to sacrifice the victims in their possession, because they were not the
heads of the conspiracy, but as expressed in this paper, " a few threads at
the end of it."
Gentlemen, I could wish that such feelings and compassion had come upon
the prisoner at an earlier day. . . .   I could wish that he had reflected sooner,
that by heading that furious mob, which burst from Thomas Street, more
human blood must be sacrificed than could be shed by this Commission
were it to sit for a year.   Three times a greater number of his rebel friends
fell upon that fatal evening than has since been devoted to the offended
justice of their country.
But how shall I speak of the loyal and unoffending ?   That rebellion lasted
but a little hour, and within that short period it deprived our country of
more virtue than this commission could strip it of were its administration
to be eternal.

All through the rest of that long day those words were to
linger in Emmet's mind and were to be answered in his own
speech from the dock.

I do however sincerely lament with him [Mr. O'Grady went on], that
some of those who have been hitherto brought to justice were comparatively speaking, insignificant persons.   But it will be found absolutely
necessary that the unhappy instruments, as well as their principals, must
atone for the mischief they have committed.   For though it is true that
there would be no rebellion if there were no conspirators so it is equally
true that there would be no conspirators if there were no instruments to be
worked on.   If perpetrators were not easily supplied [Here Wickham's
voice echoes again, this time taking up his second principle that the leaders
must appear to have sacrificed the common people to satisfy their personal
ambition] and if some unhappy people were not too ready to connect
themselves with the avarice and ambition of others treason could not be
harboured for a moment, even in the most heated imagination, and therefore, examples among the lower orders are as necessary sacrifices of justice,
as the first conspirator in the land.

Having thus accomplished his multiple commission, the
Attorney-General pressed upon the jury, as he professed to
have pressed upon preceding ones, an admonition to mildness,

clemency, and moderation. With his tongue in his cheek, figuratively speaking, he asked the jury not to let anything that had fallen from him have any other effect upon them than to help them understand the evidence that had been presented. His statement in itself was not to make any impression upon them.

Then, withdrawing his tongue, he promptly reversed himself:

If I have said anything to incite you with an additional indignation against the crime, I am not sorry for having done it. But I do not mean in expressing my horror of the crime to prejudice the criminal. On the contrary, in proportion to the enormity of the offence should the presumption be that he has not committed it.

But on the other hand, gentlemen, you have a duty to discharge to your King, and to your country. Many victims have fallen who undoubtedly may not, abstractly taken, have incurred any considerable guilt—men who, incapable of deciding for themselves, have been absorbed in the guilty ambition of others. But if it shall appear that the prisoner was the prime mover of the rebellion, that he was the spring that gave it life and activity, then I say, no false feeling of pity for the man should warp your judgment or divert your understanding. . . . Therefore, if upon the evidence you should be satisfied that this man is guilty, you must discharge your duty to your King, your country and to your God. . . .*

As he began the examination of witnesses, the Attorney-General could not know to what eloquent anger he was stirring his victim.

* The speeches of Crown officials, except Lord Norbury's, are taken from Howell's *State Trials.*

CHAPTER FORTY

Crown Witnesses

JUST in front of the dock was a large table on which stood
the witness chair. The first person to seat himself there was
an attorney, Mr. Joseph Rawlings. Emmet must have
recognised him with surprise. He had expected 'that men
who had been concerned with him in the conspiracy might
appear as Crown witnesses, but this man had had no connection with it. He had done some legal work for Dr. Emmet
shortly before his death, and Robert had had a casual conversation with him one morning at Milltown. What possible
testimony could he give ?

The Attorney-General put only a few questions to him.
They established Robert Emmet's presence in Ireland in
December of 1802, and the fact that he had been on the
continent, where he had seen his brother. Harmless, so far.

But the cross-examination developed points very useful to
the Government, and Emmet must have wondered why Peter
Burrowes made them.* The prisoner was putting up no
defence. He had told McNally that he would not bother the
Crown with any cross-examination of its witnesses unless they
misrepresented facts. He never suspected either McNally or
Burrowes, even when the latter, under the pretext of preparing
Emmet's defence, got permission to spend the last three or four
nights before the trial with Emmet at Kilmainham.

The points that Burrowes brought out were that Emmet
had said that the inhabitants of the Austrian Netherlands
execrated Buonaparte's Government, and that Emmet highly
condemned it himself. Or at least, said Mr. Rawlings diffidently, that was the impression made on his mind.

*A pamphlet copy of Emmet's trial at the National Library of Ireland, P 1048, says
that McNally cross-examined Rawlings, and that Burrowes did Fleming, just the
reverse as stated in Howell's *State Trials* and other pamphlets. The matter is of no
consequence, as Burrowes' later cross-examinations were also in favour of the Crown.

Since Emmet had sent Miles Byrne to France to get Buonaparte's assistance, these points would be much more useful
to the Crown than to the prisoner. As a matter of fact, they
fitted in perfectly with the Government's policy of doing
everything it could to make Buonaparte antagonistic to
Emmet's rising and to make him think that, if he did come to
Ireland, he would not be assisted by the bulk of the Irish
people.

The Solicitor-General, Mr. McClelland, interrogated the
next witness, Mr. Tyrrell. The evidence went to prove
Emmet's lease of the house in Butterfield Lane, and his using
a false name. McNally emphasised that point in cross-
examination.

Then Michael Frayne, Emmet's neighbour at Butterfield
Lane, was called. Mr. Plunket, who had opposed the Union
bitterly in 1800, but who had since reversed his position,
called on Mr. Frayne to show that Emmet had taken possession
of the house, that he had lived there with Dowdall and another
person, in an odd, sequestered manner, and with little furniture.

Fleming, the hostler from the White Bull Inn, then climbed
on the table, and Mr. Mayne, one of the Crown attorneys,
examined him. The evidence was to prove a conspiracy and
the preparations for it, and to link Emmet with them. Fleming
did it well, in a forthright, country manner. He had lived
at Mrs. Dillon's from harvest last, he said. He was 'ostler,
sir. He knew the depot. He had been told at first that it was
a timber yard, but afterward was told the business it was for.
He had often been there. Sometimes he was there three or
four times a day, but on days when there was a throng he did
not go in at all.

He had seen men making pikes in the depot, and later he
saw them putting heads to the poles. He had seen blunderbusses there, and pistols and firelocks. He had seen men
making ball cartridges there, more than he could describe.

" Look at the prisoner at the bar," said Mr. Mayne.

" I know him," Fleming offered. " Mr Emmet there."

" Have you seen him before ? "

" I have. The Tuesday morning after the blowing up in
Patrick Street." About five, Fleming said, he had opened the
gate of the yard to let Quigley out and had met Emmet and

old John Palmer. Emmet had wanted some sacks to put ammunition in, but Fleming had told him he had given sacks before, and they had not been returned. He would only let them have two sacks and a bag, he said. He was accountable for them ; he got them from people who had corn and other things.

Evidently, the proclamation had not impressed Fleming deeply. When Mr. Mayne asked if he had ever heard anything read in the depot, he said he had heard a little sketch. He did not take any notice of it.

" Who read it ? " Mr. Mayne asked.

" Mr. Emmet."

" What was the purpose of it ? "

" That every officer, non-commissioned officer and private, should share equally everything they got, and have the same laws as France." [This was not the case, but the answer would serve the Government by arousing the antagonism of landowners.]

" What was there to share ? "

" What they'd get when they were to take Ireland or Dublin."

He had seen uniforms made in the depot, Fleming testified. Different tailors made them. Colgan was one.

" Did you see any particular uniform ? "

" I did."

" What sort was it ? "

Fleming described it, green with gold lace, and two epaulettes. Emmet dressing in his uniform, the feathered hat, the sword, the case of pistols—the witness mentioned them all. Emmet had asked for a great-coat to disguise the uniform till he went to attack the Castle. Every sentence Fleming uttered made Emmet's conviction more inevitable. There were more men than Fleming could mention, he said, working in the depot on the twenty-third. They got arms there, and pistols and blunderbusses and firelocks, and ammunition, accordingly. They went toward Thomas Street, and at the door Fleming saw Emmet draw his sword and heard him say, " Come on boys." This was at nine o'clock at night. The lamps were lighted.*

* Pamphlet Trial P, 1048. National Library of Ireland.

In the depot Mr. Emmet was called Mr. Ellis, but Fleming was often told that he was to be *the general*, or head of the business.

" Did you hear that style given to him ? " Mr. Mayne asked.

" I did," said Fleming.

Terence Colgan, a tailor, was sworn next. He was from Lucan, up the Liffey six or seven miles from Dublin. Though it did not transpire on the stand, he was a brother-in-law to one of the Parrots of Kildare, who had been with Emmet in the mountains. His story was that he had been kidnapped while drunk and taken to the depot, where he had been required to make uniforms. Green jackets they were, with white pantaloons. The rest of his testimony corroborated Fleming's : the pikes in the depot, the ammunition, Mr. Emmet, the desk, which was there in court.

Mr. Townsend's examination was soon over. On cross-examination McNally got him to imply that the person who had taken him to the depot had done him a great wrong.

" Do you believe your friend was a great rogue ? "

" He was a great foe to me."

But he admitted that he had only given information when he was arrested, and that he had done it to get his liberty back so that he could earn bread for his family. The Government probably did not like that.

Patrick Farrell was sworn next, and Mr. Mayne took him as his witness. He was a surly, short-spoken man of middle age ; and if he had ever felt any gratitude to Emmet for having saved his life at the depot, it had long since disappeared. He told how he had been " catched " while he was listening at the depot door the evening before the rising, and that some one, thinking he was a spy, had said, " Drop him immediately." But the men in the depot had talked among themselves and had decided to wait for some one to come in. That some one was the gentleman there (here Farrell nodded toward Emmet), who came in soon after. He had said Farrell was to be taken into care and not let out.

He saw the gentleman going in and out and saw things done by his direction.

Emmet's superior position in the depot having been doubly proved, the next questions were about the preparation of arms. Farrell had seen the big beams made into chests for carrying pikes, and other big beams made into wooden cannon. For a grocer's steward his observations of these had been unusually minute. They seemed to have hollow tubes through them, he said, but here his vernacular gave way to an obviously instructed description. A hole three inches in diameter was bored at the top, into which powder was put. The tube was also filled with powder, and the stones were put on top to keep them down.

He was equally minute in his description of the bottle bombs, large and small. He had seen the gentleman in uniform that Saturday evening and had even noticed that he had two epaulettes, while the other two men in green jackets had only one each. The gentleman, too, had a cocked hat and a sword and pistols.

" Were there more people there in the evening than there were in the morning ? " Mr. Mayne asked.

" Towards evening they were gathering pretty smart into it."

" How did you get away ? "

" On that evening while they were carrying away one of those large beams, I was called down to assist, and then I made my escape."

While part of this examination was going on, Emmet had been conversing with his counsel, and as Mr. Mayne sat down, McNally addressed the bench. It is easy for one who knows McNally to have been an informer to see that his words were meant to exculpate himself in the eyes of the Government for what was to follow.

" My lords," he began apologetically, " I did not intend to ask any questions of this witness in the way of cross-examination : but at the express desire of my client I shall be excused in putting such questions as he suggests to me ; and which will be considered as coming directly from him."

The first questions concerned Quigley and Dowdall. Then : " How many men did you see who appeared to be active men, having command in different situations ? "

" There were a good many, and every man very hearty in his business."

" Did not many go in and out, who had no residence in the place ? "

" There did."

" What did they appear to be ? " McNally asked diffidently.

" Some of them country people, and some like citizens, and some well-dressed people."

" Did you see any like esquires ? "

" I cannot say."

He was seemingly as reluctant to say he had been well-treated while in the depot as McNally was to bring out that point.

" Did you hear any printed paper read ? "

" I did ; part of it only."

" What did it state ? "

" I cannot recollect it all now, but it appeared as if the man reading it said that nineteen counties were to rise."

" Was there anything said about the French ? "

" Not the smallest, as I heard. They said they had no idea as to French relief, but to make it good themselves."

" Do you recollect that any person objected to the paper when it was read, or that any observation was made as to its being proper or improper ? "

" The observation I heard, listening like another, was that *it was very good*."

" Was there no observation of any other kind ? "

" No."

" Did you hear any person object that the paper was too merciful ? "

" No, I did not hear it."

That was the last of Emmet's questions. He had been defending not his life but his intentions.

The witnesses that the Crown now presented were like actors playing old familiar parts, with Mr. Townsend giving them their cues. They were the soldiers, constables, or yeomen who, in all the preceding trials, had proved the insurrection and its extent. Lieutenant Coultman told how he had heard of the rising on the afternoon of the twenty-third and had notified his uncle and General Dunne of the report he had heard. He skipped over the fact, which had been brought out on the previous trials, that he had spent several hours in his house on the Quay before he went out, at the request of some of the men in his company, to take an active part in the fighting. He did describe most minutely how he had finally discovered the depot, and he listed accurately the military stores he had found there.

Sergeant Rice, who had been with Lieutenant Coultman when the depot was discovered, followed his officer on the stand and proved the printed proclamation declaring war on the established Government.

Colonel Vassall, the commanding officer of the 38th Regiment, testified that he went to the depot early on Sunday morning and found the floor deep in powder. He proved a copy of the small proclamation, calling the citizens of Dublin to arms.

Alderman Darley, the man who had tried to get Marsden to let him act with his yeomen early on the evening of the twenty-third and had been restrained, took the stand to testify that he had been in the depot after its discovery. He identified a letter found there addressed to Robert Ellis, Butterfield Lane, and the manuscript of the essay on the Art of War. He had given it to Lieutenant Evelyn, he said.

That officer followed Mr. Darley on the table to prove the manuscript draft of the large proclamation. Robert Lindsay, a private soldier, proved the desk as the one that had been in the depot and told how it had been loaded on an artillery car and sent to the barracks.

Emmet must have listened to all these men with interest. This was what had gone on after he had left Thomas Street. This was what had happened to all his preparations. But when Michael Clement Frayne, the quartermaster-sergeant of the 38th Regiment, stepped to the table to tell how he had taken possession of the desk when it arrived at the barracks, Emmet must have experienced another contraction of the heart. Would the man tell of the other papers he had so foolishly left in it ? One was described as a page of profiles, but no attempt was made to identify the persons sketched or to guess the artist. The Government, though it now knew Sarah's writing, still did not know that she had sketched some profiles of herself and Emmet in the front pages of her music book.

To them, fortunately, the little vignettes meant nothing. Mr. Townsend ignored them. The quartermaster sergeant left the witness table without having involved Sarah. One can imagine Emmet's feeling of relief. One can imagine, too, his weariness.

Hour after hour had passed, and there had been no halt, no break in the proceedings. As he stood there, weariness must have fallen like a shadow on his face. A friendly spectator handed him a bit of lavender, but he had not held it to his nostrils for more than a few minutes when the attention of the court was called to it. He was ordered to give it up. The smile that crossed his face as it was taken from him was slightly disdainful.*

Mr. Edward Wilson followed Sergeant Frayne. He was the peace officer who had met the rebels coming from the depot and had retreated before them. There were three or four hundred men there, Mr. Wilson testified ; and if the Attorney-General, who had insisted that the rebels never numbered more than a hundred, blushed at this, no reporter took note of it. Mr. O'Grady had heard this same sworn testimony as to the number of men in Thomas Street at every previous trial.

Mr. Wilson proved the beginning of the rebellion and also the explosion in the Patrick Street depot. Now it was Marsden's turn to blush. He had told the Lord Lieutenant that very little damage had been done there. Mr. Wilson swore that the place had been so shaken that he was afraid to stay inside the house, and he described the extent of the damage.

Lieutenant Brady took the stand to prove the fighting in Thomas Street and James's Street. That ended the Crown's case as far as establishing the rebellion went. It was afternoon now, and there were still five witnesses to tell of Emmet's flight and capture.

---

* Emmet was spared one indignity. The tatterdemalion pedlars Ryan and Mahaffy, who had cavorted so vulgarly as they helped to convict Felix Rourke and other State prisoners who had been in Thomas Street at the time of Lord Kilwarden's murder, were not called to appear against Emmet. He had left there before the murder was committed. Pat McCabe was not called either, though his name was on the original plan of the trial. Probably the Government had discovered what a real rebel he was at heart and did not trust him. On Redmond's trial, when McCabe was asked if the pikes were made for the purpose of murder, he answered indignantly " the purpose of murder ! The purpose to gain their Liberty as we call it." He admitted he had engaged in the rebellion to " be along with the people." Howell's *State Trials*, Vol. 28 .

Silky Jock Doyle tried to put some humour into his story. Heavy with drink he was when these people came up to his bed.

They were stirring and calling me, and I would not awaken at once. At last with pulling and dragging and one thing and another they wakened me sure enough but as soon as ever they did, and I saw the whole parcel of armed men about me I was frightened almost out of my wits. They wanted me to take some spirits, which I refused. They then lifted me over into the middle of the bed, and I gave them no assistance ; they lay, two of them, one upon each side of me, and one of them said I had a French general and a French colonel beside what I never had before. True enough, I never had. I lay there between them for some hours, between sleep and awake, and then I fell alistening, and I got up and stole out of bed, and I found some blunderbusses and a gun and some pistols.

Mr. Mayne established that there were fourteen men at Doyle's and a blunderbuss for each.

" Did you look at the persons who were in bed with you ? "
" I did."
" Look at the prisoner."
" I see that young man or boy or whatever you call him."
" Was he in your bed ? "
" He was, and he passed for a French officer."

Doyle had another point to make : the party had left a paper under the table when they went away. He had given it to the Barony Constable, Mr. Robinson, the next Thursday.* He could not read himself, but it was like that paper there, having iron mould on the back of it. The paper was a copy of the small proclamation.

Poor timid Mrs. Bagnell was almost in tears as she went on the table. What with having to come to town in a coach by night because her neighbours on the mountains had no use for people who gave information to the Government or testified against the rebels, and with her servant, Tom Duffy, in Kilmainham, she was nearly beside herself. She could not describe the green uniforms that three of the party had worn ; she was so much frightened that she had not observed them.

But Mayne skilfully got her to admit that they were of green, and gold laced. He got her to admit that one of the men was called general. But he could not get her to swear to

---

* Mr. Mayne did not bring out the fact, which was in Doyle's deposition, that Doyle had also shown the paper to Mr. Richard Jones. Mr. Jones' name was never mentioned publicly in connection with the capture of Emmet.

any of the men. For a person who was bound by a fine of £1,000 to prosecute, she managed to help the Government's case very little.

Briefly, Mr. Plunket questioned the Barony Constable about Doyle and the small proclamation. The copy in court was the one Doyle had given him, Mr. Robinson swore.

The Attorney-General himself examined Joseph Palmer. In the original plan of the trial his mother had also been listed to testify. But her appearance would probably have aroused even more sympathy for Emmet than her son's did, and the Crown condensed into his examination enough to hang Emmet without her. Under Mr. O'Grady's skilful questioning facts were brought out concerning the stay at Harold's Cross of a lodger who had used the name of Hewitt.

The witness could not be exact as to the time the lodger had left his mother's that spring. It was about three months before the time he was arrested, he thought. When he came back, about a month or three weeks before he was taken, he had again passed as Mr. Hewitt, and visitors had asked for him by that name.

" Do you recollect how he was dressed when he returned ? "
" Yes."
" Mention it."
" He had a brown coat, white waistcoat and white pantaloons, and Hessian boots."
" Were the pantaloons made of linen or cloth ? "
" Cloth, sir."

He admitted leaving the lodger's name from the list on the door, but it took five questions to make him admit that he had done so because the lodger had been afraid he would be taken up if it were included.

" Pray, Mr. Palmer, did he state what his cause of apprehension was ? Did he speak of the transaction of the 23rd of July ? "
" He did."
" Will you mention the amount of those conversations ? "
" I cannot unless you ask me."
" I do not wish to ask you particulars because it might have

the appearance of suggesting them to you. I wish you would mention them yourself. Did he say where he passed that evening ? "

" He said he passed part of it in Thomas Street."

" Had he any conversation with you respecting the dress he wore ? "

" He had."

" Mention it."

" He said he had the pantaloons and boots and waistcoat that I spoke of before."

" Did he mention a coat ? "

" He did."

" What coat ? "

" He said it was a very handsome uniform."

Here the jury asked whether he had said it was a military dress. Palmer said no.

" Is not a uniform a military dress ? " Mr. Plunket interposed. Palmer admitted that it was.

" Did he say anything more about it ? What the colour was ? "

" I do not recollect that he mentioned the colour, but he said it was very handsome."

Piecemeal, they dragged from the unhappy witness the admission that the lodger had spoken of a magazine, that he had said he had lost some powder there, that he had mentioned a proclamation. He admitted that the lodger had planned a mode of escape. He would not admit seeing any of his writing ; and when he was shown the letter Emmet had been writing to the Government just before he was arrested and asked where he had seen it before, he answered, " With Dr. Trevor."

He would not admit seeing the letter in his mother's house. He would not say whose hand had written it. The most Mr. O'Grady could get him to admit was that it was not his mother's or any of the family. He had to admit he knew that the lodger had been arrested by Major Sirr, though he had not been in the room at the time. He was unwell in bed, he said. The Major had come into his room.

Then came the crucial question : " Was the prisoner the person who was arrested ? "

Every eye in the court-room must have been on poor Joe Palmer as he was required to forge this final link in the long chain of evidence against Emmet. Certainly the reporter of the *Dublin Evening Post* was watching. With sympathy quite contrary to the policy of the editor he was moved to write this description of the dramatic moment : " Being called upon to identify the prisoner [Palmer] turned reluctantly towards him, and the prisoner smiled and nodded his head to him. The witness identified the prisoner"

The prosecution did not immediately call its next witness. Perhaps it felt that a little of the emotional effect of the scene that had just been enacted should be overcome first. At any rate, it now read to the jury the part of the proclamation of the provisional government which showed the object of the insurrection : to separate Ireland from England and to establish what one of the judges, in charging the Grand Jury, had called " the wretched anarchy inconsistent with all social happiness and genuine liberty which they call a republic."

They also singled out for reading a paragraph of the proclamation which indicated that the new Government would treat members of the regular forces of England who had acted conformably to the laws of war as prisoners of war, but that all Irish militiamen, yeomen, or volunteers, or bodies of Irish, or individuals who might be found in arms after a fortnight would be treated as enemies and as such committed for trial, and their property confiscated.

This gave such an incomplete picture of the intentions of the provisional government that Emmet again asked McNally to speak for him. Once more the attorney made it clear that he rose at his client's desire : Would the clerk of the Crown, he asked, please read another paragraph of the same paper ?

After some objections and delay the paragraph Emmet asked for was finally read :

No man is to suffer death by [the sentence of court martials assembled by the generals of the new Irish army] except for mutiny ; the sentences of such others as are judged worthy of death shall not be put in execution until a provisional government declares its will ; nor are court martials on any pretext, to sentence, nor is any officer to suffer the punishment of flogging, nor any species of torture to be inflicted.

Mr. Burrowes called the attention of the judges to the fact that the proclamation had appeared in several publications, from which Mr. Emmet might learn its contents. The point was not entirely in the prisoner's favour.

Major Sirr was next on the table. Emmet must have had some bad moments as the evidence drew nearer and nearer to Sarah's letters. The Attorney-General began the examination by directing the Major to tell, without disclosing the information he had received, what had happened when he reached the Palmer's house. Almost word for word, Sirr's testimony followed what he had already told Mr. Townsend at the Castle : He had heard that there was a stranger in the back parlour of Mrs. Palmer's house. He had gone there alone, but with a company of soldiers waiting at the canal bridge to be called. He had gained entrance to the house and had found the prisoner at dinner. He described the examination of Mrs. Palmer, and how during it Emmet had made a second attempt to escape.

The Major was not one to minimise his own heroic deeds. " I instantly ran to the back part of the house, as the most likely part for him to get out at," he recounted. " I saw him going off, and ordered a sentinel to fire, and then pursued myself, regardless of the order. The sentry snapped the trigger but his musket did not go off. I overtook the prisoner, and he said ' I surrender.' I searched him and found some papers on him."

" Did he say anything with regard to the wound he got ? "

" I expressed concern at being obliged to treat him so roughly. He said ' All was fair in war.' "

The Major also mentioned that he had found a paper on the chair in the prisoner's room. The Attorney-General offered extracts copied from it as evidence, but Lord Norbury ruled them out. The papers themselves, or parts of them, might be read, but copies could not be accepted as evidence.

Emmet was evidently determined to have his position and intentions made clear. He had McNally offer the copy of the paper on cross-examination. After some discussion among the judges it was finally admitted to be read, and read it was in its entirety.

If the first part, which condemned the Government's policy

of coercion and pleaded for mercy for the minor prisoners taken as a result of the rising, appeared pitifully futile in that court-room where already fourteen men had heard the sentence of death pronounced upon them, there was something prophetic in the second part which history has justified. As the Crown had deliberately chosen Emmet to be the symbol of Irish nationalism, intending to make him appear ignoble and contemptible, to be libelled and maligned, to be hanged and mutilated, his severed head held up as a warning to every man who thought that Ireland had a right to a government of her own, so his words as they were read in court epitomised the spirit of the party he represented and sounded its challenge, then and for posterity : that the Government could neither by the novelty of its punishments nor by the multitudes of its victims impress the people with terror, and that the time would come for the emancipation of the country.

Sarah's letters were then put upon the table and portions of them were read to the jury. That was bad enough for Emmet, but Lord Norbury, under a pretext of solicitude, increased his agony with a vicious thrust : " If the prisoner wishes to have any other part of these papers read, he may." Knowing Norbury, one can imagine the savage satisfaction he took in that.

" My Lord," Burrowes answered, " the prisoner is aware of that, and throughout the trial will act under that knowledge."

"*Utrumque paratus*," Emmet had told St. John Mason. But he could not have realised it would be so agonising. Strangers were fingering the pages she had written. Her words, intended for him alone, were being read aloud. And then the irony of his optimism as part of his long love letter was offered as evidence : " I have had little time to look at the thousand difficulties which lie between me and the completion of my wishes ; that those difficulties will likewise disappear I have ardent, and I trust, rational hopes. . . ."

What could he hope for now ? Already he had renounced his life and his own happiness. But he wanted so much to be remembered as he really was. He wanted the truth about

himself told. How could he do that in the little time he had
left to live ?

The Crown was closing its case. " My Lord," said McNally,
" Mr. Emmet says he does not intend to call any witnesses,
or to take up the time of the court by his counsel stating any
case, or making observations upon the evidence, and therefore
I presume the trial is now closed on both sides."

CHAPTER FORTY-ONE

The Crown Heaps Its Calumny

BUT there was one more man who could use Emmet's distress as a means of furthering his own political career and at the same time accomplish two objects very desirable from the Castle point of view. Mr. William Conyngham Plunket, one of the Crown lawyers, had been one of the most bitter opponents of the Union. He was now to announce publicly his change of principle and pledge his devotion to the Government. This could be, so Wickham hoped, " a death-blow to the anti-Union party at the bar." * He was also to heap more calumny on Emmet, along the lines of Wickham's letter of September 11.

My Lords and Gentlemen of the Jury [said the man who was shortly to be made the new Solicitor General], you need not entertain any apprehension at this hour of the day, that I am disposed to take up a great deal of your time, by observing upon the evidence which has been given. In truth, if this were an ordinary case, and if the object of this prosecution did not include some more momentous interests than the mere question of the guilt or innocence of the unfortunate gentleman who stands a prisoner at the bar, I should have followed the example of his counsel, and should have declined making any observation upon the evidence.

But gentlemen, I do feel this to be a case of infinite importance indeed. It is a case important, like all others of this kind, by involving the life of a fellow subject ; but it is doubly and ten-fold important, because from the evidence which has been presented, in the progress of it, the system of this conspiracy against the laws and constitution of the country has been developed in all its branches ; and in observing upon the conduct of the prisoner at the bar, and in bringing home the evidence of his guilt, I am bringing home guilt to a person who, I say, is the center, the life-blood and the soul of this atrocious conspiracy. . . .

* Writing next day to the Speaker of the British House of Commons, Wickham said that the speech was most eloquent and most masterly. " It was delivered on purpose to show his entire and unqualified renunciation of his former principles, his determination *on due and mature reflection*, to support the Union after having been its inveterate opposer, and to stand or fall with the present administration. You may naturally suppose that this is the prelude to closer connection, and that it will be the death-blow to the anti-Union party at the Bar." *Colchester Correspondence*, I, p. 455.

Like the Attorney-General, Mr. Plunket spoke with sarcasm of the humbleness of Emmet's companions. "Quigley, originally following the occupation of bricklayer, but he thought proper to desert the humble walk in which he was originally placed, and to become the framer of constitutions and a subverter of empires."

Like the Attorney General, he accused Emmet of personal ambition :

It will be for you to decide who was the framer of [the proclamation] the man who resided at the depot, and regulated all the proceedings there, or whether it was framed by Dowdall the clerk, by Quigley the bricklayer, or by Stafford the baker, or any of the illiterate victims of the ambition of this young man who have been convicted by this court ? Or whether it did not flow from his pen, and was dictated by his heart.

No man capable of putting two ideas together could have any doubt of the guilt of the prisoner, Mr. Plunket went on. Why then did he address them ?

Because, as I have already mentioned, I feel this to be a case of great public expectation—of the very last national importance ; and because, when I am prosecuting a man, in whose veins the very life-blood of this conspiracy flowed, I expose to the public eye the utter meanness and insufficiency of its resources.

What does it avow itself to be ? A plan—not to correct the excesses or reform the abuses of the government of the country ; not to remove any specks of imperfection which might have grown upon the surface of this constitution, or to restrain the overgrown power of the Crown, or to restore any privilege of parliament [He ignored the fact that there was no longer any parliament in Ireland.], or to throw any new security around the liberty of the subject. No. But it plainly and boldly avows itself to be a plan to separate Great Britain from Ireland, uproot the monarchy, and establish " a free and independent republic in Ireland " in its place ! To sever the connection between Great Britain and Ireland !

Gentlemen, I should feel it a waste of words and of public time were I addressing you or any person within the limits of my voice, to talk of the frantic desperation of the plan of any man, who speculates upon the dissolution of that empire, whose glory and whose happiness depend upon its indissoluble connection. But were it practicable to sever that connection, to untie the links which bind us to the British constitution, and to turn us adrift upon the turbulent ocean of revolution, who could answer for the existence of this country, as an independent power, for a year ? God and nature have made the two countries essential to each other. Let them cling to each other to the end of time, and their united affection and loyalty will be proof against the machinations of the world.

Having aimed his death-blow at the anti-Union party at

the bar, Mr. Plunket went back to the task of miring the " contemptible conspiracy." According to him, the party in Thomas Street had been stopped in its passage by the hones voice of one single peace officer. He alluded to " the miserable victims who have been misled by those phantoms of revolutionary delusion," and to " a few desperate, obscure contemptible adventurers in the trade of revolution." Most obvious of all Wickham's instructions and policy were Plunket's closing words of advice to the prisoner :

It is not for me to say what are the limits of the mercy of God or what a sincere repentance of those crimes may effect ; but I do say, that if the unfortunate young gentleman retains any of the seeds of humanity in his heart, or possesses any of those qualities which a virtuous education in a liberal seminary must have planted in his bosom, he will make atonement to his God and his country, by employing whatever time remains to him in warning his deluded countrymen from persevering in their schemes.

Much blood has been shed, and he perhaps would have been immolated by his followers if he had succeeded. They are a bloodthirsty crew, incapable of listening to the voice of reason, and equally incapable of obtaining rational freedom, if it were wanting in this country, as they are of enjoying it. They imbrue their hands in the most sacred blood of the country, and yet they call upon God to prosper their cause, as it is just !

But it is atrocious, wicked and abominable, and I devoutly invoke that God to confound and overwhelm it.

With this pious invocation as his valedictory, Mr. Plunket sat down to receive the congratulations of his colleagues and contemplate his advancing position at the bar.

It was now about nine at night. The court had been convened for twelve hours. And although Lord Norbury, in summing up, had said he would not detain the jury longer than he felt his indispensable duty required, nevertheless, he gave a long and detailed fourth variation of the case against Emmet. He went over the several overt acts of which Emmet had been guilty in all three counts of his indictment : he re-examined the evidence of the twenty witnesses and made occasional observations on their testimony. He spoke of arms and ammunition having been collected " to take away the lives of innocent fellow-creatures." The rebels, he said, " meant to put to death their fellow-creatures." He laid down the law as regards the validity of evidence of accomplices, and then added some general observations on the case as a whole.

" If I could," said Lord Norbury at the end of this summary,

" if I could with just propriety express my concern at seeing such a young gentleman at this bar, I would readily do so, but if you, gentleman, shall be of opinion that the accusation against him is well founded, it is well for the community that he is there. . . ."

As he listened, Emmet must have come to a decision. He would state his own case, not in defence of his life, which he had long ago renounced, but to clear his reputation of the slurs and falsehoods that had been hurled against it. He was going to his grave, but he would not leave unchallenged the taunts of the Attorney-General, the sanctimonious diatribe of Plunket, or the bitter jibes of the judge. Every Crown official who had spoken had increased Emmet's anger until now it was a seething thing, hot, explosive, and aching to be articulate. He, who had always played fair and had believed that every other man played fair too, in the last hours of his life, with everything lost to him, was learning that the most precious thing of all was still to be lost, his reputation. *But he would not lose it. He would speak.* McNally must get them to postpone judgment for a day. It would not be much time to prepare the oration of his life, but he could do it.

" Gentlemen," Lord Norbury was saying, " no witnesses have been called for the prisoner at the bar, and now you have your duty to perform. If you have a rational doubt—such as rational men may entertain—upon the evidence, whether the prisoner was engaged in these transactions, you should acquit him. If you do not entertain any doubt, but believe the evidence, and the criminal conduct and intentions imputed to the prisoner, you are bound to decide between the prisoner and the justice due to your country, and in that case you shall find him guilty."

The jury did not even leave the box. After a few minutes of whispered consultation the foreman addressed the court.

" My lords, I have consulted with my brother jurors, and we are all of opinion that the prisoner is guilty."

This was the time when McNally should have made his motion, but he did not rise. Instead, the Attorney-General got to his feet.

" My lord," he said, " it remains for me to pray the judgment of the court upon the prisoner."

" Gaoler," intoned the clerk of the Crown, " put Robert Emmet, Esquire, to the bar."

At last McNally interrupted apologetically. " My lords, I hope I am not intruding upon the Court, and that it is not incompatible with my duty, now that the verdict has been pronounced, to state a request of the prisoner which probably ought to be addressed to the Attorney-General rather than to the Court. It is, that the motion for judgment might not be made until to-morrow."

" My lord," the Attorney-General objected, " I have made the motion, and it is impossible for me to comply with the request."

No time now for Emmet to prepare his vindication. But ringing in his mind were all the charges that had been so unjustly flung against him : that he was selfishly ambitious, that he had betrayed his country, that he alone was responsible for all the blood that had been shed. " Guilty ambition," " General without an army," " the pusillanimous cruelty of his rabble."

He could not with honour betray the men who had been concerned with him, the ones who had called him back to Ireland and then deserted him. But he could declare that he had not worked alone. He could make clear his intentions about the French, and he could at least ask that men who did not know his mind should not pass judgment upon him.

The clerk of the Crown read the indictment again, and the verdict of the jury. As he finished, he turned toward the dock and asked the customary question :

" What have you therefore now to say, why judgment of death and execution should not be awarded against you according to law ? "

CHAPTER FORTY-TWO

Emmet Answers

FOR more than twelve hours Emmet had been in the dock. All day his heart had been tormented by fear for Sarah's safety. His body ached with fatigue. He had had no rest, no refreshment. He had not been given time to compose a reply to the accusations which had been heaped upon him by every Crown speaker, and which had purposely distorted all his idealistic intentions into a nightmare of massacre and wanton bloodshed.

But the Robert Emmet, who stood in the dock to make his first public speech since the days when he had addressed the Historical Society, was quite a different person from the boy orator of Trinity. He was a man now, defending his honour in its last stand, and the realisation steadied and inspired him. His voice, when he began to speak, was clear and distinct, perfect in its modulation and exquisite in its cadences.*

My Lords [he began, standing forward in the dock], as to why judgment of death and execution should not be passed upon me according to law I have nothing to say ; but as to why my character should not be relieved from the imputations and calumnies thrown out against it I have much to say. I have no hopes that I can anchor my character in the breast of this court. I only wish your lordships will suffer it to float down your memories until it has found some hospitable harbour to shelter it from the storms with which it is at present buffeted. Were I to suffer only death after being adjudged guilty I should bow in silence to the fate which awaits me ; but

---

* There are many versions of Emmet's speech. Those issued by the Government immediately after the trial contain references to the French ; but persons who were present, and to whom Dr. Madden talked later, were certain that these were not made by Emmet. Those issued by his friends contain other matter which it is believed was inserted by them. No one version, even those taken in the shorthand of the time, agrees exactly with another, except for the unforgettable last paragraph. Lord Norbury's interruptions, which were said by listeners to have been almost constant and pointedly abusive, are not given in any version *in toto*. Longer and more dignified statements were substituted in publications of the speech sponsored by the Government. This composite account uses only material that was printed at the time and gives, as well as any person can determine, Emmet's opinions and language. Lord Norbury's comments have been given the benefit of charity.

The Trial of Robert Emmet : a contemporary reconstruction of the scene in Green Street Courthouse

A note written by Robert Emmet to Sarah Curran. The endorsement in the upper right-hand corner is that of the British officer who found it in the arms depot in Thomas Street on the morning of July 24, 1803. *The original is in the Irish State Paper Office, Dublin*

the sentence of the law which delivers my body over to the executioner consigns my character to obloquy.

A man in my situation has not only to encounter the difficulties of fortune and the force of power over minds which it has corrupted or subjected, but the difficulties of established prejudice. The man dies, but his memory lives, and that mine may not forfeit all claim to the respect of my countrymen I seize upon this opportunity to vindicate myself from some of the charges alleged against me.

I am charged with being an emissary of France. It is alleged that I wished to sell the independence of my country. No, I am no emissary, and my ambition was to hold a place among the deliverers of my country, not in profit, nor in power, but in the glory of the achievement. Never did I entertain the remotest idea of establishing French power in Ireland.

Connection with France was indeed intended, but only as far as mutual interest would sanction and require. Were they to assume any authority inconsistent with the purest independence it would be the signal for their destruction. We sought aid, and we sought it—as we had assurances we should obtain it—as auxiliaries in war and allies in peace.

Were the French to come as invaders or enemies, uninvited by the wishes of the people, I should oppose them to the utmost of my strength. Yes, my countrymen, I should advise you to meet them upon the beach, with a sword in one hand and a torch in the other. I would meet them with all the destructive fury of war. I would animate my countrymen to immolate them in their boats before they had contaminated the soil of my country. If they succeeded in landing, and if forced to retire before superior discipline, I would dispute every inch of ground, burn every blade of grass, and the last entrenchment of liberty should be my grave. What I could not do myself, if I should fall, I should leave as a last charge to my countrymen to accomplish because I should feel conscious that life, even more than death, would be unprofitable when a foreign nation held my country in subjection. [This of course applied as much to the English as to the French, and the " last charge " was a subtle testament to other Irish nationalists.]

But it was not as an enemy that the succours of France were to land. I looked, indeed, for the assistance of France, but I wished to prove to France and to the world that Irishmen deserved to be assisted, that they were indignant to slavery, and ready to assist the independence and liberty of their country !

I wished to procure for my country the guarantee which Washington procured for America ! To procure an aid which by its example, would be as important as its valour—disciplined, gallant, pregnant with science and with experience, which would perceive the good, and polish the rough points of our character. They would come to us as strangers, and leave us as friends, after sharing our perils, and elevating our destiny. These were my objects, not to receive new taskmasters, but to expel old Tyrants !

My object, and that of the Provisional Government, was to effect a total separation between Great Britain and Ireland—to make Ireland totally independent of Great Britain, but not to let her become a dependent of France.

Here he was interrupted by Lord Norbury, who told him the court was not there to listen to treason.

When my spirit [Emmet resumed mildly] shall have joined those bands of martyred heroes who have shed their blood on the scaffold and in the field in defence of their country and of virtue, this is my hope, that my memory may serve to animate those who survive me.

While the destruction of that government which upholds its dominion by impiety against the Most High, which displays its power over man as over the beasts of the fields, which sets man upon his brother, and lifts his hand, in religion's name, against the throat of his brother who believes a little more or less than the government standard, which reigns amidst the cries of orphans and the widows it has made—

Again Lord Norbury interrupted :

Mr. Emmet, the massacres and murders committed in one night by those under your command show them to be barbarians and ruffians, to embrue their hands in the dearest blood of the country before you proceeded the length of a street, in furtherance of your vain boasting that you would take possession of the Castle of Dublin. No man who has heard this trial can doubt, but that you are guilty of high treason. The object of your depot was that you should have a quantity of arms and ammunition to enable you and the rest of the conspirators, to overturn the laws and the constitution of this realm by force.

I swear by the throne of Heaven [Emmet answered him] before which I must shortly appear, by the blood of those murdered patriots who have gone before me, that my conduct has been governed only by the convictions I have uttered, and by no other view than that of their cure, and the emancipation of my country from the inhuman oppression under which it has so long and too patiently travailed, and that I confidently and assuredly hope that (wild and chimerical as it may appear) there is still strength and union enough in Ireland to accomplish this noble enterprise. Of this I speak with confidence, of intimate knowledge, and with the consolation that appertains to that confidence. Think not, my lords, that I say this for the petty gratification of giving you a transitory uneasiness. A man who has never yet raised his voice to assert a lie, will not hazard his character with posterity, by asserting a falsehood on a subject so important to his country, and on an occasion like this. Yes, my lords, a man who does not wish to have his epitaph written until his country is liberated, will not leave it in the power of envy to impeach the probity which he means to preserve even in the grave, to which tyranny here consigns him.

For the third time Lord Norbury checked him.

Again I say, that what I have spoken was not intended for your lordships, whose situation I commiserate rather than envy ; my expressions were for my countrymen. If there be a true Irishman present, let my last words cheer him in the hour of affliction—

The court could not listen to a discourse of that kind, said the judge.

With disarming moderation Emmet picked up the theme of his discourse.*

I have always understood it to be the duty of a judge, when a prisoner has been convicted, to pronounce the sentence of the law. I have also understood that judges sometimes think it their duty to hear with patience and to speak with humanity—to exhort the victim of the law, and to offer with tender benignity his opinions of the motives by which he was actuated in the crime of which he was adjudged guilty. That a judge has thought it his duty so to have done I have no doubt ; but where is the boasted freedom of your institutions, where is the vaunted impartiality, clemency and mild-ness of your courts of justice, if an unfortunate prisoner whom your policy, and *not justice,* is about to deliver to the hands of the executioner is not suffered to explain his motives sincerely and truly, and to vindicate the principles by which he was actuated ?

Emmet's voice must here have begun to show his surging anger. The gestures that were so effective an accompaniment to his speech must have become more emphatic.

My lords, it may be a part of the system of angry justice to bow a man's mind by humiliation to the purposed ignominy of the scaffold ; but worse to me than the purposed shame or the scaffold's terrors would be the tame endurance of such foul and unfounded imputations as have been laid against me in this court. You, my lord, are a judge. I am the supposed culprit. I am a man. You are a man also. By a revolution of power we might change places, though we never could change character. If I stand at the bar of this court and dare not vindicate my character, *what a farce is your justice !* If I stand at this bar and dare not vindicate my character *how dare* you calumniate it ! Does the sentence of death which your unhallowed policy inflicts upon my body condemn my tongue to silence, and my reputation to reproach ? Your executioner may abridge the period of my existence, but while I exist I shall not forbear to vindicate my character and my motives from aspersions ; and as a man to whom fame is dearer than life, I will make the last use of that life in doing justice to that reputation

---

* Years later Dr. Madden talked to an Irish judge who had been present at Emmet's trial. He described Emmet's voice and his delivery of his valedictory : " Whenever he referred to the charges brought against him by Plunket, . . . his hand was stretched forward, and the two forefingers of the right hand were slowly laid on the open palm of the other, and alternately were raised or lowered as he proceeded." He is described as moving about the dock, as he warmed in his address, with rapid but not ungraceful motions ; now in front of the railing before the bench, then retiring, as if his body as well as his mind were swelling beyond the measure of their chains. His action was not confined to his hands ; he seemed to have acquired a swaying motion of the body when he spoke in public, which was peculiar to him, but there was no affectation in it. It was said of Tone, on his trial, by a bystander, that he never saw any one cast affectation so far behind him. The remark with equal truth might have been applied to Emmet. Madden, III, p. 457.

which is to live after me, and which is the only legacy I can leave to those I honour and love, and for whom I am proud to perish. As men, my lords, we must appear on the great day at one common tribunal, and it will then remain for the Searcher of all hearts to show a collective universe, who was engaged in the most virtuous actions, or actuated by the purest motives, my country's oppressors or—

Mr. Emmet [Lord Nurbury silenced him sternly], you have had a most patient trial. We have listened to you with great patience. It was proved in evidence that by your conduct you excited and encouraged others to join in the insurrection and rebellion. It is an insult to the judges of the land, to sit here and listen to expressions of treason. It is an insult to the law which we cannot suffer to be heard in a court of justice. You have been charged with the crime of high treason. That charge has been supported by evidence, and the jury, upon their oaths, have found you guilty. Is there anything in point of law that you can urge in your defence ?

My lords, will a dying man be denied the legal privilege of exculpating himself in the eyes of the community from a reproach thrown upon him during his trial, by charging him with ambition, and attempting to cast away for a paltry consideration the liberties of his country ? Why then insult me, or rather why insult justice by demanding of me why sentence of death should not be pronounced against me. I know, my lords, that the form prescribes that you should put the question ; the form also confers the answering. This, no doubt, may be dispensed with and so might the whole ceremony of the trial, since sentence was already pronounced at the Castle before your jury was impanelled. Your lordships are but the priests of the oracle, and I submit, but I insist on the whole of the forms.

Here he paushed, from weariness and emotion, and the court desired him to proceed.

I have been charged with that importance in the efforts to emancipate my country as to be considered as the key-stone of the combination of Irishmen, or as it has been expressed, " the life-blood and soul of this conspiracy." You do me honour overmuch ; you have given to the subaltern all the credit of the superior. There are men concerned in this conspiracy who are not only superior to me, but even to your own conception of yourself, my lord ; men, before the splendour of whose genius and virtues I should bow with respectful deference, and who would not deign to call you friend —who would not disgrace themselves by shaking your bloodstained hand.

This was insult such as Norbury had never suffered. He did not suffer it now. The prisoner was the one, he charged angrily, who was responsible for the bloodshed.

What, my lord, shall you tell me on my passage to the scaffold, which that tyranny of which you are only the intermediate minister has erected for my death—that I am accountable for all the blood that has and will be shed in this struggle of the oppressed and the oppressor ? Shall you tell me this, and must I be so very a slave as not to repel it ?

I do not fear to approach the Omnipotent Judge, to answer for the conduct of my short life ; and am I to stand appalled here before a mere remnant of mortality ? Let no man dare, when I am dead, to charge me with dishonour ; let no man taint my memory by believing that I could be engaged in any cause but my country's liberty and independence. The proclamation of the provisional government speaks my views. No inference can be tortured from it to countenance barbarity or debasement. I would not have submitted to a foreign oppression for the same reason that I would have resisted tyranny at home.

Again he was interrupted by Lord Norbury.

Mr. Emmet, you have been called upon to show cause, if you have any, why judgment of the law should not be enforced against you. Instead of showing anything in point of law why judgment should not pass, you have proceeded in a manner the most unbecoming in your situation ; you have avowed and endeavoured to vindicate principles totally subversive of the government, totally subversive of the tranquillity, well-being, and happiness of that country that gave you birth, and you have broached treason the most abominable.

You, sir, had the honour to be a gentleman by birth, and your father filled a respectable situation under the government. You had an eldest brother whom death snatched away, and who when living was one of the greatest ornaments of the bar. But you have conspired with the profligate and abandoned, and associated yourself with hostlers, bakers, butchers, and such persons, whom you invited to council when you erected your provisional government. Your sentiments and your language are a disgrace to your friends, your education, but more particularly to your father, who if alive would not countenance such opinions.

Emmet's retort to this pointed insult, if a bit vehement, was still in classic rhetorical style.

If the spirits of the illustrious dead participate in the concerns of those who were dear to them in this transitory scene, dear shade of my venerated father, look down on your suffering son, and see has he for one moment deviated from those moral and patriotic principles which you so early instilled into his youthful mind, and for which he has now to offer up his life.

My lord, you are impatient for the sacrifice. The blood you seek is not congealed by the artificial terrors which surround your victim ; it circulates warmly and unruffled through its channels, and in a little time it will cry to heaven. Be yet patient ! I have but a few more words to say. My ministry is ended. I am going to my cold and silent grave ; my lamp of life is nearly extinguished. I have parted from everything that was dear to me in this life for my country's cause, and abandoned another idol I adored in my heart, the object of my affections. My race is run. The grave opens to receive me, and I sink into its bosom. I am ready to die. I have not been allowed to vindicate my character. I have but one request to make at my departure from this world. It is *the charity of its silence.*

Let no man write my epitaph ; for as no man who knows my motives now dares vindicate them, let not prejudice or ignorance asperse them. Let them rest in obscurity and peace. Let my memory be left in oblivion, and my tomb remain uninscribed, until other times and other men can do justice to my character. When my country takes her place among the nations of the earth, then, and not till then, let my epitaph be written.

I have done.

Lord Norbury himself elected to pronounce sentence of death upon Robert Emmet. Not since the first State trial of this commission had he done so. Doubtless he had counted on making this moment the high point of the day. But he was robbed of his great scene. Anything that happened now was anticlimax. The effect that Robert Emmet's speech produced on his hearers moved even his political adversaries. Fifty years later, an Irish judge could not speak of it without tears of emotion.

As Emmet stood in the dock, ready to receive the sentence of death, he was, with few exceptions, an object of love and admiration. A young English officer who had watched the proceedings was so charmed by his personality and courage that the next day he painted from memory a little portrait of Emmet in water-colours.

He must have been a gifted young man, for the likeness he produced bears a striking resemblance to the death mask that the artist Petrie made the next night.* He must have been a generous one, too, for as soldiers wrap the bodies of their dead enemies in the flag of the country for which they died, he clothed the young rebel in his uniform of gold and green, as he imagined it must have looked.

Norbury was too much of a showman not to know with what flatness his words would fall on the ears of that audience. But emotion and artistic sensibilities cannot hinder the workings of the law and of administrative policy. To the contrary, that policy dictated that the effect of Emmet's speech be

* This little painting is now in the National Museum of Ireland and seems to possess some of the charm of personality that other sketches of Emmet, even those made from life, have not captured. The lips particularly, though they answer the description Madame de Staël gave of them, " slightly disdainful," are not unpleasant but rather seem expressive of extreme sensitivity. (For that reason, and because it has only recently become available, it has been used as an illustration for this book.)

speedily overcome.   And in pronouncing the sentence of death, the judge naturally could urge the prisoner to renounce those principles which it was so desirable from the Government's point of view that he should forsake.

Lord Norbury clothed this bit of propaganda with decent solicitude for the soul of the man he was condemning.

Be assured that I have the most sincere affliction in performing the painful duty which devolves upon me, and let me, with the most anxious concern, exhort you, not to depart this life with such sentiments of rooted hostility to your country as those which you have expressed.   Be assured that far other sentiments will better contribute to give you comfort at your departure from this life, and to obtain forgiveness and mercy in that which is to come, as well as to give you fortitude to bear that dreadful sentence which at this awful moment I must pronounce.

Emmet was to suffer death by hanging, and his head was to be severed from his body.

10

EXECUTION

CHAPTER FORTY-THREE

Final Pressure

EMMET heard the words of the sentence with dignity. He bowed in silence to the judge when he had finished, and then his gaolers took him out of court. Young Fitten of Trinity, whom he had known since he was a boy, was brave enough to shake hands with him as he left the dock, and so did some other members of the college Yeomanry Corps.*

It was now ten-thirty at night, and he had been on trial for thirteen hours. In Newgate he was given a meal, but time was short for the purposes the Government still had to achieve, and the Reverend Mr. Gamble immediately called on Emmet by official request.

"I am anxious," Lord Hardwicke wrote to his brother, Charles Yorke, "that he [Emmet] should have a fair chance of being brought to a proper temper of mind before his death." But the fact that the reverend gentleman made a report of his conversations with Emmet to both Dr. Trevor and to Mr. Marsden indicates how far political considerations outweighed any real concern for Emmet's soul.

The reports themselves are further proof of this, souvenirs of the subtle struggle being carried on against Emmet's integrity. The one made to Marsden was intended for publication, and Mr. Gamble begged Marsden to "condescend to expunge anything irrelevant or perhaps improper." It was almost entirely political. Far less attention was paid to Emmet's denial of being a deist than to what he had had to say about his plans. Mr. Gamble made a point of saying that the expression Emmet used—"I expected other resources, but found myself entangled with a rabble "—was made in the presence of two medical officers in uniform, Dr. Wade

* They got into trouble with the college authorities for having shaken hands with a convicted traitor while in the King's uniform, but Fitten at least always retained his affection for Emmet and told with pride of his connection with him.

and Surgeon Dease. That seems an uncharacteristic statement for Emmet to have made. His having lamented the death of Lord Kilwarden, as Mr. Gamble said he did, rings much more true.

He was asked again about the French, and Mr. Gamble credited him with saying that Buonaparte was the most savage and unprincipled Tyrant by whom the earth was ever disgraced. " Mr. Gamble," that clergyman wrote, " then left him to his repose and departed."

But that bit of repose was still postponed. Government had heard a rumour that efforts would be made to rescue Emmet from Newgate. An hour or so after midnight he was transferred, under heavy escort, to Kilmainham, and his old quarters on the ground floor of the gaol. As he passed by John Hickson's cell, he whispered, " I shall be hanged to-morrow."

It must have been the realisation that he had less than a day to live which made him, utterly exhausted as he was, spend part of the night in writing letters. One, to Sarah, was not delivered, and no copy of it is available. The other was to Mr. Wickham, thanking him, in veiled language, for not having brought Sarah's name forward. Also, he said he would have exonerated the Government from any blame for not having discovered the conspiracy, and he would also have done justice to the mildness of the present administration. That mildness, Emmet said, had rather accelerated his determination to make an effort for the overthrow of a Government of which he did not think equally highly. " However, as I have now been deprived of that opportunity I think it right now to make an acknowledgement which justice requires from me as a man, and which I do not feel to be in the least derogatory from my decided principles as an Irishman.

" I have the honour to be, Sir, with the greatest respect, Your most obedient, humble servant, Robert Emmet." *

Having completed this act of supererogation, Emmet slept, for the last time in his life.

Mr. Gamble was at Kilmainham early the next morning. This time he was reinforced by another clergyman, Mr. Grant of Island Bridge. There were only six hours of Emmet's life

* *Colchester Correspondence*, I, p. 457.

left now, and still he had not been induced to retract
his principles. The final battle began. The clergymen
" repeatedly urged him to those topics which were likely
to bring him to a just feeling and acknowledgement of the
crime for which he was to suffer, but were not successful in
persuading him to abjure those principles by which he was
actuated in his conspiracy to overthrow the Government."
So Dr. Trevor wrote to the Lord Lieutenant after getting a
report of the conversation from Mr. Gamble.*

The report to Marsden is even more revealing. Mr. Gamble
had asked Emmet how he could reconcile his actions to the
Christian principle. It was to that question that Emmet had
responded, according to Mr. Gamble, with his statement of
having expected other resources but having found himself
entangled with a rabble.

Finally, " wishing to bring his mind to a proper temper and
sense of religion," the clergyman administered the Sacrament
of Holy Communion to Emmet and joined him in prayer.
Mr. Gamble admitted that his behaviour was marked with
reverence and propriety. The clergyman was reading the
litany of the Established Church when McNally arrived at the
gaol at ten.

As an " indulgence " Emmet and his lawyer were allowed
to retire to another room. There, according to McNally,
Emmet heard for the first time of his mother's death. Looking
on McNally as a friend, Emmet had asked about her health,
which had been failing.

" I know you would like to see her, Robert," the attorney
answered evasively.

All the carefully concealed passion of his personal feelings
poured itself out in Emmet's reply, " Oh, how I would love
to see her."

" Have courage," the other said solemnly, pointing his finger
upward. " You will see her this night."

After a while Emmet said quietly, " It is better so."

He had struggled hard, and the traces of it were in his face.
But as he was to write Richard Curran shortly, he had " public
motives to sustain his mind." He could not make his death
the high sacrifice he was determined it should be if he went to

* I.S.P.O.

it marked with emotion, even for the death of a parent. He
did not know how much significance the Government was
attaching to his execution, and that it was intended to signify
the extinction of the national cause, but he certainly felt himself
to be an offering at the altar of liberty and justice. His reference to Algernon Sidney and Russell, the famous English
Republicans of the seventeenth century, which he shortly
made to McNally, is proof of that. The thought of them must
have lifted his heart. If he did not, as Sidney had done at his
trial before Lord Jeffries, hold out his arm to prove his steady
pulse, Emmet, by less dramatic means, displayed a courage
and composure equal to that other martyr, whom he resembled
in so many ways.

McNally's real errand, of course, was the same as Mr.
Gamble's had been, but he had no more success than the
clergyman. All the usual practices to provoke admissions
and arouse resentment against his comrades were resorted to.
He was told he had been deserted by the leaders, that he had
been imposed upon and deceived. He would not believe that
the Wexford men had failed him, and it went without saying
that he would not consider weakness in others any reason for
showing it himself. He was still firmly expecting the French
to come. He was still declaring his attachment to the United
Irishmen, and hoping for a separate Government for Ireland.

While Emmet and McNally were thus engaged, the two
clergymen must have been in conference with Dr. Trevor.
They had evidently mistaken Emmet's gentleness for weakness
and were hoping that he would eventually give in. At any
rate, at eleven the Doctor wrote a hurried note to Wickham.
To this day it carries an air of exuberant optimism :

Sir, I have the Honour to state to you that the Rev'd Mr. Grant and
Gamble two very proper Gentlemen are in attendance on Mr. Emmet. I
find they will be very likely to obtain very pleasing acknowledgements
from Mr. Emmet. They have expressed a desire that he may be conveyed
to the place of execution in a coach in which that clergymen (*sic*) proposes
to accompany him.

Mr. Gamble attends at the particular request of the prisoner, and Mr.
Grant attends from motives of Humanity.

On the cover Dr. Trevor marked, in writing emphatically
large and clear, the words " Urgent. To be delivered Immediately."

Mr. Wickham was delighted to order the carriage.

Somehow Emmet contrived to free himself for a few moments from his tormentors. He used them to write two more letters. Neither was to Sarah, but the thought of her fills them both, and her image must have been in his mind as he wrote. One to his brother was a testament of love, bequeathing his idol to his family's care :

My dearest Tom and Jane,

I am just going to do my last duty to my country. It can be done as well on the scaffold as on the field. Do not give way to any weak feelings on my account, but rather encourage proud ones that I have possessed fortitude and tranquillity of mind to the last.

God bless you and the young ones that are growing up about you. May they be more fortunate than their uncle, but may they preserve as pure and ardent an attachment to their country as he has done. Give the watch to little Robert. He will not prize it the less for having been in possession of two Roberts before him.

I have one dying request to make to you. I was attached to Sarah Curran, the youngest daughter of your friend. I did hope to have had her for my companion for life. I did hope that she would not only have constituted my happiness, but that her heart and understanding would have made her one of Jane's dearest friends. I know that Jane would have loved her on my account, and I feel also that had they been acquainted she must have loved her on her own.

No one knew of the attachment till now, nor is it now generally known, therefore do not speak of it to others. She is living with her father and brother, but if these protectors should fall off and that no other should replace them, treat her as my wife and love her as a sister. God almighty bless you. Give my love to all my friends.

Robert Emmet *

The other letter was hurriedly written to Sarah's brother, from whom he must have received some parting message.

My dearest Richard,

I find that I have but a few hours to live ; but if it was the last moment, and that the power of utterance was leaving me, I would thank you from the bottom of my heart for your generous expression of affection and forgiveness to me. If there was one in the world in whose breast my death might be supposed not to stifle every spark of resentment, it might be you. I have deeply injured you, I have injured the happiness of a sister that you love, and who was formed to give happiness to every one about her, instead of having her own mind a prey to affliction.

Oh, Richard, I have no excuse to offer, but that I meant the reverse. I intended as much happiness for Sarah as the most ardent love could have

* *Vice Roy's Post Bag*, p. 409.

given her. I never did tell you how much I idolized her. It was not with a wild or unfounded passion, but it was an attachment increasing every hour, from an admiration of the purity of her mind and respect for her talents. I did dwell in secret upon the prospect of our union. I did hope that success, while it afforded the opportunity for our union, might be the means of confirming an attachment which misfortune had brought forth. I did not look for honours for myself—praise I would have asked from the lips of no man ; but I would have wished to read in the glow of Sarah's countenance that her husband was respected.

My love, Sarah ! It was not thus that I thought to have requited your affection. I did hope to be a prop round which your affections might have clung, and which would never have been shaken ; but a rude blast has snapped it, and they have fallen over a grave.

This is no time for affliction. I have had public motives to sustain my mind, and I have not suffered it to sink ; but there have been moments in my imprisonment when my mind was so sunk by grief on her account that death would have been a refuge. God bless you, my dearest Richard. I am obliged to leave off immediately.

Robert Emmet *

* *Vice Roy's Post Bag,* p. 400.

St. Catherine's Church, Thomas Street, Dublin. Emmet's depot was at the rear of the buildings on the right

Malton's Views of Dublin

An imaginary view of Emmet's execution, published in 1877
Reproduced by the courtesy of the National Museum of Ireland

CHAPTER FORTY-FOUR

The Scaffold in Thomas Street

For the second day Dublin and its vicinity could think of nothing but Robert Emmet. Friends and foes alike flocked to the place of his execution. The colours of their clothes added brightness to the sombreness of red brick walls drabbed with dust and the cold grey of the stones of St. Catherine's. Here and there a man braver than the rest showed the corner of a green handkerchief, and more than one woman wore a bonnet tied with verdant strings. Thomas Street and all the adjoining thoroughfares were filled with people from every walk of life. Hundreds of men and boys climbed to near-by housetops where they perched in gutters or clung to yellow chimney-pots. Every window in the neighbourhood framed faces of fascinated spectators.

Raucous-voiced hawkers pushed their way through the vast throngs on the sidewalks and cobblestones, selling copies of Emmet's speech. Some had been got out by the Government and were intended both to antagonise the French and to minimise the democratic tendency of the Irish. Others had been printed by nationalists eager to carry out Emmet's "last charge" to his countrymen, and to keep alive the spirit of independence and of idealism he had evoked so dramatically at his trial.

In front of St. Catherine's Church in Thomas Street, just across from the entrance to Emmet's depot, the rudest kind of gallows had been erected. Two tall posts with a transverse beam rose from the platform of planks laid on empty barrels. Just beneath the beam and about three feet above the rough floor was a single narrow board, supported by slender props. Five feet or more above it a noose swayed gently in the mild September air. Soldiers, mounted and on foot, surrounded this instrument of death and kept the enormous crowds from pressing too closely upon it.

25—1854

At Kilmainham, Robert Emmet was leaving gaol as a guest might end his visit at the home of a friend. About one-thirty he learned with composure of the Sheriff's arrival. Mr. Gamble, looking on, had to admire his easy politeness. He thanked the Governor, Mr. Dunn, and Major Swan for their humanity and attention. He even embraced Dr. Trevor and entrusted to him two letters, the one to Tom and Jane and the one to Mr. Wickham.*

The carriage Dr. Trevor had asked for was waiting. An escort of cavalry and foot was ready to surround it on the trip to Thomas Street. As Emmet came out of the gaol, he saw, among the crowd pressing about the entrance, a priest whom he had known some time before. Impulsively, he detached from his watch fob his onyx seal, engraved with a harp and weeping willows, and presented it to his friend.†

With solemn slowness the procession moved toward Dublin. A long route to Thomas Street had been laid out, to give as many people as possible a glimpse of the condemned man. It crossed the Liffey at Island Bridge and came back to the south side of the river near the place of execution.

* The doctor delivered both letters to the Castle, where it was decided that the one to Tom and Jane Emmet should not be forwarded, but that Mr. Curran should be told of the paragraph concerning Sarah. Mr. Wickham notified him of it by letter, which drew from the ambitious man a letter full of lavish compliments and superabundant thanks. (Wickham wrote the Speaker that it was "very comical.") In it he spoke of his "warm and animated thanks of man to man"; but when he came to speak of his daughter, his tone was one of detached coldness. He described her as a poor creature that once held the warmest place in his heart, toward whom he had resolved to act with as much moderation as possible. That moderation, it developed, was just short of disowning her, and Emmet's letter, he told Wickham, had confirmed him in that resolve. He could "not let her sink so low as to become the subject of a testamentary order of a miscreant who could labour by so foul means and under such odious circumstances to connect her with his infamy, and to acquire any posthumous interest in her person or her fate.

"Blotted, therefore, as she may irretrievably be from my society, or the place she once held in my affection, she must not go adrift. So far, at least, 'these protections will not fall off.' I should therefore, sir, wish for the suppression of this extract if no particular motive should have arisen for forwarding it to its destination." *Vice Roy's Post Bag*, p. 409.

Unfortunately, Curran did not live up to even that limited promise. Sarah was banished from his home. As Tom and Jane for some years knew nothing of Robert's attachment, she did not find with them the haven her sweetheart had hoped for. If it had not been for the kindness of friends in Lismore and Cork who took her in for a while, there is no telling how much actual privation she might have suffered before she finally became the bride of an English officer.

Her father was made Master of the Rolls in Ireland.

† This was probably the same seal Emmet had used when sending Miles Byrne to France. Later, the priest bequeathed it to Dr. Madden, who gave it to Dr. Thomas Addis Emmet of New York. *Memoir of Thomas Addis and Robert Emmet*, II, p. 235.

The two clergymen were still urging Emmet to retract his principles, but they never could get him to admit he had been in the wrong. Even when they asked him whether he would have persisted in his attempt to overthrow the Government if he had foreseen the blood that would be spilt, he answered that no one went to battle without being prepared for that. He considered his attempt free from moral reproach because of the purity of the motives that produced it.*

Even as the carriage drew up beside the gallows, fenced off by a solid line of redcoats from the pressing mob, the clergymen persisted in urging Emmet to forsake his principles and to give them some of the " pleasing assurances " they had hoped for. It was no use. For fifteen minutes the talk went on, as the crowd watched curiously, and the Sheriff and the hangman waited. To the spectators it seemed a quiet conversation. They could not know that they were witnessing the triumphant end of Emmet's long ideal. In spite of temptations and pressures he had not given in. Instead of being ashamed of dying on the gallows, he was proud to be giving his life for his country. He had not renounced his principles. To the contrary, he wanted to address the crowd in support of them.

" What did he wish to say ? " the clergymen asked hopefully, thinking perhaps that the sight of the gallows and the swinging noose had weakened him.

They had not. He intended to say, Emmet told his questioners with simple dignity, that he had never taken any oath but that of the United Irishmen, and by that oath he meant to abide.

Ruefully the clergymen looked at one another, defeat admitted in their eyes.

" Such an address," they explained hurriedly, " might produce tumult and bloodshed, and it could not be permitted." Emmet acquiesced without appearing to be disturbed or agitated.† He had done what he could. In time his life would speak for itself.

* I.S.P.O.

† Mr. Gamble's account of Emmet's last moment, written for Marsden, said that " at the place of punishment he [Emmet] expressed a wish to address the crowd, from which he was dissuaded by Mr. Sheriff Walsh and Major Swan, who represented the impossibility of his being heard."

Mr. Gamble made a fuller report to Dr. Trevor, who wrote it out and sent it to the Castle. "At the place of execution he was desirous of addressing the people. He

Emmet's hands were tied, and the Sheriff and Major Swan
helped him up the ladder to the rude platform. Before they
pulled the black cap over his head or put the noose about his
neck, Emmet looked down on the thousands of faces turned
up to him and in his lovely silvery voice spoke his short
valedictory : " My friends, I die in peace, and with sentiments
of universal love and kindness toward all men."

The fall from the little ledge was not enough to break
Emmet's neck. His body hung motionless for a moment,
then began to writhe and struggle. When it was quiet, the
executioner cut it down, and the last part of the sentence was
carried out. From an upper window in a house just opposite
the gallows a horrified woman saw the head severed from the
body with a common knife, and Emmet's blood spurt forth
like a gory fountain. His heart must still have been beating.

The hangman rose from the planking, holding Emmet's
head by the hair. Walking the length of the platform and
turning from left to right so that every one might see, he
lifted it up to the crowd. " This is the head of a traitor,
Robert Emmet," he chanted. " This is the head of a traitor."

Slowly the people who had witnessed the execution dispersed. Some went exulting that Lord Kilwarden's death
had been avenged again. Many grieved for the young man
who had died and mourned that their cause had lost a leader.
More than one, it was said, loitered about and, when the
guards were not looking, darted furtively to the dark pools
that had collected under the planking to dip their handker-
chiefs in Emmet's blood. An hour later, a woman who lived
near by saw dogs lapping it up.

When the street was quiet, a cart came for Emmet's body
and took it to Newgate. There it was kept till eleven that
night, then sent to Kilmainham. When the artist George
Petrie went there to ask permission to make a death mask,
he saw the body, coffined in a thin penal shell, on the floor
of the entry. There was no one about, and, thinking that he

intended to have declared that he had never taken any oath but that of the United
Irishmen, and by that oath he meant to abide. The clergymen who were present
explained to him that an address to that effect might produce tumult and bloodshed,
and that it ought not to be permitted. He was therefore obliged to acquiesce, and he
did so without appearing to be disturbed or agitated."
Both these accounts are in the I.S.P.O.

could work better at home, he took the head away. When he returned with it an hour later, the body and shell had vanished.*

Just down the road from the entrance to Kilmainham was the public burying-ground known as the Hospital Fields. There, all the other State prisoners who had been executed had been interred, and there about midnight Emmet's body was buried near that of Felix Rourke's. If the common practice of the time and place was followed, only a few inches of earth lay over it.

But the headless body was not to stay there long. A little later, it was secretly removed and taken elsewhere. To this day no one knows definitely where it lies.†

---

* Petrie carried the head away again, and for many years it was in his possession. Copies of the death mask he made are in the National Gallery of Ireland and in the National Museum. They bear a great resemblance to the little water colour portrait painted that day by the English officer which is used as the frontispiece for this book.

† Many places in Dublin claim the honour of holding Emmet's body : the grave-yards of St. Michan's, St. Peter's, and the vaults of St. Ann's. The quiet little burying-ground in the shadow of the church at Glasnevin, made famous by its association with Dean Swift, has a stone which is said to cover Emmet's body. But when investigations were made at these places about a hundred years after Emmet's death, nothing was found to confirm the rumours.

In 1904 the vault of Dr. Trevor's family, in St. Paul's Church, King Street, Dublin, was opened. For a long time there had been a story that a headless body rested there. The Parish Registry had entries for only four bodies for this vault. The remains of five were found. One, enclosed in a thin penal shell, was the headless skeleton of a young man about Emmet's build.

II

USING THE RISING

CHAPTER FORTY-FIVE

Infamy and Arrests

EMMET's death ended nothing but his own personal ordeal; and though he had come out morally and spiritually triumphant, the public was told just the reverse. In fact, the most important phase of the pursuit of Robert Emmet took place after his death, the pursuit of his reputation. It was necessary to picture the symbol as defeated, degraded, and weak, and this, contrary to all truth and decency, was done *ad infinitum.*

The people assembled to see him die could buy distorted versions of his speech from the dock, warning the Irish people to have nothing to do with France. A large newspaper supplement (also issued in colours at one shilling and sixpence) pictured Emmet on his trial and added a text that combined every feature of Wickham's policy. In it Emmet was described as an insane enthusiast, leading a handful of deluded followers to their death. According to that account, Emmet had issued from the depot on the evening of July 23.

. . . at the head of a contemptible band of nefarious assassins, who, after committing the most disgraceful atrocities, were at length dispersed by a small body of the army and yeomanry and fled different ways, but have been since apprehended, and suffered the punishment due to their crimes. Strange infatuation ! that can still prompt the poor to risk their lives in the service of leaders who either, as in the rebellion of 1798, turn king's evidence and betray them or, as on the present occasion, sacrifice them to vain expectations, and feed them with the hopes of being joined by rebel forces, which have no existence but in their own imaginations. When we behold this arrogant young man, seated in state on the floor of a Malt-house, surrounded by Lieutenant-Generals Dowdall the Clerk, Stafford the baker, and Quigley the Brick-layer, assuming the title of General, and giving laws to thirty or forty deluded mechanics and labourers, half of whom were killed in the first attack he led them to, and the remainder hanged in the course of a few weeks after. (*sic*) When we consider the misery, the disgrace and the destruction his mad attempt brought on those whom he prevailed on to join him, mingled emotions of contempt for presuming audacity, and pity for misguided ignorance arise in the mind, and we doubt whether most to despise or to compassionate the ravings of insanity of the leader, or credulity of the victims he conducted to the gallows. . . .

Nevertheless, the report went on, the deluded young man had been wise enough to see the miseries brought upon the countries subject to France and had, in his speech from the dock, warned his countrymen to have nothing to do with them and to repel them with their dying breaths.

The *Dublin Evening Post,* in the first issue after Emmet's trial, printed Plunket's entire speech, gave a version of Emmet's along the lines of Wickham's policy, and editorialised sanctimoniously :

We lament that such talents as Mr. Emmett (*sic*) possessed were not directed to better purposes ; but while his death has furnished an awful example to others, his trial is fraught with much useful and satisfactory information to the public : it has disclosed the late conspiracy in all its parts, and confirmed our uniform opinion of it, that it was contemptible and inefficient, and stood isolated and detached from popular sympathy and cooperation. . . . The whole turns out to be the last effort of expiring sedition, which by its attempt to overthrow, has contributed to the firmer establishment of our excellent constitution.

Mr. Emmet had dinner in Newgate and asked to see the gentleman who had defended him. To him, it is generally rumoured, he made a full disclosure of all the means he had used to effect the late insurrection, and authorised him to make it known to Government. He declared himself the chief mover and instigator of that attempt to effect a revolution, and solemnly denied having any associates in this country of either property or respectability. He also denied having solicited or received any assistance from the French government, and protested that were this country invaded by Frenchmen from his information of their principles or conduct wherever they were, that he would be one of the most zealous in the expulsion of such rapacious and sanguinary miscreants.

When Mr. Gamble's account of Emmet's last moments finally appeared in print on September 24, sections of it credited Emmet with sentiments directly opposite to what the clergyman had originally reported. It now began : " The execution of Emmet may be well deemed a deathblow to conspiracy and rebellion in this metropolis, as it was stated on his trial he was the life and soul of it which indeed he acknowledged." With equal disregard for the truth, Emmet was credited with having said that, if he had foreseen the great

evils which had ensued from his " desperate enterprise," he
would never have engaged in it.   Mr. Gamble himself, one
regrets to say, later tried to get admissions from McIntosh
(and probably from other State prisoners) by saying that
Emmet had " confessed " certain things to him.

Mr. Gamble's original account had admitted Emmet's
reverent behaviour and his acknowledgement of being a
Christian.   But one Dublin paper declared that the two
clergymen had tried in vain to win Emmet from his deistical
opinions.

In short, he behaved without the least symptoms of fear, and with all the
effrontery and nonchalance which so much distinguished his conduct on his
trial yesterday.   He seemed to scoff at the dreadful circumstances attendant
upon him ; at the same time, with all the coolness and complacency that
can be possibly imagined, though utterly unlike the calmness of Christian
fortitude.   Even as it was, I never saw a man die like him, and God forbid
I should see many of his principles.

The *London Chronicle* reprinted the account in its next issue.
On September 27, the *Dublin Evening Post* again emphasised
the obscurity and contemptibility of the people who had taken
part in the rising.   Ignoring the fact that one of the State
prisoners, John Russell, of Mountjoy Square, a wealthy
builder, was about to be released from gaol on £10,000 bail,
it claimed that no one but a few needy adventurers living in
vagrancy and dependence had been concerned in it.   It spoke
of " an outlawed bricklayer, and such contemptible creatures
as an outlawed clerk [Dowdall], hodmen, hostlers, old clothes
men, etc. . . . "

Wickham achieved his greatest success in using Robert
Emmet as a symbol the day after his trial when Luke White,
a banker, called at the Castle and said he would immediately
take £500,000 in Exchequer-bills at par.*

The account of the transaction appeared in all the Dublin
papers three days later, elaborated in such a way as to make
use of its great morale-building qualities.

We understand that the morning immediately following the trial and
conviction of Emmet, Luke White, Esq., waited on the Right Hon. Mr.
Wickham, and proposed a loan of half a million ster. to government upon

* *Colchester Correspondence*, I, p. 456.

Mr. Wickham's own terms, an offer which we believe has been accepted. As Mr. White may properly be considered the representative and organ of the monied interest in Ireland, this circumstance manifests two things—the one justly complimentary to an individual, the other highly assuring to the public ; it evinces the deserved confidence placed by the property of the country in Mr. Wickham and generally in Lord Hardwicke's administration, and it shews that the monied part of the community, altho' the soonest and easiest affected by alarm, consider the late insurrection (as it appears from Emmet's trial) to have been such a contemptible ebullition of confined and partial treason, as should excite no general or well-grounded apprehensions to the public mind.

Indeed, it was one of those efforts of mob-like riot and licentiousness which mad enthusiasm can almost at any time, with the aid of a little money, rouse the desperate profligacy of a great capital, and while we may lament some of its consequences it can have no other effect than invigorating our spirit and accelerating our preparations to repel the actual dangers with which we are threatened by a foreign foe.*

In writing to the Speaker about the loan, Wickham said that he had been working himself almost to the bone in his endeavours " to make use of the late conspiracy as a means of securing the capital at least, and its vicinity, a fair prospect of solid and permanent tranquillity." Practically, this meant the imprisonment of every potential rebel possible, as well as men suspected of having been concerned with the events of July 23. It meant the execution of men too dangerous to be allowed to live. It meant exile for others who might in the future take up the old struggle for Irish independence. It meant getting every bit of information about the rising from spies, informers, and such prisoners as could be induced to talk. With the knowledge of how and with whom the rebels had acted, the Castle could easily frustrate any future attempts the disaffected might make.

On the day of Emmet's execution Anne Develin was one of those questioned about him, on the sound psychological

---

* Mr. Cody of the *Dublin Evening Post*, who was drawing a secret-service allowance of £100 a quarter, of course printed the story in his papers, and dozens of others along the same lines. In October he also helped to earn his allowance by bringing out a pamphlet titled *The Insurrection of July 23rd*. This was an account tailored to suit the Castle propaganda programme. Wickham's policy letter of September 11 is especially noticeable in the introduction, one paragraph of which said that the " treason had been found contemptibly narrow in its scope and contemptibly mean in its instruments and resources. Without morality in its principles (if morality could combine with treason), without political sagacity in its system or its views, and without property, respectability or physical strength to carry it into effect, it was incapable of aspiring to any distinction, but the horrible preeminence of ferocity and crime. . . ."

assumption that the death of some one she had known so intimately might have shaken her nerves. It had not, and so the next day, before being questioned again, she was taken to Thomas Street and forced to look at the gallows on which Emmet had been hanged. Even the gruesome sight was not enough to make Anne give the information the Castle wanted ; thus she was sent back to Kilmainham and put off the State allowance.*

John Patten was transferred to Kilmainham that day and put into Emmet's old cell. Since his arrest in August, he had been kept in the house of a King's messenger. His transfer to the gaol was timed so as to let him meditate on the uncertainty of human life. The room was just as Emmet had left it the day before. Even the bed-clothes lay rumpled as he had risen from them. But though the effect was calculated to be demoralising, Patten, a philosophical soul with ideals of honour as high as Emmet's own, remained calm and refused to say anything.†

Not so Jimmy Farrell, the friend of John Allen, Tom Russell, little brown jugs, and light-hearted ladies. Much less debonair than usual, he was brought to Dublin from London a few days after Emmet's execution and set to work helping the Government catch some of his old friends. He was not committed to gaol but lived privately at Government

---

* That meant that she was reduced to the almost starvation diet which ordinary, not political, prisoners received : two loaves a week, a pint of milk daily, and water. Tom Duffy, Mrs. Bagnell's servant, and Michael McDonagh, her neighbour, were also put off the State allowance that day. Anne was restored to it a week later, but McDonough and Duffy were not restored till November 7.

Anne's confinement was especially severe, partly owing to her stubbornness and partly, no doubt, to her vituperative tongue. Certainly she suffered greatly and was ill with erysipelas and rheumatism for long afterward. If it had not been for Mrs. Dunn, the wife of the turnkey, who used to smuggle Anne into her kitchen and give her food, she would have been much worse off. When she was sent back to the Tower, in 1806, so that she would not have to be released with the other State prisoners after the expiration of the Suspension of the Habeas Corpus Act, it was Mrs. Hanlon, widow of a former keeper, then taking her husband's place in the Tower, who obtained her release.

† When he continued to refuse to give information, he was put into solitary confinement. In 1805 he was given the chance of regaining his freedom. But though the negotiations between him and the Castle were carried on by his uncle, Mr. William Colville, a governor of the Bank of Ireland, with all the dignity due to the old gentleman's position, the terms resolved themselves into the old familiar ones of giving information. Patten was to name the persons he knew who had offered Robert Emmet any kindness either before or after the rising. He declined and remained with most of the important State prisoners in Kilmainham till the Suspension of the Habeas Corpus Act expired shortly after Pitt's death in 1806.

expense, charged to the secret-service fund. Since he had been in Paris the year before and knew intimately most of the important United Irishmen in London, Liverpool, and Dublin, Wickham found him invaluable in rounding out the general picture of the conspiracy.

On September 30, the mysterious Malachy Delaney, who had gone to France with Emmet in 1800, was arrested and committed to Kilmainham, charged with high treason. Where he had been before his arrest and what, if anything, he told the Government in the four months he was in gaol has not transpired. But when he was released in January of 1804, it was by Mr. Wickham's order, and he had made terms that called for his surrender in case of invasion. But he was not obliged to give bond to keep the peace, as most prisoners were on their release. This fact, coupled with his strange acquittal from the charge of murder the spring before, is additional reason to suspect that he too was helping the Government develop the conspiracy. William Ainslie Houlton, the would-be hero of the Pigeon House attack, was in Kilmainham at this time, and he too, still acting as a spy, was charged with high treason, as Delaney had been.

Pat Finnerty, one of the carpenters who had worked in the depot on Thomas Street, was released from gaol for the purpose of " setting " (i.e., trapping) Henry Howley. On learning that he was working in a certain carpenter's shop Finnerty led Major Sirr there. Hanlon, the Keeper of the Tower, was killed in the capture, but it gave the Government another man to be tried in Green Street as an example to the common people. Howley followed Emmet in the dock in Green Street court-house on September 27 and was executed the next day.

John McIntosh and Thomas Keenan of the Patrick Street depot were arrested at this time in Arklow and promptly brought to Dublin for trial. McIntosh was put into the dock the first of October, convicted the same day, and hanged the next.

The *Dublin Evening Post's* account of McIntosh's trial claimed that he had been " truly penitent for his crimes, and particularly lamented that he had abandoned the Kirk of Scotland, in which he had been bred, for the Church of Rome, which he had adopted since his coming to Ireland. He made many important communications to Mr. Sheriff Pounden. . . ."

But the truth was, as the Lord Lieutenant admitted to his brother soon after, that McIntosh died a Roman Catholic and had refused to give any information, though he might have saved his life and returned to his own country in perfect safety.*

On October 1, Robert Carty was brought over to Dublin from London and handed over to the Castle. Wickham's insistence that he be there to give information from day to day had finally triumphed over the scruples of Mr. Yorke. Carty had been promised that no one would know that he was giving information, and that he would not be required to come forward as a witness against any one. However, Wickham purposely spread the news that he was in communication with the Government in order to terrify other prisoners and so thoroughly convinced Carty himself that he would be hanged if he did not help convict some of the other men he had known that he at once agreed, provided his own life were spared, that he would prosecute Philip Long. Later he went back on that promise, but for the years he was in prison Wickham had him within call whenever a point came up where his knowledge would be useful.

Early in October Mr. Pollock, Colonel Wolfe, and the Solicitor-General sorted out the most important prisoners from among the thirty-eight then in Naas gaol and sent them to Kilmainham, charged with rebellion. They were Patrick Dunn, Richard Scott, William Andrews, Daniel Brophy, Mathew Dodd, and Edward Scully.† Most of them were kept in prison for years. Naas gaol continued to hold other important rebels, and additions to their ranks continued to be made for a long time. Other Kildare prisoners were in gaol in Athy.

Admiral Pakenham was scouring the county so thoroughly that one of the Maynooth rebel leaders, tired of being hunted and harried, went to Colonel Aylmer and gave himself up. His surrender and his unsuspected desertion to the ranks of

---

* *Vice Roy's Post Bag*, p. 377.

† A Black Book in the I.S.P.O., made up about 1806, before most of these men were liberated, says that Scott, a very turbulent man, " declares he will not die till he has satisfaction, and that if he is liberated he will shoot Colonel Wolfe."

informers netted the Castle one of the most important prizes
of the whole rising. Through him, Quigley, Stafford, and
the Parrots were arrested in County Galway, where they had
taken refuge disguised as spade labourers, and brought to
Dublin. Wickham thought that Stafford was one of the
finest-looking men he had ever seen, but Quigley immediately
impressed him as being by far the cleverest of all the rebels
he had conversed with. He was more than that. He was the
key man to the County of Kildare. He had been engaged
with the disaffected since 1798. He had been in France and
knew many of the Irish exiles there and in the cities of England
where he and Hamilton had stopped on their return to Ireland.
He had met Emmet early in March and had conducted all the
transactions for the Kildare men. He had been in charge of
the depot in Thomas Street and had built the false walls in
Patrick Street. He had visited the house in Butterfield Lane.
He had gone to the mountains with Emmet and knew who
had sheltered him there. He had had communications with
Emmet after their separation on July 28.

The Government had no intention of losing this source of
information by executing the man. Quigley's landlord from
Ardfry in County Galway had come to Dublin and was also
in custody. From him as well as from all the informers who
had been at the depot, the Government took down enough
evidence against Quigley to hang him. Then Wickham went
to work. All the usual pressures were applied. He was told,
of course, that he had been betrayed by his companions.

On October 22 he and Stafford were arraigned before Lord
Norbury, ostensibly as a prelude to trial. Then the pair had
to face the judge in the privacy of his own home. Lord
Norbury must have done a thorough job of intimidating the
two men, for a few days later Quigley had completely reversed
his political principles. He no longer wanted a separation of
Ireland from England. He thought that " with his knowledge
of affairs " he would be of use to the Government. He asked
for a conference with Mr. Wickham. But he could not have
been willing to make the unqualified submission the Government was insisting upon, for it was not until the twenty-eighth
that he finally gave in and threw himself upon the mercy of
the Government. The delay is explained in a paragraph of a

letter that Wickham immediately sent to London with the good news.

The question of shewing mercy to Quigley has been well and deliberately discussed. It was determined from the first, considering the very important part he had acted in the conspiracy, not to hear of any terms or stipulations of any kind that he might attempt to insist upon, either for himself or others. This was so distinctly signified and so often repeated to him, in answer to every condition he wished to attach to the disclosures he offered to make that he yesterday threw himself upon the mercy of government, and immediately gave me some *local* information of considerable importance, the substance of which will be communicated to you from time to time for Mr. Yorke's information. At present we are very busily employed in acting upon it.*

There was one good thing to be said for Quigley. His submission had included a strong request for the lives of five of the men he had led into the rising. The Government allowed them to live.

Of the five he has named [Wickham explained], viz, Stafford, the two Parrots, Frayne and Condon,—two are already secretly in the services of the government (one of them being the very man who betrayed Quigley himself) ; against the third there is no evidence ; the fourth has a young wife and eight small children, and both the third and fourth are the sons of an Englishman of as good and loyal a character as any man in the United Kingdom. When the father removed to the county of Galway as gardener and land surveyor to Mr. Blake of Ardfry, a gentleman of very large property in that county, he unfortunately left these young men behind in the neighbourhood of Maynooth, where they fell into the hands of Lord Edward Fitzgerald, whose attentions to them they were unable to resist, and so entered deeply into the Rebellion.

Wickham thought that the knowledge that Quigley was giving information to the Government would do more toward pacifying the country and terrifying the disaffected than the execution of twenty men of his rank and station in life.

And Kildare still needed pacifying, as indeed all Ireland did. All the wishful thinking of the Government that had found its way into print about the quietness of the country and the loyalty of the majority of the people was just the opposite of the truth. Colonel Wolfe, writing to the Castle that he was sending up six more prisoners from Naas to Dublin, felt that he could not lose the opportunity of endeavouring to impress the great extent of disaffection in his part of the

* *Vice Roy's Post Bag*, p. 437.

country and the great importance of hunting it out. It was more important to do so in his county than any other part of Ireland, he thought, except perhaps in the City and County of Dublin. What progress had been made was only in the neighbourhood of Maynooth [thanks probably to the salty Admiral]. The extensive local and personal knowledge possessed by Quigley and Quigley alone, the Colonel suggested, made it very advantageous to the Government to allow Quigley to communicate what he knew to the Government, if he felt so disposed.

The first information Quigley gave that is now available was taken down by Dr. Trevor and is headed

Doctor Trevor's conversation with Quigley, October 28 :
About September 1802 part of the arms for the Louisiana scheme were purchased. Lord Cloncurry was constantly in company with Surgeon Lawless and W [witness, Quigley] believes but is not certain that he (Lord C) contributed to the purchasing of arms. Quigley and McDermot lived in the Rue St. Denise when McCabe came to tell them they were to go to Ireland. McCabe had been employed by A. O Connor to organize Ireland. . . .

The paper also contained some local information that is doubtless what Wickham had referred to in his letter to London.*

The next day Dr. Trevor had another conversation with Quigley along the same lines, and another the next. Each time he sent his report to the Castle. On November 1, Quigley was taken there himself and underwent a full-dress examination. It covered everything he had done from the time he was released from Kilmainham in the summer of 1802.

Later, Quigley began to make almost daily reports, and there are dozens of them still at the Castle. Some are written in a tall awkward hand that may have been his own ; others were transcribed by Dr. Trevor. Between them they put on paper everything Quigley remembered and, when the first rumours that he had turned informer had been dispelled, everything he could gather from the conversation of his fellow-prisoners and—very important point—from the conversation

---

* This is no longer at the I.S.P.O., but I have had access, through the kindness of Dr. Charles Dickson, to transcripts of it and other Quigley material, which are believed to be accurate.

of visitors to the prison. From them particularly the Castle received hints that led to the capture of many Kildare rebels.

The Government at first hoped to get Quigley to prosecute some of the more important State prisoners, but he absolutely refused to appear in court. Dr. Trevor, who had a large variety of inducements at his disposal, thought he could bring him round but failed. However, Quigley was probably more useful to the Castle as an unsuspected informer. He could pump his comrades for information that they would not give to an avowed agent of the Government. For years he kept the Castle informed of the very thoughts of his fellow-prisoners. When the Suspension of the Habeas Corpus Act finally expired in 1806 and they were released, he opened a public house in Dublin that became a rendezvous for the disaffected. What Quigley learned from them he handed on to the Castle.

The North was " pacified " in the same manner as Kildare. Aided by secret agents, McGucken, of course, still being the most important, yeomen went about arresting every one they could find who had been concerned with Russell's attempt to raise that part of the country. In October, Russell himself was sent to Downpatrick for trial before a Special Commission appointed to clear the gaols of Antrim and Down.* Some of the loyal gentlemen there had wanted the pacifying effect his execution would have on the disaffected ; and the Castle, having insisted so often that the rising had been merely the brief rioting of a contemptible rabble on Thomas Street for which Robert Emmet alone was responsible, could hardly produce in Dublin a figure of so much prominence and try to prove that he had been the centre of a co-ordinated conspiracy in the North, even though it had failed.

And Russell had to die. He had proved that more than five years of imprisonment had not altered his devotion to democracy and the ideal of Irish freedom. Like Emmet, he was

* Wickham would have liked to try Russell for having returned from transportation, as an example to some of the exiles in France who were only waiting for a favourable opportunity to come to Ireland. But that would have brought up the discussion of the written agreement by which the State prisoners of 1798 had bound themselves to transportation for life in exchange for the cessation of State trials. That agreement was so notoriously at variance with the Banishment Bill that the discussion would have exposed the bad faith of the Government. Wickham tacitly admitted this and said that it was fortunate that they had Mr. Curran so completely in their power, and that Mr. Plunket was life and soul with them. P.R.O.L.

quite willing to die for his principles.* The last weeks of his life, in fact, followed almost exactly the same pattern that Emmet's had. He refused to give information even for the sake of people he loved. St. John Mason planned an escape for him, as he had for Emmet. It ended, as Emmet's had, by the betrayal of the turnkey. McNally was sent to probe him for secrets. What he learned was more disturbing than helpful to the Government. Wickham had already heard from Emmet how widespread the seeds of disaffection were spread among English working tradesmen and labourers. He was so alarmed at Russell's insistence on this point that he immediately sent a secret and confidential letter to officials in London, warning them of the danger.

At another interview Russell told McNally what the Castle, though it would not admit it, already knew : that as many tears were being shed for Emmet as would bathe him, and that he would be considered a martyr by the people.

The Reverend Mr. Archer, the Inspector-General of Prisons, administered the Holy Sacrament to him and wrote his account of Russell's conversation for the Castle.

As Mr. Bell had taken Crown witnesses to Kilmainham to look at Emmet, so Mr. Forde, the High Sheriff of County Down, sent men to Dublin to identify Russell. Among them was James Witherspoon, at whose house Russell had held meetings. But though Witherspoon had acknowledged, when he was first arrested, his connection with Russell, he refused to identify his friend when he realised he would be helping to convict him and from that time on was no further help to the Government. Other friends of Russell's, however, had not Witherspoon's courage or loyalty, and by the time that Russell, accompanied by Major Sirr and Dr. Trevor, reached Downpatrick gaol, the Crown attorneys had a list of witnesses as long as Emmet's.

* Russell used the same expression that Emmet used about being willing to serve his country by dying on the gallows. He was equally brave, as his attempt to rescue Emmet proved, but there was a time when his mind was much agitated, and Wickham wrote to England that he was by no means so stout-hearted a man as Emmet. This, however, was in a secret letter to London. Wickham also expressed privately his respect for the plan of military operation Emmet and his associates had recommended to the French Government. It showed " talent and judgment when considered with a reference to the hopes and preparations of the disaffected at the time that the plan was submitted to the French government," he said in a letter to London written at the time when Emmet was being publicly stigmatised as weak, ineffectual, and deluded. P.R.O.L.

Russell, like Emmet, was under pressure up to the very last moments of his life. Like him, he made a stirring speech in the dock in defence of his principles. Like Emmet he was hanged and beheaded. Even Wickham admitted privately that he had behaved with firmness and propriety. But many of the newspapers spoke of him as though he were almost a monster.

At the time of Russell's trial, Wickham, still working desperately hard making use of the rising, decided it would be helpful to have the Trinity boy "Jones" on hand for questioning. "Jones" was then serving as Lieutenant in an English Militia regiment, but officials in Whitehall arranged a leave for him, and he was secretly sent over to Ireland. Since the disaffected still looked on him as one of themselves, his presence in Dublin could not be known. He lived with a State messenger, at the Government's expense, for several weeks.

Since June, and perhaps before then, "Jones" had been sending the Castle biographical sketches of important United Irishmen at home and abroad. His political career with the Society had given him a particularly widespread acquaintance, and he had of course kept up his connections in Dublin, in spite of a slight cloud of suspicion that had once hung over him.

"Jones" was in Ireland about a month, and though only one written report that he made at this time still survives at the State Paper Office, he probably wrote others. Short as his stay was, it resulted in secret-service payments to him totalling £300.

The one surviving report concerned a man who had been in Paris from 1798 on, and who had been a great friend of Emmet's both there and during Trinity days. He was Michael Farrell of County Longford (no relation to the debonair Jimmy, who originally came from County Waterford). Farrell had gone to England that summer from France, "Jones" thought for the purpose of helping Emmet's rising, and had been arrested some time later. Now he was sent over to Ireland in the custody of a King's messenger and in company with William St. John, sometimes known as Johnston. There is no indication that Michael Farrell gave any useful information to the Castle, but St. John probably did. He had been helpful to the British Government while he was on the continent in 1799, and there is reason to suspect that his presence in Ireland during the summer of 1803 was known to the Castle. At any rate, while he was in Kilmainham he was supported, not as most of the State prisoners were, by funds provided through the Crown Solicitor's office, but through the Treasury. The only other prisoner supported in this way was Robert Carty, who is definitely known to have given most useful information. Jimmy Farrell said in one of his informations that St. John had been a great democrat but was then loyal.

The Kerry and Limerick man-hunts had not brought in many of the men General Payne was most interested in, and the Castle evidently felt that he was a little too scrupulous in making arrests.* They sent down a spy of their own, one Captain James Fitzmaurice, who had good family connections in the county. He was introduced among the disaffected of both Limerick and Kerry as a person who would help them throw off the English yoke. The idea was that, when he had learned the names of all those who would be willing to join an insurrection, he would provide officials with lists of names and help superintend wholesale arrests. But Fitzmaurice, though he spent the Government's money and roused the people almost to the point of insurrection by talk of providing them with arms, never did turn in a rebel of any note.

Worse than that, he informed various gentlemen of the country that he was a spy, mentioned men in high places as being his confidants, and even embroiled members of the British cabinet in his unorthodox antics. He was General Payne's *bete noire* for months.† But though his informations

---

* He wrote Marsden that autumn, when some warrants had been sent down to him which he neglected to use, that " were I to give in to all the alarms, apprehensions, private resentments and private objects of all around me, I should repeatedly fill the gaols of the district, distress individuals, and increase the spirit of disaffection without benefiting our cause. However, I assure you that I am not supine in my exertions to man his Majesty's Fleet and with a race of sturdy Ruffians who have the old proverb in favour of their never being drowned. . . ." I.S.P.O.

† The General finally became so exasperated at him that he wrote Marsden a saucy letter, decorated with several blots that indicate that his audacity was of the vinous variety. " I look upon you, sir," he told Marsden, " as the author of your own misfortunes by having increased the number (tho' not having added to the respectability) of my acquaintants. I hardly dare feel that I am called upon to make you any apology of the intrusion [the many letters General Payne had had to write the

were not useful to the Castle, they are now valuable to students of Irish history. In one of them he indicated that the elder Fitzgerald of Kerry, father of the British spy, David Fitzgerald, and himself suspect, was the head of the business in that county. If he was, Kerry was quiet on July 23 for the same reason that the North was.*

The Castle knew very well that Wicklow would never become loyal as long as Michael Dwyer was at liberty there. In fact, he constituted a major menace to the peace of the whole country. So all autumn, larger and larger detachments of soldiers, spies, and informers were sent to the mountains to try to trap him. The Government even offered to let him "retreat from the kingdom" with all his immediate family. The offer was carried down by his aunt, Anne Develin's mother.

In explaining this to the Home Secretary in London, Lord Hardwicke admitted that there was very little hope of being able to apprehend Dwyer by ordinary means. His having taken an active part in the insurrection of July 23, so Hardwicke said, seemed a fair pretext for removing from the country, "by an act of lenity and indulgence which the loyal part of the country could not possibly disapprove," a very dangerous rebel. Of course, Dwyer had not actually done a thing at that time, but the offer was a tacit admission on the part of the Government of Dwyer's importance and their own failure to capture him. It also showed the importance they attached to Emmet.

Dwyer turned the offer down, perhaps because he was then still hoping for a French landing and perhaps because it made no provision for any of his followers, whom he would not desert.

On November 8 a reward of £500 was offered for his capture, and he was formally outlawed. A reward of £100

Castle concerning Fitzmaurice] and if I may add one remark to this very unreasonable letter it is that the removal of Fitzmaurice from the Province of Munster would relieve us from present and future troubles." I.S.P.O.

* With no publicity at all one John Farrell, a Limerick prisoner, was executed in February, 1804, for treason. John Dwyer and Dennis Murphy, charged with high treason and treasonable practices, respectively, were in Limerick gaol from August 8, 1803, and March 8, 1804, up to the time in 1805 when lists were prepared of all prisoners then in Ireland who had been arrested since July 23, 1803, on charges connected with the rising. They probably were kept in gaol until the Suspension of the Habeas Corpus Act expired in 1806. There is no return of Kerry gaols now available.

was promised for information about those who concealed or harboured him. Two or three soldiers were billeted in every house where he could possibly shelter, and they watched every move of the inhabitants. They were also an intolerable burden to the community, because their unwilling hosts were not reimbursed for their upkeep.

One by one Dwyer's relatives who were still at large were arrested. Even his brothers and sisters, his aunts, uncles, and cousins were taken up and sent to Dublin. The men went to prison ships in the bay, the women to Kilmainham. Their sufferings, even more than his own discomfort and frustration, must have swayed Dwyer. Early in December he and some followers were hiding in a cave near Wicklow Gap. The snow was deep, the cold severe, the men were truly wretched. Dwyer told them he meant to surrender. He proposed to give himself up to the Government on terms that would take care of his family and his immediate followers, with the understanding that they would be sent to the United States. All but one of the men who were with him were willing to accept such terms.

This news was relayed to Mr. Hume of Humewood, a magistrate of the County of Wicklow, and a week later he and Dwyer met to discuss terms. Dwyer wanted assurance that he, his wife and children, Big Arthur Develin, and two other followers would be pardoned for all past misdeeds and sent to the United States, and that all the people who had been arrested merely on his account would be liberated.

Mr. Hume had been in contact with the Government, and he promised Dwyer that these conditions would be fulfilled. Word was sent to the other men included in the terms to come in. There was some delay in their surrender ; and, after waiting for them for three days, Mr. Hume and Dwyer, escorted by the local yeomen cavalry, set off for Dublin without them.

On Wednesday evening last [the *Dublin Evening Post* for December 17 reported], the robber Michael Dwyer, wearied and hunted down by the activity of the troops sent to scour the mountains sent notice to Captain William Hume of his wish to surrender himself, at a place he mentioned. Captain Hume accordingly repaired, with a party of his yeomanry to the appointed spot, where he took him into custody and brought him a prisoner to Humewood. The remainder of this ruffian's desperate gang, which has so long eluded public justice in the fastnesses and bogs of Imail and Augha-vanagh, must be expected immediately to surrender as the vigorous measures now adopted have deprived them of their former resources of plunder and driven them into the bleakest and most barren part of the mountains.

Another newspaper styled Dwyer " a plundering disciple of the Mountain Nymph Sweet Liberty." But Wickham told the truth in a " most secret " letter written to England on December 26. " The capture of Dwyer will make the difference of an army to us. Had this man remained in the fastness of the county of Wicklow at the time of the landing of an enemy there is no doubt that a most formidable insurrection requiring a powerful force to put it down would have instantly broken out there." He was still uneasy about Cork, Limerick, and Kerry.*

Big Arthur Develin surrendered soon after this and was immediately sent up to the Castle. He was of course urged to give information. He did not, but to frighten some of the other State prisoners it was hinted that he had. To give colour to the tale he was daily taken into the Castle Yard in company with Fleming the hostler from the White Bull, Finnerty, and Pat Farrell, whose status as Crown witnesses was now well known.

Both Dwyer and Big Arthur were examined at the Castle on January 11. Dwyer evaded giving any answers that would injure men in captivity or help the Government find those who were still at large. He gave an incredibly low estimate of the men he might have raised for Emmet. He even said that it would then be impossible to raise the County of Wicklow if the French did come, a statement that Wickham knew quite well was ridiculous.†

He was, of course, questioned about Russell and Emmet and his conferences with them at Butterfield Lane. He dismissed them as briefly as he could. Of Emmet he said, with what candour it is impossible to state, that " if he had brain to his education he'd be a fine man." Perhaps it was a realist's estimate of an idealist whose pursuit had not been so obvious as Dwyer's own. He had evidently thought Emmet too

* P.R.O.L.

† The examinations are not now at the I.S.P.O., but they have been made available, in transcripts, through the kindness of Dr. Charles Dickson of Dublin.

enthusiastic and optimistic but had been much impressed with Russell's judgment.

Instead of sending Dwyer and his followers to America as they had been promised, the Government kept them in prison for more than two years and finally badgered them, by threatening to bring them to trial, into accepting Australia as a place of exile.*

The surrender of Dwyer was the last of the widely publicised accounts of the taking of any of the leaders concerned with Emmet. It was held up to the people as securing finally and definitely the peace and loyalty of Wicklow and the country adjoining, and as removing the last leader capable of acting effectively with the French in case of invasion.

As a matter of fact, though the Government (through McNally, writing over the initials J.W. in the *Dublin Evening Post* for December 1, 1803), was still calling the insurrection " The mere ebullition of a few fanatical politicians, stimulated to destruction and disgrace by an inconsiderate youth," hundreds of men were then in gaols in all parts of Ireland and in prison ships in Dublin Bay, charged with being concerned in the rising. Only a few of the leaders known to have been connected with Emmet had escaped (John Allen and William Dowdall being the most notable exceptions), and many more men than has ever been suspected were engaged in it.

By the time of Dwyer's surrender, Kilmainham gaol alone held fifty or more important State prisoners, and others had been executed, released, or transferred elsewhere. John Palmer had been there since shortly after the rising. So had John Stockdale, the printer the Government suspected of having printed Emmet's proclamation. Emmet's cousin St. John Mason was in solitary confinement, as were Philip Long and John Patten. Even the wealthy son of old Napper Tandy had been arrested when it transpired during the examinations of some prisoners that he had given Dowdall and others of the disaffected, letters of introduction to his father in France.

Anne Develin, her father and mother, a young broker, and two sisters were confined in Kilmainham. (Many other

---

* Their imprisonment served a very useful purpose. Quigley and other unsuspected informers picked their brains day by day, thereby enabled the Castle to learn the names and hiding places of other rebels and generally to round out the picture of the conspiracy.

relatives of the Develins and Dwyers were on prison ships in Dublin Bay.) Quigley, Stafford, the Parrots, and Nicholas Grey, who was to have been the general in Kildare, were also prisoners there. The more important Naas men were sent there to be probed by officials and spies. By March of 1805, when a return of political prisoners was compiled, more than two hundred men and women had been within its thick grey walls since July 23, 1803, charged with high treason, rebellion, or treasonable practices.*

Newgate gaol had received thirty-eight State prisoners during that time, including several who were executed. Miles Byrne's half-brother, Edward Kennedy, a well-to-do gentleman, was a prisoner there till May of 1804, when he was transferred to Kilmainham.

Thirty-one had been imprisoned in the Provost of Belfast, including James Scott, the man mentioned by McGucken in May of 1803 as having come to Dublin to see Emmet, and who had met Russell at James Witherspoon's just before the rising. John Shaw, who had been host to the little spy Houlton

---

* Barney Doogan, the dark-visaged little Northerner who had been one of Emmet's most confidential conspirators, was committed to Kilmainham in February of 1805. After he had shot at Mr. Clarke of Palmerstown on the evening of July 23, Doogan had escaped to the County Galway. He had been with Quigley and his party at Ardfry and had narrowly missed being taken up with them. For eighteen months he had stayed in the west, mostly in the County Galway, travelling a great deal and meeting all the disaffected of the district. It made him, with his natural shrewdness and intelligence, an ideal person for a spy, and when, on his return to Dublin, he was arrested, he was only too anxious to become one.

Mr. Townsend drew up a case against him, getting evidence from Quigley and the other men who had become informers since the rising, Fleming the hostler, Finnerty, and Condon. Meanwhile, tortured with fear and suspence, Doogan was giving Dr. Trevor the name of every person he had ever known among the disaffected, particularly the Galway rebels. He was also writing to friends outside that he had " undergone all the tortures that the government could inflict in order to extort information from me, but as you would expect, without effect thanks be to God."

The story of his sufferings made such an effect on his friends outside that for nearly forty years Doogan remained unsuspected. During that time he kept the Government informed of all the seditious activities in Ireland that he could learn of, and after his release, with the other State prisoners in 1806, he travelled the country looking for them. Besides that, he was sent to England and to France, always in the guise of an Irish patriot, to learn what was going on among the Irish exiles. He gave information about the Catholics when O'Connell was working for their emancipation ; he spied on O'Connell's Repealers. He spied on the Young Irelanders when those brave young idealists set out to follow in Emmet's footsteps. One of the greatest uses of Emmet's rising was the spies it produced which enabled the Government to suppress other patriotic efforts that inevitably followed.

In 1840, Doogan's duplicity was discovered, through an information of his which was then in the possession of Major Sirr's son, the Reverend James Darcey Sirr, and which was seen by the editor of a Repeal paper. Sirr, however, would not allow Doogan to be publicly exposed, and he was allowed to leave the country.

on his trip to Belfast was also there, and several men against whom, as a report in the State Paper Office admits, there was no evidence but who were known to have been remarkably active in attempting to incite rebellion on July 23.

Carrickfergus gaol had received twenty-two political prisoners by March of 1805, including David Porter and Andrew Hunter, who were hanged shortly after Russell's execution for their activity at Carnmoney on the night of the twenty-third ; William Rodgers, the fourteen-year-old boy who would not tell from whom he had got Russell's proclamation ; Isabella Shaw and Margaret Munro, who had been deceived by Houlton ; and Joseph Tannahill, in whose house in 1797 had been found a declaration of principles that closely resembled the American Declaration of Independence.

Downpatrick gaol had had eight State prisoners during that period, including Thomas Russell and his Northern companion James Drake, both of whom were executed.

Seven State prisoners were confined in the County Limerick gaol, including John Farrell, who was executed. (There are no returns for the city of Limerick gaol, or for the county gaols of Kerry or Clare, where many of the Munster prisoners must have been confined.)

The gaol of Athy, in the southern part of County Kildare, had had fourteen prisoners, including the informer-brother of B. Senior, John B., and his pseudo-French companion who had gone to the farm of the Careys in Kildare just before the rising and had been with the family on Thomas Street. On July 25 the two spies had gone to Athy, where they were arrested and put into gaol. John B. evidently cultivated his fellow-prisoners there and learned from them so much of the activities of the disaffected of the district that he was busy there for years. Mr. Bell, who generally took down his information in his open easy script, had by then been made a justice of the peace for the counties adjoining Dublin, and he and John B. worked successfully in rounding up some very important men in the County Carlow.

Philipstown gaol, in King's County, had one political prisoner, Wexford one, the city of Waterford one, the County of Waterford four, Longford two, Enniskillen one, County Carlow fifteen (most of them due to John B.'s activity there), Mullingar, County Westmeath, twelve, Naas gaol, eighty-six.

In all nearly fifteen hundred names are listed from all parts of the country. But as the returns of many gaols known to have held suspected rebels are not included in the published reports, and as the prison ships, which probably held hundreds of men, are not represented, the number of people who suffered imprisonment as a result of the rising, even taking into account those who were arrested more than once, or who were transferred from one gaol to another, must have been in the neighbourhood of three thousand.

This, and not the publicised official estimate of a few score ragged beggars, led by an ambitious fanatic, was the true measure of the men concerned in Robert Emmet's rising. Rich men, poor men, bakers, millers, farmers, these had had one thing in common, a great and burning love of liberty.

CHAPTER FORTY-SIX

Pitt's Fight for Office

FROM the very first announcement of Emmet's rising, Pitt and his friends had used it as a means of discrediting the Addington administration. Ever since Pitt had retired as Prime Minister in March, 1801, ostensibly because George the Third had refused to consider any measures that would put Irish Catholics on an equal political footing with Protestants, he had been anxious to get back into office.* He had assumed that his successor, his old friend Henry Addington, would take his place only temporarily and would resign when Pitt wished. But Addington, once he became Prime Minister, was so enchanted with his position that he could not bear to renounce it. Nor could Pitt, who had promised to support the new administration, go into open opposition without

---

* In 1798 Lord Cornwallis, who had been sent to Ireland to bring about the Union, had discovered that the measure could not possibly pass the Irish Parliament if the Catholics opposed it. On the slim ground of a promise from Pitt that the Act of Union would contain no clause that would prevent Catholic relief from being taken up later, Cornwallis contrived to make them think that they would benefit from the Union. Pitt encouraged him to do so, though he had privately promised the Protestants that the Catholics would gain nothing from the Union. Even so, the measure did not pass on its first introduction, and at the second try Cornwallis found it necessary to buy votes by promises of peerages and pensions to obtain the necessary majority. Marsden helped him with the most delicate negotiations.

Pitt did not inform the King of his intention to introduce any Catholic relief measures for months and left office when the King, assuming that he meant to resign if the Catholic measure was not passed, asked Addington, then Speaker of the House of Commons, to form a cabinet. However, it is now known that Pitt would have given up the Catholics if the King had asked him. He later told his friend George Canning that he had gone out of office " Not on the Catholic question simply as a measure on which he was opposed, but from the manner in which he was opposed, and to which, if he had assented, he would as a minister have been on a footing totally different from what he had ever been in his cabinet." (Malmsbury, *Diary and Correspondence*, IV, p. 75, October 20, 1802.)

The King had been glad to get rid of Pitt as Prime Minister. For years the two had fought one another for supremacy, and the King considered Pitt insolent and ambitious. Of a bad set, he once told the Prince of Wales, Lord Grenville was the best.

The research necessary to fit Emmet's rising into its proper place in imperial politics has brought to light so much new and important material that it cannot all be presented here. It will shortly be published as a separate book.

displeasing the King to such an extent that he would never have recovered his old position with him. Pitt's strategy in forcing Addington out of office was to create the impression (which he and his friends Lord Grenville, Mr. Thomas Grenville, Mr. William Windham, and Mr. George Canning did whenever possible) that the ministry was a weak one, incapable of carrying on the ordinary business of the country and much less capable of carrying on a war with France.

When, immediately after the rising, the British Parliament had been asked to suspend the Habeas Corpus Act in Ireland, Pitt's party had used the debate to attack the Addington administration but had voted for both bills. (It is quite possible that Pitt, anticipating his return to office and not believing that it would be delayed so long, had incubated the rebellion for the purpose of obtaining this legislation.) The winter session of Parliament brought on the necessity of obtaining an extension of the bills, and again Pitt and his party planned to use the rising as a means of attacking Addington. Other critics were threatening to ask for an official investigation to find out who had been to blame for it—General Fox for not having taken the necessary precautions, or the Castle for not having discovered what the rebels were up to.

This put Marsden in a desperate position. He could not possibly allow the public to learn how much he had known of the rebel's plans. He could not risk letting the Lord Lieutenant know that he had kept important information from him. Any investigation, even any discussion, of what had gone on at the Castle was extremely dangerous. Wickham, too, was involved and was equally anxious to avoid an investigation.

So many reports reached Dublin that Marsden was being blamed in London for almost having lost the Irish capital to the rebels and that the opening of Parliament would bring on a demand for an investigation that Marsden and Wickham decided that they needed a champion there. Lord Castlereagh was a perfectly natural choice for them to make—he was still Pitt's grateful protégé though serving as one of Addington's ministers—but, as it turned out, it was a most unfortunate one.

Castlereagh undertook the role of defender with seeming

affability. He wrote Marsden that it would be full of embarrassment to take the discussion on the ground of admitting blame and arguing where it should be attached. Therefore, he wanted Marsden to send him the best case the facts would warrant to prove that reasonable precautions had been taken and that upon the whole enough was done.

Not too pleased with this policy, Marsden answered that it would not be easy to shape such a case in the way Castlereagh wished, but that he should have it both ways. Except in the instance of not discovering the depot, he claimed, no fault existed.*

This correspondence took place early in November, while Marsden and Wickham were both busy examining Quigley, Jimmy Farrell, Carty, Malachy Delaney, and all the other men who were "developing" the conspiracy; thus the written "defence" was held up for a time. Then Wickham became ill, and all the work fell on Marsden. On November 15, however, the important paper was finished and put into the hands of the Lord Lieutenant's brother-in-law, the Reverend Charles Lindsay, who had lately been made Bishop of Killaloe. The Bishop, armed with many letters of introduction to officials in London, was instructed to do his best to put off an official investigation.

Not content with having the Bishop and Lord Castlereagh working to ward off the threatened danger, Wickham and Marsden got the Lord Lieutenant, who still had no idea of how he had been deceived by them, to connive at some not-too-subtle blackmail. From his sick-bed Wickham sent a memorandum to Lord Hardwicke which was to be incorporated into a letter for Mr. Charles Yorke.†

* The Castle always claimed that they had not known the location of the depot in Thomas Street until after the rising. But in 1805 Mr. Thomas Clarke, writing to the Castle about Barney Doogan, who has just been arrested, disclosed that Sirr had had men watching the depot all the day of July 23, and that they had seen Doogan when he left it both in the morning and afternoon.

† The memorandum in Wickham's hand is now at the Irish State Paper Office and has the endorsement : "Copy of a note from Mr. W. Original sent in a letter to Mr. Yorke 18 Nov 1803." Mr. Yorke evidently received the memorandum, for the Bishop referred to it in a letter to Marsden a few days later. He said that he had that morning seen a note transmitted to Mr. Yorke by the Lord Lieutenant, "in which Mr. Wickham gives some very curious views of certain persons with whose secrets you are too well acquainted to be blessed with their love. I had touched on this spring before, but Wickham's note was kind and forceable coming well on the back of what I had said." I.S.P.O.

In writing to Mr. Yorke on the subject of the personal attack that is intended to be made upon Marsden your Excellency will perhaps do well to call his attention to these points.

1st. Marsden was the person who conducted the *secret part* of the Union. *Ergo* the price of each Unionist, as well as their respective conduct and character is well known to him.

Those who vapor away and vapor in so great a stile in London are well known to him. They live in hourly dread of being unmasked and they all consider him as the person who opposes their interested views and jobs by his representation of the whole truth.

2nd. Marsden as a lawyer is supposed to be the person who gives the Government the opinion that is asked upon the legal appointments.

He is therefore supposed to be the man who has stood in the way of our filling the Bench and the Confidential Law Situations under the Crown with improper persons by giving a fair and right interpretation to the Union Engagements. [In plain English no person hoping for a future engagement in Ireland should forget that Marsden was in a position to block the appointment of anyone who opposed him in the matter of the proposed investigation.]

3d. Many of the persons who make a great figure at the Levee or on the Bench of either House in London really dare not look Marsden in the face. I have often witnessed this and been diverted by it.

With your Excellency and with me they have an air of uncomfortable greatness, but with him they quite shrink away.

Lord Castlereagh, the Bishop found in London, was intending to make such a feeble defence of Marsden (not going into any detail about the rising, but " keeping the subject clearly standing on its own narrow base of a contemptible rabble without means or respectable leaders ") that, notwithstanding Wickham's illness, Marsden decided to go to London himself. He too was armed with letters of introduction, and his intention was to persuade as many powerful people as possible to vote against an investigation.

The new speaker, Mr. Abbot, one of the men Marsden called on, though not uncritical of both Castle and military authorities, was willing to pass the incident over in silence.

The first debate on the Irish bills took place in the House of Commons, with Marsden anxiously listening in the gallery. Of course, Marsden and Wickham were both anxious to have the measures pass, but their introduction to Parliament would be the most opportune time for Marsden's enemies to bring up the matter of an investigation. As it was, the Castle came in for some inevitable criticism. The King's speech from the throne had claimed, with the glossy optimism usual on such

occasions, that Ireland was in a state of perfect tranquillity.
The obvious inconsistency of asking for martial law in a
peaceful country and denying its citizens the right of the
Habeas Corpus Act was an invitation to any member of the
House hostile to the administration. Mr. Yorke compounded
the inconsistency by placing the necessity for the measure on
the connection of the Irish rebels with France, those same
rebels who had so often been referred to as a mean and contemptible rabble.

Pitt was not yet acting openly in his fight to get back into
office, but the Grenvilles and their friends were only too glad
to use this as a means of discrediting the ministry. The most
brilliant and significant speech for the Pitt faction was made
by Mr. William Windham. With accomplished sarcasm he
asked the King's ministers to tell the House, when they had
made up their minds, whether the late insurrection was really
a contemptible riot, a mere effervescence of the moment and
confined to the spot on which it had originated, or whether
it had spread to a greater extent and had taken deep root in
the country. The honourable gentlemen of the other side
of the House were seeking to have the benefit of suppositions
both of which could not be true. They were like the student
who, when asked whether the sun revolved about the earth
or the earth about the sun, said " Sometimes one way and
sometimes the other."

It was true, he continued, that arbitrary and despotic power
might in some cases have their advantages ; but as it seldom
fell to their lot to have angels to exercise it, mankind was
generally content to forego those advantages and take up
the safer and slower operation of laws and free governments.
He could place no confidence at all in those ministers who now
wished for those arbitrary powers, as their representations of
the State of the country had hitherto been fallacious. Only
the week before the rising, they had congratulated themselves
on the tranquillity of Ireland. The Irish Government appeared
to prefer the charge of having been negligent to that of having
been taken by surprise. There was, however, every appearance of surprise.

Out of the defences that ministers tried to make for both
Lord Hardwicke and General Fox there arose new troubles

for the administration and a new opportunity for opposition. Admiral Berkeley, a kinsman of General Fox, thought he saw an aspersion to his relative in some reference to the precautions the Lord Lieutenant had taken and gave notice that he would, at an early date, move for papers to exculpate the Commander-in-Chief. The General's brother, Charles J. Fox, also took up arms by criticising the whole policy of the Government in Ireland.* He considered the method of governing the country a negation of political liberty and one of the weak points of the imperial structure.

It is significant that, though many members used the bills as a means of speaking against the administration, they voted for the measures, and both bills passed the House of Commons on December 7.

In the House of Lords the Grenville party used Windham's points with great effect. Lord Grenville referred to the absurdity of representing the rising first as a most formidable conspiracy and then as a contemptible riot, and asking for measures of such magnitude when the only official information that the House had was in the King's speech from the throne, which claimed that Ireland was in a state of undisturbed tranquillity. This drew from Lord Limerick a bit of unintentional honesty. Lord Limerick had been one of the most violent of Marsden's critics in August but had later aligned himself with the Castle. (He was also one of those gentlemen with whom Marsden had negotiated at the time of the Union.) The tranquillity of Ireland, Lord Limerick blurted out, was due to the presence of large numbers of troops there. The State trials in Dublin had gone forward peaceably because there were 12,000 armed men in the city. If they had taken place in the remoter districts, the contrary would have been the case.

Lord Sligo, the Mayo peer who kept up a constant correspondence with the Castle, and who was currently hoping to be advanced to the British peerage, put forward a most ingenuous explanation : the insurrection was a most

* The great Whig leader had long opposed Pitt's coercive measures against the democrats of both England and Ireland. He called them an absolute surrender of the rights of the people. He had championed Muir when that Scotsman was tried for sedition for advising a man to read Paine's *Rights of Man*. He had rejoiced in the early success of the French Revolution, but now Buonaparte seemed a menace to that love of political liberty that was the idol of his heart. His opposition to France now removed one barrier that had separated him from Pitt.

contemptible and abortive effort in point of numbers, but the principle on which the rebels acted was separation from England. Therefore he was in favour of the measures. They both passed the House of Lords.

More fearful than ever that there might be an investigation of his conduct, Marsden went back to Ireland.

Charles Fox's change of attitude toward France had removed one of the principles on which Pitt and Fox had differed ; and though the great Whig still distrusted Pitt, he had even less respect for the abilities of Addington and was anxious to have him displaced. Pitt's friends wanted to gain all the strength that a coalition with him would bring, so on January 26, Mr. Thomas Grenville paid Fox a two-hour visit. He suggested that the Grenville family and their friends co-operate with Fox and his friends in a system of opposition for the purpose of destroying the Addington administration and of substituting in its place one based on comprehensive lines. Besides the Grenville family, they proposed to bring in Lord Carlisle, Lord Spencer and Lord Fitzwilliam, Mr. Windham, and probably Lord Morpeth. They did not know about Canning or Lord Stafford. There was to be no compromise of former opinions by either party, and nothing was settled as to " future arrangements." This covered the assumption on the part of the Grenvilles and Fox, at least, that the Whigs would be looked after in the new cabinet.

The first move of the proposed coalition would be to have some of the Grenvilles suggest an inquiry into the matter of July 23, then to oppose Addington's bills about English Volunteers, and present others along the lines of a more effective general defence against French invasion.

The suggestions were perfectly agreeable to Fox, and he promised to write some of his friends. When he did write his most particular confidant, General Fitzpatrick, he added to the outline of the new scheme a doubt which both he and the Grenvilles shared, and which was not confined even to them. It was that after having ousted Addington, Pitt might return to power ; and after having proposed terms " in vain " to some of the opposition, he would put himself at the head of the present weak administration. This was admitted to be an objection to the plan.

Pitt, though he was co-operating with the Grenvilles and delighted to acquire the voting strength of Fox and his followers, was still reluctant to come out into active opposition to the ministry. He contented himself with letting the new coalition do the actual fighting in the House of Commons and with weakening Addington's prestige by speaking of him privately with spleen and ill humour.

When Parliament met after the Christmas recess, the new opposition made its first move. Sir John Wrottesley, acting for them, charged the Irish administration with the grossest neglect and inattention in some quarters on July 23 and gave notice that he would bring in a motion for the production of some papers that had passed between the Lord Lieutenant and General Fox on that day.*

Mr. Yorke did his best to avoid such an inquiry, but Sir John and his party were not to be put off.

Lord Sligo hurried to warn Lord Hardwicke that a discussion of the twenty-third would infallibly be brought up in Parliament, and to ask that any other papers that might help the defence be sent over immediately. Lord Sligo also confided the news of the new coalition to Marsden and said that they meant to use the attack as a means of getting into power.

It was arranged that, if the inquiry could not be stopped before it got to Parliament, Lord Dunlo should make a speech against the motion in the House of Commons, and Lord Sligo in the House of Lords.†

* These were the papers General Fox used to document his case. See p. 201. It was just at this time that the debate brought up the mention of the letters that Peter Burrowes had sent the Honourable George Knox about the conspiracy and Lord Hardwicke learned how much information both Marsden and Wickham had kept from him. *Vice Roy's Post Bag*, p. 451.

† Lord Dunlo, as Richard Trench, had been member for Galway in the Irish House of Commons. He had voted against the Union in the session of 1799, when it was defeated, and for it in 1800, when it passed. His father, Lord Kilconnel, had supported the measure in the House of Lords and had been rewarded with a promotion in the peerage, to be Viscount Dunlo in 1800. In 1803 he was further promoted to the Earldom of Clancarty, and his son assumed the courtesy title of Lord Dunlo.

The papers Marsden sent over to London at this time later served him well. In 1805 the Princess Augusta, in speaking to Lady Sligo, mentioned Marsden as having nearly lost the country because of his negligence on July 23. Lord Sligo, always delighted to serve the administration, gave the Princess a copy of the account of the rising which Marsden had got up. The many " official " accounts of the rising were circulated so assiduously in London and Dublin and reprinted in so many historical works, that the erroneous impression they gave is still noticeable.

On March 7, Sir John opened the attack. He moved for an investigation of the rising of July 23. His speech paid little attention to the actual events of that day. He spoke briefly of Emmet's return to Ireland in December of 1802 to join a conspiracy already formed ; he recalled the preparations the rebels had made. He spoke of the conference at the Castle between Marsden, General Fox, and the Lord Lieutenant, and of the note Marsden had written to the General later that evening, expressing his doubts as to whether the rising would take place or not. He disclaimed wishing to exonerate General Fox. If there was any cause to blame his conduct, he said, that could be brought forward in an investigation. The public had a right to the particulars of the transaction they were discussing.

In considering the case, he said, he had wished to trace some principle upon which the Government had acted, and the only consistency appeared to be a determination to avoid giving alarm. It was therefore necessary to say a few words upon the propriety of that determination. It had always been admitted that it was better to *prevent* than to *punish* crimes. It was impossible that the Government could have intended to wait until the insurrection took place with a view of discovering the authors. The risk that every loyal man must have run, the placing the lives of his Majesty's subjects, even for the shortest period, in such a state of danger would of itself be deemed highly criminal, and the impropriety of such a measure could not be more fully exemplified than in the unfortunate occurrence that actually took place. But, it had been argued, the melancholy circumstance of Lord Kilwarden's death had been " accidental," the rising only " a contemptible riot."

But can it [Sir John asked, warming to his task] be deemed contemptible which has for its object the separation of Ireland, to deprive us of her valuable assistance at a moment when we are called upon to make every exertion for the defence of these kingdoms ? Which was evidently undertaken in concert with the enemy, who had probably contributed to the powerful means which they had of carrying their plans into execution ?

Can it [and here Sir John dropped inflated oratory for solid truth and gave voice to words that stand unsurpassed to-day as just and honest comment on Robert Emmet's rising] be a contemptible riot which induced you to pass bills, giving the greatest possible power to the government of that country, and after a period of four months, deliberately to renew them? Which obliged you to place the Yeomanry of Ireland on permanent duty for three months, at an expense of above four hundred thousand pounds to be defrayed by the two countries? No, sir.*

The government of Ireland found itself embarrassed. To justify these strong measures, they were obliged to represent it in its true light : they then perceived that if it was important and extensive, they should have been better prepared against it, and what they call in their proclamations " daring and rebellious outrages in persecution of a rebellious conspiracy " dwindles into a " contemptible riot." But let us not differ on terms. Grant a full and fair investigation. Let us have authenticated papers, and persons at the bar. Let us have the facts, and the appropriate name will be easily found. I therefore move " that this House do resolve itself into a committee of the whole House to enquire into the conduct of the Irish government relative to the insurrection of the 23rd of July, and the previous conduct of that government as far as it relates to the said insurrection."

It was doubtless just as well for Marsden's peace of mind that he was not there to hear that attack upon him, which he had been dreading for so many months. It was just as well, too, that he was spared hearing the speech with which Lord Castlereagh ostensibly defended him. Though he stood up as one of Addington's ministers, the feebleness of his defence and his subsequent course of action inevitably create the impression that Castlereagh was acting at Pitt's man. What he had admitted to Dr. Haliday in 1793 was never more evident, that he was " Pittised " with a vengeance.

Castlereagh opened his answer to Sir John Wrottesley with the statement that the Baronet based his motion on the supposed criminal neglect of the Irish Government in regard to the rising on July 23. Sir John, he said, assumed that blame attached itself to the Irish Government, civil or military. He was mistaken. His Majesty's ministers never had made that concession. Therefore, there was no need for the investigation.

He agreed with Sir John that preventive measures were preferable to punishment, but he thought that that principle might be carried too far.

It was very material [he said] not to urge the rebels to postpone their attempt by any appearance of too much precaution and preparation. The Honourable baronet might laugh, but it was expedient that the precautions should not have been carried out to such an extent as to alarm the fears of the rebels, and thereby induce

* Sir John might well have added the item of £92,000 spent by the Government in buying up all property contigent to Dublin Castle, and the cost of other military preparations made in Dublin after July 23.

them to delay their project. If patrols had been sent out, if such extraordinary measures of precaution had been adopted as would have induced the rebels to lay aside their design, the consequence would have been that government would have been the laughing stock of the country, for they would not have believed that any danger existed. In that case, how could the government of Ireland have applied to Parliament for any extraordinary power? Besides, it was desirable that the measures afterwards applied for should be claimed on ostensible, not arguable grounds.* The conduct of administration in Ireland, both at the time and since, had been that of a wise, provident and vigorous government.

This was, of course, a tacit admission that the Castle had allowed the rebellion to ripen, a complete desertion of Marsden, whom Castlereagh had promised to defend, and a covert attack on the administration of which he was a minister. His speech as a whole was held to have done more harm to Addington than those from any hostile quarter. From that time on ministerial majorities dwindled, and Pitt was emboldened to come into the open as a member of the opposition.

In writing to his old colleague, Henry Dundas, now Lord Melville, on March 29, Pitt outlined his plans and asked Melville to come to London for the final attack on Addington.† He also asked the support of other Scottish peers and even summoned members of Parliament from Ireland. He went farther than that in his efforts to secure a victory; he became reconciled to an old enemy, Mr. John Foster. He had once been party to a most malicious joke played on Foster when the Union was being debated in the Irish House of Commons; yet Foster evidently succumbed to the devastating charm that

---

* The italics are mine. H. L.

† He would not take part in any Government of which he was not head, he bluntly stated to Melville, but claimed that he was prepared to " put aside the recollection of former differences [with Fox] if a cordial union could be found for the future." However, he immediately qualified that good intention by finding an excuse for excluding from his cabinet not only Fox and his friends but even the Grenvilles. Fox was *persona non grata* with the King not only because of his liberal politics, but for personal reasons. The King thought Fox was responsible for the loose behaviour of the Prince of Wales, over whom he had great influence. The Grenvilles had expressed a desire to help the Catholics. The King, Pitt told Melville, should not have forced upon him men to whom he had long been opposed. The Melville letter is printed in an unpublished booklet prepared from manuscripts at Melville Castle, for private distribution, " Secret Correspondence Relative to Pitt's Return to Office in 1804."

It seems impossible to look on Pitt's offer to " put aside the recollection of former differences " as genuine when one remembers that for three years the King had been violently opposed to Pitt himself, and he was prepared to force himself on the King if no other way was possible. That it was personal ambition and not danger to the country which made him resolve to take office can be seen in his refusal to take part in any Government of which he was not the head.

Pitt usually reserved for his intimate friends but sometimes called on in political emergencies.*

Backed by his own friends, a large contingent of Fox's followers, and many members who had deserted Addington after Castlereagh's speech about the rising, Pitt forced the Prime Minister to resign early in May. Castlereagh, of course, was given a post in the new cabinet, but the King objected to Fox, as Pitt had known he would.† In spite of the great help Fox had been to him, Pitt made no effort to overcome the King's objections.

With characteristic lack of resentment the old Whig asked the Grenvilles not to let his exclusion keep them from entering the cabinet. They felt, however, that two important points were at issue. They had no wish to join a cabinet based on exclusion, and, in spite of the fact that there had been no

* " By the bye," Edward Cooke, who was then in London helping Pitt roll the drums, wrote to Mr. Beresford in Dublin, " they [Pitt and Foster] are now reconciled, and Foster acts with him.

The reconciliation probably related to the incident of 1799. Foster, then Speaker of the Irish House of Commons, had refused to be cajoled by Pitt into giving up his opposition to the Union. In fact, he had become a leader in opposing it. So many Irish people were pleased with his fight to save the Irish Parliament that a subscription for him was started in Dublin.

This was insult added to deep injury as far as Pitt was concerned, and steps were taken in London to stop the collection. Wickham, then in London, helped Canning concoct the frustrating scheme. In February of 1799 Canning wrote Wickham : " I have stated to Mr. Pitt and Lord Grenville the idea which seemed to amuse you so much, of the motion to be made in the Irish House of Commons in bar of the Speaker's subscription, and they both agree with me in thinking it might be carried into effect with great advantage. . . .

" It strikes me that a very serious and imposing argument might be raised on the impropriety of any member of the House of Commons, particularly the Speaker (whose purity and impartiality etc etc ought to be *above all suspicion*) receiving the wages of a Party out of doors, for his conduct on any particular question.

" The motion might be worded, and introduced in a manner not only highly respectful to the Speaker, but such as to evince a particular tender regard for his honour and feelings. The mover would of course assure the House that what he had to offer the House was offered *without the concert,* or even the *knowledge*, of the Right Honourable Gentleman to whom it might seem particularly to refer : but that as on the one hand it would have been extremely indelicate to implicate him in a proceeding which went to damp the generous though mistaken ardour of his fellow citizens. . . .

" Pitt has a notion that there can be found no member in the Irish House of Commons to execute so malicious a joke with sufficient gravity. But I am very much mistaken if there is not that in the style of at least half a dozen out of the twenty-seven speakers, whose speeches were reported in the first night of the session, which would suit the idea exactly." *Wickham Correspondence*, II, p. 94.

† Pitt attended a dinner at Lord Stafford's on April 29 at which a list of his new cabinet as he then envisaged it was handed around. The Grenvilles, Lord Melville, and Canning were taken care of, and most of Pitt's other supporters. But the name of Charles Fox did not appear, nor did the names of any of his friends. Stanhope's *Pitt,* IV, p. 160.

express arrangements made between Fox and themselves, they felt it would be dishonourable to accept office without him.* Even Pitt's closest friends admitted privately that the means he had used to get into office were hardly creditable.

Was such a man capable of instigating a rising, even though it meant the shedding of blood, so that coercive measures could be asked for " on ostensible, not arguable, grounds " ? It seems no more out of character than his use of Fox and the Grenvilles, whom he had all along been ready to give up.

Was he capable of employing Marsden and perhaps Wickham as well to forward his own personal schemes, and then feel no scruples at deserting them when they were attacked ? We have the word of Fox, who was charitable as well as keen, that " Pitt was not a man capable of acting fairly and on a footing of equality with his equals." Fox had written that to his friend Fitzpatrick weeks before his exclusion from the new cabinet.† It would have been as easy for Pitt to have been amused at Marsden's predicament as he had been at the joke played on Mr. Foster.

But if he had taken sardonic pleasure in thinking that he was using Robert Emmet's blazing nationalism as a means of keeping enslaved the country the young patriot meant to free, he certainly had not foreseen an even more sardonic jest of which he himself became the butt. In making use of every means that offered to effect his own ends he had for once overstepped himself. He had invited Robert Emmet home to win an immortality even more enviable than the one he himself achieved and had thereby furnished Ireland with an everlasting source of inspiration and national pride. The idealist who, in spite of every pressure that could be put upon him, had adhered to the motto " Constans " gained the final victory over his covert enemy.

Robert Emmet's speech from the dock soon became a classic. It was printed in school readers and collections of

* " The efficacy of Fox's aid became so apparent that it seems to have attracted Pitt at last and encouraged by the prospect of success for union of *all* he came forward unequivocally, and not only concurred in common measures but *concerted* them with all the other parties, Fox included." *Diary and Correspondence of Lord Minto*, III, p. 329.

† In March, when Castlereagh was being berated by Dublin Castle officials for having deserted them by his weak defence, Fox wrote his friend Fitzpatrick, " I suspect he [Pitt] has treated Castlereagh roughly, but he will bear anything." *Life and Letters of C. J. Fox*, IV, p. 26.

oratory in America as well as Ireland. Young Abraham Lincoln read it by the fire-light of his Kentucky cabin. All the world sang the songs Thomas Moore wrote about his young friend. The presses never stopped printing new ballads about Emmet : " My Emmet's No More," " Emmet's Grave," " Emmet's Farewell to his Love "—the titles ran into thousands. They are still being written, still being sung.

Nor did artists ever cease to picture his trial, his execution, and his march into Thomas Street arrayed in all the glory of his green uniform. The engraver who portrayed him holding aloft his plumed hat and added as a caption four lines of Moore's song, " She Is Far from the Land Where Her Young Hero Sleeps," touched the popular fancy to such an extent that he sold thousands of copies that still adorn cottage walls in every corner of Ireland.

But most of all, Emmet's likeness was engraved on the hearts of the Irish people and became, perhaps unconsciously on their part, a symbol of the national spirit. If such an undeniable statement needs documentation, aside from the hundreds of babies who are still being named in his honour, one might as well select a significant incident that took place in 1867. It was an aftermath of the Fenian rising of that year, when Irish rebels had tried again to set their country free. Some of the executions following the frustrated attempt took place in England, and Manchester gave its name to three young martyrs.

In Dublin, on December 18, a huge procession followed three empty hearses, each of which carried a banner displaying the name of one of the dead men. It was a quiet, orderly assembly, but the men who had organised it were arrested. The marchers, it was claimed by the Castle, had sung a seditious song called " Tramp, Tramp, the Boys Are Marching " and had worn green ribbons.

Preparing its case against the organisers of the procession, police officials took down the depositions of many people who had witnessed it. One of them was given by Acting-Sergeant Thorpe. He was on duty, he said, in Thomas Street, Dublin, on December 18, 1867, close to St. Catherine's Church.* He saw the three hearses and horsemen following them. He saw

* The place of Emmet's execution.

marchers, thousands of them, some wearing crepe and some badges of green ribbon.

When the procession came near the church, the sergeant heard people say, "Remember Emmet," and then they cheered. Some time after (there were twenty or thirty thousand in the procession), the sergeant noticed among the marchers a young man wearing a green sash with yellow stripes and carrying a white wand.

He held up the stick [Thorpe's deposition reads] and put his two hands up, and as he motioned they stepped easy ; he took off his hat, and the others took off their hats, and turning to Catherine's Church I could hear the name "Emmet" used. After that party passed a band in the procession halted at the end of Catherine's lane in Thomas Street. They nearly all took off their hats when they came up to the place. I heard some in the procession ask "What are they taking their hats off for ? " I heard some people in the procession say, "Emmet."

Index

A

A.B., French informer, 80n, 81n
A.B., Limerick informer, 155
Abbey Street, Dublin, 66
Abbot, the Honourable Charles (later Lord Colchester), 210n, 215n, 347n, 370n, 380, 401
Abercrombie, Sir Ralph, 88
Addington, Henry, 122, 151n, 398, 399, 404, 407, 409
Age of Reason, by Thomas Paine, 53
Alexander, William, 209
Allen, John 81, 84, 86, 106, 142n, 143, 162, 165n, 170, 189, 191, 208, 213, 276, 285, 394
Allingham, William, 96
Altamont, Earl of (later Lord Sligo), 58
America, 3, 6, 30, 55, 57, 97, 110, 120, 122, 134, 142n, 306, 315, 353, 394, 411
American Ambassador to France (Livingston, Robert R.), 122
American Museum, The, 7
American Revolution, vii, 7, 47, 142
Americans, 150
Amsterdam, 121
An t-Oglach, 201n, 214n
Ancient Britons, the, 89
Ancient Irish Music, by Edward Bunting, 44
Andrews, William, 170, 188, 196, 255, 383
Andrews, Mrs. William, 188, 196
Anglo-French war, xi, 99, 120, 150
Annadorn, 181, 182
Antrim (county), 94, 109, 182, 387
Antrim Castle, 156
Apennines, the, 117
Archer, Mr., Inspector-General of Prisons, 388
Archives Nationales, Paris, 67n
Ardagh, Arthur, 76
Ardfry, County Galway, 384, 385, 395n
Armagh (county), 56–58
Arms, 10, 29, 31, 32, 58, 109, 182, 189, 224n, 227, 229, 245, 260, 289, 323 333, 349
Armstrong, of Newry, 165n
Armstrong, Captain John, 91
Army, British, 30, 144, 177
Army Headquarters, Royal Hospital, Kilmainham, 199–202, 213
Arnold, Benedict, 47

Artillery Barracks, Royal, 190, 221, 224, 266, 315
Asgill, Sir Charles, 200, 202, 212, 213n, 219
Associated Scoundrels, 20
Astley's Theatre, Dublin, 85
Athy, County Kildare, 227, 383
Athy gaol, 396
Atkinson, William, of Belfast, 193, 197
Attorney-General of Ireland (*see* O'Grady, Standish)
Auckland, Lord (William Eden), 33n, 47n, 94n, 102
Augereau, General Pierre-François-Charles, 116
Aughavanagh, County Wicklow, 393
Aughrim, battle of, 118
Augusta, Princess of England, 405n
Australia, 142n, 394
Austria, 118, 253n
Aylmer, Sir Fenton, 136, 137, 255
Aylmer, Lieutenant-Colonel Michael, 194, 229, 255, 257, 383
Aylmer, William, 253n

B

B., John, brother of B., Senior, 60n, 157, 171, 185n, 193, 216, 256, 396
B., Senior, 50, 58, 59, 60n, 91, 157, 171, 185n, 193, 256, 396
Bagnell, Mrs. Rose, 250, 254, 325, 340, 381n
Bagot, of Limerick, 154, 237
Ballinagarry, County Limerick, 154
Ballinahinch, battle of, 181
Ballinamuck, battle of, 101
Ballinascorney, Breaks of, 250, 251, 252
Ballitore, County Kildare, 92
Ballymena, County Antrim, 177, 179, 231, 232
Ballynameece, 249–254, 281
Banishment Bill, 387
Bank of Ireland, 193n
Bannon, 215n
Bantry Bay, 66n, 100, 236
Barlow, Joel, 118, 261n
Barlow, Ruth, 118, 261n
Barrett, of Tubberbui, 154
Barthélemy, M., 47n
Bastille Day, 19
Beard, Henry, 110, 111

413

Beckwith, Colonel F., 251n, 266
Bedford, Duke of, 86
Belfast, 13, 18, 19, 31, 33, 34, 44, 60, 61, 68, 82, 89, 107, 110, 126, 151, 180, 193, 197, 230, 231n, 232, 269–275, 395
Belfast gaol, 270n
Bell, Hugh, 84
Bell, John, 208, 210, 251n, 253n, 258, 283, 284n, 292, 325, 388, 396
Beresford, John, 189, 409n
" Beresford Packet," 135
Berkeley, Admiral George C., 403
Berne, 49
Berney, Michael, 167
Berthier, Alexander, 151, 261n, 320
Bird, William, alias Smith, John Henry, 49, 59, 161n
Black Book of the North, 179
Black Horse Bridge, 197
Bohernabreena, 252
Bolton-le-Moor, 135n
Bolton, Lyndon, 117
Bond, Oliver, 34, 75, 188
Bonfield, Caitlín, xvi
Bordeaux, 127, 318
Botany Bay, 51, 153
Bouch, J. J., xvi
Bourney's Bridge, County Kildare, 195
Bow Street, London, 128
Boyne, battle of, 11, 118
Brady, Lieutenant Felix, 211, 213, 314, 339
Brest, 65, 100, 105
Bridewell, Dublin, 105
British Constitution, 16, 348
British Government, 120, 121, 293n
Brophy, Daniel, 170n, 188, 383
Broughshane, County Down, 180, 232
" Brown," secret informer, 275–276
Brown, Wogan, 253n
Browne, Colonel, 211–212, 247
Browne, the Honourable Denis, 241n
Browne, John, of Belfast, 110
Browne, Nason, 191
Bruce, Robert, 11
Bruxelles, recte Brussels, 121–123, 134, 138
Bunting, Edward, 44, 181
Buonaparte, Napoleon, 8, 49, 116, 119, 137n, 142, 150, 151, 158, 253n, 261n, 304, 319, 320n, 323, 332, 333, 364, 403n
Burchell, Benjamin, 170n
Burke, Trinity student, 315n
Burke, Sir Bernard, viii, ixn, 123, 124, 131
Burke, Martin, 144, 146
Burrowes, Peter, 115, 157, 158, 312, 314, 325, 332, 344, 345, 405n
Burton, barrister, 290, 296, 306, 312

Burton, lumberyard clerk, 166
Butler, the Honourable Simon, 24, 34
Butterfield Lane, 145, 149, 161, 185, 186, 199, 209, 215n, 239n, 245, 249, 254n, 283n, 301, 333, 384, 393
Byrne, deserter, 253n
Byrne, Billy, of Ballymanus, County Wicklow, 97, 98
Byrne, Darby, 148, 166, 169
Byrne, Edward, 22, 80
Byrne, Henry, of Union Hall, Dundalk, 271
Byrne, Hugh, 146
Byrne, James, of Naas, 171, 314
Byrne, John, of Union Hall, Dundalk, 271
Byrne, Miles, 93, 127n, 141–143, 147, 161n, 166, 170, 211n, 224n, 260, 261, 265, 285, 291n, 302, 318–320, 333, 370n, 395
Byrne, Patrick, of Union Hall, Dundalk, 270, 271

C

C, informer, 251n
Camden, Lord (John Jeffries Pratt), 15, 46, 47, 54n, 59, 80n, 94, 132
Campbell, Brigadier-General Colin, 230, 232, 275
Canal Harbour, Dublin, 140, 195, 196, 208, 213
Canning, George, 398n, 399, 404, 409n
Captain Stout, 46
Carey, Patrick, 60, 60n, 157, 171, 185n, 193, 216, 256, 396
Carey, W. P., 52n
Carey, William, 256
Carhampton, Lord (Luttrell), 47, 68, 73, 136, 204, 269
Carlisle, Lord, 404
Carlow (county), 93, 156, 157, 396
Carnegie Students' Library, Dublin, xvi
Carnmoney, Co. Antrim, 180, 231, 234, 374
Carnot, M., 47n
Carolan, Edward, 134
Carrick-on-Suir, 238n
Carrickburne, County Wexford, 93
Carrickfergus, 47, 49, 61
Carrickfergus Assizes, 108
Carrickfergus Castle, 107n
Carrickfergus gaol, 270n, 274n, 396
Carton (castle), 30, 226, 228
Carty, Robert, 133, 160n, 165–167, 293, 383, 390, 400
Cashel, County Tipperary, 154n
Casino, 107, 109, 115, 120n, 121n, 145n
Castle, the (see Dublin Castle)
Castlebar, Races of, 101

Castlereagh, Lord, 61, 87, 88, 91, 93, 97, 99, 110, 115, 120n, 132n, 154n, 253n, 276n, 399-401, 407-409, 410n
(*See also* Stewart, Robert)
Castlereagh Correspondence, 109n, 198n
Catholic Church, 10
Catholic Committee, 21, 271n
Catholic Relief Measures, 398
Catholics, Irish, 8, 11, 12, 15, 19-22, 23-26, 33-36, 46, 52-58, 77, 132, 142, 146, 395n, 398n
Cave Hill, Belfast, 231n, 232
Celbridge, 227, 228, 255
Chambers, John, 66
Chancellor, the (*see* Lord Chancellor)
Charlemagne, 117
Charlemont, Earl of, 14, 15, 25, 36, 57, 58
Charlemont Mss., R.I.A., 14n, 21n, 36n, 62n, 68n
Charles Edward, Prince (the Young Pretender), 58
Chart, Dr. D. A., xvii
Church of Rome, 382
Clane, County Kildare, 92
Clare (county), 154, 235, 396
Clare, Lord, Lord Chancellor, 76-79, 88, 91n, 94n, 99, 154n, 315n
(*See also* Fitzgibbon, John)
Clare, Walter, 269
Clare County gaol, 396
Clarke, Edward, 192, 198, 199, 218, 220, 395n, 400n
Clarke, General (*see* Cullinane, Daniel)
Clarkson (*see* Cullinane, Daniel)
Clergymen, Catholic, 58, 314
Protestant, 314, 363-366, 371n, 378,379
Cloncurry (Valentine Lawless), 74, 123, 386
Clondalkin, County Dublin, 216
Clones, County Monaghan, 57
Cloney, Thomas, 142, 143, 146n, 152, 162, 165, 166, 293n
Cockayne, John, 37, 38, 53
Cody, H. B., 158n, 247, 380n
Coffey, Diarmuid, xv
Colbert, Jean Baptiste, 58n
Cole, Lois Dwight, xvii
Colgan, Terence, 172, 223, 334
College Green, Dublin, 86
College of Physicians, Dublin, 5
Collins, Thomas, 41, 51, 52
Collis, John, 155n
Collis, John, of Dublin, 41
Collison, Daniel, 137, 227, 230, 256n
Colonists, American, 95
Colville, William, 16, 381n
Commander-in-Chief of Army in Ireland, 1796-1797 (*see* Carhampton, General Lord)

1797-1798 (*see* Abercrombie, Sir Ralph)
1798-1801 (*see* Cornwallis, General Lord)
1801-1803 (*see* Meadows, General)
1803 (*see* Fox, General Henry E.)
Commons, James, 249, 251, 252n
Condon, Edward, 141, 171, 187, 205, 207, 385, 395n
Connaught (province), 94, 107, 146, 240-242
Connemara, 240-242
Connolly, Carter, 227-229
Conway, Timothy, 239n
Cooke, Edward, 53, 58, 82, 84, 85, 89, 93, 98, 101, 108, 133n, 238, 409n
Cooke, Thomas, 7
Coombe, the, 144, 209n, 210, 214n, 254n, 262n, 266, 293
Coombe Barracks, 210, 214
Cope, William, 74n, 75n
Corballis, Edward, 159
Corbet, Thomas, 78
Corbet, William, 65
Corbett, William, publisher-informer, 50, 60n, 72
Corbett's Hotel, Dublin 135
Cork (city), 4, 53, 54n, 89n, 90, 238 gaol, 240
Cork (county), 76, 89, 162n, 238, 240, 370n, 393
Cork County gaol, 240
Cork Gazette, 238
Cork Street Barracks, 209
Cormick, John, 122
Cornwallis, General the Marquis Charles, xi, 95-99, 101, 104, 115, 119, 132, 142n, 398n
Cornwallis Correspondence, 97n-98n, 104n
Corsican corporal, *i.e.* Buonaparte, 8
Costello, Margaret, 195
Costigan, Sylvester, 207, 209
Cotton, Colonel, 202, 212
Coultman, Lieutenant Wheeler, 202n, 221-224, 337
Council of State, Ireland, 29
Courts and Cabinets of George III, by the Duke of Buckingham and Chandos, 47n
Cox, John, of Kildare, 195
Cox, Walter, 73, 309
Coyle, Bernard, 111
Craigvally (Craigbilly ?), 231
Crauford, Sir James, 70
Croagh Patrick, 242
Croce, Benedetto, xiii
Croker, Crofton, 66n
Cromwell, Oliver, 3
Crops, 89, 238
Cullen, Brother Luke, xvi, 144n, 253n, 302

Cullinane, Daniel, *alias* Father Murphy, General Clarke, Clarkson, M. Thorington, M. Lordonnier, 154, 179, 238.
Cumber, 232
Cummins, of Market Hill, 58
Cunningham, *alias* Emmet, 270, 282, 286
Cupples, the Reverend Samuel, 233
Curragh, the, of Kildare, 92
Curran, Amelia, 305
Curran, Gertrude, 159
Curran, Jane, 305
Curran, John Philpot, 102, 115, 131, 265, 296, 299, 303, 305, 307, 312, 329, 367, 387n
Curran, Richard, 160, 305, 365, 367
Curran, Sarah, 159-161, 172, 185, 186, 199, 205, 224, 254, 260, 262, 265, 285, 296, 303, 310, 328, 329, 338, 352, 364, 367, 370n
Custom House, Dublin, 91
    old, 202n
Cuxhaven, 121

D

Daley, Thomas, 136
Dalrymple, General William, 58
Dalton, Adjutant-General, French Army, 319, 320
Dalton, Michael, 136, 140n
Daly, Timothy, 229
Darley, Alderman Frederick, 201, 220-223, 338
D'Artois, Comte, 80n
Dease, Surgeon, 364
Declaration of Independence, American, 7, 396
Decrès, Admiral, 261n
Defenders, the, 12, 33, 35, 46, 50, 56, 59, 60, 136, 177, 192
Delaney, Malachy, 92, 110, 116, 117, 123, 125, 126, 382, 400
Denniston, Hans, 167n
Depot, Patrick Street, 144n, 147n, 161n, 165, 166, 187, 190, 191, 248, 261, 268, 320, 328, 339, 384
    South King Street, 147n, 149
    Strawmarket, 147n, 149
    Thomas Street, 122n, 140, 147, 163n, 165, 166, 170, 172, 186, 189, 190, 198, 203, 209, 210, 213, 220, 227, 235, 239, 247, 293, 311, 325, 328, 333, 377, 384, 400n
    Winetavern Street, 147n, 149
Derry (county), 7, 57, 60, 68
Derry, Bishop of, 311n
Desmond, 16th Earl of, 11, 226
De Steigeur, M., 47n
De Valera, Eamon, xv

Develin, Anne, 145, 159, 161, 162, 165, 185, 198, 209n, 245, 246, 254, 262, 265, 277, 293-296, 301, 302, 380, 381, 394
Develin, Arthur (Big Arthur), 144, 145, 147, 164n, 165n, 167, 169, 185, 191, 215, 245, 246, 248n, 252, 253n, 293, 393, 394
Develin, Arthur (Little Arthur), 144, 145, 161, 245
Develin, Bryan, 145, 147, 246, 248, 296, 394
Develin, Mrs. Bryan, 248, 296, 391, 394
Develin, Edward, 296
Develin, John, 296
Develin, Judith, 296, 394
Develin, Mary, 296, 394
Diamond, the, Armagh, 56
Diary and Correspondence of Lord Colchester, 139, 179n, 215n, 347n, 364n, 379n
Diary and Correspondence of Lord Malmsbury, 398n
Diary and Correspondence of Lord Minto, 410n
Diary of Sir John Moore, 88n, 89n
Dickson, Dr. Charles, xvii, 184n, 386n, 393n
Dickson Transcripts, 147n, 162n, 165n, 179n, 189n, 196n, 393n
Dillon, Beau, 118
Dillon, Mrs. Mary, 140, 204, 333
Dillon of Bride Street, 74
Dillon of Parliament Street, 74
Dissenters, 19, 53, 238
Dobbs, Francis, 106n
Documents Relating to Ireland, edited by Gilbert, Sir John T., 66n, 93n, 94n
Documents Relating to Ireland (Mss.) National Library of Ireland, 94n
Dodd, Mathew, 383
Dolan, Biddy, 295
Dolphin's Barn, Dublin, 140n
Donnelly, Mathew, 195
Donnybrook, 145n
Donnybrook Hurling Club, 267, 275
Donovan, schoolteacher of Tralee, 155n
Doogan, Barney, 141, 171, 194, 195, 199, 218, 395n, 400n
Dos Passos, John, 118n
Double Inn, Winetavern Street, 147n
Douglas, Lieutenant Stewart H., 214
Dowdall, William, 82, 104, 143, 146, 162, 186, 190, 223, 275, 276, 283n, 290, 328, 336, 348, 377, 379, 394
Down (county), 57, 69, 94, 109, 181, 387, 388
Downpatrick, 232, 311, 387
Downpatrick gaol, 388, 396
Downs, Judge William, 32
Downshire, Lord, 13, 53, 61, 62
Downshire Letters, The (Mss.) P.R.O.B., 53n, 54n, 67n

Doyle, John, Jr., 249, 251
Doyle, John, Sr., 249–251, 281, 292, 329, 340, 341
Doyle, Simon, 254, 276, 281
Doyles of Athgoe, County Kildare, 185
Drake, James, 181, 396
Drennan, Nancy, 103
Drennan, Dr. William, 8, 13, 16, 18, 19, 23, 25, 31–35, 39, 52, 74, 79, 82, 89, 274
Drennan Letters, The, 17n, 32n, 34n, 52n
Drum, County Monaghan, 57
Drury, Mr. Justice, 214n
Dublin, vii, ix, 3, 12, 16, 20, 25, 29, 34, 49, 76, 80, 81, 86, 89, 91, 101, 104, 105, 107, 111, 117, 119, 124, 127, 131, 135, 136, 141, 149, 155, 157, 161, 166, 176, 180, 185n, 189, 193, 195, 196, 198, 219, 223, 226, 227, 229, 231, 233, 234, 235, 238, 240, 246, 248, 250, 252, 256, 257, 266, 272, 275, 276n, 286, 308, 320, 323, 324, 369, 370, 381, 384, 385, 387, 389, 392, 395, 399, 411
    City Libraries of, xvi
Dublin (county), 150, 386
Dublin Castle, viii, ix, 20, 21, 24, 29, 32, 38, 39, 49–54, 56–60, 66, 68, 71, 74, 81, 82, 85, 86, 89, 91, 92, 99, 103–110, 115, 116n, 125, 126, 127n, 133, 134, 136, 139, 143, 147, 152, 154n, 157, 158n, 159, 163, 165n, 169, 172, 173, 176, 179, 187, 190, 192, 194, 195, 197–202, 205–208, 215, 217, 223, 224, 227, 230, 236–240, 247, 251n, 252, 269, 272, 273–277, 282, 285, 292n, 295, 297, 302–303, 304, 308, 314–316, 324, 328, 354, 370n, 379, 381–391, 393, 399, 400n, 401, 403, 406, 407n, 410n, 411.
Dublin Castle Tower as prison, 110, 293, 296, 383
    as State Paper Office, viii, ix, 55n, 69n
    (*See also* State Paper Office Irish)
Dublin Corporation, 74n
Dublin Evening Post, 158n, 167, 170, 172, 191, 247, 258, 275, 313n, 343, 378, 379, 380n, 382, 392, 394
Dublin Post Office, 116n
Duffin, Mrs., xiv
Duffy, Thomas, 251, 340, 381n
Dumouriez, General, 47n
Dunboyne, priest of, 193
Dundalk, 266, 269, 271–274
Dungannon, 233
Dunkirk, 100
Dunlo, Lord (Richard Trench), 405
Dunn, George, 298, 299, 303, 304, 308, 381
Dunn, Mrs. George, 381
Dunn, John, 298, 299, 370
Dunne, Brigadier-General, 192, 202, 221, 337

Dunne, Charles, xiii
Dunne, Patrick, 170, 188, 204, 255, 383
Dwyer, John, 391n
Dwyer, Michael, 96, 102, 144, 146, 147, 150, 154n, 157, 162, 167, 177n, 185, 205, 247, 253n, 254, 391–395

E

Edinburgh, 7
Edwards, Captain John, 87
Elizabeth, Queen of England, 11, 153
Ellis, Robert, *alias* Emmet, Robert, 145, 223, 254n, 283n, 286, 293, 294, 329, 335, 338
Emancipation, Catholic, 50, 71, 395n
Emerson, John, 309, 310
Emmet, Dr. Christopher, 3
Emmet, Christopher Temple, 3, 5, 7, 16, 39
Emmet, Elizabeth Mason (Mrs. Robert Emmet), 4, 5, 16, 120, 145n, 312, 365
Emmet, Jane Patten (Mrs. Thomas Addis Emmet), 16, 45, 75, 121, 123, 367, 370
Emmet, Miss Lydia Field, xv, 123
Emmet, Mary Anne (Mrs. Robert Holmes), 5, 16, 145n, 312
Emmet, Rebecca Temple (Mrs. Christopher), 3
Emmet, Robert, vii–xii, xiv, xv, 3, 5–9, 12, 13, 16, 25, 29, 31, 42, 43, 44, 60n, 65, 66, 70, 71, 74–80, 86, 99n, 102–111, 115–126, 131–136, 140–150, 152, 154n, 159–164, 165, 166, 170–174, 179, 185, 186, 188, 189, 190n, 191, 196, 198, 199, 203, 204, 206, 210n, 214n, 223, 225–227, 239, 242, 245–251, 252, 253, 254–255, 257, 260–267, 275–277, 281n, 282, 283–291, 292, 293, 294, 296, 298–304, 306–310, 311–320, 323–359, 363–373, 377–382, 387, 393–398, 406, 410–412
    (*See also* Ellis, Robert)
Emmet, Judge Robert, of New York, 123, 367
Emmet, Dr. Robert, State Physician of Ireland, xii, 3–6, 13, 17, 45, 74, 78, 105, 120, 124, 133, 145n, 323, 332
Emmet, Thomas Addis, xi, xii, 5, 7, 16, 24, 25, 29, 34, 38–40, 52, 65, 66, 71–76, 81n, 90, 97, 98, 99, 102–104, 106, 109, 115, 120, 121, 123, 134, 138, 141, 145n, 149, 151, 157, 173, 189n, 204, 209n, 225, 239, 260, 261n, 262n, 291n, 315, 319, 367–370
Emmet, Dr. Thomas Addis, of New York, viii–x, xv, 39, 124, 370
Emmet Family, The, by Dr. Thomas Addis Emmet, viii, xv
Emmet family motto, 3, 298, 388

England, x*n*, 9, 17, 30, 33, 54, 58, 66*n*,
    80, 86, 93, 99*n*, 103, 109, 111, 115, 117,
    120*n*, 127, 133, 142, 146*n*, 154, 157,
    165, 203, 240, 242, 253*n*, 255, 270*n*,
    293, 343, 384, 388, 395*n*, 403*n*
English Fleet, 101
Enniscorthy, County Wexford, 93
Enniskillen gaol, 396
Erin's Call, 8
Erskine, Thomas, 83
Essay on the Art of War, by Robert
    Emmet, 172, 223, 338
Evelyn, Lieutenant Henry, 223, 338
Expedition to Ireland (*see* Invasion,
    French)

F

Falkiner, C. Litton, 94*n*
Fane Mss., I.S.P.O., 26*n*
Farrell, James, 106, 107, 108*n*, 143, 381,
    389, 390, 400
Farrell, John, 391*n*, 396
Farrell, Michael, 66, 389
Farrell, Patrick, 187, 189, 206, 206*n*, 293,
    335, 393
Farrell, William, 180
Farrington, Dr. Anthony, xiv
Fermanagh (county), 269
Ferriter, Pierce, 153
" Fine Hand," 49*n*, 116*n*, 125, 292, 315,
    318*n*
Finglas, County Dublin, 221
Finlay, Mr., 250, 281*n*
Finlay and Co., 281*n*
Finnerty, Patrick, 141, 171, 187, 382, 393,
    395*n*
Fitten William Henry, 324, 363
Fitzgerald, father of David Fitzgerald of
    Kerry, 236–238, 391
Fitzgerald, David, " General Fitzgerald,"
    alias Martin, 236, 237, 239, 391
Fitzgerald, David, nephew to Philip
    Long, 199*n*, 202*n*, 308
Fitzgerald, Lady Edward (Pamela), 30,
    69
Fitzgerald, Lord Edward, 29-31, 59, 65,
    66, 69, 90, 99, 116*n*, 118*n*, 127, 138,
    145*n*, 236, 323, 385
Fitzgerald, Lord Henry, 12, 13, 29
Fitzgerald, John (Qu : David of Kerry ?),
    239
Fitzgerald, Maurice, 11
Fitzgerald, Thomas (Silken Thomas), 11,
    30, 226
Fitzgerald, Thomas Judkins, High Sheriff
    of Tipperary, 87, 97, 154*n*
Fitzgibbon, Lord John, Lord Chancellor
    of Ireland, 15, 23, 24, 30, 33, 35, 43, 71
    (*see also* Clare, Lord)
Fitzharris, Patrick, 257

Fitzmaurice, Captain James, 390
Fitzmaurice, Ulysses, 155*n*
Fitzpatrick, of Loughlin Island, 182,
    231*n*
Fitzpatrick, General Richard, 404, 410
Fitzpatrick, William J., ix*n*, 69*n*, 75*n*,
    158*n*
Fitzwilliam, Lord, 404
Flanagan, Terence, 271
Fleming, John, 140, 166*n*, 188, 207, 293,
    294, 333–335, 393, 395*n*
Fleming, Patrick, 146
Flinn, Joseph Thomas, 78
Flint, Charles, 173, 236*n*, 291
Flood, Andrew, 136
Flood, Michael, 136, 204
Flood, Nicholas, 255
Fontenay, Marquise de, 119, 120
Foote, Mr., 257
Forde, Mr., High Sheriff of County
    Down, 388
Fort George, Scotland, 109, 115, 120,
    122, 125, 134, 135, 143, 178, 239, 262*n*,
    318, 319.
Fortescue Mss., 20*n*, 22*n*, 33*n*, 48*n*.
Foster, the Honourable John, 408
Fowler, Richard, 257
Fox, Hon. Charles James, 37, 47, 83,
    402-404, 408*n*, 409
Fox, General Henry E., viii, 191, 197,
    200–202, 212, 213*n*, 219, 266, 399,
    402, 405, 406
Fox and Geese, 251*n*
France, Republic of, 3, 10, 30, 33, 37, 49,
    54, 59, 60, 67, 81, 84, 99, 116, 119, 120,
    126, 127, 133, 137, 154, 157, 165, 233,
    251*n*, 260, 261*n*, 271, 272, 286, 293, 334,
    353, 378, 382, 384, 387, 395*n*, 403*n*, 404
    army of, 100
    Directory of, 37, 49, 59, 81, 99, 100,
        142, 151, 156, 157, 311*n*, 318
    fleet of, 105, 137, 261*n*
    Ministry of Finance of , 100*n*
Franklin, Benjamin, 14, 33
Frayne, Michael, 146, 333
Frayne, Michael Clement, 338
Frayne, Thomas, 136, 140, 165, 277, 228,
    256, 385
Frazier (name used by Emmet and also
    by Dowdall), 146
Freeman's Journal, 92*n*, 247
French, 84, 87, 154, 166, 196, 240, 242,
    261*n*
Frenchman, a, 49, 80*n*
" Frenchman, the," 60, 157
French Revolution, 16, 20, 119, 326,
    403*n*
Fry, Mr., 257
Fugitive Bill, 126*n*
Fulton, Robert, 118, 261*n*

G

G., James, 60n, 171, 216, 256, 396
Gaelic culture, 4, 10
Gaelic Ireland, 153
Gaelic language, xvn, 153, 181, 329
Gaelic poets, 58
Gallagher, Patrick, 117, 150
Galway (county), 21, 240, 241, 384, 395n
Gamble, the Reverend Thomas, 363–366, 370, 371n, 378, 379
Gardiner, the Widow, 232
Genlis, Madame de, 30
George III, King of England, xi, 47, 94, 155, 398n, 403, 407n, 409
Geraldines, the, 11, 30, 226
Gibbons, John, 241
Gibbons, John, Jr. (Johnny the Outlaw), 241
Gibbons, Thomas, 241
Gilbert, Sir John T., 66n, 93n
Gill, M. H. and Son, Ltd., Dublin, xvii
Glasnevin Churchyard, 373n
Glyn, Knight of, 236n
Goddard, Miss Betty, 18
Gogan, Liam, xvi
Golden Bottle, the 140n, 188
Golden Rock, the, County Kerry, 153
Goodwin, William (recte Godwin), 65n
Goossens, Nicholas, 271
Gordon, Major, 222, 223
Granard, 257
Grange, of Dublin, 170n
Grant, the Reverend Mr., 364, 370, 371n
Grattan, Henry, 12, 13, 30, 82, 143
Great Britain, viii, 87, 120n, 353
Green, friend of Houlton, 273
Green, John, of Cave Hill, 231n
Green Street Court House, 299, 323, 324, 382
Grenville, Lord (William W. Grenville), 20, 22, 23, 48n, 398n, 399, 402, 403, 404, 407n, 409
Grenville, Thomas, 399, 402, 404, 409
Greville, Major, 223, 224
Grey, Nicholas, 143, 162, 165, 188, 227–229, 293n, 315n, 395
Grierson, George, 164n, 168, 248, 309
Ground We Stand On, The, 118n
Groze, General, 142n

H

H., Leonard, 82
Habeas Corpus Act, Suspension of, Ireland, x, 48n, 109, 151n, 220, 236n, 240, 248, 320, 381n, 387, 391n, 399, 402
Hacketstown, County Carlow, 96
Hacketstown Fair, 324
Hale, Nathan, 7

Haley, or Healy, Bernard, of Dundalk, 273
Haley, or Healy, Peter, of Kildare, 195
Haliday, Dr. Alexander, 14, 15, 21, 36, 57, 61, 68, 407
Halpin, Thomas, 293
Hamburg, 50, 69, 116, 125, 251n, 275, 276n
Hamilton, William, 117, 134–137, 145, 146, 148, 162, 170, 175, 179, 189, 231, 269, 274n, 285, 384
Hanlon, Keeper of the Tower of Dublin Castle, 294, 382
Hanlon, Mrs., 294, 381n
Hanna, Joseph, xvi
Harding, Dr. Robert, 177n
Hardwicke, Lord (Philip Yorke), viii, 48n, 124, 132, 138, 167, 191, 193–195, 197, 200, 201, 219, 220, 226n, 242, 285n, 294, 304, 305, 312, 314, 339, 363, 365, 380, 391, 399, 400, 402, 405, 406
Hardy, General Jean, 100
Harold's Cross, 145n, 210, 254, 258, 262n, 264, 276, 281–283, 328, 341
Hart, Mr., of Belfast (probably John Shaw), 270
Hart, John, 267
Haussonville, Countess d', 119
Havre, 134
Hay, Edward, 165n
Hayes, Sir Harry, 177n
Hayes, Dr. Richard, Director of the National Library of Ireland, xvi
Hayes, Richard, M.D., xvii, 66n, 100n
Hayes-McCoy, Dr., xvi
Hazel Hatch, County Dublin, 185
Hedge schools, 10, 153n
Henry, Patrick, 7
Henry II, King of England, 10
Henry VIII, King of England, 11, 30
Hevey, Henry, 143, 246, 248, 253n, 261
Hewitt, name used by Emmet at Harold's Cross, 264, 282, 286, 341
Hewson, Edward, alias of James Farrell, 107, 108
Hibernian Telegraph, the, 72
Hickey, Arthur, 165n
Hickson, John, 364
Higgins, Francis, ixn, 50, 69, 90
Hill, Sir George, 60
Hillsborough, County Down, 179
Hinchy, Arthur, 143
Historical Society of Trinity College, Dublin, 3, 42, 44, 65, 246, 352
History as the Story of Liberty, xiii
Hoar, James, 155n
Hobart, Lady Emilia (later Lady Castlereagh), 36
Hobart, Major Robert, 20
Hoche, the, 101

Hoche, General Louis-Lazare, 59, 66n, 100, 236n
Hodgestown, County Kildare, 136, 137
Holland, 116n, 161n
Holland, Lady, 37
Holland, Lord, 83
Holmes, F., of Croagh, County Limerick, 155n
Holmes, Robert, 140n, 145n, 267
Home Office, London, 80, 236n, 284, 297
Hope, James, 132n, 133, 146, 149, 151, 154n, 162, 163, 165, 169, 175, 231, 233n, 239n
Hope, Rose (Mrs. James), 162, 165, 245
Hospital Fields, 373
Houlton, William Ainsley, 269–275, 382, 396
Howley, Henry, 141, 187, 223, 382
Howth Hill, 269–272
Hudson, Edward, 44, 71
Hughes, Henry, 143, 162, 315n
Hughes, John, 180
Humbert, General Jos. Amable, 107n, 117, 122, 134, 137n, 142n, 151
Hume, William Hoar, 392
Hunter, Andrew, 232, 396
Hyde, Dr. Douglas, 241n

I

Imail, Glen of, County Wicklow, 393
"Independent Northern Whig, An," i.e. T. W. Tone, 18
India, 95
Informers, 46, 66n, 154n, 391, 395
Insurrection, Emmet's plan of, 316
of 1798, 87–94
Insurrection Bill, 67
Invasion, French, of Ireland, 65–67, 96, 105, 108, 117, 122, 137, 142, 150, 155, 230, 261n, 264, 285, 320, 327, 366, 391, 404
Ireland In the Eighteenth Century, by W. E. H. Lecky, 111n
Irish language, 163n, 181, 241n, 329 (See also Gaelic)
Irish Magazine, The, 73n
Italy, 10

J

J.W., i.e. McNally, Leonard, 52, 394
Jackson, the Reverend William, 37, 53
Jacobite wars, 58
James, Alderman William, 137, 327
James II, King of England, 11, 56
James's Street Barracks, 212, 213n
Jeff, Sergeant, 222
Jefferson, Thomas, 7, 119, 315

Jeffries, Lord, 23, 366
Johnston, probably St. John, William, 148, 161n, 166, 389
Johnston, A., 57
Johnstown, County Kildare, 136
"Jones," 66n, 71n, 100n, 117, 125, 171, 253n, 281n, 293, 389
Jones, Richard, 250, 281n, 340n
Jones, William Todd, 143
Jordan, Valentine, 241
Journal and Correspondence of Lord Auckland, 102n
Junius, i.e. Burrowes, Peter, 158

K

Kearney, Edward, 212, 314
Kearney, William, 252, 253
Kearney, Mrs. William, 281
Keating, Colonel, 54
Keenan, John, 166, 167, 268
Keenan, Thomas, 187, 268, 382
Keith, Lord, 236n
Kells, 180, 231
Kelly, 85
Kennedy, Sir John, 185
Kennedy, William, 185
Kennedy, Edward, 395
Keogh, Cornelius, 131
Keogh, John, 22, 71, 131
Keregan, Thomas, 165, 227, 228
Kerry (county), 4, 71, 153, 154, 205, 234, 236, 240, 267, 390, 391, 393
Kerry, Knight of, 236
Kerry gaols, 391, 396
Kildare (county), 29, 31, 60n, 74, 92, 94, 116, 125, 132, 135–138, 140, 141, 150, 157, 162, 165, 170, 171, 187–189, 193, 195, 196, 205, 218, 219, 226, 229, 235, 251n, 253n, 255, 259, 281n, 316, 335, 383, 385, 387, 395, 396
Kildare, Earls of, 11, 30
Kildare, 9th Earl of, 11
Kildare Hunt, the, 136, 255
Kilgobbin, County Dublin, 257
Kilkenny (county), 93
Killala Bay, 99, 101, 117, 270n
Killarney, 155n
Kilmainham gaol, 97, 105, 135, 198, 267, 275, 277n, 281n, 291, 292, 295, 298, 308, 309, 312, 315, 319, 323–325, 332, 340, 364, 370, 372, 381–383, 386, 388, 390, 392–394
Kilmainham Papers (Mss.) Nat. Lib. Ire., 178n, 266n
Kilmainham Register, 296
Kilwarden, Lord (Arthur Wolfe), 215n, 216, 218, 220, 246, 247, 264, 323, 339n, 364, 372, 406

Kilwarlin, 13
King, Mr. Thos., 163
King's Bench, Court of, 105
King's County, High Sheriff of, 88
King's County Regiment, 91n
King's Inn Library, Dublin, xvi
Kinehan, Miss, xvi
Kirk of Scotland, 382
Knight, Richard, 194
Knockbracken, County Down, 179, 181, 231n
Knox, the Honourable George, 157, 405n
Kohen, Frederick, 272, 273
Kosiosko (recte Kosciuszko, Tadeusz), 122

L

Lacy, 277n
Lake, General Gerard, 60, 67, 89
Lake Mss., Nat. Lib. Ire., 68n
Landed Gentry of Ireland, by Burke, Sir Bernard, 236n
Lansdowne, Marquis of, 163n
Larevellière-Lépeaux, M., 100n
La Rochelle, 100
" Lass of Richmond Hill, The," 51
Last Invasion of Ireland, The, by Richard Hayes, xvii, 66n
La Touche, Captain, 252
Lawless, Surgeon, William, 74, 117, 134, 386
Lawless, John, 71
Lawless, the Honourable Valentine, 109n, 117 (See also Lord Cloncurry)
Lawson, 110
Leary, 81
Lecky, W. E. H., ixn, 54n
Lessons, the, 74
Leinster (province), 158, 235
Leinster, 2nd Duke of, 12, 30, 34, 226, 228, 229
Leinster United Irishmen (see United Irishmen, Society of)
Leitrim (county), 21
L'Estrange, Colonel, 91n
" Let Erin Remember," 44
Lewins, Edward, 116
Lexington, battle of, 6
Liberty Rangers, 246, 262n
Life of Anne Devlin, by Brother Luke Cullen, xvi, 146n, 185, 215n, 262n, 281n, 302
Life and Journals of Theobald Wolfe Tone, 18n
Life and Letters of C. J. Fox, 410n
Life of Michael Dwyer, by Brother Luke Cullen, xvi, 144n, 146n, 253n, 302
Liffey, River, 84, 192, 370
Limerick (city), 154, 158, 236n, 238

Limerick (county), 154, 155, 163n, 234, 236, 390, 391n, 393
Limerick, Treaty of, 11
Limerick, Lord, 403
Limerick County gaol, 156, 391n, 396
Lincoln, Abraham, 411
Lindsay, the Reverend Charles, Bishop of Killaloe, 400, 401
Lindsay, Private Robert, 338
Lisburn, 61, 65n, 232
Lismore, 270n
Little Hastings, 133n
Littlehales, Sir Edward, 257
Liverpool, 85, 142, 143, 382
Locke, John, 7, 25
London, 7, 15, 37, 41, 47, 49, 51, 66n, 69, 80, 81, 84, 98, 104, 108, 109, 118n, 123, 126n, 133n, 148, 155n, 248, 261n, 276n, 293n, 313, 323, 324, 382, 383, 388n, 391, 399, 408
London Chronicle, the, 379
London Corresponding Society, 236n
London Courier, 68
London Tower, 109n
Londonderry, Lady, 36
Long, Philip, 143, 165, 189, 199, 202n, 254, 260, 265, 268, 275, 276, 285, 308, 383, 394
Longford (county), 167n
Longford County gaol, 396
Longford Inn, Dublin 140n
Longueville, Lord, 66
Lord Chancellor of Ireland, 1789–1802 (see Fitzgibbon, John and Clare, Lord) 1803 (see Redesdale, Lord)
Lord Lieutenant of Ireland, 1790–1795 (see Westmorland, Lord)
1795–1798 (see Camden, Lord)
1798–1801 (see Cornwallis, Lord)
1801–1806 (see Hardwicke, Lord)
1876 (see Marlborough, 7th Duke of)
Lord Mayor of Dublin, 218, 248
Lordonnier, M. (see Cullinane, Daniel)
Loughin Island, 181, 230, 231n
Loughlin, Patrick, 250
Louis XIV, King of France, 58n
Louisiana scheme, 134, 386
Louth (county), 134, 271n
Lucan, County Dublin, 172, 235
Lynch, Patrick, 181
Lyons, Owen, 165, 227–229

M

McCabe, Patrick, 170, 189, 213, 214, 215, 268, 293, 339n
McCabe, Thomas, 33n, 126
McCabe, William Putnam, 116n, 126, 127, 134, 161, 170, 262n, 292n, 386

McCan, Mr., 186
McCance Collection of Mss., P.R.O.B., 179n
Macartney, A. C., 76, 77
McClean, Archibald, 233
McClelland, James, 170n, 180n, 283, 325, 333, 383
McCormick, Richard, 52
McCracken, Henry Joy, 308
McCracken, Mary Ann, 308
McCreath, Donough, 215–217, 218
McDaniel George, 148, 187, 199
McDermott, William, 255
MacDonagh, Michael xv
McDonnell, James J., 117, 150n, 241
McDonough, Michael, 250–252, 381n
McGucken, James, 52n, 82, 103–111, 115, 123, 151, 154n, 169, 176, 178–181, 193, 197, 230–233, 237, 269, 274n, 387, 395
McIntosh, John, 148, 166, 187, 268, 379, 382
McLaughlin, Peter, 78
MacMahon, Rory, xiii
McNally, Leonard, 37, 50–55, 72, 73, 80, 82, 89n, 116, 126, 152, 193, 238, 269, 300, 312, 314, 325, 332, 333, 335, 336, 343, 346, 350, 351, 365–366, 378, 388, 394
MacNevin, Captain Andrew, 47
McNevin, Dr. James, 98, 105, 106n, 262n, 319
McPhea, of Belfast, 150n
McTier, Samuel, 18, 19, 32, 230
McTier, Mrs. Samuel (Mattie Drennan), 16, 31, 89, 103, 274
Madden, Martin, 184
Madden, Dr. Richard R., 132n, 162n, 164, 239n, 277n, 295, 308n, 352, 355n, 370n
Magan, Francis, 50, 90, 138
Maguan, Nicholas, 69, 94, 179n, 180
Maguire, Hugh, 11
Mahaffy, Michael, 268, 339n
Mahon, of Carrick-on-Suir, 238n
Mahon, John, 136, 170, 187, 245, 253n
Maidstone, 82–86
Malmsbury, Lord, 47n
Malone, County Down, 232
Man of Ulster, i.e. Alexander Marsden, 158
Manchester, 411
Manders, Alderman, 192
Mansion House, Dublin, 218
Margate, 81–84
Marie Antoinette, Queen of France, 118
Market Hill, County Armagh, 58
Market House, Thomas Street, 211n, 266
Marlborough, 7th Duke of, viii

Marsden, Alexander, viii, x, 48n, 73n, 123, 124, 125, 135n, 138, 139, 156–158, 167, 168, 171, 180, 188, 191–195, 197, 198, 199, 218, 219–221, 230, 233, 236, 240, 246, 247, 248, 256–258, 283–286, 287–289, 294, 310, 314, 338, 339, 363, 365, 371n, 390n, 398n, 399–401, 403, 405–408, 410
Marshall, of Tralee, 155n
Marshalsea prison, 206, 210, 222
Martial law, 92, 97, 258, 402
Martin, (see Fitzgerald, David, of County Kerry)
Martin, Belle, 50, 68, 253n
Martin, Richard, 240, 241
Mason, Elizabeth, 4.
Mason, St. John, 71, 267, 298, 299, 324, 345, 388, 394
Massarene, Lord, 156
Mayne, Mr., 325, 333–336, 340
Maynooth, County Kildare, 136, 137, 165, 226, 227, 229, 247, 255–257, 383, 385
Maynooth Castle, 30, 226
Mayo (county), 21, 240, 242, 403
Meath (county), 60, 163n, 239n, 258, 259
Meath, Earl of, 246
Melville, Lord (formerly Henry Dundas), 408, 409n
Memoir of Miles Byrne, 142n, 260n, 319n
Memoir of Thomas Addis and Robert Emmet, xvii, 71n, 119n, 120n, 151n, 318, 320n, 370n
Memoirs of Thomas Moore, 43n
Memoirs of the Whig Party, by Lord Holland, 83n
Mernagh, John, 146
Merrion Square, Dublin, 38, 91
Metcalf, William, 151, 176, 179–181
Militia, 59, 68, 91, 137
Milltown, County Dublin, 107, 132
Minchen, Humphrey, 310
Minis, William, 178
Minto, Lord, 47n
Moira, Lord (later the Earl of Hastings), 15, 58, 83, 87, 207
Monaghan Militia, 68
Montpellier, 6
Montanus, i.e. Emmet, Thomas Addis, 72
Moore, Sir John, 46n, 88, 89
Moore, Thomas, vii, 12, 42–44, 71, 76, 411
Moran, John, 137
Morpeth, Lord, 404
Mountgarret, Lord, 24, 34
Muir, Thomas, 37, 403n
Muley, Daniel, 308–310
Mumford, Captain Lewis, 49, 133n

Munro, Margaret, 274, 396
Munster (province), 90, 94, 153, 154n, 156, 162, 196, 239n, 390n, 396
Murdock, Robert, 68
Murphy, of Bull Alley, 167, 285
Murphy, Denis, 391n
Murphy, Father (see Cullinane, Daniel)
Murphy, George and sister, 264, 283
Murray, John, Ltd., xvii
Myers, General William, 239

N

Naas, County Kildare, 92, 136, 137, 165n, 170, 188, 194–196, 219, 255, 257, 314, 395
Naas gaol, 163n, 256, 267n, 268, 383, 385, 397
National Gallery of Ireland, 373n
National Library of Ireland, vii, xvi, 178n, 214n, 332n, 334n
National Museum of Ireland, xvi, 358n, 373n
Neilson, Samuel, 61, 65n, 98, 107n, 109
New Geneva prison, 142n
Newell, Edward, 68
Newgate gaol, Dublin, 7, 30, 34, 37, 38, 73n, 90, 97, 104, 106n, 267, 275, 308, 325, 363, 364, 372, 378, 395
Newmarket on the Coombe, 254n
Newmarket Watchhouse, 211
Newry, 31, 89, 179, 267
Ní Dhomhnalláin, Máirín, xvi
Niall of the Nine Hostages, 11
Noonan, John, 155, 155n
Norbury, Lord, formerly John Toler, 193n, 300, 326, 331n, 344, 345, 349, 350, 352n, 354–359, 363, 384
Norfolk, Duke of, 83, 86
Norris, William, 140, 141, 156, 162, 193, 239, 239n
North, the (Ulster), viii, 6, 12, 31, 32, 33, 56, 58–62, 116, 133, 150, 154n, 156, 162n, 170, 175, 177–182, 196, 205, 230, 232, 237, 269, 274, 387, 388, 391
Northern Star, The, 35, 68, 176
Northern Whig Club, 15
Nugent, General George, 274n

O

O'Connell, Daniel, 395n
O'Connor, Arthur, 66, 73, 81–86, 98, 103–106, 109, 127, 128, 134, 143, 150, 158, 261n, 262n
O'Connor, Patrick, xvi
O'Donnell, Hugh, 11

O'Grady, Standish, 275, 283, 286, 287, 305, 313, 325–332, 339, 341, 344, 348, 350, 351
O'Hanlon, 108, 109–111, 115
Oldtown, County Wicklow, 87
Omagh, County Tyrone, 35
O'Moloney, Bishop John, 58n
O'Neill, Donal, 10
O'Neill, Hugh, 11
O'Neill, John (later Lord O'Neill), 13, 14, 15, 36
O'Neill, John, deserter, 253n, 262n, 293
O'Neill, Owen Roe, 11
O'Neill, Shane, Earl of Tyrone, 11
Orange Order, the, 56
Orange Society, 78
Orangeism, 92
Orangemen, 56, 58, 132, 142, 163n, 248n
Orleans, Duke of, 30
Ormsby, Henry, 206n, 222
Ormsby, Philip, 187n
O'Rourke, Bryan, 140n
Orr, George, 66n
Osborne, Albert S., xviii, 122n
O'Sullivan, Owen Roe, " Owen of the Sweet Mouth," 153
Oxford, Lord, 83

P

P., Kildare informer, 256
Paine, Thomas, 19, 37, 53, 92, 118n, 238, 403n
Painestown, County Kildare, 253n
Pakenham, Sir Thomas, 136, 245, 256, 383
Palmer, Mrs. Ann, of Harold's Cross, 145n, 254, 262n, 264, 276, 277, 281n, 282, 283, 290, 341
Palmer, Biddy, 161, 309
Palmer, Jemima, 264, 277, 282, 283, 290, 344
Palmer, John, Jr., 116n, 127, 145n, 161
Palmer, John, Sr., 116n, 161, 166n, 167, 168, 191, 267, 290, 334, 394
Palmer, Joseph, 264, 276n, 283, 285, 325, 341–343
Palmerstown, County Dublin, 188, 192, 198, 218, 395n
Paris, viii, xii, 30, 37, 100, 116, 117, 118n, 119, 121, 122, 125, 134, 135, 137, 139n, 144, 149, 154n, 165, 253n, 260, 261n, 276n, 291n, 292, 315, 318, 382
Parliament, British, 33, 36, 124, 132, 151n, 248, 399, 405
  House of Commons of, 12, 198n, 401, 403, 406
  House of Lords of, 87, 403, 405

Parliament, Irish, 8, 15, 22, 29, 30, 33, 34, 53, 95, 96, 115, 132, 204, 398n, 405n, 408, 409n
  Committee of Secrecy of, 33–35
  House of Commons, of, 7, 12, 15, 18, 20, 22, 30, 39, 115, 131, 405n
  House of Lords of, 24, 30, 33, 405n
Parrots, the, John and William, 252n, 262n, 335, 384, 385, 395
Patten, Jane (Mrs. T. A. Emmet), 16, 17
Patten, John, 45, 121–123, 125, 138, 140n, 239, 260, 265, 276, 283, 290, 318, 320, 381, 395
Pattison, Captain, 197
Payne, General William, 154, 156, 235–238, 390
Peep of Day Boys, 12, 56
Pelham, Thomas (later Lord Pelham and Earl of Chichester), 59, 67, 69, 93, 219, 236n, 248
Pelham Transcripts, P.R.O.B., 59n, 67n
Penal Laws, Ireland, 12, 15
Peppard, Thomas, 253n
Personal Narrative, by Thomas Cloney, 142n
Petrie, George, 324, 358, 372, 373n
Philipstown, King's County, 138, 396
Pichegru, General, 47n
Pigeon House, Dublin, 171, 200, 269–272, 314, 316, 382
Pitt, William, the younger, viii–xi, 15, 16, 20, 21, 26, 32, 33n, 33–37, 48, 50, 56, 66n, 70, 94, 95, 122, 124, 138, 191, 285, 381n, 398, 399, 402, 405, 407, 408, 410
Plunket, Colonel, of County Roscommon, 149
Plunket, William Conyngham, 115, 325, 333, 342, 347–349, 355n, 387n
Poddle, the, Dublin, 161, 167, 215n
Poets, Irish, 10, 58
Police Commissioners, Dublin 137n
Pollock, John, 31, 32, 39, 50, 52, 61, 72, 82, 83, 104, 108–111, 116, 140n, 163n, 170n, 188, 195, 197, 239, 255, 258, 275, 312n, 383
Ponsonby, George, 299
Porchester gaol, 236n
Porter, David, 396
Portland, Duke of, 37, 47
Potato diggings, 60
Pounden, Mr. Sheriff, 383
Power, David, 76, 162n, 239
Prendergast, the Reverend Myles, 241
Presbyterians, 19, 57
Press, the, Dublin 71–74
Priory, The, 159, 160, 186, 260, 304, 305, 309, 312
Prison conditions, 34, 267n
Prison ships, 107n, 371, 373, 375

Privy Council, Irish, 258, 273, 291n, 294, 296, 305, 306, 318
Proclamation of the Provisional Government, large, 203, 204, 222, 247, 267, 283n, 286, 320, 328, 334, 337, 338, 343, 348
  small, 203, 204, 240, 338, 340, 341
Prosperous, County Kildare, 92, 205, 244
Protestant Ascendancy, 11, 21, 26, 56, 94
Protestant Boys, 56
Protestants, 11, 15, 19, 21, 46, 56, 57, 94, 111, 398n
Provisional Government, 231, 239, 260, 320, 328, 353
Provost of Trinity College, Dublin, 77
Provost Prison, Belfast, 106n, 395
  Dublin, 258, 266–268, 296
Prussian Army, 177
Public Record Office, English (abbreviated as P.R.O.L.), x, xv,ixvi, 54n, 81n, 82n, 86n, 91n, 93n, 100n, 109n, 111n, 116n, 128n, 133n, 135n, 160n, 165n, 196n, 201n, 214n, 228n, 236n, 283n, 311n, 312n, 313n, 317n, 387n, 388n, 393n
  Irish (abbreviated as P.R.O.D.), vii, x, 49n
  of Northern Ireland (abbreviated as P.R.O.B.), xvi, 59n, 67n, 179n
Putnam, General Israel, 7

Q

Quigley, the Reverend James, 81, 82–85, 132n
Quigley, Michael, 135–141, 147n, 150, 162, 165, 171, 179n, 187, 188n, 189, 196, 199, 206–210, 223, 229, 238n, 245, 246, 249, 251, 253n, 255, 262n, 264, 274n, 333, 336, 348, 377, 384, 387, 394n, 395, 400
Quin, of Dublin, 110

R

Raleigh, Sir Walter, 153
Ranaghan, Patrick, 182
Randalstown, 35n
Rathangan, County Kildare, 138, 259
Rathcoffey, County Kildare, 136
Rathcoole, County Dublin, 185, 188, 277–279
Rathdrum, County Wicklow, 145, 164n
Rathfarnham, County Dublin, 145n, 159, 164n, 186, 224, 257, 262n, 293, 304, 309, 328
Rathfarnham Cavalry, 252
Rawlings, Joseph, 332
Red Cow Tavern, 197

Redesdale, Lord (formerly Sir John Mitford), 273*n*, 275, 283, 286, 305
Redmond, Denis Lambert, 167, 190, 206, 211*n*, 267, 293, 339*n*
Reform, Parliamentary, Ireland, 8, 12, 13, 15, 17–19, 35, 38, 47, 49, 71
Reformation, English, 11
Reilly, Jenny, 272, 273
Reynolds, Dr. James, 24, 38, 53
Reynolds, Thomas, 74*n*, 75, 188
Rice, Sergeant Thomas, 338
Richardson, Samuel, 264
Richmond, Duke of, 30
Ridgway, Mr. Wm., 325
Rights of Man, The, 19, 37, 53, 92, 403*n*
Roberts, *alias* of Samuel Turner, 276*n*
Robertson, Major, 211, 212, 215*n*
Robinson, John, 250, 281*n*, 240, 341
Rochambeau, General, 142
Roche, Sir Boyle, 21
Roche, Maxwell, 314
Rockets, 148, 162
Rodgers, William, 234, 396
Ronan, the Very Reverend Myles V., xvi, 144*n*, 146*n*
Roscommon (county), 21, 46, 50, 149
Rouen, 99, 127, 135
Rourke, Felix (sometimes called O'Rourke), 140, 170, 188, 195, 215*n*, 268, 299*n*, 300*n*, 301
Rousseau, Jean-Jacques, 25
Rowan, Alexander Hamilton, 23, 27, 38, 53
Royal Exchange, Dublin, 266, 276*n*
Royal Irish Academy, vii, x, xvi, 16, 66*n*, 170*n*, 173*n*, 281*n*
Royal United Services Institution, London, xiv, 94*n*
Russell, Lord John, 83
Russell, John, of Limerick, 155*n*
Russell, John, of London, brother of Thomas, 311
Russell, John, of Mountjoy Sq., Dublin, 359
Russell, Margaret, 311
Russell, Thomas, 18–20, 34, 44, 52, 61, 78, 90, 99*n*, 102, 103–107, 117, 122, 134, 139, 142*n*, 145, 148, 162, 163, 164, 165, 170, 175, 178–182, 205, 230–234, 239*n*, 269, 274*n*, 285, 294, 308–312, 320, 387–389, 393, 394
Russell, Lord William, 366
Ryan, James, 132
Ryan, John, 268, 339*n*
Ryan, Mrs., of Thomas Street, 268, 339*n*

S

S, informer, 90
St. Ann's, Dublin, 373*n*
St. Catherine's, Dublin, 369, 412

St. John, William (sometimes called Johnston), 116, 148, 161, 276, 292*n*, 389, 390
St. Michan's, 373*n*
St. Patrick, 14, 242
St. Patrick's Cathedral, Dublin, 208
St. Paul's, 373*n*
Saintfield, County Down, 69, 178, 274*n*
Sallins, County, Kildare, 137
Sands, Nicholas, 155*n*
Saratoga, battle of, 7
Sarsfield, Patrick, 11
Scotland, 7, 36, 49, 79, 127, 180
Scott, James, 176, 179, 374
Scott, Richard, 170, 188, 255, 383
Scott brothers, of Kildare, 204
Scully, Edward, 383
Seal of United Irishmen, 74, 75, 261, 318, 319, 370*n*
Secret Correspondence Relative to Pitt's Return to Office in 1804, 408*n*
Secret papers, viii, ix, 54*n*, 125
Secret Service, British, 32, 47, 49, 50
Secret-Service money, 66*n*, 133*n*, 138, 139, 158*n*, 193*n*, 258, 281*n*, 312*n*
Secret-Service Money Account Book, 139, 281*n*
Secret Service Under Pitt, by W. J. Fitzpatrick, ix*n*
Shamrock and the London Pride, The, 70
Shannon, Lord, 36
Shaughnessy, 144
Shaw, Isabella, 270, 271, 274, 376
Shaw, John, of Belfast, 274, 395
Shaw, Robert, 252
Shaw, William, of Belfast, 274*n*
Sheares, Henry, 91
Sheares, John, 91
Sheridan, Richard Brinsley, 83
Sheridan, William, 140*n*
Sheriff of Dublin, 370, 372
Sidney, Algernon, 3, 34, 47, 366
Simms, Robert and William, 178, 180
Sir Charles Grandisson, by Richardson, 264
Sirr, Charles Henry, Town Major of Dublin, 66, 106*n*, 110, 122*n*, 133, 134, 137, 138, 144, 160*n*, 168, 191, 194, 217, 218, 248*n*, 262*n*, 270, 271*n*, 272, 273, 275, 277, 281*n*, 282, 287, 294, 295, 299*n*, 304, 309, 310, 312, 314, 323, 329, 342, 344, 382, 388, 395*n*, 400*n*
Sirr, the Reverend James, 374*n*
Sirr Papers (Mss.), T.C.D., 18*n*, 144*n*, 160*n*, 194*n*, 300
Sligo, Lady, 405*n*
Sligo, Lord (formerly Lord Altamont), 58*n*, 241, 242, 403–405
Smith, Hall, 252*n*
Smith, Henry, of Annadorn, 181

Smith, John *alias* of William Bird, 49, 59, 161*n*
Smith, Patrick, of Annadorn, 181
Society of Constitutional Information, of England, 118*n*
Society of Friends of the Constitution, Liberty and Peace, of Dublin, 38
Society of United Irishmen (*see* United Irishmen, Society of)
Solicitor-General of Ireland, 1792 (*see* Toler, John)
    1803 (*see* McClelland, James)
Spain, 10
Speaker of House of Commons, English, 1803 (*see* Abbot, Charles)
Spencer, Lord, 404
Staël, Madame de, 119, 358*n*
Stafford, Lord, 384, 409*n*
Stafford, Nicholas, 172, 206, 207, 245, 246, 251, 253*n*, 328, 348, 377, 384, 395
Stamp Tax, 7
State prisoners, Irish, 97-99, 103, 105, 107, 109, 120*n*, 125, 318*n*, 379, 386, 395
State trials, 403
Steeven's Hospital, Dublin, 169
Stephen's Green, Dublin, 3, 13, 25, 45, 74, 76, 91*n*, 107, 118, 323
Stephenson, Patrick, xiv
Stewart, Robert, 13, 14, 15, 25, 36, 46 (*See also* Lord Castlereagh)
Stockdale, John, 267, 394
Stokes, Dr. Whitley, 78, 181
Straffan, County Kildare, 185*n*
Stratton, Major, 273
Strawmarket, Dublin, 147, 149
Stuart, Lieutenant-Governor of Fort George, 121
Studies (Irish Quarterly Magazine), 67*n*
Studies in Irish History, by C. Litton Falkiner, 94*n*
Suffolk, Lord, 83
Swan, Major, 137, 201, 370, 372
Sweeney, John, of Belfast, 180
Sweeney (Swiney), John, of Cork, 122, 134, 150*n*, 239, 240
Sweetman, John, 105
Swift, Jonathan, 5, 209, 373*n*
Switzerland, 48*n*, 59, 80

T

Taghmon, County Wexford, 93
Tallaght, County Dublin, 188
Tandy, James N., 394
Tandy, Napper, 12, 13, 20-24, 37, 52, 66*n*, 100*n*, 127, 171, 394
Tannahill, Joseph, 396

Tarbert, County Kerry, 155
Tate, Minor, 155*n*
Teeling, Bartholomew, 65*n*, 107, 179
Teeling, Charles Hamilton, 61, 107*n*
Teeling, George, 107, 107*n*, 179
Teeling, Luke, 107*n*
Temple, the, London, 7, 17
Temple, Lord (George Nugent Temple, later Marquis of Buckingham), 4
Temple, Sir John, 74
Temple, Sir Thomas, 1st Baronet, 3
Temple, Sir William, 3
Templehoff, Colonel, 173
Ten Mile House, 229
Thanet, Lord, 83
Thompson, David, 274
Thorington, M. (*See* Cullinane, Daniel)
Thorpe, Sergeant, 411, 412
Thwaites, Austin, 106
Tipperary, High Sheriff of, 97, 154*n*
Toler, John, 22, 23, 71, 326 (*See also* Norbury, Lord)
Tone, Matthew, 100, 101
Tone, Theobald Wolfe, 8, 17-22, 24, 31, 35, 38, 52, 53, 55*n*, 59, 65, 67, 78, 99-101, 157, 178, 204, 271*n*, 323
Tone, Mrs. Theobald Wolfe, 74*n*
Townsend, John, 275, 294, 325, 335, 337, 344, 395*n*
Tregony, 36
Trench, General, 188
Trevor, Dr. Edward, 267*n*, 295-298, 301, 303, 314, 342, 363, 365, 366, 370, 373*n*, 386, 387, 388, 395*n*
Trinity College, Dublin, xii, 17-19, 25, 42, 65, 76, 111, 131, 181, 239, 240, 292*n*, 315*n*, 323, 352
Trinity College Library, vii, x, xvi, 18*n*
Trinity College Yeomanry Corps, 324, 363
Turner, Samuel, *alias* Furnes, Roberts, and Richardson, 69, 70, 84, 98, 104, 116, 126, 126*n*, 271*n*, 276*n*
Turner's Public House, Ballsbridge, County Limerick, 234
Twomey, Dr., 299
Tyrone (county), 34
Tyrrell, George, 333

U

Ulster (*see* North, the)
Union, legislative, between Ireland and England, viii, ix*n*, xi, 15, 26, 95, 98, 102, 115, 124, 132, 141, 157, 160, 204, 233, 347*n*, 398*n*, 399-401, 403, 405*n*, 408
Union Star, the, 73, 108*n*
United Britons, 81

United Irishmen, Society of, xii, 19, 22–26, 29, 31–40, 47, 49, 51–55, 59–61, 65, 66, 68, 71–75, 80, 81–83, 85, 90–92, 96, 98, 102, 109, 111, 116, 123, 125, 128, 131, 150, 156, 157, 173, 188, 239, 261n, 271n, 315, 329, 366, 371, 382, 389
   Belfast, 19, 65n, 107
   Dublin, 19
   Executive Directory of, 66, 102–104, 107n
   Kildare County Committee of, 136
   Leinster, 90
     Executive of, 74
   Northern Provincial Committee of, 271n
   Ulster Executive of, 104
United Irishmen, The, by Madden, R. R., 43n, 45n, 92n, 127n, 132n, 149n, 162n, 196n, 199n, 209n, 308n, 355n
United States, 118n, 392

V

Vannlet, M., 100n
Vassal, Lieutenant-Colonel Spencer, 202, 224, 225n, 338
Vaugirard, Rue, Paris, 118
Vauquelin, M., 118, 122
Vernon, Captain, 272
Vienna, 48n
Villars, Le Maréchal de, 17
Vinegar Hill, battle of, 93, 96
Vint, John 234
Visitation of Trinity College, 77
Volney, Constantin, 144
Volunteers, English, 404
Volunteers of Belfast, 18, 33
Volunteers of Dublin, 29, 31, 37

W

Wade, Dr., 363
Wale, Colonel, 274n
Wales, Prince of (later George IV), 398n, 408n
Wall, Stephen, 231
Walsh, John, 256
Walsh, Miss Roisin, xvi
Washington, George, 33, 315, 353
Waterford (county), 106n, 389
Waterford city gaol, 396
Waterford County gaol, 396
Weir, Miss, 256
Weir, William, 256
Westmeath County gaol, 397
Westmorland, Lord (formerly John Fane), xi, 20, 21, 24, 26, 30, 36, 47, 52
Wexford (county), 92n, 93, 96, 116, 133, 141–143, 147, 164n, 165, 166, 190n, 316, 366, 396

Whig Club of Dublin, 15, 53, 54n, 80
   of London, 15, 83
Whigs, 7, 12, 15, 36, 47, 404
Whinnery, of Belfast, 230, 233
Whipcord, 72
Whitbred, Samuel, 83
White, General, 33
White, George, 264, 283
White, Luke, 379
White Bull Inn, 135, 140, 143, 166n, 188, 203, 204, 293
White's Restaurant, Paris, 30, 118n
Whitehall, 81, 117, 128, 135n, 138, 389
Wickham, William, x, 47n, 49, 59, 67n, 69, 80, 82, 84, 85, 89, 95, 99n, 101, 104, 108, 111, 116n, 124, 126, 139n, 150n, 158, 161n, 172, 191, 210n, 215n, 220, 238, 253n, 261n, 266, 275, 283–285, 292, 293n, 294, 296, 298, 299n, 304–305, 310, 311, 313, 314, 318n, 323, 328, 377–386, 388n, 389, 393, 399–401, 409n, 410
Wickham Correspondence, 49n, 409n
Wicklow (county), 92–94, 102, 106n, 142, 144–147, 150, 154n, 164, 190n, 282, 295, 316, 391, 392
Wild Geese, the, 118
Wilde, Miss, 254
Wilde, Thomas, 136–138, 170, 187, 188, 245, 253n
Wilkenson, —, 82
William of Orange, 11, 56
Wilson, Edward, 194, 207–211, 220, 262n, 339
Wilson, Hugh, 318
Windgate Hill, County Kildare, 229
Windham, William, 399, 402, 403
Witherspoon, James, 179, 231n, 233, 234, 388, 395
Wolfe, Miss Elizabeth, 216, 218, 220, 221
Wolfe, Colonel John, 170n, 194, 219, 255, 383n, 385
Wornall, Richard, 208, 214n, 249
Worthington, Sir William, 246
Wright, Dr. Thomas, 110, 111, 269
Wrottesley, Sir John, 405–407
Wycomb, Lord (John Henry Petty Fitzmaurice), 163n

Y

Yellow Bottle, 140n, 195, 198
Yeomanry, 58, 201, 220, 221, 234, 246, 254, 258
Yorke, Charles, 124, 293, 315n, 363, 383, 385, 401, 402, 405
Yorktown, battle of, 7
Young Irelanders, 395n

MADE AND PRINTED IN IRELAND BY BROWNE AND NOLAN LIMITED
THE RICHVIEW PRESS DUBLIN